Retiring Men

Manhood, Labor, and Growing Old in America, 1900–1960

Gregory Wood

UNIVERSITY PRESS OF AMERICA,® INC.
Lanham • Boulder • New York • Toronto • Plymouth, UK

Copyright © 2012 by
University Press of America,® Inc.
4501 Forbes Boulevard
Suite 200
Lanham, Maryland 20706
UPA Acquisitions Department (301) 459-3366

Estover Road
Plymouth PL6 7PY
United Kingdom

Library of Congress Control Number: 2011935886
ISBN: 978-0-7618-5679-5 (clothbound : alk. paper)
eISBN: 978-0-7618-5680-1

For Mihaela and John Michael

Contents

Tables

Acknowledgments

Like many of the workers and retirees that I write about in *Retiring Men*, I gained more than just a few gray hairs as I toiled. This book first began in the early-to-mid 2000s as a dissertation in the history department at the University of Pittsburgh. Throughout that time, and in the years since I completed my Ph.D. in 2006, I enjoyed growing older with this project. We matured together as I conducted additional research, addressed colleagues' suggestions, and rewrote the manuscript at least twice—all while teaching numerous classes at three universities, moving from Pennsylvania to Maryland, and starting a family.

From the beginning, I benefited immeasurably from the wisdom and continuous support of Richard Oestreicher, my dissertation advisor at Pitt, who patiently and expertly showed me how to become a better researcher, writer, editor, and teacher. His suggestions ultimately helped to make the completion of this book possible (and rewarding). While we get to talk far too seldom, Maurine Greenwald's influence during graduate school continues to shape my work. As I teach my own students the labors of research, writing, and critical thinking, I often hear myself echoing much of Maurine's original advice to me: read closely, good writing means rewriting, think carefully about evidence, and challenge yourself and your students. Lisa Brush showed me how theory energizes and enriches the study of history; and much of what I know about conceptualizing gender and masculinity I credit to her teaching.

In the years since graduate school, several individuals offered very helpful feedback as I transformed the dissertation into a book. I spent a long time working through Steve Meyer's and Colleen Doody's methodical and important critiques of Chapter 1 at the Newberry Library's Labor History Seminar. Laurie Matheson and Deborah Gershenowitz offered substantive comments on the entire manuscript, as well as very insightful views from the publishing marketplace on why books and dissertations are not the same. I presented portions of my research at several conferences since the dissertation defense and received excellent advice. In particular, the commentators and audience members at the Popular Culture Association/American Culture Association (PCA/ACA) and the Economic and Business Historical Society (EBHS) deserve a special nod—especially James W. Stitt of High Point University in North Carolina.

Portions of Chapters 1 and 3 appeared in an earlier form as "Beyond the Age of Earning: Masculinity, Work, and Age Discrimination in the Automobile Industry, 1916–1939," in *Labor: Studies in Working-Class History of the Americas,* Vol. 3, Issue, 2, pp. 91–120. Copyright 2006, Duke University Press. Reprinted by permission of the publisher. Also, I published a previous draft of material from Chapter 3 as "Forty Plus Clubs and White-Collar Manhood during the Great Depression," which appeared in *Essays in Economic & Business History*, Vol. 26, pp. 21–31 (© 2008 Economic and Business Historical Society). For their help with the necessary permissions, I thank Lynne Pierson Doti and Janice M. Traflet at *Essays* and Diane Grosse of Duke University Press.

An incredible network of colleagues sustained me with their support and friendship over the past five years as I transitioned from graduate school into full-time teaching. At Penn State Erie, where I taught as a visiting professor in 2006–2007, I warmly thank Richard Aquila, Michael Christofferson, Ralph Eckert, Dan Frankforter, and John Rossi for their collegiality and hospitality. They made a home for me in the history program, and I think of them often. At Frostburg State University in western Maryland, where I've been since 2007, I am grateful to many colleagues for their friendship, collaboration, and support since arriving on campus. I especially thank Alem Abbay, Gina Alderton, Amy Branam, Natalia Buta, Paul Charney, Maureen Connelly, David Dean, Judy Dieruf, Shelley Drees, Charlie Ewers, Mary Gartner, David Gillespie, Steve Hartlaub, Cindy Herzog, Joe Hoffman, Nicole Houser, Liz Keller, Brent Kice, Dori Kice, Jesse Ketterman, John Lombardi, Melanie Lombardi, Randall Lowe, Jeff Maehre, Jean Marie Makang, Michael Mathias, Marc Michael, Mary Mumper, MaryJo Price, Elesha Ruminski, Maria Luisa Sanchez, Daniel Silver, Steve Simpson, Joanna Skelley, Gerry Snelson, Sheri Whalen, Pamela Williams, and John Wiseman. My very good friend in the music department, Mark Gallagher, insisted on having his own sentence, so here it is: "Thank you for being a friend." Our next-door neighbors and very close friends, Sue Gerhard and Paul Gerhard, have become our extended family here in Maryland; and in nearby Morgantown, Elizabeth Fones-Wolf and Ken Fones-Wolf of West Virginia University have been great colleagues and become good friends.

At home, everyone is growing up and growing older. My dad, James Wood, retired last year and my mom, Janis Wood, is soon to follow. Their enthusiasm for retiring from work disproves one of my book's main arguments; but alas, I am very grateful to them for the many years of love and support that made this entire endeavor possible. My sister, Erin Evers, grew up, got a job, and got married as I wrote the dissertation and then the book. I thank Erin and Tim Evers for welcoming me home whenever I've returned to Warren, Michigan. In Romania, where my retired in-laws live, I was always made to feel welcome as a new member of the Gainusa family. Multumesc, Mama si Tati, pentru dragostea si sprjinul vostru. Si multumesc Mihai, Ioana, Eva, si Andrei pentru gazduirea in Bucuresti.

Finally, I owe more debts than I could ever fully repay to my wife, Mihaela Wood, for everything she has done for me and for our family over the past eight years. Miha not only accepted my marriage proposal after three dates, but sustained me in every way since. She is always abundantly loving, generously caring, and unselfishly encouraging; she keeps me going when I'm frustrated; she brings me much-needed calm. (And Miha is a superb editor, colleague, and critic.) I'm proud that we are growing old together, and quite relieved now that she finished her own Ph.D. in Eastern European history last year. In July 2009, our son John Michael was born a few short hours after Miha retired the first draft of her dissertation. He gives real meaning and joy to the lives of his busy parents. He is our little goose, our little bear, and our little quackeroo. We love you tons and tons, John Michael.

Introduction:
Manhood and Its Discontents

No other technique for the conduct of life attaches the individual so firmly to reality as laying emphasis on work; for his work at least gives him a secure place in a portion of reality, in the human community.

—Sigmund Freud, 1930[1]

As he lay in a dentist chair undergoing a procedure on a sore tooth, Austen A. Ettinger, an aging New York advertising executive of the 1980s, talked with the dentist (another professional man) about his upcoming retirement. The dentist asked Ettinger if he knew Freud's thoughts on the subject. "You know what he said, of course," the doctor cautioned. When Ettinger said he had no idea what Freud had written about retirement, the dentist briskly walked away, retrieving from his office a worn copy of Freud's 1930 *Civilization and Its Discontents.* "Solemnly," according to Ettinger, the man read aloud: "'No other technique for the conduct of life attaches the individual so firmly to reality as laying emphasis on'—a dramatic pause—'*work*; for his work at least gives him a secure place in a portion of reality, in the human community.'" The dentist closed the book and announced to his prone patient, "I'll never retire."[2] How could Austen Ettinger even *consider* retirement? Without work to safeguard a sense of purpose, define his relationships with others, and, most significantly it would seem, provide "him a secure place in a portion of reality," the dentist believed the ad man risked the loss of his rank in society and even his very existence. Without productive work, a man became a non-entity: without self, community, or purpose, and as Freud's wording suggested, without gender.

Retiring Men shows that as retirement from work and their twilight years beckoned, older men of the twentieth century redefined their identities as

men in ways that diverged substantially from the more forceful and aggressive masculinities of young men and adolescents. Historians, sociologists,
anthropologists, and journalists have focused almost entirely on how men
construct gender identities during their younger years.[3] This book broadens
our understanding of the history of masculinities by focusing on *aging* men
and their special relationship to work. Productive manhood, or men's need
to show their worthiness as men through labor, became a constant refrain in
men's pursuit of masculinity throughout their life spans during the twentieth
century. Productive manhood represents the essential ingredient of twentieth-
century masculinity, as opposed to the youth-driven excesses found among
practitioners of turn-of-the-century physical culture for example, or the more
modern post-adolescent inhabitants of what sociologist Michael Kimmel
calls "Guyland": a "perilous world" of video games, college fraternities, and
entry-level jobs where former boys try to become adult men.[4]

As *New York Times* reader Walter Spieth of Bethesda, Maryland, wrote in
1969 to the paper, "The most vital characteristic of male adulthood is doing
real work for pay."[5] By implication, the absence of a job posed a direct threat
to the core of adult masculinity. Both Spieth and Austen A. Ettinger's dentist
pointed to what fundamentally defined masculinity throughout the twentieth
century: manhood hinged on a man's ability to sustain life-long ties to labor.
Gainful employment provided the most crucial path to masculinity, allowing
men to separate themselves from the feminized space of the home by laboring in factories and offices, cultivate identities as breadwinners by securing
incomes that guaranteed subsistence to dependents, and define their social
status in relation to other men. Freud briefly noted the ties between labor
and manhood in his book *Civilization and Its Discontents*; and Ettinger's
later choice to retire seemed to reject work as the basis of male identity—an
unwise or even dangerous decision, at least according to his well-read, psy-
choanalytic dentist.

The dentist's insistence that work was the premise of manhood suggests
that ideals of masculinity had changed considerably since the late-nineteenth
century. This productive manhood of the twentieth century challenged late-
nineteenth century masculinities and their legacies, which emphasized that
men needed to embrace physical aggression, reject modernity and "civilization," and retreat into bastions of male exclusivity. While gainful labor had
been celebrated as a basis of adult male identity and a benchmark of male
achievement since the early-nineteenth century, this connection would appear
to be overwhelmed by late-nineteenth century men's ambivalence toward
modern industrial work discipline, the convenience of urban living, the di-
versity of mass society, and the "closing" of the Western frontier as "civilization" advanced westward and forward into the new century. In response,

as historians have rightly shown, men of the late 1800s and early 1900s embraced physical prowess, human mastery of nature, the conquering of new frontiers, and homosocial relations as ways to achieve and ensure male uniqueness, authority, and power. Men of the late nineteenth century associated steady employment with the ease and comfort of "civilization," which for many undercut the physicality and toughness that defined the new man. At the turn of the twentieth century, men struggled to prove manliness by immersing themselves in hazardous sports such as boxing and football, seeking outdoor adventures, joining male-exclusive organizations such as college fraternities and social clubs, and even waging wars of imperial conquest.[6] As several historians of manhood suggest, employment became something of a social and economic obligation, not a path to real manhood.[7]

This book examines an historical irony: how adult men's struggles with aging, retirement, and gender helped create new and enduring connections between working and manhood throughout the twentieth century. The widening of the life span over the twentieth century created new physical, social, and chronological spaces ("old age") where manliness was not certain and needed to be redefined. The average duration of life in the United States increased by 30 years during the twentieth century, from 47 in 1900 to 77 in 2000; and the percent of men and women over the age of 65 also expanded considerably: from 4.1 percent of the US population in 1900 to 12.7 percent in the 1990s.[8] Despite lengthening life, the reality of aging bodies (and biases toward them) would limit the ways older males could demonstrate their worth as men. As this book shows, working would ironically become the path to manhood throughout the adult life course, despite age discrimination in the workplace, mandatory retirement to fixed incomes, and physical changes and limitations that accompanied growing old. Older retired men, both blue- and white-collar, did not look not to the physical aggression of the grid iron or the pranks of the college fraternity as sites where they could secure manhood, but rather to ongoing productivity: to somehow preserve the connection between the labors of their working years and masculinity as they aged. Former working men would often struggle to find new "occupations," both literal and figurative, in their later years, and this process of making a male culture of a "busy" old age and retirement would, in turn, solidify personal productivity as the basic path to masculinity throughout the life cycle. Aging men's efforts to remain productive in their twilight years ensured that work would fundamentally define manhood during the twentieth century, more so than any other social or physical activity or relationship.

However, most historians and other scholars are guilty of focusing too often on the politics of gender among the young and the reckless—subsequently ignoring the old and the restless.[9] While historians, sociologists, and other writers often discuss the age transitions that drive young people's uncertainties about gender, their sensitivity to age ends in adulthood. Scholars of gender and labor frame adulthood too statically, often implicitly focusing on younger people's gender politics and ignoring the age transitions that jeopardize and even undermine gender identities during the adult years. By focusing on masculinity in ways that favor younger subjects and disregarding the adulthood transition into later life and old age, scholars fail to see not only how men and women relate to gender politics as they age, but also the significant historical impact of older men and women's actions and attitudes on the making of gender's history in the twentieth century. Aging men responded to their uncertainty about retirement by looking for ways to stay at work. A friend of Ettinger told the soon-to-retire advertising man that "You are what you produce," even in retirement. Despite advancing years, the friend insisted "we live in a society where our work defines us."[10] Staying busy, remaining industrious: men looked for ways to work throughout adulthood—including the phase of life when men were in the final years of their lives and most disadvantaged in the labor market. Retirement could not be restful. As a result, I argue that older men and those who wrote about them would ensure that working equaled true manhood not only in later life but for adult men of all ages.

Since the 1960s and 1970s, social and cultural historians have fruitfully illustrated how class, race, and gender function as structures of power and building blocks of identities. These power structures have, as scholars point out, limited the civil rights and economic opportunities of working people, persons of color, and women, among other social groups. However, scholars' treatment of class, race, and gender relations ignores the importance of age hierarchies as components of these social identities and relations, the ways identities and social relations change over the life course, and how aging shapes anxieties and conflicts over gender and class. Historians do not typically recognize anxieties about growing old as a basic feature of gender and class identities, nor do they consider how these categories intersect with and contest the others. Citing a 1990 conference paper by Thomas Holt, historian Earl Lewis once described race, class, and gender as an "iron triangle" in historical scholarship. While these concepts have enriched historical knowledge, they also can, as Lewis points out, limit "the range of our imagination."[11] This study takes historians' view of intersecting social categories and identities into another direction, highlighting gender, class, and aging as overlapping and contesting identities and social relations in the twentieth-century past.

By studying the intersections of aging, class, and gender, this book is intended to contribute to labor, masculinity, and women's historians' interests in (1) the construction of gender within the contexts of work and class, organized labor, the family, and the welfare state; and (2) how men and women's responses to economic and social change draw upon, challenge, or reinforce ideas about gender. This study simultaneously builds on gender and labor historians' investigations into the issues of gender identity and sexual difference in working-class life, while urging scholars to explore how the expanding prevalence of growing old in the twentieth century, a period when youth became a building block of popular culture and managerial ideology, contributed to worries about gender in blue-collar and white-collar working-class life, as well as how men (and women) responded to their uncertainties about the relationships between gender and aging. Manhood is not only a key theme in the study of male workers, but later life and old age became essential twentieth-century arenas where men struggled to fabricate and sustain manhood more broadly.

Retiring Men draws and builds upon the insights of numerous earlier scholars in women's history, labor and working-class history, and the history of masculinities. Women's historians first introduced the analytic category of gender to labor, social, and cultural history. Beginning in the 1970s, feminist labor historians challenged the centrality of male workers in the field. They showed that women had always worked in a variety of settings (both paid and unpaid), organized labor unions, and struck for higher wages and better working conditions. In the process, they illustrated how women had never been confined to homes or been passive recipients of historical change. Women's historians also demonstrated how the sexual division of labor was a major component of the social and economic changes wrought by industrialization.[12] Before 1800, men and women typically worked together on farms and in commodity production to support their households; but throughout the 1800s, the industrial revolution divorced "work" from family, moving production to towns, cities, and factories.[13] In addition to the marginalization of women in the market economy, women's labor historians examined the barriers to women's employment by showing how employers and male workers constructed skills and occupations as male. While women did work in textile factories and the sweated needle trades, men predominated in manufacturing employment. Working-class women mostly worked in domestic service and later clerical work. Women's historians showed how gender *and* class (as well as race and ethnicity) defined women's experiences as workers.[14]

Masculinity studies were a direct consequence of scholarship in women's history. To understand men's opposition to feminism and women's employment, scholars looked at how anxious males constructed gendered identities as "men." The subordination of women to male authority, in part, defined these identities. Early works by historians Peter Filene and Peter N. Stearns, written amidst the second wave of American feminism, focused on the social construction of a male gender role in middle-class culture, as well as men's anxieties about women's political activities and male vulnerability.[15] During the 1990s, the masculinity literature expanded considerably. These studies focused on middle- and working-class men, and their responses to social and economic change. Ava Baron's 1990 edited collection *Work Engendered* was a benchmark in labor history. This collection of essays highlighted how men's responses to changing labor processes and unemployment reflected not only a politics of class, but also gendered conceptualizations of work, union, and community.[16] The essays showed how working men have historically constructed class identities that were gender-specific, as well as acted politically to uphold social boundaries between themselves and women. Roger Horowitz's collection of essays in *Boys and Their Toys?* (2001) nicely complemented *Work Engendered*. This compilation of articles by historians of labor and technology focuses on how working men constructed masculinities through professionalization, the socialization of boys, and the design of new technology during the early twentieth century.[17]

The most well-known works on the broader history of masculinity in the United States focus on middle-class men, particularly in the late-nineteenth century. To understand the roots of modern sexism, E. Anthony Rotundo, Michael Kimmel, and Gail M. Bederman, as well as Clifford Putney, John F. Kasson, and Nicholas L. Syrett, argue that nineteenth-century middle-class men constructed ideals about manhood that have long endured: in particular, male authority in the workplace and politics, domesticity for women, and the expression of male power through physicality, sexuality, and exclusivity. Since the market economy was a site of stifling boredom (or worse, possible failure), violent sports and bodybuilding, for instance, provided ways for men to affirm notions of male power on their own terms. Trapped in the modernity of the twentieth century, unable to escape to the western frontier, men used sports to test their courage, stamina, and brawn.[18] Also, Gail Bederman, Kristin Hoganson, and Glenda Elizabeth Gilmore highlighted the late-nineteenth century intersections of manhood and race, linking men's unease about gender to racial violence and the New Imperialism.[19]

As women's labor historians and historians of masculinities collectively suggest, nineteenth- and twentieth-century economic change—especially industrial capitalism and class formation—determinedly shaped conflicts and male gender anxieties. The consequences of capitalist development have been central to historical analyses of manhood in the women's history literature and the masculinities literature. Historically, men's struggle to affirm manhood has been a significant response to the economic, personal, and familial upheavals and transformations brought about by industrialization.

There are four main lines of inquiry in the literatures which deal with working-class and middle-class manhood since roughly 1800. First, historians frequently describe how men battle to protect politics and the workplace as male territory: for instance, they have often opposed women's presence in factories and offices, unions, and politics.[20] Second, in factories and offices shared by men and women, men have emphasized careful boundaries between "men's" and "women's" work. Men have frequently classified "their" jobs and skills as masculine, using gendered conceptualizations of work to marginalize and exclude women from hiring and promotion.[21] Working males also used the labor movement to protect their economic and social interests as men, utilizing organization to defend their jobs as the foundation of manhood and the "manliness" of their occupations.[22] As historians of gender and labor have argued, "class" has been very much about gender, for both men and women. Working men not only struggled with employers over their economic and social status as "workers"; more specifically, they defended their status as "working-class men." Third, in addition to the workplace, men have utilized what might be termed "after-hours" activities—religious organizations, fraternities, sex, hobbies, and sports—as paths to masculinity and secure bastions to protect their manhood.[23] The socialization of boys and adolescents into "men" is the fourth major theme in the historiography on masculinity. Nineteenth-century middle-class "boy culture" and adolescence took shape within the context of separated spheres ideals and industrialization. Male youth worked out masculine identities in the streets—away from the parlors and playrooms at home. Boys also mimicked their fathers' occupations, and learned the values of competition, self-mastery, and strength through fighting and sports. Boyhood prepared young males for manhood in a modern world: to thrive and succeed in the volatile adult male world of business. Historians revealed how boys were thus socialized to accept and endorse conceptualizations of men's and women's different (and unequal) social roles.[24] As the various literatures on gender suggest, economic development during the era of the industrialization created new social spaces (such as factories, craft unions, offices, clubs, and fraternities) where men would struggle to impose order in the form of gender boundaries, as well as raised questions about gender, order, and authority in the familiar sites of home and community.

But what happens when men grow old?

The following chapters detail two related lines of argument: (1) the ways that the increasing prevalence of growing old and retirement during the twentieth century ironically re-affirmed work, and more broadly productivity, as the requisite paths to manhood—a kind of masculinity that I call productive manhood; and (2) how productive manhood became the foundation of retirement

culture and successful aging. During the early twentieth century, new celebrations of youth and speed as cardinal virtues in the American industrial
economy jeopardized older men's foothold in the labor market, bringing into
relief the fragile connections between work and the male breadwinner ideal.
As men aged on the job, the question of the ability to work in later life assumed utmost importance. Discussions of manhood now centered on work
and the ability of a man to sustain identities as worker and breadwinner over
the expanding life cycle. Men would continue to look for ways to maintain
their personal productivity—even in retirement: the period of life when they
would presumably no longer work. Even as bodies, abilities, and health
would ultimately wane near the end of the life cycle, men remained committed to productivity as the true path to manhood.

Initially, at the start of the twentieth century, discussions of manhood, age,
and work began in industry and centered on working-class men. Chapter
1 explores older working men's struggles in the labor market of the early
twentieth century. Men on the job confronted a glaring contradiction: powerful industrial employers of the early 1900s demanded youth and speed from
laborers to match the increasing pace and vaunted newness of their mass
production assembly lines and mechanized factories, at a time when working-
class men now lived longer lives than ever before. How could an aging male
retain an identity as a "working man" if his employer regarded him as redundant, out-of-date, and unqualified in the new era of modern mass production?
Working men of the early twentieth century confronted extensive patterns of
age discrimination in American workplaces that fundamentally jeopardized
manhood, especially later in life. The prevalence of ageism in the factory
fueled ongoing criticisms of industrial management among working men,
unionists, and reformers, and a widespread affirmation of work as a foundation of manhood throughout the life cycle.

Worries about the instability of breadwinning and manhood for older
workers propelled demands for pensions from the state during the 1920s
and 1930s. Chapter 2 explores why state pensions emerged as the principal
way to address what pension scholar Gorton James described in 1921 as "the
problem of the old man." During the 1920s, social provision experts, working
men, and craft unionists concluded that only pensions from the state could
uphold the masculinity of the aging male breadwinner. Working men, experts
argued, could not count on earning good wages and accumulating savings for
old age due to employers' disregard for older workers. Other possible solutions were not acceptable because they undermined manhood—aging men
disliked institutionalization and relying on children because these support
systems failed to sustain independent households headed by a male breadwinner. In addition, pensions from industry would not suffice since so few em-

ployers offered them. Working men and experts viewed state pensions as just and deserved rewards for older workers after a lifetime of work. Widespread concerns about the social and economic foundations of masculinity propelled the unfolding support for old-age assistance and the nascent American welfare state during the interwar period. And in the decade before the 1930s and the creation of the Social Security Act, experts and workers had already concluded that only pensions from the state could sustain manhood when men would no longer be allowed to work.[25]

The Great Depression was the most extensive challenge to the connection between labor and masculinity during the twentieth century. The economic collapse of the 1930s undermined working-class manhood on a massive scale, as roughly 25 percent of the US population was out of work in 1932 alone. As observers and historians have noted, the extensiveness of unemployment was thought to be the cause of a "crisis" of masculinity. However, as Chapter 3 shows, aging men, politicians, unionists, and reformers pursued numerous strategies to somehow ensure manliness in the dangerously unmanly context of joblessness. Politicians passed the Social Security Act in 1935, in part, to honor the labors of aging working men after life-long careers, promising to uphold, at least to some extent, his earned identity as a worker and breadwinner. Struggling, jobless white-collar men formed new organizations such as Forty Plus Clubs that reconstructed the culture and practices of the male-dominated office, and agitated for new job opportunities for older men. In other settings, workers and unionists labored to strengthen the bonds between employment and masculinity. In mass production factories, the new Committee for Industrial Organization (CIO) made aging working men's struggles on the shopfloor a cornerstone of labor's politics during the 1930s, pushing for seniority clauses that would protect older men's ties to the workplace as they aged. Also, aging men explored ways to secure manhood by looking for possible ways in the consumer marketplace that might bring them back to the workplace. During the Great Depression, companies offered products and advice that promised to give aging men the youthful pep, vigor, and healthy looks that would help them hold on to their jobs, or find new ones, in the unstable and merciless labor market of the decade.

Chapters 4 and 5 examine the making of postwar retirement culture. During the 1940s and 1950s, on the foundations of an expanding Social Security program and a widening system of workplace pensions, the new economic and cultural institution of "retirement" took shape. Americans expected older men to retire at sixty-five. However, prevailing ideals about postwar manhood now hinged on new middle-class standards of living and personal productivity, while the culture of the early Cold War celebrated team work and service to the nation as core male values. As observers embraced the idea that the United

States was now a middle-class nation, they no longer discussed blue collar working-class men and matters of economic justice, but envisioned the typical aging male worker as a financially well-off white-collar professional. Aging men struggled to secure manhood at a time when productivity, status, and professional success mattered more than ever. As Chapter 4 shows, men's uncertainties about productive manhood in later life could be seen in frequent discussions of sudden death, illness, isolation, the disruption of separated spheres for men and women, the loss of sexual ability, and uncomfortable retirement ceremonies that signaled the end of men's careers.

Chapter 5 explores how a new generation of retirement advice authors, magazine writers, sociologists, and gerontologists established a retirement culture after World War II on the basis of perpetual activity and productivity. Experts described how retired men could maintain productivity in retirement through rigorous new routines of leisure, home improvement activities, yard work, and strategic retreats to dens, home offices, and garage or basement workshops. To be "men" without gainful employment, "successful" retired males needed to work hard (and well) at having fun and maintaining a healthy distance from women. Golf, shuffleboard, and fishing, for example, were not avocations; for retired men they became new professions—and pathways out of the stifling and feminizing domesticity of the household. Some men, however, refused to play and rejected retirement outright, as many uneasy retirees struggled to rejoin the labor force, while others tried to launch new businesses. As the writings and spoken words of culture producers, scholars, and retirees demonstrated, successful retirement paradoxically centered upon the maintenance of a manly work ethic.[26] Austen A. Ettinger confronted the continuing and powerful intersections of manhood and labor in postwar retirement culture in the decidedly ordinary setting of a dentist's office. His dentist (and other men he knew) insisted that he would have to continue working in his retirement—*at something.*[27]

Later life thus became a key site during the twentieth century where men (and women) struggled to make sense of shifting gender boundaries and identities, aging bodies, and changing economic circumstances. Like workplaces and other sites, aging men labored (often literally) to establish hierarchies of gender in their old age, and women would be symbolically and politically sidelined by the preeminence of men in discussions of retirement and aging for much of the twentieth century. However, like workplaces, unions, and other sites, women's actions would challenge the masculinity that prevailed throughout so much of postwar retirement culture.

Even though later life constituted a cultural space that privileged men, the formations of productive manhood in later life subtly challenged the masculinities of youth. Old age necessitated reformulations of gender that were, by comparison, less belligerent, more flexible, and more welcoming to women than those found in the college fraternity, on the football field, or in the rough culture of the factory or saloon.

By studying the history of men, manhood, and growing old, it is my hope that historians and other scholars will take away a more dynamic and nuanced view of identities and social relations. Gender "as a category of analysis" originally showed us how to locate and deconstruct power and inequalities rooted in the concepts of sex and class; but this book pushes historians' often ageless, sometimes youth-driven, formulations of gender and class into a lesser-known frontier: the twilight years of historical actors' lives.

We begin in the early-twentieth century, in the new era of mass production. When they interviewed aging working men and women for *Middletown: A Study in American Culture* (1929), the sociologists Robert S. Lynd and Helen Merrell Lynd heard numerous remarks concerning the troubled relationship between growing old and men's ties to the workplace. "In general," they observed, "it appears that male members of the working class start to work from fourteen to eighteen, reach their prime in the twenties, and begin to fail in their late forties."[28] If shops and factories favored young workers, how could industrial veterans sustain identities as working men? The first chapter begins in the 1900s, 1910s, and 1920s, when managers reorganized work around youth and speed—and aging men began to "fail."

NOTES

1. Sigmund Freud, *Civilization and its Discontents*, trans. James Strachey (1930; repr., New York: WW Norton & Company, 1961), 27.

2. Austen A. Ettinger, "The Retiring Kind," *New York Times*, 28 May 1989, 18.

3. In addition to the works by academic historians discussed below, see David D. Gilmore, *Manhood in the Making: Cultural Concepts of Masculinity* (New Haven: Yale University Press, 1990); RW Connell, *Masculinities* (Berkeley: University of California Press, 1995); and Susan Faludi, *Stiffed: The Betrayal of the American Man* (New York: HarperCollins Publishers, 1999).

4. Michael Kimmel, *Guyland: The Perilous World Where Boys Become Men* (New York: HarperCollins, 2008). For related themes from American history, I recommend Nicholas L. Syrett, *The Company He Keeps: A History of White College Fraternities* (Chapel Hill: University of North Carolina Press, 2009).

5. Walter Spieth, "Adolescence Forever," *New York Times*, 30 November 1969, SM38.

6. See Elliot Gorn, *The Manly Art: Bare-Knuckle Prize Fighting in America* (Ithaca: Cornell University Press, 1986); E. Anthony Rotundo, *American Manhood:*

Transformations in Masculinity from the Revolution to the Modern Era (New York: Free Press, 1993); Gail Bederman, *Manliness and Civilization: A Cultural History of Gender and Race in the United States, 1880–1917* (Chicago: University of Chicago Press, 1995); Michael Kimmel, *Manhood in America: A Cultural History* (New York: Free Press, 1996); Clifford Putney, *Muscular Christianity: Manhood and Sports in Protestant America, 1880–1920* (Cambridge: Harvard University Press, 2001); John F. Kasson, *Houdini, Tarzan, and the Perfect Man: The White Male Body and the Challenge of Modernity in America* (New York: Hill and Wang, 2001); Kristin Hoganson, *Fighting for American Manhood: How Gender Politics Provoked the Spanish-American and Philippine-American Wars* (New Haven: Yale University Press, 1998); John Pettegrew, *Brutes in Suits: Male Sensibility in America, 1890–1920* (Baltimore: Johns Hopkins University Press, 2007); and Syrett, *Company He Keeps*. Richard Briggs Stott argues that American men's rough culture of manliness was in noted decline by the late nineteenth century. See Stott's book, *Jolly Fellows: Male Milieus in Nineteenth-Century America* (Baltimore: Johns Hopkins University Press, 2009), esp. 1–3.

7. A key exception is Jacqueline M. Moore, *Cow Boys and Cattle Men: Class and Masculinities on the Texas Frontier, 1865–1900* (New York: New York University Press, 2010), esp. 60, 68.

8. "The Senior Profile," *USA Today*, 20 July 1995, 1.

9. There are some noteworthy exceptions. See Carole Haber and Brian Gratton, *Old Age and the Search for Security: An American Social History* (Bloomington: Indiana University Press, 1994); Laura Davidow Hirshbein, "The Transformation of Old Age: Expertise, Gender, and National Identity, 1900–1950" (PhD diss., Johns Hopkins University, 2000); Toni M. Calasanti and Kathleen F. Slevin, *Gender, Social Inequalities, and Aging* (Lanham, MD: Rowman & Littlefield, 2001); Toni Calasanti, "Bodacious Berry, Potency Wood and the Aging Monster: Gender and Age Relations in Anti-Aging Ads," *Social Forces* 86:1 (2007): 335–355. The broader historiography on aging and the aged in the United States is not primarily concerned with gender as a category of analysis. See David Hackett Fischer, *Growing Old in America* (New York: Oxford University Press, 1978); W. Andrew Achenbaum, *Old Age in the New Land: The American Experience Since 1790* (Baltimore: Johns Hopkins University Press, 1978); William Graebner, *A History of Retirement: The Meaning and Function of an American Institution, 1885–1978* (New Haven: Yale University Press, 1980); and David Van Tassel and Peter N. Stearns, eds., *Old Age in a Bureaucratic Society: The Elderly, the Experts, and the State in American History* (New York: Greenwood Press, 1986). For a brief discussion of aging male bodies in masculinity studies, see Stephen M. Whitehead, *Men and Masculinities: Key Themes and New Directions* (Cambridge, UK: Polity, 2002), 199–202.

10. Ettinger, "Retiring Kind," 18.

11. See Earl Lewis, "Invoking Concepts, Problematizing Identities: The Life of Charles N. Hunter and the Implications for the Study of Gender and Labor," *Labor History* 34:2–3 (1993), 295–296; as well as Evelyn Nakano Glenn, "Protest, Resistance, and Survival in the Jim Crow South," *Labor History* 39:2 (1998): 173; and Christopher Tomlins, "Why Wait for Industrialism? Work, Legal Culture, and the

Example of Early America—An Historiographical Argument," *Labor History* 40:1 (1999): 7–8. Major books throughout the 1990s–2000s by historians of race and labor underscore scholars' long-standing and ongoing interest in the intersections of race, gender, and class. See, among many other great studies, David R. Roediger, *The Wages of Whiteness: Race and the Making of the American Working Class* (New York: Verso, 1991); Robin DG Kelley, *Hammer and Hoe: Alabama Communists during the Great Depression* (Chapel Hill: University of North Carolina Press, 1990); George Lipsitz, *Rainbow at Midnight: Labor and Culture in the 1940s* (Urbana: University of Illinois Press, 1994); Neil Foley, *The White Scourge: Mexicans, Blacks, and Poor Whites in Texas Cotton Culture* (Berkeley: University of California Press, 1997); Amy Dru Stanley, *From Bondage to Contract: Wage Labor, Marriage, and the Market in the Age of Slave Emancipation* (New York: Cambridge University Press, 1998); Tera Hunter, *To 'Joy My Freedom: Southern Black Women's Lives and Labors After the Civil War* (Cambridge: Harvard University Press, 1998); William P. Jones, *The Tribe of Black Ulysses: African American Lumber Workers in the Jim Crow South* (Urbana: University of Illinois Press, 2005); Julie Greene, *The Canal Builders: Making America's Empire at the Panama Canal* (New York: Penguin Books, 2009); Katherine Benton-Cohen, *Borderline Americans: Race and Labor War in the Arizona Borderlands* (Cambridge: Harvard University Press, 2009); and Cynthia M. Blair, *I've Got To Make My Livin': Black Women's Sex Work in Turn-of-the-Century Chicago* (Chicago: University of Chicago Press, 2010). For a recent overview of intersectionality in studies of race, class, and gender, see Ava Baron and Eileen Boris, "'The Body' As a Useful Category for Working-Class History," *Labor: Studies in Working-Class History of the Americas* 4:2 (2007): 23–43. For key examples of major studies of the intersections of gender and race, see Bederman, *Manliness and Civilization*; Glenda Elizabeth Gilmore, *Gender and Jim Crow: Women and the Politics of White Supremacy in North Carolina, 1896–1920* (Chapel Hill: University of North Carolina Press, 1996); Kathleen M. Brown, *Good Wives, Nasty Wenches, and Anxious Patriarchs: Gender, Race, and Power in Colonial Virginia* (Chapel Hill: University of North Carolina Press, 1996); Naoko Shibusawa, *America's Geisha Ally: Reimagining the Japanese Enemy* (Cambridge: Harvard University Press, 2006); and Crystal N. Feimster, *Southern Horrors: Women and the Politics of Rape and Lynching* (Cambridge: Harvard University Press, 2009). Scholars have urged historians to pursue other forms of identity, including age. These works, however, continue to focus largely on questions of class, race, and gender. See Lewis, "Invoking Concepts, Problematizing Identities," 295–296; and Gunja Sengupta, "Elites, Subalterns, and American Identities: A Case Study of African-American Benevolence," *American Historical Review* 109:4 (2004): esp. 1105. Ava Baron cites age as a key category of analysis for gender and labor historians. However, Baron is predominantly interested in younger working-class men and boys. See Ava Baron, "Questions of Gender: Deskilling and Demasculinization in the US Printing Industry, 1830–1915," *Gender & History* 1:2 (1989): 180; and idem, "An 'Other' Side of Gender Antagonism at Work: Men, Boys, and the Remasculinization of Printers' Work, 1830–1920," in *Work Engendered*. A 2004 essay, which examined young women as national symbols in *fin-de-siecle* France, also argued for discussions of age in gender history. This article, however, focuses on young women. See David M. Pomfret, "'A Muse for the Masses': Gender, Age, and Nation in France, Fin de Siecle," *American Historical Review* 109:5 (2004): 1441–1442. For further considerations of gender and age, see Shibusawa, *America's Geisha Ally*.

12. For useful introductions to the field of US women's history, see Ava Baron, "Gender and Labor History: Learning from the Past, Looking to the Future," in *Work Engendered: Towards a New History of American Labor*, ed. Ava Baron (Ithaca: Cornell University Press, 1990), 9–14; Vicki L. Ruiz and Ellen Carol DuBois, eds., *Unequal Sisters: A Multi-Cultural Reader in US Women's History*, 2nd edition (New York: Routledge, 1994); Jane Sherron De Hart and Linda K. Kerber, "Introduction: Gender and the New Women's History," in *Women's America: Refocusing the Past*, fifth edition (New York: Oxford University Press, 2000), 3–24; and Linda Gordon, "US Women's History," in *The New American History*, ed. Eric Foner (Philadelphia: Temple University Press, 1997), 267–273. On gender as a category of analysis, be sure to begin with Joan Wallach Scott, *Gender and the Politics of History* (New York: Columbia University Press, 1988).

13. For an overview of working-class women in the nineteenth and twentieth centuries, see Alice Kessler-Harris, *Out to Work: A History of Wage-Earning Women in the United States* (New York: Oxford University Press, 1982); as well as various sections of Nancy Cott, ed., *No Small Courage: A History of Women in the United States* (New York: Oxford University Press, 2000). On the early industrial revolution and ideas about women's work, see Christine Stansell, *City of Women: Sex and Class in New York, 1789–1860* (Urbana: University of Illinois Press, 1987); Thomas Dublin, *Women at Work: The Transformation of Work and Community in Lowell, Massachusetts, 1826–1860* (New York: Columbia University Press, 1979); Mary H. Blewett, *Men, Women, and Work: Class, Gender, and Protest in the New England Shoe Industry, 1780–1910* (Urbana: University of Illinois Press, 1988); and Jeanne Boydston, *Home and Work: Housework, Wages, and the Ideology of Labor in the Early Republic* (New York: Oxford University Press, 1990).

14. There is a rich literature on the construction of gender and the sexual division of labor during the nineteenth and twentieth centuries. See, for instance, Maurine Greenwald, *Women, War, and Work: The Impact of World War I on Women Workers in the United States* (Westport, CT: Greenwood Press, 1980); Maurine Greenwald and Richard Oestreicher, "Engendering US History: Rethinking Masternarratives," essay in the author's possession, 2001; SJ Kleinberg, *The Shadow of the Mills: Working-Class Families in Pittsburgh, 1870–1907* (Pittsburgh: University of Pittsburgh Press, 1989); Ruth Milkman, *Gender at Work: The Dynamics of Job Segregation by Sex during World War II* (Urbana: University of Illinois Press, 1987); Blewett, *Men, Women, and Work*; Stansell, *City of Women*; Dublin, *Women at Work*; Boydston, *Home and Work*; Susan Porter Benson, *Counter Cultures: Saleswomen, Managers, and Customers in American Department Stores, 1890–1940* (Urbana: University of Illinois Press, 1986); Sonya O. Rose, *Limited Livelihoods: Gender and Class in Nineteenth-Century England* (Berkeley: University of California Press, 1990); Kathy Peiss, *Cheap Amusements: Working Women and Leisure in Turn-of-the-Century New York* (Philadelphia: Temple University Press, 1986); the essays in Baron, ed., *Work*

Engendered; Patricia A. Cooper, *Once A Cigar Maker: Men, Women, and Work Culture in American Cigar Factories, 1900–1919* (Urbana: University of Illinois Press, 1987); Sharon Hartman Strom, *Beyond the Typewriter: Gender, Class, and the Origins of Modern American Office Work, 1900–1930* (Urbana: University of Illinois Press, 1992); Stanley, *From Bondage to Contract*; and Elizabeth Faue, *Community of Suffering and Struggle: Women, Men, and the Labor Movement in Minneapolis, 1914–1945* (Chapel Hill: University of North Carolina Press, 1991).

15. Peter G. Filene, *Him/Her/Self: Sex Roles in Modern America* (1978; repr., Baltimore: Johns Hopkins University Press, 1986); Peter N. Stearns, *Be a Man! Males in Modern Society* (New York: Holmes & Meier Publishers, 1979).

16. Baron, ed., *Work Engendered*. *Work Engendered* was immediately preceded by Elliot Gorn's study of nineteenth-century boxing, Alice Kessler-Harris' 1989 article on male breadwinner ideology during the Great Depression, and the 1989 *Gender & History* "Formations of Masculinity" forum. See Gorn, *The Manly Art*; Alice Kessler-Harris, "Gender Ideology in Historical Reconstruction: A Case Study from the 1930s," *Gender & History* 1:1 (1989): 31–49; Cynthia Cockburn, "Introduction," *Gender & History* 1:2 (1989), 15163; Keith McClelland, "Some Thoughts on Masculinity and the 'Representative Artisan' in Britain, 1850–1880," *Gender & History* 1:2 (1989), 164–177; Baron, "Questions of Gender," 178–199; and Ella Johansson, "Beautiful Men, Fine Women and Good Work People: Gender and Skill in Northern Sweden, 1850–1950," *Gender & History* 1:2 (1989): 200–212. For other key analyses of working-class manhood during the 1990s and 2000s, see Elizabeth Faue, *Community of Suffering and Struggle: Women, Men, and the Labor Movement in Minneapolis, 1914–1945* (Chapel Hill: University of North Carolina Press, 1991); Alice Kessler-Harris, "Treating the Male As 'Other': Redefining the Parameters of Labor History 34:2–3 (1993): 190–204; Lisa M. Fine, "'Our Big Factory Family': Masculinity and Paternalism at the Reo Motor Car Company of Lansing, Michigan," *Labor History*, 34:2–3 (1993), 274–291; George Chauncey, *Gay New York: Gender, Urban Culture, and the Making of the Gay Male World, 1890–1940* (New York: Free Press, 1994); Steve Meyer, "Rough Manhood: The Aggressive and Confrontational Shop Culture of US Auto Workers during World War II," *Journal of Social History* 36 (2002): 125–147; idem, "Workplace Predators: Sexuality and Harassment on the US Automotive Shop Floor, 1930–1960," *Labor: Studies in Working-Class History of the Americas* 1:1 (2004): 77–93; Joshua R. Greenberg, *Advocating the Man: Masculinity, Organized Labor, and the Household in New York, 1800–1840* (New York: Columbia University Press, 2008); and Moore. *Cow Boys and Cattle Men.*

17. Roger Horowitz, ed., *Boys and Their Toys? Masculinity, Class, and Technology in America* (New York: Routledge, 2001). See also Greenberg, *Advocating the Man*; Gregory L. Kaster, "Labour's True Man: Organised Workingmen and the Language of Manliness in the USA, 1827–1877," *Gender & History* 13:1 (2001): 24–64; Steve Estes, "'I AM a Man!' Race, Masculinity, and the 1968 Memphis Sanitation Strike," *Labor History* 41:2 (2000): 8–32; Frank Tobias Higbie, *Indispensable Outcasts: Hobo Workers and Community in the American Midwest, 1880–1930* (Urbana: University of Illinois Press, 2003); and Brian P. Luskey, *On*

the Make: Clerks and the Quest for Capital in Nineteenth-Century America* (New York: New York University Press, 2010).

18. See the studies cited in note 6 above.

19. Bederman, *Manliness and Civilization*; Hoganson, *Fighting for American Manhood*; Gilmore, *Gender and Jim Crow*.

20. Baron, "Questions of Gender," 178–199; Kimmel, *Manhood in America*; Faue, *Community of Suffering and Struggle*; Stansell, *City of Women*, Kessler-Harris, *Out to Work*, Rotundo, *American Manhood*; Milkman, *Gender at Work*; Gilmore, *Gender and Jim Crow*.

21. Milkman, *Gender at Work*; Gabin, *Feminism in the Labor Movement*; Strom, *Beyond the Typewriter*; Blewett, *Men, Women, and Work*; Benson, *Counter Cultures*; Cooper, "Faces of Gender"; Gregory L. Kaster, "Labour's True Man: Organised Workingmen and the Language of Manliness in the USA, 1827–1877," *Gender & History* 13:1 (2001): 24–64; Kevin Boyle, "The Kiss: Racial and Gender Conflict in a 1950s Automobile Factory," *Journal of American History* 84:2 (1997): 496–523; Jim Rose, "'The Problem Every Supervisor Dreads': Women Workers at the US Steel Duquesne Works during World War II," *Labor History* 36:1 (1995): 24, 40–43; Wayne A. Lewchuk, "Men and Monotony: Fraternalism as a Managerial Strategy at the Ford Motor Company," *Journal of Economic History* 53:4 (1993): 824–856.

22. Faue, *Community of Suffering and Struggle*; Gabin, *Feminism in the Labor Movement*; Rose, *Limited Livelihoods*; Stansell, *City of Women*; Greenberg, *Advocating the Man*; Kimmel, *Manhood in America*, esp. 56–57.

23. Bederman, *Manliness and Civilization*, esp. 16–17; idem, "'The Women Have Had Charge of the Church Work Long Enough': The Men and Religion Forward Movement of 1911–1912 and the Masculinization of Middle-Class Protestantism," *American Quarterly* 41 (1989): 432–465; Kristen Haring, "The 'Freer Men' of Ham Radio: How A Technical Hobby Provided Social and Spatial Distance," *Technology and Culture* 44:4 (2003): 734–761; Gorn, *Manly Art*; Timothy Gilfoyle, *City of Eros: New York City, Prostitution, and the Commercialization of Sex, 1790–1920* (New York: Norton, 1992); Michael Kaplan, "New York City Tavern Violence and the Creation of a Working-Class Male Identity," *Journal of the Early Republic* 15 (1995): 591–617; Faludi, *Stiffed*; Chauncey, *Gay New York*; Putney, *Muscular Christianity*; Kasson, *Houdini, Tarzan and the Perfect Man*; Kimmel, *Manhood in America*; Rotundo, *American Manhood*; Syrett, *Company He Keeps*; Theresa E. Runstedtler, "Journeymen: Race, Boxing, and the Transnational World of Jack Johnson" (PhD, diss., Yale University, 2007); Stacy L. Lorenz and Geraint B. Osborne, "'Talk About Strenuous Hockey': Violence, Manhood, and the 1907 Ottawa Silver Seven-Montreal Wanderer Rivalry," *Journal of Canadian Studies* 40:1 (2006): 125–156.

24. Rotundo, *American Manhood*, chs. 2–3; Kimmel, *Manhood in America*, esp. 162–164; Bederman, *Manliness and Civilization*, 77–120. See also Moore, *Cow Boys and Cattle Men*, esp. 43–67. For additional historical analyses of the boyhood/adolescent transition to manhood in US history, see various essays in Horowitz, ed., *Boys and Their Toys?* as well as E. Michelle Kilbourne, "Self-Made Men: The Margins of Manliness Among Northern Industrial Workers, 1850–1920" (PhD diss., Emory University, 2000). Scholars in anthropology and sociology also focus heavily on the

socialization of boys. See Gilmore, *Manhood in the Making*; R W Connell, *The Men and the Boys* (Berkeley: University of California Press, 2001); and Michael Messner, "The Life of a Man's Seasons: Male Identity in the Life Course of the Jock," in *Changing Men: New Directions in Research on Men and Masculinity*, ed. Michael Kimmel (Newbury Park, CA: Sage Publications, 1987), 53–67.

25. On the origins, politics, and social ramifications of Social Security, be sure to begin with the diverging viewpoints presented in Jill Quadagno, *The Transformation of Old Age Security: Class and Politics in the American Welfare State* (Chicago: University of Chicago Press, 1988); and Graebner, *History of Retirement*; as well as Ann Shola Orloff, *The Politics of Pensions: A Comparative Analysis of Britain, Canada, and the United States, 1880–1940* (Madison: University of Wisconsin Press, 1993).

26. On the culture of the Protestant work ethic during the nineteenth century, see Daniel T. Rodgers, *The Work Ethic in Industrial America, 1850–1920* (Chicago: University of Chicago Press, 1978).

27. Ettinger, "Retiring Kind," 18.

28. Robert S. Lynd and Helen Merrell Lynd, *Middletown: A Study in American Culture* (New York: Harcourt, Brace, and Company 1929), 34–35.

Chapter One

Growing Old at Work during the Early Twentieth Century

Whenever you get old they are done with you.

—Unnamed working-class woman and wife of a
factory worker, age 40, in Muncie, Indiana, 1929[1]

In only a few words, the woman in Muncie summarized a grave problem that plagued so many working people in 1929, including her own husband: As industrial workers aged in the new era of mass production, employers no longer wanted to employ these supposedly slower and less efficient individuals. This hardening bias against older laborers struck hard at the foundations of gender and identity among members of the respectable adult working class. Working men of the early twentieth century viewed steady work and the family wage as core fundamentals of adult male identity; they assumed that factory work was to be reserved for adult men who would use their earnings to provide for a wife, dependents, and an independent household. However, the instability of men's employment over the lengthening life course insured that respectable working-class manhood became too fragile, if not altogether unsustainable, because of, as the social commentator Stuart Chase put it, "the apparently increasing difficulty with which men over forty retain their jobs, and the even greater difficulty with which they find a new job once they have lost an old one."[2]

After 1900, the rapid transition to mass production labor processes in basic industries such as steel and automobile manufacturing, combined with the lengthening of the average human life span in the United States, challenged men's long-term ties to labor. Working men faced a troubling contradiction: They would live longer and longer lives in the new century, but managers were less inclined to provide employment for them in their later years. Grow-

18

ing old was an overriding source of anxiety in working-class life, more central to working-class men's concerns than other sources of male angst: the recent "closing" of the Western frontier, women's suffrage activism, the Nineteenth Amendment, the proposed Equal Rights Amendment, the prominence of women in factories, offices, movies, and stores, the visibility of "flappers" in the media, and concerns about the effeminizing effects of "civilization."[3]

Age discrimination was rampant in the early twentieth century. In modern industry, young men became employers' favorite kind of working man. Young men's agile bodies allowed them to work long hours at grueling physical tasks carried on at high speeds, and they could be paid less to work the assembly lines and operate new machines. To build a youthful labor force that could sustain employers' demands for efficiency, lower labor costs, and maximum production, managers implemented hiring age limits and various systems of dismissal to weed out those they regarded as the weakest. As a result men struggled to keep going, as workers and breadwinners, in the lengthening and uncertain terrain of longer life.

MANHOOD: "THE WORKING PERIOD"

Beginning in the early 1800s, ideals about working-class male identity hinged on productive work, the male breadwinner ideal, the notion of a family wage in an industrializing economy, functional bodies, and the power they gave men within the home and the public. The images of the "heroic artisan" of the United States and the "representative artisan" of England, for instance, celebrated physical ability, "honest" toil, and the ability to provide for a household. With his sleeves rolled up and an apron tied around his waist, the adult working man shouldered a hammer and forged his value in the market and the workplace.[4] Organized labor pointed to these themes, such as the mighty arm-and-hammer symbol adopted by the General Trades Union of New York City in 1836. The ability to complete gainful labor—either as a wage earner, or more ideally as an independent proprietor—was the primary indicator of a man's worth. As the Detroit branch of the Greenback Labor Party noted in a broad 1881 definition of the working man: "By 'workingmen' our organization means every man, who by his own legitimate and honest industry, provides for himself and his family."[5] In 1854, Henry David Thoreau noted during a lecture, "Work, work, work . . . It would be glorious to see mankind at leisure for once." "Work and days were offered us," he said, "and we chose work." Also, historians Daniel T. Rodgers and Nick Salvatore wrote of labor in the American culture during the nineteenth century that there was a "commitment to the moral primacy of work."[6]

Even in the early nineteenth century, men recognized aging as a threat to their ability to work and earn. An aging male might retain some status as a font of wisdom during the 1800s, but this was not necessarily enough to fit the ideal of a "man." In the 1840s, for example, men in the shoe industry feared that limited job prospects and low wages denied them a "competence": enough money for economic stability, personal independence, and sustenance in old age. To forcefully call attention to older workers' troubles, antebellum unionists wrote about the most dire and desperate cases. Union men in Lynn, Massachusetts, reprinted the content of a suicide note written by a struggling older shoe cutter who took his own life in 1848. "As I grow old, and my health fails, and I find myself less able to provide for myself and live as I want to, and not be dependent on others," the dying man wrote, "I take the method you will find when it happens."[7] These anxieties never dissipated as industrialization advanced. In 1875, another working man in Massachusetts explained that he was unable to envision a future as an older person in industry. "With present conditions of business," as quoted by historian David Hackett Fischer, "I don't want to live to sixty-five." Using more moderate language, other workers discussed their physical struggles with growing old amidst the industrial revolution, while others pointed to the emerging problem of age discrimination. An ironworker in 1875 remarked in the *National Labor Tribune* that boilers were "old" at forty as a result of "declining strength." Because of the demanding work, and constant exposure to intense heat, it was difficult to work in the mills for so many years. In 1884, resentful workers at International Harvester in Chicago petitioned company chief Cyrus H. McCormick about a factory superintendent who targeted older men for dismissal. "It only pains us to relate to you," workers wrote, "that a good many of our old hands is not here this season and if Mr. Evans is kept another season a good many more will leave."[8]

Certainly, work and masculinity were deeply connected, but by the late nineteenth century youthful bodies had become crucial to the expression of strength, vitality, and the execution of productive labor. By the turn-of-the-twentieth century, men worried increasingly about strength and longevity, as they believed "civilization" and modernity rendered them economically, socially, and physically vulnerable. As more and more men lived in crowded cities and worked in sedentary office jobs or exhausting factories, they agonized over the erosion of their bodies due to abuse and disuse. By 1900, men were advised to invest heavily in new ways to strengthen their bodies and protect their health. In advice books and advertisements, self-anointed experts urged men to exercise, drink elixirs, engage in outdoor activities, and surgically "rejuvenate" their glands in order to stay virile, strong, and young.[9] This emphasis on sustaining robust health suggested that maintaining youth could protect masculinity. In contrast, growing old evoked worries about physical decline and the loss of manhood. Experts lamented the aging male's supposedly declining physical and mental capabilities. Upon on his own retirement, William Osler, a famous professor in the Johns Hopkins University medical school, stated in 1905 that men over forty no longer ranked among the productive elements of society.[10] Men cherished what young bodies could accomplish; in later life, men's older bodies would someday fail them. An aging Ernest Hemingway, struggling with cancer and depression, understood this too well. Just before his suicide in 1961, Hemingway mourned: "What does a man care about? Staying healthy. Working good . . . I haven't any of them."[11]

Men in the United States and Great Britain celebrated young bodies and their physicality through sport. As the industrial revolution supposedly robbed men of their vigor, both working-class and middle-class men embraced sport to get it back. Men flocked to prizefights and football games as new ways to celebrate male bodies and their strength. Successful boxers, football players, and wrestlers embodied the virtues of aggression, competition, strength, and fair play. When the famous prizefighters Jack Johnson (a black man) and Jim Jeffries (a white man) squared off in a racially charged bout in 1910, white men's admiration of Jeffries and black men's praise of Johnson collectively affirmed how the fighters' size, strength, and athleticism represented the highest forms of masculinity. Jeffries also used the fight to prove he was still a *young* man, coming out of retirement to challenge Johnson. Body builders were other manly models; they personified the male body's potential. Eugene Sandow, a weightlifter who toured the US and Europe and published numerous photos of his physique, successfully marketed himself as the finest specimen of adult males' physical potential. Sandow excited audiences with his strength and his body. He possessed massive arms and a chiseled back; there were no sagging chins, flabby arms, or skinny legs on his finely tooled frame. Sandow was "the perfect man."[12]

By the interwar period, as the average life expectancy in the US expanded dramatically, the idealized male body remained very youthful. In addition to the boxing ring and the gridiron, the movies became a new site where men and women could revel in young male bodies. In 1920s cinema, the youthful physicality of Douglas Fairbanks and Rudolph Valentino allowed them to become idolized men, reflecting yet also reinforcing the Jazz Age as a period of "obsession with all things youthful." Valentino exuded a macho sexuality, coupled with a robust physical presence on the silver screen. By the same token, audiences reveled in Fairbanks' handsome looks and "vibrancy."[13] Labor iconography of the period also showed how model men were young, physically robust men. In the *Detroit Labor News*, a publication of the Detroit Federation of Labor, illustrations from the 1920s most frequently depicted brawny laboring men, battling against foreign Communist unionism, low wages, and emasculating yellow dog contracts.[14] Working-class men of the 1930s affirmed ideals of powerful manhood through class struggle and unionization. To build strong unions and protect their jobs, unionists in Minneapolis, for example, implied that powerful young male bodies would lead the charge. Labor publications celebrated the muscular young man in cartoons. Armed with his youthful brawn, the working man wrenched social and economic justice from his employer.[15]

Just as culture producers celebrated youth, so did employers. Beginning in the late-nineteenth and early-twentieth centuries, managers of industry deliberately reorganized work around the harnessing of youth and speed. Mass production required the fastest, most efficient production techniques and young workers who could keep up with the speedy pace. The cachet of youth and speed began among the members of management and filtered down to the shop floor. At US Steel, for example, Andrew Carnegie described his managers as "Young Geniuses." He believed that young college-educated men brought dynamism and energy to a rapidly changing business environment. They did not have the biases toward "old ways," as well as the supposed lethargy of older executives; and managers at US Steel banished aging staffers from their ranks. When executives aged and became supposedly less effective, they were simply released from their employment.[16] This attitude towards older ages extended down to the lowest ranks of the industrial workforce. During the 1920s discharge records at a Midwestern factory, for instance, indicated that managers dismissed senior laborers between the ages of 40 and 60 for being "slow" and "physically unadapted."[17] Foremen and managers on the shop floor, obsessed with efficiency themselves, consistently sought out young men.

Men faced new conditions at work throughout the late 1800s and the early 1900s. For the bulk of the nineteenth century most factories were small, and workers and bosses often labored in close proximity to one another. By 1900, however, the situation had changed. Industrial workplaces were now often hierarchical and large, characterized by expanding physical, social, and financial distances between managers and laborers. Faced with intense competition in a crowded industrial economy, managers of the second industrial revolution embraced a doctrine of efficiency, striving to enhance profits, maximize productivity, and minimize operating costs. Low labor costs and control over production provided their means to the desired ends. Skilled workers, upon whose expertise manufacturers often depended, stood in the way of managers' desires for full control over their businesses. Managers wanted to end their dependence on skilled workers' knowledge in building products such as Flivvers or metal beams, pursuing ways to undermine what David Montgomery has described as "workers' control." In meatpacking, employers used the assembly line and subdivided tasks to gain control over production. In steel, Bessemer Converters allowed manufacturers to undermine puddlers' expertise. In the auto industry, assembly lines and mechanized tools helped employers undermine skilled men's autonomy. As mechanization advanced, workers' influence in the factory waned.[18] Managers took control, and many older men lost the security they wielded earlier. By using unskilled (and often younger) labor, manufacturers cut back the employment of veteran men, who usually earned higher wages. "As to machinists, old-time, all-round men, perish the thought!" a pair of engineers observed in a 1919 book. "The Ford Company has no use for experience." In fact, by the 1920s, a study conducted at Ford reported that "most [jobs] could be satisfactorily filled by women or older children."[19]

Uneasiness and concern about adult working men's vulnerability fueled experts and unionists' critiques of mass production and scientific management. Observers and workers pointed to numerous factors that weakened working-class male security: the loss of skilled positions and the eroding status of skilled workers, erratic wages, the decline of organized labor, increasing work paces, and the persistence and severity of unemployment cycles and recessions. Due to their inconsistent employment and limited earnings, unskilled men often had to rely on their children for financial contributions to the household in the 1800s and early 1900s. And in addition to taking in boarders, more and more wives pursued employment in stores, factories, and offices.[20] Unskilled men—married and unmarried—struggled to work steadily. By the interwar period, the transitory reality of employment was a common refrain in worker fiction. In Jack Conroy's *The Disinherited*, layoffs pushed Larry Donovan from job to job throughout the 1910s, 1920s, and early 1930s: he worked in a rail yard, did turns in a steel mill, tolerated the smell in a rubber factory, and labored as an assembly line worker in the auto industry. Thomas Bell, in *Out of This Furnace*, illustrated how steelworkers and their families experienced frequent bouts of unemployment in the early twentieth century.[21]

For older working-class men, the difficulties that accompanied unemployment were even more acute because of the ways that industry made age an impediment to employment. With employers' systematized preferences for young men and high production speeds, older workers found themselves in a vulnerable situation. Unpredictable wage rates, workplace accidents, sickness, the lack of seniority, the weakness of unionism, and frequent bouts with unemployment hindered the ability of the aging working-class man to build a stable economic future. As the pension advocate Abraham Epstein noted in 1922, "[T]he great mass of wage earners in this country lead continuously a precarious and hand-to-mouth existence."[22] This fragile situation was not a feasible long-term basis for male identity.

Men lived longer than ever in the early-to-mid twentieth century, while at the same time employers embraced young men as the best laborers for mass production. In 1900, the average American lived 47 years. By 1920, the average life span was 54 years. Twenty years later, life expectancy had risen to 63 (Table 1.1). The largest increases in twentieth-century life expectancy occurred between 1900 and 1960, where the average length of human life increased by more than 2 decades. Throughout the first three decades of the century, observers worried that if rationalization and mass production symbolized the present and the future of industry, then the future held no place for working men. "While life has been lengthened," AO Wharton, president of the International Association of Machinists (IAM), lamented in 1929, "it has not been matched by a proportionate increase in the working period."[23]

"AGILITY IS AT A PREMIUM"

Obsessed with maximizing efficiency and increasing productivity, employers in automobile manufacturing and steel, among other industries, accelerated work paces with assembly lines and new machine tools during the early years of the twentieth century. "The motto of life in America in our twentieth century would seem to be: Speed—more speed—top speed," writer EK Parkinson noted in 1922. "For speed is impressed and drilled into our youth."[24] Despite Frederick Winslow Taylor's celebrated philosophy of "scientific

Table 1.1. **Average Life Expectancy in the United States, 1900–2000***

Year	Number of Years
1900	47
1920	54
1940	63
1960	70
1980	74
2000	77

*Averages include men and women.
* Numbers are rounded.

Sources: US Department of Commerce, *Historical Statistics of the United States: Colonial Times to 1970* (Washington, DC: Government Printing Office, 1975), 55; National Center for Health Statistics, *Health, United States, 2004, with Chart Book on Trends in the Health of Americans* (Hyattsville, MD: US Department of Health and Human Services, 2004), available at http://www.cdc.gov/nchs /data/hus/ hus04trend.pdf#027.

management," which emphasized how technology would ease workers' burdens and expand production in the shop, mass production work fostered considerable resentment within the ranks of labor. For example, as the Ford Motor Company transitioned to mass production during the early 1910s, working-class men on the new assembly lines expressed a "natural revulsion" as they grappled with "the new kind of work." In response to the intense pace, routinization, and strict managerial control, many men voted with their feet and walked off the job, creating a persistent labor turnover problem. Since Henry Ford's version of modern management, Fordism, would not dominate the auto industry until the 1920s, working men of the 1910s hoped to find more agreeable conditions elsewhere. However, autoworkers quickly discovered that the unfolding transition to mass production was not unique to the Ford Motor Company. Rather, employers' passion for mass production transformed manufacturing itself during the 1910s and 1920s.[25]

In this new era, no one struggled more with the transition to mass production than veteran workers. Labor in the auto industry and steel was now done at incredible paces, and work processes, which were now driven and dictated by machines, assembly lines, and pushy foremen, still required a great degree of lifting and a range of constant and often repetitive movements. For men in their 40s, 50s, or even 60s, whose bodies might be less agile and less durable than their younger co-workers, labor became particularly burdensome and even dangerous. The speed and heavy work wore down men's physical abilities and health over time. "When the line would be speeding up," a four-year Ford veteran noted in 1933, "the pusher [foreman] would keep after me . . . ." "This was happening on the job when I went to Ford's four years ago, and it is worse today," he continued. "The speed-up is so great that . . . I am at present suffering pain as a result of the high tension I have been working under."[26]

Observers complained that mass production made older men's experience, ability, and knowledge redundant, as managers and machines now dictated work methods and rules. Managers had no need for aging bodies that could not withstand the new demands of work, nor did they see veteran experience as an intrinsic asset in the shop. "As it [industry] scraps machinery so it scraps human beings," remarked author Edward T. Devine in 1909. From management's point of view, the right type of man was a young, brawny man in his twenties or thirties. As pension advocate Abraham Epstein summarized in 1928, "With the introduction of new machinery, skill and experience are no longer of importance. Each new invention and the introduction of each new machine diminishes the value of the old mechanics' experience and renders it worthless." Quoting Devine's work, Epstein concluded, "Only the young, the adaptable, and the supple of limb are desired."[27] For example, auto industry craftsmen of the 1910s and 1920s experienced the steady advance of de-skilled work and employers' retreat from reliance on individual men's skills. At Cadillac in Detroit, Mort Furay remembered the destruction of his father's career as a result of employer-induced erosion of trimming as a skilled trade. His father, who individually measured and stitched fabric trim inside of each car on the assembly line, steadily lost his individualized work to standardized processes. Furay observed that mechanized upholstery cutting and sewing machines made his dad a redundant item around the plant. "Gradually," Furay recalled, "he lost all of the components of his trade," as managers systematically looked to machines to replace mind, eye, and hand. "This was a lamentable thing," he remembered, "for a child to see his father's job, the source of income, the security of the family taken away, as it were, piece by piece, to have your father reduced to the status of other men in the neighborhood who were just plain ditch-diggers."[28]

The high degree of physicality of labor in the steel and auto industries dominated discussions of aging men and the transition to mass production. In 1910, Progressive reformer John Fitch concluded that older men could barely keep up with the new speed of mass production work conditions. In Pittsburgh's finishing mills, employers coveted speediness. Fitch described a situation in *The Steel Workers* where he:

> watched the heater's helper before the furnace, pulling out billet after billet and throwing them along the steel floor to the "rougher" . . . the sweat was pouring from his body and his muscles stood out in knots. The rougher was leaping at his work, thrusting the red billets almost in a stream through the first pair of rolls, and yet before he could turn back there was always another billet on the floor behind him . . . they went at an ever increasing speed and with ever increasing strength.

He argued that only strong, young men could work in the industry's mass production facilities. "They are the younger men who work at these mills," Fitch observed. "Here is where agility is at a premium and where a false step may possibly mean death, there is no room for the man whose joints are stiff or whose eye is not keen." Even in the open-hearth mills of the early twentieth century, where the production of steel was entirely mechanized, heavy physical labor predominated on the peripheries of the mill workplace. As the massive open-hearth furnaces roared and erupted with fire, it was unskilled men's brawn that loaded raw materials in rail cars and moved them from one machine to the next.[29]

Men would have to be young because, as John Fitch argued, the rigors of mass production labor seemed to make men age more quickly. Men became "old" at forty, as long hours in an intense work environment led to physical decline, injury, and exhaustion. Even though a man might be in his early forties, Fitch lamented that so many aging steel workers looked far older than their actual age; many more closely resembled men in their final moments. In the steel industry, working men struggled with chronic fatigue, burns, stooped backs, seared eyes, and sullen demeanors, which made them reportedly look and act "old" before their time. "Often I was told by workmen of forty and forty-five," Fitch noted, "that they had been at their best at thirty years of age, and that at thirty-five they had begun to feel a perceptible decline in strength."[30] Many other workers and authors agreed. "After a man passed thirty, he plodded like the oldest, shoulders slumped, legs heavy, bloodshot eyes burning in a blackened face," novelist Thomas Bell wrote in *Out of This Furnace.*[31] In Jack Conroy's *The Disinherited*, a steel mill manager tells the aging Robert Lee "Bun" Grady, a struggling casual laborer, that a "man has to be spry, and it takes a young man to stand the gaff."[32] Whether young or old, mass production labor demanded more than mere human flesh could ultimately provide. Mistakes or missteps, however small, could mean injury, disability, or death, since fire and metal—the literal tools of the trade—tore and crushed skin, bones, and organs.

Mass production pushed many aging men beyond their physical limits, causing chronic injuries to the body. During the 1920s, John Szymanski, who worked at the Auto-Lite factory in Toledo, Ohio, saw many older men struggling to remain on the job as increasing physical limitations and injuries threatened their ability to work. In an oral history interview conducted during his later years, Szymanski noted, "I found that my sympathy always went out to my fellow worker, especially if I was working with an older person." He described a specific incident: During 1929, he and an older man assembled starter frames, and the pace of work was intense and difficult. The job took a frightening toll on the aging co-worker. "Why, you were bouncing around like a rubber ball," Szymanski recalled. "And this guy's doing the same thing." During a break one day the man tried to eat his lunch, but chronic muscle spasms made it too difficult to even sit. Szymanski told interviewers that he "felt sorry for these people" because if the older man could not work, he would be summarily fired.[33]

For men with chronic health troubles, mass production labor was unbearable. At Packard Motors in Detroit during the 1920s, an autoworker and writer named Robert L. Cruden met an aging body polisher struggling with chronic stomach pain. The assembly line workers called him Frenchie: The speedups plagued all of the men, but Frenchie in particular struggled to keep up with his assigned duties. The intense pace of the line worsened his abdominal discomfort. When Cruden asked Frenchie why he stayed at Packard, the aging man said he *had* no choice. He had a family to take care of, and he believed he would not find another job.[34] As working men aged and developed what one doctor described as "the silent sickness"—heart, kidney, and lung conditions—their ability to do physical work diminished considerably.[35] Worse, the combination of heavy physical labor and unhealthy bodies could prove fatal. A sudden heart attack or stroke could abruptly kill or incapacitate them.

As Frenchie's experience suggested, aging men tried to remain stoic in the face of such adversity. An aging man who worked on a Bessemer converter in a Pittsburgh steel mill ("one of the oldest men in his mill") told John Fitch that "his strength is not up to what it was, say, fifteen years ago." The man had a lengthy history of terrible accidents: eye injuries, a shattered leg, and severe burns. But he kept a stiff upper lip, taking pride in his ability to keep working; his (many) injuries, he claimed, were mere "trifles." On the other hand, the majority of his co-workers, the men his own age, had long since succumbed to industrial attrition. "The men who went to work with him as young men," Fitch wrote, "are nearly all dead."[36]

By World War I, the men of Amalgamated Association (AA) locals spoke openly and frequently about worries regarding the ways aging jeopardized steelworkers' long-term employability. For example, steelworker H. Dewees wrote to the *Amalgamated Journal* in 1918: ". . . you will find the workman at his place of toil every day and makes no complaint so long as he gets a fair day's wages for his toil and a chance to lay by a little for such a time as he will not, be able to toil as hard as he does today, for as he becomes older his ability to toil becomes less, and then comes to the time," he continued, "when the employer will show his hand. We have seen it time and time again. If you can't do it, I [management] will get some one who will, so out you go."[37] Hugo the Third, an aging steelworker from West Virginia was more blunt. "Today," he wrote, "men that work dread the thoughts of getting old."[38] Feelings of "dread" remained with Hugo. In 1924, he visited fellow Amalgamated members in Wisconsin and published a poem he thought would resonate among other aging men throughout the industry. Its first lines told a story that was supposed to be familiar to many: "There is a man now old and slow/Whose aching heart is filled with woe/The foreman said: 'He'll have to go.'" "He's out of luck in spring or fall," the poem continued. "He sadly waits the final call."[39]

Employers certainly noticed older men's weaker bodies, including their apparent need to frequently use the restroom. Auto industry managers such as those on the shop floor at Cadillac, monitored how many times assembly line workers left their places to use the bathroom. Whenever a man used the toilet, the foreman (dubbed the "pusher") had to substitute for him. Aging men, more so than the young, required frequent bathroom breaks, disrupting production in the process. These older fellows' bladders (or possibly their desire for a cigarette and some time away from the noise and commotion of the assembly line) undermined managers' demands for constant motion and efficiency. As the former autoworker Steve Nelson recalled in his autobiography, employers did not appreciate aging men's general inclination to steal away to the bathroom. "That's why they didn't hire old guys," he said.[40]

Because so many Americans depended on the industrial economy for their living, working-class persons knew all too well that growing old did not mean a quiet retirement to the rocking chair, surrounded by adoring grandchildren and sufficient savings. Aging was a liability. In one of several interviews for *Middletown: A Study in American Culture* (1929), the manager of a local factory reported to Robert S. Lynd and Helen Merrell Lynd that older men did not fair well in the new era of "speeding up" and "the eliminating of the human factor by machinery." The manager observed there was "less opportunity for older men in industry now than there used to be," the result of the fact that strength and speed "are at a premium." While his company did not have a specific policy of firing older men, he noted that aging workers struggled to keep up: "we find that when a man reaches fifty he is slipping down in production." Employers repeatedly told the Lynds that older workers were the wrong kind of man for the new rigors of mass production. "The age dead line is creeping down on those men," noted the superintendent of another factory. "I'd say by forty-five they are through."[41]

The new mass production firms' treatment of aging laborers differed greatly from older manufacturers that relied more on workers' knowledge and less on assembly lines. The superintendent of a metal shop told the Lynds that skilled iron molders worked well into their sixties. "After a man reaches forty to forty-five he begins to slow down," the boss noted, "but these older, experienced men are often valuable about the shop." This certainly did not apply to the new factories. "There a man is harnessed to a machine and he *can't* slow down," the superintendent continued. "If he does, his machine runs away with him." The older factories were in the minority, such as "Plant I," a shop that dated back to the late nineteenth century. Plant I was regarded as "one of the few places in town" that valued aging labor.[42]

Industry's preference for young bodies puzzled James J. Davis, the US Secretary of Labor, who read numerous letters from veteran workers urging him to do something about their struggles to remain employed.[43] A former ironworker himself, Davis believed that managers should have embraced older laborers since machinery was now supposed to do the work that was once done by human exertion. "With the infinite number of our industrial operations coming to be done by machinery ever more automatic and easier for human hands to run, the reasons for firing the older workers fade to almost nothing," Davis argued. "Where machines do so much and the worker so little, the worker of 60 becomes as able as the one of 20." Age was no longer supposed to matter.

Davis told managers they were overlooking older men's value. Aging working-class men lacked the recklessness and unreliability that hindered the work habits of younger men; they remained at their jobs—rather than hire in, work for a while, and move on. Older men were the best men. Davis condemned employers' disregard for aging men's manly steadiness. "Now we hear and more and more," he noted, "of the worker whose employer is willing to release him [the older man], whatever his skill and value, for no other cause than that he has reached an age beyond which it is thought he is, or will be, useless."[44]

Following Davis' lead, the American Federation of Labor helped make aging working men's shop floor struggles something of a national issue. In its 1929 symposium on "The Older Worker" in the *American Federationist*, AFL leaders reported on how new technologies weakened older working men's employment prospects. Highlighted in the symposium, the bottle industry reflected trends in steel or auto manufacturing. James Maloney, the president of the Glass Bottle Blowers Association, argued that new machines in his industry had led to the displacement of aging skilled men, as employers now no longer needed their experience and expertise. Mechanization destroyed older men's livelihoods and a long tradition of workers' control. He began with a discussion of the glass blowing craft's proud tradition, noting that his organization began in 1846 when skilled men made glass by hand.[45] During the old days, Maloney insisted that age discrimination never occurred. "As far as our information goes," he wrote, "there never was any discrimination on the part of employers . . . there was no age limit beyond which men could find employment."[46] However, the Owens Automatic Bottle Machine, invented in 1905, changed production techniques—and glass workers' fortunes. By 1906, there were 5 machines in operation, producing an estimated 95 to 105 gross of bottles each day. The machines, Maloney lamented, "eliminated the skilled bottle blower." In the new era of mechanization, there were "very few" of the old guard, "the old skilled craftsmen," still working in the industry.[47] Bottle production became mass production.

The AFL found equally poor prospects in the textile industry. In Southern factories, updated machinery—urged on manufacturers by technical consultants—allowed employers to drastically accelerate production in order to maximize volume (and profits) at a moment when prices for cloth had drastically declined. At the same time, consultants told employers to hire new younger workers who could keep up with the new machines. Thomas F. McMahon, the president of the United Textile Workers, claimed that textile industry managers abruptly fired many older men and women, while forcing the remaining young workers to run the machines at break-neck speeds. The imposition of mass production destroyed the employment of aging men and women, who previously received stable work "because of experience and skill." McMahon estimated that mass production led to the loss of 150,000 jobs and the intensification of labor throughout the industry during the 1920s. Managers told anxious job applicants to throw a hand brush down the length of the looms. When the brush landed and finally slid to a stop, managers would tell their charges, amidst the din of the machinery, "All right! The job is yours. You run all these looms."[48] The new worker would have to race up and down the row of noisy machines, keeping them all running simultaneously.

During the 1910s and 1920s, mechanization and increasing speed on industrial shop floors made it difficult for older men to secure and retain employment. Seeking to build a younger workforce that could keep up with their quickening ambitions, manufacturers instituted systems of dismissal and hiring age limits, both formal and informal, to remove older workers from the factory and to keep senior job seekers away.

AGE DISCRIMINATION IN HIRING AND FIRING

The physical demands of mass production assembly line labor jeopardized older men's staying power on the job, but age discrimination kept many out of the factory completely. When the young Len de Caux sought work at a Chicago electrical firm during the 1920s, for instance, a manager told him that "Western Electric is looking for young men like you." In 1927, a struggling steelworker in Canton, Ohio, confronted many hiring managers who also looked for younger workers. "All the shops and factories in this town," he grumbled, "strictly enforce the age limit which is 45 and 50 years and anyone on the shady side of 50 cannot secure employment in any shop or factory."[49] Hiring age limits, as well as arbitrary dismissals of aging laborers, were the second pillar of older men's struggles at work during the early twentieth century. Men's problems with age limits and dismissals exploded across the pages of writings by workers, unionists, industrial relations scholars, and social provision experts during the 1920s and 1930s. Hiring age limits not only affected the employment of the oldest workers, but employers often refused to hire men past the age of forty. Age quickly became a problem in adult men's lives.

The 1930 census reports tellingly indicate that mass production employers preferred to hire younger men. Possibly in response to more than a decade of public debate on the subject of older working men's struggles to secure work, the US Census bureau provided 4-year brackets (20–24, 25–29, etc.) in the Fifteenth Census, which yielded a more nuanced view of age and labor force participation.[50] In automobile manufacturing, the most prominent mass production industry of the 1920s and 1930s, the workforce was significantly younger than the national average for men employed. Over 70 percent of male operatives (Table 1.2) and 65 percent of male laborers (Table 1.3) were under 40 years old. For the country as a whole, however, the numbers were more balanced. Just over half (52 percent) of all men listed as employed were under 40 (Table 1.4).

The number of jobless older men was probably higher than reported. In 1930, President Herbert Hoover ordered census takers to revise their statistics, reflecting a lower (and to his view, more realistic) portrait of the unemployed population. The president insisted that men who refused to seek work and seasonal workers between jobs should not be included with the "actual" unemployed population.[51] The US Census underestimated joblessness in

Table 1.2. Men Employed As Operatives in the Auto Industry, 1930

Ages	Number	Percent
18 to 39	100,337	70.2
40 to 69	40,767	28.5

Total given in census (N) = 142,925

Source: US Bureau of the Census, *Fifteenth Census of the United States, Population, Vol. IV: Occupations, By States* (Washington, DC: Government Printing Office, 1933), 48–49 (Table 22).

Table 1.3. Men Employed As Laborers in the Auto Industry, 1930

Ages	Number	Percent
18 to 39	78,564	65.4
40 to 69	39,601	33.1

Total given in census (N) = 120,150

Source: US Bureau of the Census, *Fifteenth Census of the United States*, 50–51 (Table 22).

Table 1.4. Men Listed As Employed Throughout the United States, 1930

Ages	Number	Percent
18 to 39	20,139,580	52.8
40 to 69	15,616,110	41.0

Total given in census (N) = 38,077,804

Source: US Bureau of the Census, *Fifteenth Census of the United States*, 44–45 (Table 22).

1930. Also, a variety of additional sources yield data that suggests older men could not hire into the auto industry: for instance, nearly 75 percent of the men at Ford's Highland Park plant during the early 1920s were under 40; of 2,677 Mexican men hired at Ford Motor Company between 1918 and 1933, only 2.2 percent were over 40 (75.3 percent were between 20 and 29); and only 2 percent of the men at Chrysler in 1928 were over 35.[52]

Employers' own statistics subtly pointed to discrimination on the basis of age. In *Moving Forward* (1930), Henry Ford proudly gave numbers to prove that his firm employed many aging men. He insisted that 34 percent of his workers were between 40 and 69 (Table 1.5). However, the vast majority of the men in the 40–69 age bracket were in their early 40s, and the numbers precipitously declined thereafter. While some older men certainly worked for Ford, his statistics demonstrated that the majority were 40 and younger.

Table 1.5. Men Employed at the Ford River Rouge Factory, February 1930

Ages	Number	Percent
18 to 39	57,621	62.4
40 to 69	31,356	34.0

Total given in source (N) = 92,208

Source: Henry Ford, with Samuel Crowther, *Moving Forward* (Garden City, NY: Doubleday, Doran & Company, 1930), 93–94.

Likewise in the steel industry, statistics point to a hiring bias. However, steel managers were not so brazen as their counterparts in automobile manufacturing; the numbers were lower. For the "operatives" category in the 1930 census, the number of men between the ages of 18 and 39 constituted 63.2 percent of the total. Men between the ages of 40 and 69 only formed 35 percent (Table 1.6). However, like the auto industry, the numbers were more imbalanced when compared to the overall national statistics (Table 1.4).

Table 1.6. Men Employed As Operatives in the Steel Industry, 1930

Ages	Number	Percent
18 to 39	65,459	63.2
40 to 69	36,154	35.0

Total given in source (N): 103,575

Source: US Bureau of the Census, *Fifteenth Census of the United States*, 48–49 (Table 22).

Numbers for laborers in steel were closer to the national average. Men classified in this category, between the ages of 18 and 39, rested at 59.2 percent (Table 1.7), whereas the national average for men's employment equaled

52.8 percent.[53] However, the census probably overestimated the number of steelworkers actually employed, and other sources indicate that older men certainly struggled to hire into the steel industry throughout the 1910s and 1920s. Industry analyst Horace B. Davis, for instance, found disturbing numbers in a 1930 New York state study: Less than ⅓ of 212 new hires in steel were over the age of 45, and only 3 of the men were first-time steelworkers.[54]

Table 1.7. **Men Employed As Laborers in the Steel Industry, 1930**

Ages	Number	Percent
18 to 39	138,827	59.2
40 to 69	90,884	38.8

Total given in source (N): 234,524

Source: US Bureau of the Census, *Fifteenth Census of the United States*, 50–51 (Table 22).

In addition, steelworkers testified time and time again in the *Amalgamated Journal* (and other publications) throughout the 1910s, 1920s, and early 1930s how they confronted age discrimination on a consistent basis or witnessed other older men struggling to get a job. For instance, in Fort Wayne, Indiana, steelworker Samuel Craig noted that "jobs are scarce, especially for men that are up in years," while the wife of a pattern maker downstate in Muncie reported, "They [managers] always put in the young men."[55] James J. Davis reported hearing from jobless veteran steelworkers that "the mills won't take on anybody over 40."[56] If we use the census in a cautious way to gauge hiring patterns, and augment this material with data from other sources, it becomes clear that auto and steel manufacturers discriminated against older men.

The census numbers provide a suggestive way to analyze employment patterns according to age and occupation. Patterns of age discrimination in the workplace become clearer when we compare the numbers for both workers and management. The Fifteenth Census indicated that proportionally fewer working-class men could be found on the job over the age of forty when compared with younger men; however, there were significantly higher numbers for "manufacturers, managers, and officials" who were on the job at forty years old and up. Only 40.2 percent (202,657) of the 504,524 men who occupied the managerial tiers of manufacturing concerns were between 20 and 39 years of age (Table 1.8). The majority (59.5 percent) of manufacturers and men in management were over 40—well above the national average of 41 percent of the total workforce. In other words, aging did not jeopardize the careers of men in managerial positions, as it did for working-class men.

Table 1.8.   Men Employed in Manufacturing as
"Manufacturers, Managers, and Officials," 1930

Ages	Number	Percent
20–39	202,657	40.2
40 and up	300,366	59.5

Total given in census (N) = 504,524

Source: US Bureau of the Census, *Fifteenth Census of the United States, Unemployment, Volume II: Unemployment by Occupation* (Washington, DC: Government Printing Office, 1932), 259, 271 (Table 13).

Beginning in the early 1900s and 1910s, and reaching a crescendo during the late 1920s and 1930s, aging men confronted an extensive web of hiring age limits, arbitrary dismissals due to age, and frenetic work paces that made their long-term employment prospects in industry seem very grim. Yet was the situation so bad? Some aging workers surely did benefit from longer lives and rising wages, while others made the most of opportunities to start their own small businesses after leaving the factory. For those who were permanently superannuated due to physical inability or declining health, they probably received assistance from their grown children. Others were offered jobs as sweepers and watchmen in the factories where they had spent most of their careers.[57] But in reality, these individuals were atypical. "The above is an exception," a steelworker noted of aging factory sweepers."[58]

Older working-class men could not usually find steady work or establish a stable business in the final years of their lives, lamented the diminished earnings and status that came with lower-paying jobs, and regretted the loss of independence that accompanied relying on children. In New York during the 1910s, for example, the wife of a struggling aging man told a social worker that "It would set him [her husband] crazy if he had to be dependent on his sons."[59] It may have been custom for nineteenth-century industrial employers to offer easy jobs as informal pensions to the oldest men, but the informality of the practice did not suffice in the era of the large mass production factory where large numbers of men worked. Employers did not need so many sweepers and watchmen, and foremen often protected only their favorites.[60]

Formalized hiring age limits constituted the most evident form of age discrimination in mass production industry during the early decades of the twentieth century. Looking at the use of these policies during the early twentieth century, Leo Wolman and Gustav Peck concluded in *Recent Social Trends* that "there is much evidence to support the growing belief that industry is honey combed with strict hiring age rules."[61] Employers in the steel industry, for instance, used hiring age limits to regulate which workers would be eligible for a pension. Managers did not want to hire men only to pay them a pension a short time later. Employers used hiring age limits to ensure that the men who received pension benefits had worked for a very long time, usually 20 or more years. For job-seeking older men, however, pensions and age limits restricted the number of places they could work. If a 55 year-old man applied for work at a firm that provided pensions, he would reach 65 years of age (the usual pension age) in only 10 years; from management's point of view, it was unprofitable to offer pensions to these men who had not worked for the company for at least 2 or 3 decades. Companies favored young men because they would theoretically spend their entire adult lives with the firm. As Stuart Chase observed, when an older man "comes seeking work in a plant which has a pension plan, there is a strong economic motive to discriminate against him if he is past his prime. The older he is, the nearer he will be to the pension provision, hence the more costly to the company."[62]

Despite their rising notoriety after 1900, hiring age limits had a lengthy history in the US and Europe. Pension scholar Murray Webb Latimer discovered that age limits had originated long before the era of welfare capitalism; he traced them back to the industrial revolution of the early 1800s. In Great Britain, men in the needle trades complained that employers disregarded their "usefulness" after a certain age, favoring cheaper young workers over men with experience. Throughout the nineteenth century, numerous industries adopted hiring age limits, and by 1900 age limits existed in mining, maritime trades, textiles, and other industrial occupations. Given the absence of pension programs in nineteenth-century England, Latimer implied that employers had long instituted deliberately ageist hiring policies.

On the other side of the Atlantic, in the United States, formal hiring age limits took hold first in railroads during the later part of nineteenth century.[63] After 1900, age limits quickly became customary in new mass production industries where the fast-paced labor of assembly line production prevailed. Hiring age limits appeared early on in meatpacking, inspiring Upton Sinclair to conclude that age discrimination "was the rule everywhere in America."[64] The steel industry followed, institutionalizing their fondness for youth: In 1902, American Steel and Wire announced "no experienced person over forty-five years shall hereafter be taken into the employ of the company," while Carnegie Steel managers promised "to accept no more men over forty" in 1904. By 1929, at least 21 steel companies ("including some of the largest," according to Horace B. Davis) had established hiring age limits.[65]

The announcements in steel led to serious "dissatisfaction." In Chicago, where steel and meatpacking were major industries, the Chicago Federation of Labor was quick to condemn the expanding system of hiring age limits. In 1904 the Federation, probably in response to the Carnegie Steel announcement, threatened to withdraw all "police and legal protection" from factories that practiced age discrimination. The Chicago Federation of Labor's complaint reached the editors of the *Wall Street Journal*, who, surprisingly, sympathized with the unionists. While they disagreed with the union's promise to interfere with "the right of all" to police protections, the newspaper endorsed the contention that ageism was offensive. "To discharge a man," the *Journal*'s editors wrote, "who is skillful, faithful, sober and experienced simply because he has reached a certain age or was first employed after he had reached the age of 35, seems entirely unsound in policy and unfair in its effects."[66]

Complaints were not confined to the mainstream labor movement. In 1905, the same year William Osler proclaimed that men over 40 were useless and the Industrial Workers of the World (IWW) was formed in Chicago, and a year after the Chicago Federation of Labor voiced its opposition to ageism, struggling men in Chicago formed an organization called the Anti-Age Limit League. Many of the men in the group were struggling veterans of the recent Spanish-American and Philippine-American Wars, who had looked for work after mustering out of the service but could not find it due their age. They complained that industry, like the military, imposed strict age limits on "enlistment." For example, the League resented Admiral Dewey's recent comments about older men as members and leaders of the United States Navy: he complained that unless young men rose to positions of prominence, the US navy "assuredly will meet with disaster." Military campaigns and empire-building, as well as industry, he suggested, required vital younger men who were ready for ongoing fighting and perpetual struggle. The members of the League were disgusted; they vowed to wage their own fight on behalf of working men to end the "cruel and unnatural" practice of "age ostracism." "Of all the obstructions to a man's right to earn a living," the organization proclaimed, "the ban put upon labor by the 45 year age limit is the cruelest, most obnoxious, and most absurd . . . The floors of the league are open to all honest and industrious and reputable men, especially those who have passed the . . . age limit of 45 years. It [the League] will lead the fight."[67]

The group highlighted the gendered underpinnings of their program, arguing that men would "be considered first" in the organization's struggle against hiring age limits. "The league announces that it does not intend to antagonize the employment of women," members said, "but holds that man possesses the inherent right to be considered first as the head and bread-winner of the family."[68] League president James F. Downey said the group would make a "dignified, manly plea" for jobs. "God knows that the situation with many a man is tragic enough," he noted, "but we want no favors, merely fair play."[69] Despite the League's bold and compelling rhetoric about justice and fairness for aging laborers, the organization quickly faded from the Chicago newspapers in 1905 and from the other major newspapers that had picked up the story.

However, the public announcement of the league's creation led to the disclosure of individual working men's worsening experiences with discrimination. The *Chicago Daily Tribune* profiled leading members of the League in October 1905, whose narratives pointed to long histories of encounters with employers who told them they were too old to be hired. The president of the Anti-Age Limit League, James F. Downey, told a reporter that his struggles with the "'Osler theory' as applied to the industrial situation" began in 1898, when he turned 60. Then an "old time printer" and editor who had lived for years in Philadelphia, he sought a new job only to be told, for the first time in his life, that he was "too old to work." "I shan't forget it in a hurry," he told the reporter, "though I have heard it many times since." Downey noted that 1898 marked a "turning point" in his career. "Nobody wanted me," he remarked of his waning days as a working man of the City of Brotherly Love. He and his spouse left for Chicago, where he once again confronted complaints about his advancing age. Downey sought work in printing, but heard other men (including older ones like himself) report that employers wanted "young blood here." Quickly he reached his "last straw." Downey described a verbal altercation with the aging manager of a printing firm. After the man told him that his company wanted a transfusion of youthful blood, Downey leaned over the desk and angrily shook his fist. "You old fool," he seethed, "you must be almost a hundred. Old!. . . I can do more work in twenty minutes than you have been able to pump out in the last eighteen puerile years you have spent here." Frustration, desperation, and forced residence at his son's Chicago home led him to take action. Along with ex-bankers, railroad workers, and even men from the clergy, Downey threw himself into the organization of the new League.[70]

According to the *Chicago Daily Tribune*, the first man to join was MS Thornton, an "old time" railroad conductor, age 47. The Chicago Great Western line laid him off in 1900, and he found himself unable to find work in the five years since. Thornton told the reporter that his hastily whitening hair continually betrayed his age. "Premature white hair told heavily against me," he said. "At 35 I was gray and at 40 I suppose I looked like a man of 50." Still, Thornton insisted he was an effective and reliable worker, but his employer abruptly began to favor younger men and he soon lost his job as a result. The "quick decision" of a superintendent at the railroad led to his termination. "You must go," the boss told the man.[71]

Discussions of age discrimination in the Chicago press proliferated, as journalists now began to carefully report employer policies that favored younger men. For example, changes in the Chicago police department's hiring age requirements (from 35 to 30 years) for new applicants became front-page news in 1906. The reporter for the *Chicago Daily Tribune* perhaps quoted directly police chief John M. Collins' words as a way to raise questions about the growing obstacles to the employment of older men in the city, and the chief himself appeared to be responding to the likelihood of public criticism. "I believe the department is entitled to the advantage that goes with the acquisition of young, vigorous men," he told the reporter for the *Tribune*. "We want men who run without puffing like a steam engine. We want men who can climb a tree if necessary. We want athletes, young, spry, slender men." However, the chief worried enough about public criticism that he tried to downplay the department's youth movement. "Elderly policemen are all right," he claimed, "if they are not too fat and sluggish."[72] Several months later, however, the police commissioner announced he would consider revising the department's age requirements yet again after three "boyish" hires savagely assaulted a prisoner in one of his local jails. "Their youthfulness and lack of self-control," a reporter noted, were major problems for the police. Youth was not always an asset.[73]

But discrimination against aging working men continued unabated in Chicago. By 1911, another organization called the "Anti-Forty-Five-Year Age Limit League" launched into the pages of the *Chicago Daily Tribune*. Mirroring the demands of the aging Chicago workers who formed the 1905 Anti-Age Limit League, they vowed to fight for aging men's foothold in industry and combat employer favoritism of younger men. Behind the "cry" of "Abolish Oslerism," the new League held a mass meeting in Chicago on November 28 to rally new members, and "there were so many present that some had to stand up." Since March 1911, the men who launched the Anti-45 League had been wearing "Anti-45" buttons on their jackets as they walked the streets of the Windy City.[74] The League lambasted Chicago employers for "UJUST," "UNREASONABLE," ILLOGICAL," "BARBAROUS," and "INDEFENSIBLE" hiring policies that undermined a man's ability to provide for his children, robbed him of the ability to be professionally active in the "meridian of life," and consigned him to "the army of the unemployed."[75] They promised a nationwide campaign, as well as a new headquarters that would serve as an employment agency and a place where aging men could find "solace" and "help."[76] The rally drew workers from as far away as Indianapolis. JH Lawrence, an aging black worker from Indiana who was then working in Chicago, stood up during the rally of (white) men and asked whether or not the League would accept black members. "I see that I am the only man of my race here tonight," he remarked. "I want to ask you if you won't take the negro in. You have a great idea behind this league, but it won't be a success unless you recognize the brotherhood of man." The assembly "applauded."[77] Despite the proclaimed racial openness, energy, and sincerity of the group, the new League would flounder and quickly disappear from the Chicago newspapers; the organization is never mentioned again after 1911.

In Chicago and beyond, hiring age limits were industry norms by the mid-to-late 1910s. When industrial relations scholars traveled to factories to study welfare capitalism measures during the 1910s and 1920s, they encountered working men who complained about the power politics of age limits. During a visit to the Colorado Fuel and Iron Company's Minnequa Steel Works, for example, Ben M. Selekman discovered that a 1917 hiring age limit instituted with the new pension plan was "severely condemned by the men."[78] Working men and Employee Representation Plan (ERP) representatives complained the age limit not only affected workers already employed, but threatened other needy men who came to Colorado Fuel and Iron in search of work. "It is not just to a man to refuse him employment simply because he is past the age of forty-five," an ERP representative noted. "Men have to live and support their families after they are past this age, regardless of a pension plan."[79] Colorado Fuel and Iron instituted the same age limits in its coal division. Ben Selekman (and collaborator Mary Van Kleeck) discussed the "bitterness" among miners at CF&I. They "met no coal miner who was in favor of the age limit." While older men were "taciturn," as the visiting scholars described them, the young men were openly angry about the age limit and the pension plan.[80]

The ubiquitous culture of hiring age limits at work during the early-twentieth century even shaped the age requirements of the federal government's 1917 Selective Service Act, which required all men of the ages of 21–31 to register for the draft. Young men would be the ideal soldiers as the United States entered the war against Germany. As a result of "their youth and strength and enthusiasm" a pair of editorials in the *Washington Post* argued, "vigorous" young men equaled "what military experts consider the best possible material for an effective army."[81] The ageism of the draft law and youthfulness of the new US military frustrated some older men. "In my opinion," an observer wrote to the *Chicago Daily Tribune*, "there are plenty of people about the 40 to 50 age limit right here in Chicago simply aching to get into action, but are barred by the rules." When Congress modified the age range to 18–45 in August 1918, men in their later 40s still remained formally "too old" for military service. Even valuable professional men, such as medical doctors, who wanted to serve confronted Uncle Sam's formal age preferences. J. Wohlfarth, a physician over the age of 55, wrote to the *New York Times* in 1917 to complain about the "ubsurdity [sic] of the present age limit" in the army's medical service. Since he was "physically able" despite his more than 55 years of age, he saw no reason why he should be prevented from serving overseas. After all, "some men are old at 40," Wohlfarth noted, while "some are young at 60 or even 70." Congress did add a proviso to the August 1918 bill that allowed men up to age 55 to serve in specific roles (such as physician or quartermaster) "so that younger men may be released for more active positions"; however, Wohlfarth and other older men of Chicago, for instance, were still too aged.[82] While the government did modify its age limit for military service, there were those men such as Dr. J. Wohlfarth who would never be young enough to join the military as soldiers, sailors, or even doctors—despite their loud proclamations of physical ability, professional capability, and desire.

In addition to the codified patterns of age favoritism that were related to pension programs and the wartime draft, informal patterns of age-based discrimination were common in early twentieth-century industry. A range of sources related to the steel and auto industries indicate that employers hired younger men whatever their company's policies, pension or otherwise. Horace B. Davis concluded that "workers well know that employment officers in hiring, discriminate against older workers, limit or no limit, and that they operate more by their own estimate of a man's age than by his statement."[83] At Colorado Fuel and Iron, physicians systematically examined older men who returned to work after a lay-off. The physical exam required a working man to remove all of his clothes, "even to his socks." To be poked and prodded by a company doctor offended laborers and their designated representatives. "I think it is an injustice to him," ERP representatives concluded. Worse, management used the pretext of a physical exam to dismiss any unwanted and redundant men of suspect physical health and questionable stamina: "I have been asked by some our old employes [sic] to see what could be done with regard to them. Many times these men who have passed the age limit have to stand an examination before they can go back to work; they go over there and of course are turned down because of their age." If a man was in less than what the company vaguely referred to as "reasonable condition," he could not return.[84]

The 1919 Steel Strike underlined the prevalence of age discrimination practices in major factories, as scattered discussions of employer discrimination emerged at important steel mills in Johnstown and Duquesne, Pennsylvania. Employers fired large numbers of older men in 1919 and 1920. As a general rule, steel employers preferred younger men; and at the same time, they wanted to be rid of the veteran Amalgamated Association (AA) leaders. In March 1919, a man in Johnstown (perhaps the Communist union organizer William Z. Foster who visited the city in 1919) reported: "The company began to discharge union men. Somebody decided to leave the new men alone, but to discharge the old-timers, men of 15 to 40 years service, men who cannot get places in other mills." This went on for some time. "All winter long," the writer reported, "we have stood aside while veterans were discharged."[85]

At Cambria Steel in Johnstown, William Z. Foster called attention to the link between the employer assault on unionism and the precarious status of older men. He reported to the AFL that the company "declared war on the unions . . . They are picking out and discharging the oldest employees they have who belong to the unions . . . Many of the men have from 10 to 35 years in point of service."[86] For the veteran men at Cambria, the strike brought about a new, coldly deliberate form of age discrimination:

> The men sacrificed were the Company's oldest and best employees. Men who had worked faithfully for ten, twenty or thirty years were discharged at a moment's notice. The plan was to pick out the men economically most helpless; men who were old and crippled, or who had large families dependent upon them, or homes half paid for, and make examples of them to frighten the rest.

These superannuated men "could never hope to work in the steel mills again."[87] Similar claims appeared in McKeesport, near Pittsburgh. US Steel targeted older men as a way to bully its extensive workforce. "In addition to all this [company opposition to the union], men are being discharged from the plant in wholesale lots," the *Amalgamated Journal* reported. "Most of them are among the oldest employes. This reveals a double purpose on the part of the company. They hope to intimidate the men and prevent their joining the union and also to be relieved from the payments of old age pensions, under which plan these men would soon become beneficiaries."[88]

Hiring age limits made it difficult for unemployed aging men to secure new jobs, essentially allowing employers to threaten older workers with permanent layoff. Cambria Steel accused forty-year veteran Joseph Yart of union organizing, but Yart denied the allegation "and protested" to his supervisors. Management fired him anyway. Industry-wide hiring age limits insured that Yart would have a tough time finding a new job and continuing a career as a steelworker. And if he was a union man, he would not be able to continue his "agitation," as managers alleged. After leaving Cambria, Yart fell on hard times as he struggled to find a new job. The Interchurch World Movement, a religious organization who conducted their own investigation of the 1919 Steel Strike, concluded, "Mr. Yart has been unable to find another job ever since and has been out of work now for the past eight months, as every place he goes to his age handicaps him in securing a job." Cambria Steel managers insisted that older workers were leaders and organizers of the striking Amalgamated locals. Yart was not the only aging man to be fired, as fellow Cambria steelworker Bernard Heeney met the same fate. "The oldest employee in the department," the assistant superintendent dismissed Heeney for alleged union activity during the strike. This surprised the older man. When Heeney asked why he was fired, the manager said, "I don't know—we have orders here to take you off."[89]

In her book *Men and Steel*, published in 1920, labor journalist Mary Heaton Vorse took readers into the homes of these superannuated men of steel, where wives worried silently in cramped homes, children now supported their down-and-out fathers, and aging patriarchs lamented the loss of their jobs and family status. She spoke with a man known as Old Steve, who "had not been taken on again" after the strike debacle of 1919. The company rehired his sons, but they passed on the aging father. Steve "had been scrapped," as Vorse explained. In Braddock, Pennsylvania, Vorse visited an aging man named Shapiro during a tour of the town with a local Catholic priest. She introduced readers to a kind older man, who had lost a long, almost heroic battle to maintain a respectable home. When Vorse and the priest, Father Kazinci, arrived, Mrs. Shapiro asked right away, "What will we do, Father? They won't give him back his job." Vorse, Father Kazinci, and the Shapiros talked about their recent struggles after the strike. Shapiro only wanted to work, to support his family as other men did. "They won't take me back," he told the visitors, "They said, 'No work for you.'" He could only watch his daughter leave home each day to work in a glass factory. "One could see he had understood nothing," Vorse wrote. "The industrial machine of America had caught him up."[90]

After the 1919 Steel Strike, some AFL unions outside of the steel industry began worrying about age discrimination in their own sections of the economy. During 1921, for instance, older men who ran streetcars for the Detroit United Railway company complained about rumors of an impending dismissal. In only "a few weeks," the city government would take over operations, and, as part of the conversion, the city allegedly intended to fire the "old employes" and hire younger men. In response, the Detroit Federation of Labor issued a stern proclamation: "it is rumored that the old employes now operating these lines are to be dismissed from the service and new and inexperienced men placed in charge of the operation . . . . we . . . do hereby take up the situation and make a full investigation and see if it is not possible to have an understanding that these men who have for years performed this labor to the best interests of the public . . . may be retained." The mayor quickly insisted the rumor was false, and "the men now employed . . . have no grounds for fear."[91] But the DFL was clearly worried about age discrimination, as mere rumors led to calls for an official investigation of the issue.

Members of the AFL in Detroit also probably had one eye on the automobile industry. Beginning in the 1910s, when mass production was still very new to the auto industry, the pioneering Ford Motor Company actively recruited young men. In 1916, Ford established the Henry Ford Trade School, where managers instructed teenage boys in mechanical engineering and industrial praxis. Boys not only studied in the classroom; they worked on the assembly lines at the new River Rouge plant, gaining first-hand knowledge of the latest machines and tools. They were officially students, but they completed the same factory labor as the regular employees. The typical student-worker earned $7.20 a week—much less than the vaunted "five dollar day." The creation of the school showed that Henry Ford favored the training of young males for jobs within his company and he readily used them in the factory. Harold L. Brock, a graduate of the school, wrote in his memoir about the jobs he learned to complete during the 1920s and 1930s: "My training included drafting, tool and die making, pattern making, foundry practice . . . I became knowledgeable in . . . manufacturing processes." Between the 1910s and 1940s, the trade school graduated 8,000 teenage boys.[92] Older working men often cast an anxious eye towards these precocious youngsters. A veteran autoworker alleged that Ford replaced older men with the "high school boys" who earned "learner's wages"—thus guaranteeing an even larger profit margin for the great man who owned the auto giant.[93]

The Ford Motor Company had a "natural liking" for young men. In 1917, the firm organized laborers into four categories: Honor Roll, Class A, Class B, and Class C. The classifications all hinged on thrift, reliability, and sobriety (or the lack thereof). Ford deemed these virtues to be crucial if men were to be included in profit sharing plans, the Five Dollar Day, and promotion. Men in Class C were "problem" workers; these men drank alcohol and missed work. The upper tiers honored workers who practiced good habits; they were sober family men who saved their pay. To join the Honor Roll, however, men needed to be more than thrifty and ascetic. They needed to be 30–35 years old.[94]

While Henry Ford endorsed younger men as his ideal autoworkers, he also valued the better judgment and familial commitments associated with more mature men. He wanted to combat chronic absenteeism and labor turnover, which he believed was most prevalent among younger men.[95] The 30–35 year-old age bracket Ford associated with the "Honor Roll" men reflected his contradictory goals of attaining both youth and speed on the new assembly line and workforce stability. He wanted men who were young enough to endure the physicality of assembly line labor, yet he wanted men who were old enough to be reliable employees. Despite Ford's interest in dependable workers, the firm's labor policies consistently favored youth and brawn, not age and restraint.

By the late 1920s, the patterns of age discrimination at Ford extended throughout the industry. After researching his *Labor and Automobiles*, Robert

W. Dunn characterized the auto industry in 1929 as "a young man's industry." He specifically indicted Ford, Hudson, and Packard in his study. Dunn argued that in 1928 managers at Ford quietly dismissed many aging men who earned six dollars per day, handing their jobs over to young men at a lower pay rate. At Hudson Motors, superintendents laid off many older men during the 1928 model changeover. When production resumed, Hudson "hired for the new production thousands of young workers." At Packard, managers laid off veteran men who earned 75 and 80 cents per hour, and the company brought in young men who received 52 cents. Dunn's research notes documented complaints of ageism at other companies. At a factory in Flint, a man named Jones remarked: "Flint. workers scrapped at 40 [sic]." Elsewhere, a manager reported there was "no actual age limit in hiring but try to take young, for more agile." Age discrimination saturated the industry, making it "almost impossible for a man over 40 to get a job."[96]

Robert L. Cruden, a young first-hand observer of auto industry conditions, concurred with Robert Dunn. Under his own name and the pseudonym James Steele, he wrote several essays and a novel, *Conveyor: A Novel* (1935), about men's experiences in the auto industry. Cruden went to work for Packard on the assembly line in 1928 to support the family after his aging father lost his job, but the difficult conditions he witnessed compelled him to write about auto workers' struggles. His writings provided a gritty look at ageism in the shops. For example, while filling out paperwork at the Packard office, the eighteen year-old Cruden observed "that the older men were being turned away." He also commented on men's problems in other factories. When Henry Ford vowed in 1926 to end delinquency in Detroit by creating new jobs for young men, Cruden argued that the company only wanted to jettison older workers. "The young men, new and former employees, were taken on," he wrote. "The old men, the men whose hair had whitened in the service of Ford, were refused employment . . . These old men were made to understand that they are nothing but old rusty tin cans on the garbage heap of society."[97]

Managers sometimes transferred aging workers to departments where the work was more demanding, knowing that older men's inability to cope with the faster paces and heavier work would provide a convenient pretext for firing them. In October 1929, a man at Ford wrote to the Communist-led Auto Workers Union (AWU) about a series of transfers at the River Rouge plant. In an unnamed department, the work was relatively light and many older men worked there. Then, managers began transferring the men to another department where jobs were more strenuous. Since many of them could not keep up, managers fired them. "In this way," the man wrote, "Ford is able to get rid of many of us [older men] in a nice way." At Chrysler, the AWU pointed out, a forty-five year-old man who worked in the inspection department lost his job because he could not work at faster paces. At Packard, management increased the body workers' job quota from six auto bodies to eight. The increased workload led to a bloodletting in the department; only the young and strong survived. "Old men fired," Robert Dunn noted.[98]

When employers updated work departments to advance mass production, they sometimes used the hiatus to oust older men. Working men in Toledo, Ohio, argued that the Auto-Lite company retooled various departments to promote "efficiency" and conveniently release aging and redundant men. Reflecting on his experiences at Auto-Lite in 1928, Carl Leck, a former stockroom worker, told two historians that his bosses did not openly fire older men. However,

> Some economy engineer says we [management] can do better to lay off all the men in the stockroom and move directly from the receiving dock up to final assembly and let them take care of it. We used to have at one time thirty men in that stockroom. When they wound up, they had one man. And these older men, that were too old at that time, where would they go for a job? They couldn't get a job.

Aging men constituted a significant part of the stockroom staff. Management effectively (and quietly) removed twenty-nine older, higher paid men from their payrolls. Workers did not accuse management of blatant discrimination; however, they grasped management's goal. The interviewers asked, "Did the company try to get them [aging men] back in the operation there some way?" Leck responded, "No, no way."[99]

When experienced (and generally older) men qualified for higher pay rates, employers moved quickly to lay them off. At Packard, Robert Cruden noted it was "a general rule" that older men received higher wages than young men. However, an aging body polisher, probably Frenchie, explained to Cruden "how this works out." Once an older man reached the high seventy cents per hour rate, the foremen began scrutinizing his work. If any defects were noticed, the older worker would be fired. The aging polisher was in the midst of his own tug of war with the boss. "This old polisher's panic when his foreman found a spot on a body," Cruden reported, "was sufficient proof for me that this was no fiction of his imagination."[100]

Since the early twentieth century, visible gray hair had been a source of trouble for working men. The AWU made a link between layoffs and men whose hair was gray in a 1929 article about Dodge, where a union organizer noted, "Now Dodges, too, is beginning to lay off men on account of . . . gray hair." According to the AWU organizer, three aging men approached their boss to ask for a change of shifts. They worked the late shift and complained that managers would not transfer them to the day shift. Now, the superintendent targeted the men for dismissal; they brought themselves to his attention. They soon lost their jobs. "These three men," the AWU lamented, "find themselves laid off because of gray hair . . . , gotten in the service of the Dodge Motor Company."[101]

If they wanted to remain employed, older working men knew they had to keep their age a secret. Clearly worried about employers' preferences for younger men, aging workers in a wide range of occupations—including autoworkers, steelworkers, and machinists—colored their hair in the hope of protecting their toeholds in the labor market. In 1929, Robert W. Dunn pointed out that "Detroit workers have been known to dye their hair to disguise their age." Some men even "applied shoe polish to conceal gray hair." Other observers of industry in the late 1920s, such as Stuart Chase and Warren B. Catlin, talked about struggling machinists who "touch[ed] up their gray"; and the Secretary of Labor James J. Davis wrote about older men in the steel industry who "darkened" their gray hair with "soot from the furnace."[102]

Men who tinted their hair during the 1920s had possibly met or heard of veteran workers who once colored their own during the 1900s and 1910s. Throughout the early twentieth century, aging men colored their hair to conceal the physical signs of advancing age, and newspaper articles often commented on the trend. In 1909, a writer in Chicago visited several drug stores to ask about the extent to which older men purchased hair dyes. A druggist on the North Side of Chicago told the reporter that men purchased more than 75 percent of the dyes sold in his store. At drug stores found in "industrial neighborhoods," hair dye advertisements typically hung in the windows. "I do not ask the men what their object in dying their hair is," the druggist noted. "But I know what causes them to resort to hair dye."[103]

During the 1900s and 1910s, the fashionable moustache became an Achilles heel for aging men. It was the first site on the face that grayed, and working men needed to be cautious about the conspicuous transformation of its color from dark to gray. "This is a remorseless time in industry," the *New York Times* observed of aging men's troubles in 1904. "Many elderly men dye their mustaches first, if they wear mustaches, as the mustache become gray sooner than the hair on their heads."[104] Anxious working men nearing their 40s often visited the barber and asked for their stylish (and graying) mustaches to be trimmed off completely, disposing of this dangerous sign of advancing age. At work the next day, "Mr. Smith" would tell his co-workers that he shaved off the mustache on a whim, but in reality "the real cause is in the fact that mustache was turning stage's evidence against him, and testifying that Mr. Smith is getting old, and, consequently, is approaching industry's dead line."[105]

Companies that manufactured hair dye during the early twentieth century were, by the 1920s, marketing their wares to both men and women. In

Chicago, the Kolor-Bak company asked newspaper readers of the New Era: "Why fear gray hair?"[106] Kolar-Bak was a clear, colorless liquid that, as the company claimed in its ads, magically transformed gray hair into the "right shade" of blonde, auburn, black, or brown. (The company boldly insisted that its product was also healthy for the scalp, as it supposedly cured dandruff, stopped itching, and prevented hair from falling out.) The company began marketing its product in the 1910s, and by 1924 ads featured regular references to "men and women."[107]

Hair dyes, however, could be dangerous. In 1909, for instance, the Municipal Court of Los Angeles ruled on a lawsuit put forward by Kate J. Moeser, who sued Charles H. Grimley—a maker and distributor of hair dye—for making her seriously ill. As Moeser alleged, the dye she bought at the drug store "poisoned" her scalp and caused a loss of sight that "lasted several days." Initially, she had hoped that the product "would restore gray hair to its original beauty and give to the middle aged the appearance of youth." However, the product caused injuries to such an extent that she "had not yet entirely recovered" by the time her case went to court. The packed courtroom was "filled with the representatives of the manufacturers of hair dyes and restorers," who closely followed the witnesses' testimony. Grimley did have his supporters, including "patrons" such as Marmaduke Dorian who claimed on the stand that he "owed all his happiness in life to the effects of the defendant's hair dye." In the end, however, the Municipal Court ruled against Grimley, citing negligence on his part. The court awarded Moeser the sum of $500 for her pain and suffering.[108] Discussions of toxic hair dyes continued into the 1920s. In 1927, for example, physicians with the American Medical Association reported there were 111 known incidents of hair dye poisoning.[109]

For those who worried about the noxious compositions (and results) of manufactured hair dyes, there was a market of advice for alternatives; however, these concoctions were by no means organic. In 1902, the *Los Angeles Times'* "Milady's Beauty Table" column printed a letter from someone who asked about how she could change her hair color without dying it. "Milady" offered the following "recipe," supposedly given to her by a doctor.

Sugar of lead [sic], ½ ounce
Lac sulphur, ½ ounce
Essence of bergamot, ½ ounce
Alcohol, ½ gill [sic]
Glycerine, 3 ounces
Tincture of cantharides, ½ ounce
Ammonia, ½ ounce

Mix all in a pint of soft water. Apply to the roots of the hair, which must be perfectly clean, once a day.[110]

For older men and aging ladies, daily newspaper ads and articles offered (risky) solutions to the problem of changing hair color.

In addition to coloring their hair, older men of the 1920s often lied about their age when they applied for work, struggling to subvert the gaze of age-wary managers. As an employment officer told Bun Grady, the struggling older man introduced to us by worker/writer Jack Conroy, "get wise on that age deal. Never be a day over thirty-nine." Unskilled aging men who desperately needed jobs could never disclose their real age to the boss. For an older man like Grady to get a job, any job, he would need to be as adept as possible at foiling managers' attempts to ascertain his true age. While Grady was visibly older than other job applicants, he was somehow able to convince a steel mill manager to try him out as a laborer. Managers' frustrations with deceptive and reticent older men emerged in a handful of sources from the 1920s. Millicent Pond, a manager at the Scovill Manufacturing Company, remarked in 1929 "that the employment interviewer has the difficult problem of determining whether a man is telling the truth or not when he says he is 42, 47, or 50 years of age, over a range of individuals who look as if they were from 50 to 70." At an auto factory in Pontiac during 1929, a manager asked one applicant where he was born, his age, and, oddly, "whether he was older or younger than his grandmother."[111] The manager could not readily identify the man's age.

Despite managers' preferences for young workers, older men never completely disappeared from the factory. Some concealed their age, while other men's brawn helped them remain attractive to employers. Still, men always worried how long their employment in a given factory might last. The Ford Motor Company hired the fifty year-old William McKie, a skilled metal worker (and veteran unionist) from Scotland, in 1927. (Known as "Big Bill," McKie's size, in addition to his skills, might explain why Ford gave him a job.) During his tenure as a River Rouge worker during the interwar period, McKie noted that older men's employment was never secure. "Men over forty lived in daily fear of losing their jobs," his biographer wrote. "Men over fifty in production were knocked off day by day."[112]

Men worried greatly about the gender connotations of work during the early twentieth century, as concerns over age discrimination emerged simultaneously with unionists' worries about working women in the auto plants. Discussions of "girls" (who, some union organizers argued, needed to relinquish their jobs and return to the home) appeared alongside discussions of older workers troubles in labor newspapers. In a 1927 letter to the *Auto Workers News*, a middle-aged man at Ford described Detroit as a "She-Town" because of the increasing prominence of women in industry. (In reality, the number of women in Detroit's auto factories increased slowly during the interwar years, never exceeding 6 percent.)[113] Some men, such as the author of the "She-Town" lament, blamed rival working women for their troubles, but many more workers, unionists, and experts pointed to age discrimination as the chief threat to working-class men's claims to jobs in mass production industries.

Unionists and observers never spoke about women's troubles with age discrimination in the automobile industry. However, women who sought employment certainly confronted managerial preferences for young labor. The 1930 census suggests that when manufacturers did hire women they preferred young women under the age of 35. Of 19,858 women employed as "semi-skilled" workers in auto factories and 3,690 listed as "unskilled," over 77 percent of the women in each category were in their teens, 20s, and early 30s (Tables 1.9–1.10). In addition to racism and sexism, women confronted the problem of ageism. Observers, however, only discussed age discrimination as a threat to men, building on the inaccurate assumption that the only women who needed factory work were young women in pursuit of "pin money."[114]

Table 1.9. Women Employed As Semiskilled Workers in the Auto Industry, 1930

Ages	Number	Percent
10 to 34	15,398	79.0
35 to 74	4,449	22.4

Total given in census (N) = 19,858

Source: US Bureau of the Census, *A Social-Economic Grouping of the Gainful Workers of the United States* (Washington, DC: Government Printing Office, 1938), 156–157 (Table 33).

Table 1.10. Women Employed As Unskilled Workers in the Auto Industry, 1930

Ages	Number	Percent
10 to 34	2,865	77.6
35 to 74	818	22.2

Total given in census (N) = 3,690

Source: US Bureau of the Census, *Social-Economic Grouping of the Gainful Workers of the United States*, 156–157 (Table 33).

Mary Heaton Vorse, Abraham Epstein, James J. Davis, and the American Federation of Labor popularized Samuel Gompers' concept of the "industrial scrap heap" to condemn employers' disregard for older men.[115] The "scrap heap" encapsulated numerous themes affecting aging men of the early twentieth century—especially the end of men's much-needed careers and the ideal of the male breadwinner and the family wage, as well as physical decline and dependency. Manhood was fragile, as underlined by the widespread problems of hiring age limits, arbitrary dismissals, and intense work paces. After more than a decade of talk about "the scrap heap" in the labor press, a 1928 *Detroit Labor News* illustration summarized what lie ahead for men in modern industry. The "industrial world," black and gloomy, used up and discarded men once they were no longer desirable. After years of service, older men were likely cast out, forced to walk a lonely road away from the factory—the site of their manhood.[116] With only tattered coats, slumping shoulders, sullen eyes, and worn brows, aging males could no longer work and earn as men. During the early twentieth century, working-class men certainly understood there were few guarantees in later life: only a small minority of workers received pensions from their companies, and seniority privileges hinged on employers' goodwill.

As the theologian Reinhold Niebuhr watched Detroit workers confront the new regime of mass production labor during the 1920s, he wrote: "According to the ethics of our modern industrialism men over fifty, without special training, are so much junk."[117] Prevalent fears that aging and unskilled working men would be callously tossed on the industrial scrap heap, as expressed by Niebuhr and so many others, led to forceful calls for action in the labor press, the literature on social provision and industrial reform, and the mainstream press during the 1920s and 1930s. While numerous possibilities for old age economic support existed during the early twentieth century (including union, religious, and fraternal society old age homes, state-run poorhouses and poor farms, industrial pensions, reliance on children, and liquidating personal assets), it was the state pension concept that became the most popular. American men and women believed the state should protect respectable working-class manhood and womanhood from the challenges of "growing old" in a society now dominated by the values and practices of mass production industry. Already by the late 1920s, the worker turn towards state pension schemes—and thus a nascent welfare state—had begun.

NOTES

1. Robert S. Lynd and Helen Merrell Lynd, *Middletown: A Study in American Culture* (New York: Harcourt, Brace, and Company 1929), 34.

2. Stuart Chase, "Laid Off at Forty," *Harpers Magazine*, August 1929, 340.

3. Karen Manners Smith, "New Paths to Power,1890–1920," in *No Small Courage: A History of Women in the United States*, ed. Nancy F. Cott (New York: Oxford University Press, 2000), 374–412; Sarah Jane Deutsch, "From Ballots to Breadlines, 1920–1940," in *No Small Courage*, 413–446; Gail M. Bederman, *Manliness and*

Civilization: A Cultural History of Gender and Race in the United States, 1880–1917 (Chicago: University of Chicago Press, 1995); Richard Briggs Stott, *Jolly Fellows: Male Milieus in Nineteenth-Century America* (Baltimore: Johns Hopkins University Press, 2009), esp. 4–5; John Pettegrew, *Brutes in Suits: Male Sensibility in America, 1890–1920* (Baltimore: Johns Hopkins University Press, 2007); Nicholas L. Syrett, *The Company He Keeps: A History of White College Fraternities* (Chapel Hill: University of North Carolina Press, 2009), esp. 226–227.

4. John Tosh, "What Should Historians Do With Masculinity? Reflections on Nineteenth-Century Britain," *History Workshop Journal* 38:1 (1994): 185–186; Martha May, "The Historical Problem of the Family Wage: The Ford Motor Company and the Five Dollar Day," *Feminist Studies* 8:2 (1982): 400–403; Michael Kimmel, *Manhood in America: A Cultural History* (New York: Free Press, 1996), 28–33, 144; McClelland, "Some Thoughts on Masculinity and the 'Representative Artisan' in Britain, 1850–1880" *Gender & History* 1 (1989): 164–177.

5. Richard Oestreicher, *Solidarity and Fragmentation: Working People and Class Consciousness in Detroit, 1875–1900* (Urbana: University of Illinois Press, 1989), 133. On work and the family wage principle during the late-nineteenth century, see also Lawrence B. Glickman, *A Living Wage: American Workers and the Making of Consumer Society* (Ithaca: Cornell University Press, 1997).

6. Daniel T. Rodgers, *The Work Ethic in Industrial America, 1850–1920* (Chicago: University of Chicago Press, 1978), xii (for "the moral primacy of work"), 1 (for Thoreau quote); Nick Salvatore, *Eugene V. Debs: Citizen and Socialist* (Urbana: University of Illinois Press, 1982), esp. 19, 23.

7. Paul G. Faler, *Mechanics and Manufacturers: Mechanics and Manufacturers in the Early Industrial Revolution: Lynn, Massachusetts, 1780–1860* (Albany: State University of New York Press, 1981), 172–173, 116; Bruce Laurie, *Artisans Into Workers: Labor in Nineteenth-Century America* (1989; repr., Urbana: University of Illinois Press, 1997), 57; Mary H. Blewett, *Men, Women, and Work: Class, Gender, and Protest in the New England Shoe Industry, 1780–1910* (Urbana: University of Illinois Press, 1990), 76.

8. "The Boiler," *National Labor Tribune*, 18 January 1875, 2; David Hackett Fischer, *Growing Old in America* (New York: Oxford University Press, 1977), 163; Herbert G. Gutman, "Work, Culture, and Society in Industrializing America, 1815–1919," *American Historical Review* 78 (1973): 564–565.

9. John F. Kasson, *Houdini, Tarzan, and the Perfect Man: The White Male Body and the Challenge of Modernity in America* (New York: Hill & Wang, 2001), esp. 21–76; Bederman, *Manliness and Civilization*, 175–184; E. Anthony Rotundo, *American Manhood: Transformations in Masculinity from the Revolution to the Modern Era* (New York: Basic Books, 1993), 186–193, 223–224; Laura Davidow Hirshbein, "The Transformation of Old Age: Expertise, Gender, and National Identity, 1900–1950" (Ph.D. diss., Johns Hopkins University, 2000), 128–166.

10. Hirshbein, "Transformation of Old Age," 40–43.

11. Quoted in Betty Friedan, *The Fountain of Age* (New York: Touchstone, 1993), 225.

12. Patrick F. McDevitt, *May the Best Man Win: Sport, Masculinity, and Nationalism in Great Britain and the Empire, 1880–1935* (New York: Palgrave, 2004), 58–79; Frederick Cople Jaher, "White America Views Jack Johnson, Joe Louis, and Muhammad Ali," in *Sport in America: New Historical Perspectives*, ed. Donald Spivey (Westport, CT: Greenwood Press, 1985), 155–157; Theresa E. Runstedtler, "Journeymen: Race, Boxing, and the Transnational World of Jack Johnson" (PhD diss., Yale University, 2007); Matthew Lindaman, "Wrestling's Hold on the Western World before the Great War," *Historian* 62 (2000): 779–797; Kasson, *Houdini, Tarzan, and the Perfect Man*, 21–76. See also James Gilbert, *Men in the Middle: Searching for Masculinity in the 1950s* (Chicago: University of Chicago Press, 2005), 16–17; and Stacy L. Lorenz and Geraint B. Osborne, "'Talk About Strenuous Hockey': Violence, Manhood, and the 1907 Ottawa Silver-Seven-Montreal Wanderer Rivalry," *Journal of Canadian Studies* 40:1 (2006): 125–156.

13. Lynn Dumenil, *Modern Temper: American Culture and Society in the 1920s* (New York: Hill & Wang, 1995), 92–93. On the 1920s as a decade of "obsession with all things youthful," see Syrett, *Company He Keeps*, esp. 262; and Paula S. Fass, *The Damned and the Beautiful: American Youth in the 1920s* (New York: Oxford University Press, 1977).

14. Gregory Wood, "The Paralysis of the Labor Movement: Men, Masculinity, and Unions in 1920s Detroit," *Michigan Historical Review* 30:1 (2004): 78, 81.

15. Elizabeth Faue, *Community of Suffering and Struggle: Women, Men, and the Labor Movement in Minneapolis, 1914–1945* (Chapel Hill: University of North Carolina Press, 1991), 70, 75–76, 80–81, 85, 93.

16. David Brody, *Steelworkers in America: The Nonunion Era* (1960; repr., Urbana: University of Illinois Press, 1998), 25.

17. Chase, "Laid Off at Forty," 341.

18. See Daniel Nelson, *Managers and Workers: Origins of the Twentieth-Century Factory System in the United States, 1880–1920* (Madison: University of Wisconsin Press, 1995); David Montgomery, *Workers' Control in America: Studies in the History of Work, Technology, and Labor Struggles* (Cambridge, UK: Cambridge University Press, 1979); Brody, *Steelworkers in America*; and Steve Meyer, *The Degradation of Work Revisited: Workers and Technology in the American Auto Industry, 1900–2000*, http://www.autolife.umd.umich.edu/Labor/L_Overview/L_Overview1.htm (accessed 13 March 2009).

19. Horace Lucien Arnold and Fay Leone Faurote, *Ford Methods and the Ford Shops* (New York: Engineering Magazine Co., 1919), 41–42, quoted in Joyce Shaw Peterson, *American Automobile Workers, 1900–1933* (Albany: State University of New York Press, 1987), 36. Second quote appears in Wayne A. Lewchuk, "Men and Monotony: Fraternalism as a Managerial Strategy at the Ford Motor Company," *Journal of Economic History* 53 (1993): 831.

20. Alice Kessler-Harris, *Out to Work: A History of Wage-Earning Women in the United States* (New York: Oxford University Press, 1982), 22, 31, 124–125.

21. Jack Conroy, *The Disinherited: A Novel of the 1930s*, introduction by Douglas Wixson (1933; repr. Columbia: University of Missouri Press, 1991); Thomas Bell,

Out of this Furnace: A Novel of Immigrant Labor in America, afterward by David P.
Demarest, Jr. (1941; repr., Pittsburgh: University of Pittsburgh Press, 1976).

22. Abraham Epstein, *Facing Old Age: A Study of Old Age Dependency in the
United States and Old Age Pensions* (New York: Alfred A. Knopf, 1922), 142.

23. AO Wharton, "Age Limits for Industrial Workers—Then What?" *American
Federationist*, July 1929, 807.

24. EK Parkinson, "After Fifty—What?" *Outlook*, 13 September 1922, 62.

25. Harry Braverman, *Labor and Monopoly Capital: The Degradation of Work in
the Twentieth Century* (New York: Monthly Review Press, 1974), 149–150.

26. Peterson, *American Automobile Workers*, 56.

27. Abraham Epstein, "You After Forty," *Forum*, February 1928, 267–268; Edward T. Devine, *Misery and Its Causes* (New York: Macmillan Company, 1911), 125.

28. Mort Furay quoted Peterson, *American Automobile Workers*, 38.

29. Edward Slavishak, *Bodies of Work: Civic Display and Labor in Industrial
Pittsburgh* (Durham: Duke University Press, 2008), 31.

30. John Fitch, *The Steel Workers* (1910; repr., Pittsburgh: University of Pittsburgh Press, 1989), 51, 183.

31. John Fitch, "Old Age at Forty," *American Magazine*, March 1911, 655–664;
Bell, *Out of this Furnace*, 167.

32. Conroy, *Disinherited*, 137. On industrial labor and worker injury, see Nelson,
Managers and Workers, 28–33; Sara F. Rose, "'Crippled' Hands: Disability in Labor
and Working-Class History," *Labor: Studies in Working-Class History of the Americas* 2:1 (2005): 27–54; and Slavishak, *Bodies of Work*.

33. Philip A. Korth and Margaret R. Beegle, *I Remember Like Today: The Auto-
Lite Strike of 1934* (East Lansing, MI: Michigan State University Press, 1988), 49–50.

34. Cruden, "No Loitering," 697.

35. "The Problem of Middle Age in Industry," *Monthly Labor Review*, March
1930, 541.

36. Fitch, *Steel Workers*, 12–13.

37. H. Dewees, Report of Girard Lodge No. 95, PA, *Amalgamated Journal*, 31
October 1918, 10.

38. Hugo the Third, Report of Crescent Lodge No. 8, WV, *Amalgamated Journal*,
14 November 1918, 19.

39. See "The Speed Merchant," *Amalgamated Journal*, 11 December 1924, 11.

40. Steve Nelson, James R. Barrett, and Rob Ruck, *Steve Nelson, American Radical* (Pittsburgh: University of Pittsburgh Press, 1981), 30.

41. Lynd and Lynd, *Middletown*, 33, 34–35, 31.

42. Ibid., 32, 33.

43. Davis refers to these letters in "Why Should Workers Be Fired at 50?" *Detroit
Labor News*, 31 August 1928, 9.

44. James J. Davis, "'Old Age' at Fifty," *Monthly Labor Review*, June 1928, 1097,
1095, 1098, 1099–1100. See also James J. Davis, "Setting an Age Deadline for Industry," *Baltimore Sun*, 21 April 1929, SM7.

45. On mass production in glass, see Slavishak, *Bodies of Work*.

46. James Maloney, "Glass Bottle Blowers," *American Federationist*, July 1929, 803.

47. Ibid.

48. Thomas F. McMahon, "Textile Workers," *American Federationist*, July 1929, 810, 811; Irving Bernstein, *The Lean Years: A History of the American Worker, 1920–1933* (Boston: Houghton-Mifflin, 1960), 4.

49. Len de Caux, *Labor Radical: From the Wobblies to CIO, a Personal History* (Boston: Beacon Press, 1970), 108; GR Price, Report of Nimishillen Lodge, 32, OH, *Amalgamated Journal*, 27 October 1927, 9.

50. In the earlier 1920 census, the Census Bureau organized the adult age brackets into 5 categories: 18–19, 20–24, 25–44, 45–64, and 65 and up. The large 25–44 and 45–64 brackets distort the substantial drop in job prospects that began when men reached their 40s.

51. See Bernstein, *Lean Years*, 268; and Harry Weiss, "New Models—Old Workers," *American Federationist*, January 1936, 84.

52. Thurber M. Smith, "The Unemployment Problem: A Catholic Solution" (PhD diss., St. Louis University, 1932), 85–86; Zaragosa Vargas, "Mexican Auto Workers at Ford Motor Company, 1918–1933" (PhD diss., University of Michigan, 1984), 56; Zaragosa Vargas, *Proletarians of the North: A History of Mexican Industrial Workers in Detroit and the Midwest, 1917–1933* (Berkeley: University of California Press, 1993), 61; Robert W. Dunn, "Youth Demanded on Speeded Up Auto Belt," press release, 22 November 1928, Folder 26, Box 2, Dunn Papers, Reuther Library.

53. A closer look at the numbers shows that a precipitous drop-off takes place at the age of 50. The number of "laborers" in steel drops from 24,326 (ages 45–59) to 16,667 (ages 50–54)—the greatest reduction for all ages in this category. See US Bureau of the Census, *Fifteenth Census of the United States, Population, Vol. IV: Occupations, By States* (Washington, DC: Government Printing Office, 1933), 50–51 (Table 22).

54. Horace B. Davis, *Labor and Steel* (New York: International Publishers, 1933), 22.

55. Samuel Craig, Report of Fort Wayne Lodge, 17, IN, *Amalgamated Journal*, 11 October 1928, 19; Lynd and Lynd, *Middletown*, 35.

56. Davis, "Setting an Age Deadline for Industry," SM7.

57. Brian Gratton, "The Poverty of Impoverishment Theory: The Economic Well-Being of the Elderly, 1890–1950," *Journal of Economic History* 56:1 (1996): 39–61; Ransom and Sutch, "Labor of Older Americans," 1–30; Roger L. Ransom and Richard Sutch, "The Labor of Older Americans: Retirement of Men On and Off the Job, 1870–1937," *Journal of Economic History* 56:1 (1986): 5–38. Other research acknowledges that age discrimination was a much more significant problem during the early twentieth century. See Carol Haber and Brian Gratton, *Old Age and the Search for Security: An American Social History* (Bloomington, IN: Indiana University Press, 1994), esp. ch. 3; Jill Quadagno, *The Transformation of Old Age Security: Class and Politics in the American Welfare State* (Chicago: University of Chicago Press, 1988), 78; and Dora L. Costa, *The Evolution of Retirement: An American Economic History, 1880–1990* (Chicago: University of Chicago Press, 1998), 100.

58. Sam T. Baker, "The Reward for Faithful Service," *Amalgamated Journal*, 4 November 1926, 21; see also Quadagno, *Transformation of Old Age Security*, 78.

59. Mabel Louise Nassau, *Old Age Poverty in Greenwich Village* (New York: Fleming H. Revell Company, 1915), 29.

60. Gorton James, "The Problem of the Old Man," *Survey*, 16 September 1921, 672.

61. Leo Wolman and Gustav Peck, "Labor Groups in the Social Structure," in *Recent Social Trends in the United States: Report of the President's Research Committee on Social Trends*, foreword by Herbert Hoover (New York: McGraw-Hill, 1933), 811.

62. Chase, "Laid Off at Forty," 344.

63. See Murray Webb Latimer, *Industrial Pensions in the United States and Canada* (New York: Industrial Relations Counselors, 1932), 790–798.

64. Upton Sinclair, *The Jungle* (1906; repr., New York: Bantam Books, 1981), 43.

65. Fitch, *Steel Workers*, 183–184; "The Age Limit in Steel Mills," *New York Times*, 27 September 1904, 8; "Age Limits Revised," *New York Times*, 26 August 1905, 6; Davis, *Labor and Steel*, 22.

66. "The Age Limit," *Wall Street Journal*, 18 October 1904, 1.

67. "The Anti-Age Limit League," *New York Times*, 20 October 1905, 8; "Fight the Old Age Limit," *Chicago Daily Tribune*, 18 October 1905, 1; "Form Age Limit League," *Chicago Evening Post*, 18 October 1905, 10; "Age Limit Stirs Gray Haired Men," *Chicago Daily Tribune*, 19 October 1905, 4.

68. "Fight the Old Age Limit," 1.

69. "Age Limit Stirs Gray Haired Men," 4.

70. Ibid.

71. Ibid.

72. "Want Policemen Under 30," *Chicago Daily Tribune*, 14 March 1906, 1.

73. "Fires Policemen for Being Brutes," *Chicago Daily Tribune*, 13 December 1906, 1.

74. "Age Limit Foes Plan Big Fight," *Chicago Daily Tribune*, 27 November 1911, 1; "Meet to Oppose 45-Year Limit," *Chicago Daily Tribune*, 29 November 1911, 1; "Protest Against Age Limit," *New York Times*, 27 November 1911, 3; "Men Join to Fight 45-Year Age Limit," *Chicago Record-Herald*, 27 November 1911, 1. The buttons are referred to in "Look Out for an Anti-Forty-Five," *Chicago Daily Tribune*, 24 March 1911, 5.

75. "Men Join to Fight," 1. Emphases in original.

76. "Age Limit Foes," 1.

77. "Meet to Oppose," 5.

78. Ben M. Selekman, *Employes' Representation in Steel Works: A Study of the Industrial Representation Plan of the Minnequa Steel Works of the Colorado Fuel and Iron Company* (New York: Russell Sage Foundation, 1924), 134. For background on the Colorado Fuel and Iron firm, see Thomas G. Andrews, *Killing For Coal: America's Deadliest Labor War* (Cambridge: Harvard University Press, 2008); and Jonathan Rees, "What If a Company Union Wasn't a 'Sham?' The Rockefeller Plan in Action," *Labor History* 48:4 (2007): 457–476.

79. Selekman, *Employes' Representation in Steel*, 134.

80. Ben M. Selekman and Mary Van Kleek, *Employes' Representation in Coal Mines: A Study of the Industrial Representation Plan of the Colorado Fuel and Iron Company* (New York: Russell Sage Foundation, 1924), 198–199.

81. See "New Draft Ages," *Washington Post*, 3 August 1918, 4; and "A Young Men's War," *Washington Post*, 17 August 1918, 4.

82. "Two Bills to Make Draft Age 18 to 45," *New York Times*, 25 June 1918, 5; "Raising the Draft Age," *Chicago Daily Tribune*, 28 July 1918, D4; "Doctors Barred by Age Limit," *New York Times*, 18 July 1917, 7; "New Draft Bill Passed by Senate," *New York Times*, 28 August 1918, 1; "New Draft Passes," *Washington Post*, 28 August 1918, 5.

83. Davis, *Labor and Steel*, 22.

84. Selekman, *Employes' Representation in Steel*, 136, 137, 138. On the history of physical examinations in early-twentieth century workplaces, see Sarah Rose, "No Right To Be Idle: The Invention of Disability, 1850–1930" (PhD diss., University of Illinois at Chicago, 2008), 211–214.

85. Unsigned, Report of Conemaugh Val. No. 112 PA, *Amalgamated Journal*, 27 March 1919, 29.

86. Quoted in Brody, *Labor in Crisis*, 87.

87. William Z. Foster, *The Great Steel Strike and Its Lessons* (1920; repr., New York: DaCapo Press, 1971), 43–44.

88. Report of National Committee for Organizing Iron and Steel Workers, *Amalgamated Journal*, 24 July 1919, 8.

89. Interchurch World Movement, *Report on the Steel Strike of 1919* (New York: Harcourt, Brace & Howe, 1920), 214–215.

90. Mary Heaton Vorse, *Men and Steel* (New York: Boni & Liveright, 1920), 168–170.

91. "Men Employed on Day-to-Day Lines Fear Losing Jobs," *Detroit Labor News*, 14 October 1921, 1; "Men Employed on Day-to-Day Lines Will Retain Jobs," *Detroit Labor News*, 28 October 1921, 1.

92. Ford Motor Company, *A Tour of the Remarkable Ford Industries during the Days When the End Product Was the Matchless Model A, with 150 Photographs* (1929; repr., Lockport, NY: Lincoln Publishing Company, 1961), 38; Harold L. Brock, *The Fords In My Past* (Warrendale, PA: Society of Automotive Engineers, 2000), 6; Peterson, *American Automobile Workers*, 63; Frank Marquart, *An Auto Worker's Journal: The UAW from Crusade to One-Party Union* (University Park: Pennsylvania State University Press, 1975), 6.

93. Phillip Bonosky, *Brother Bill McKie: Building the Union at Ford* (New York: International Publishers, 1953), 43. On Bill McKie's organizing career, see also Wendell Phillips Addington, "Reds at the Rouge: Communist Party Activism at the Ford Rouge Plant, 1922–1952" (MA Thesis, Wayne State University, 1997).

94. Ford's "natural liking" for young men is referenced in Allan Nevins and Frank Ernest Hill, *Ford: Expansion and Challenge, 1915–1933* (New York: Scribner, 1957), 534. On age and the Ford laborer classifications, see Steve Meyer, *The Five Dollar Day: Labor Management and Social Control in the Ford Motor Company, 1908–1921* (Albany: State University of New York Press, 1981), 145–146.

95. Peterson, *American Automobile Workers*, 95–96.

96. Robert W. Dunn, *Labor and Automobiles* (New York: International Publishers, 1929), 71, 72; "Young Workers in Hudson's," *Auto Workers News*, April 1928, 3; Cards 2, 4, and 6, Box 1, "Young Workers" section, Robert W. Dunn Papers

(hereafter Dunn Papers), Walter P. Reuther Library, Wayne State University (hereafter Reuther Library).

97. Robert L. Cruden, "No Loitering: Get Out Production," *Nation*, 12 June 1929, 696; idem, "Ford's Flimflammery," *Labor Age*, July 1928, 16; Dunn, *Labor and Automobiles*, 72.

98. "Many Men Fired in 'B' Building," *Auto Workers News*, October 1929, 1; "A Dodge Worker Speaks on Cutting Down Overhead," *Auto Workers News*, June 1929, 1; Card 12, Box 1, "Speed-up and Productivity" section, Dunn Papers, Reuther Library.

99. Korth and Beegle, *I Remember Like Today*, 62–63.

100. Cruden, "No Loitering," 697.

101. "Human Scrap Pile Grows," *Auto Workers News*, July 1929, 3.

102. Dunn, *Labor and Automobiles*, 72; Warren B. Catlin, *Labor Problem in the United States and Great Britain* (New York: Harper & Brothers, 1935), 88; Chase, "Laid Off at Forty," 340; Davis, "'Old Age' at Fifty," 1096.

103. Elias Tobenkin, "Gray Hair Terror to Worker," *Chicago Daily Tribune*, 9 May 1909, D9.

104. "Youth Crowding Out Even Middle Age," *New York Times*, 30 October 1904, 5.

105. Tobenkin, "Gray Hair Terror to Worker," D9.

106. "Why Fear Gray Hair?" *Chicago Daily Tribune*, 28 January 1929, 4.

107. See "No Need To Tolerate Gray Hair Any Longer," *Chicago Daily Tribune*, 20 November 1924, 6; as well as "No Need To Tolerate Gray Hair Any Longer," *Chicago Daily Tribune*, 12 June 1925, 12; "No More Gray Hair," *Chicago Daily Tribune*, 17 September 1926, 39; and "Gray Hair Unnecessary," *Chicago Daily Tribune*, 23 January 1927, 7.

108. "$500 for Hair Dye Injuries," *New York Times*, 25 June 1909, 18.

109. "Poisonous Dyes," *Chicago Daily Tribune*, 24 March 1927, 8.

110. "Recipes for Milady's Beauty Table," *Los Angeles Times*, 17 August 1902, 7.

111. Conroy, *Disinherited*, 138; Latimer, *Industrial Pensions*, 807; "Let It Sink In!" *Auto Workers News*, April 1929, 4; James Steele [Robert Cruden], *Conveyor: A Novel* (New York: International Publishers, 1935), 116.

112. Bonosky, *Brother Bill McKie*, 34–35.

113. Wood, "Paralysis of the Labor Movement," 73–82, 75 (statistic).

114. "The Auto Industry and its Workers," *Labor Age*, April 1929, 3; *Buick Worker* clipping, Box 1, "Women and Wages" section, Dunn Papers, Reuther Library.

115. Samuel Gompers, *Labor and the Employer* (New York: EP Dutton & Company, 1920), 142; Vorse, *Men and Steel*, 168–170; Epstein, *Facing Old Age*, esp. ch. 2; Davis, "'Old Age' at Fifty," 1098.

116. See "The End of the Trail," *Detroit Labor News*, 6 July 1928, 1.

117. Reinhold Niebuhr, *Leaves from the Notebook of a Tamed Cynic* (Chicago: Willet, Clark & Colby, 1929), 149.

Chapter Two

Old Age Poverty, Pension Politics, and Gender during the 1920s

What must we do for them? Shall we, by our weakness, permit them to go to poorhouses and homes for the infirm and aged? Are they not worth more than that?

—Sam T. Baker, steelworker in Canonsburg, Pennsylvania, 1926[1]

Several questions lingered in Sam T. Baker's mind after he read about the end of a fellow steelworker's long career and the suicide that followed. His acquaintance had worked for more than thirty years at the American Sheet and Tin Plate Company, building a respectable working-class life that included a steady income, a home, and educations for his children. Now facing his twilight years, the man intended to remain on the job in order to continue providing for his spouse and the household they shared. The children had offered to help and he knew he could depend on them, but the veteran steelworker was "too proud" to ever accept their "charity." His job was not only the core of his daily life, but more importantly, made everything important in his life possible; he intended to remain at work.

One day in the mill, however, the aging worker injured his back. For several months, a company doctor tended to him, and while the aging man's condition improved he could never carry out the heavy steel labor he had once done. The man needed light work. Once he was up and around, he visited the superintendent and asked for a transfer to a new job; however, the manager told him curtly "that his services were no longer required." Now facing permanent layoff, as well as the likelihood of having to depend on his children, or worse, the possibility of institutionalization for himself and his wife, the man went into his basement and hung himself. Tragically, his spouse found him. Rather than face the loss of his coveted status as a worker

59

and breadwinner, the aging man took his own life. "He had released society of a burden," Sam Baker wrote, offering his own interpretation of the man's actions. Baker believed the tragedy could have been avoided, however, if the aging steelworker knew that an old-age pension was waiting for him once he could no longer work. Pensions might sustain the social and economic foundations of manhood (productive labor, the family wage principle of the primacy of the male breadwinner, and the maintenance of an independent household via wage labor) when men could no longer work, if established as justly earned rewards after a lifetime of labor. Specifically, Baker hoped state governments would "pension these 'Old-Timers' so that he can retire to his little cottage and, with the mate who has struggled by his side, live in happiness and pleasant memories of his past successful efforts."[2]

The discussion of the Canonsburg man pointed to widespread anxieties during the 1920s about the erosion of gendered notions of working-class respectability and personal independence as working men and women faced their later years. As life spans increased during the early twentieth century, where could aging men and women find economic support in their twilight years? Could they count on a pension from their employer? Would they have savings and assets that might maintain them? Could they turn to their children for help? Would they have to move to a county poorhouse or poor farm? By committing suicide, the man in Canonsburg sternly rejected many these choices. He would not turn to his children, he probably could not afford a private old age home (nor would he want to live in one), and the man did not have savings. (After all, he paid for his children's education.) Finally, he would not move to the dreaded poorhouse; these institutions, he probably thought, were more like prisons than homes. With nothing left, the man chose death. To make matters worse, his widow now faced the prospect of losing their home and the independence she had known for years. The widow would surely have to ask her children for help, something her laboring husband had long tried to prevent. These anxieties about the destruction of manhood, womanhood, and the family unit in old age propelled experts' and workers' interest in state intervention. During the 1920s, workers, labor leaders, reformers, and politicians came to view pensions for the aged as the best way not only to provide economic assistance to the aged, but also to protect ideals of respectable working-class manhood and womanhood in later life.

These anxieties about gender in later life transformed attitudes toward social welfare politics and the idea of an American welfare state. Popular and political support for the 1935 Social Security Act began with these 1920s discourses about aging, gender, and poverty. Social provision experts, industrial reformers, and craft unions pressed for state pensions throughout the decade, but the movement failed to achieve its immediate goals. However, this movement established the legitimacy of the state pension idea, and its gendered foundations, which would shape the creation of Social Security in the next decade. The state pension movement, with its focus on aging men, showed how welfare state advocates were beginning to concern themselves with bolstering manhood throughout the life course, moving away from an earlier Progressive Era "maternalist" orientation that focused on working-class women's (and children's) struggles with poverty, labor, and mother-hood.[3] The importance of aging men in interwar social welfare thought furthers historians' understanding of why 1920s–1930s welfare state politics slighted women as workers, mothers, and citizens. Because of the dire problem of age discrimination in industrial employment, 1920s pension advocates believed state pensions were the only acceptable safety net that could catch aging working men if they fell; state pension programs, they believed, could defend the men's independence and the male breadwinner role against the vicissitudes of permanent layoff and the physical inability to work. Because alternatives (savings, industrial pensions, depending on children for help, poorhouses, and private old-age homes) provided no guarantees, were not available or accessible, or bore the mark of stigmatization, state pensions became the most attractive way to uphold notions of manhood in later life.

While several possibilities for economic support did exist in the social and economic landscape of 1920s America, reformers, experts, unionists, and workers successfully promoted state pensions as the best way to preclude the uncertainty of gender in later life. This discussion extended into politics, as states tentatively explored new pension legislation—especially toward the end of the decade. While the 1920s state pension movement failed to secure many legislative successes, the movement did much to legitimize social provision and old-age assistance in the United States, ultimately making the later 1935 Social Security Act possible. Attention to gender helps us to more clearly see the connections between failed 1920s state pension demands and the later old-age provisions of the Social Security Act: Before the creation of the New Deal welfare state, social provision experts, unionists, workers, and politicians had by 1929 already concluded that any government pension system would be intended to uphold the manhood of the aging male breadwinner. As sociologist Ann Shola Orloff argued in *The Politics of Pensions*, the 1920s state pension movement was a "dress rehearsal" for the later New Deal.[4] However, workers', unionists', and reformers' concern for masculinity amidst the gender anxieties of later life underpinned this political and cultural development.

SAVINGS? FAMILIES?

Some affluent citizens of the 1920s encouraged older men and women to buy their own houses, arguing that home ownership constituted the "best form of old-age pension." George A. Martin, president of the Railroad Cooperative Building and Loan Association, told readers of the *New York Times* that the "beginning of each man's provision for his sunset years should be a home of his own." If men prudently bought their own houses in their younger years, he sagely suggested, they would possess the ability to maintain themselves and their spouses in old age. They would benefit from living "rent free" in later life—a time when aging men and women would need every dollar and cent the most.

However, Martin failed to explain how older men and women, especially of working class backgrounds, could acquire the capital needed to purchase their own homes.[5] Men and women certainly wanted homes of their own, but 1920s economic realities repeatedly undermined many working-class men and women's abilities to save funds in the long term. As historians Alexander Keyssar and Susan Porter Benson have pointed out in their work, personal debt, low wages, lay-offs, and unemployment undercut worker budgets.[6] John R. Commons and John B. Andrews's remarks about older workers' problems in 1916 proved to be prophetic. "Failing health, inability to find employment, lack of means, often absence of friends willing or able to help him," they wrote in *Principles of Labor Legislation*, "such is the prospect which confronts, in the great majority of cases, the aged worker."[7]

Working-class men's problems acquiring savings were a common refrain in discussions of state pension demands. While most would not secure it, working-class men wanted a "competence": enough savings, earned through wage labor, to support a man and a spouse in old age. In Washington, Pennsylvania, steelworker Bill G. Boswell wrote that all working men wanted "[a] competence against old age. In other words, the position of labor is this":

> A worker who works so many hours a day regularly, for such a number of years regularly, at such and such a steady useful job, is entitled to receive in return, his political and religious independence. All the necessaries and a fair share of the luxuries of life, reasonable opportunities for his family, a fair proportion of recreation, and an independent old age.[8]

However, any economic downturns or periods of unemployment endangered working men's abilities to work, earn, and save for their later years. In Altoona, Pennsylvania, aging steelworker Fred Caswell observed that the local mill's episodic operations struck hard at local pocketbooks, as the mill remained closed between August and October 1924. "This is no good," Caswell wrote to the *Amalgamated Journal*, "and a mill man will never be able to lay away a nest egg for his old age with this kind of working."[9] As historian David Hackett Fischer pointed out, "The problem of old age was primarily a problem of poverty."[10]

Men of the 1920s worried that most industrial firms would never provide the kind of steady employment that was a prerequisite for savings. Otto P. Deluse, president of the Fraternal Order of Eagles (FOE), which called for state pensions to support aging Americans, argued that industry's refusal to provide sufficient earnings and savings overwhelmingly justified state pension demands.[11] A working man in Tennessee agreed with the stand of the FOE. He wrote in the *Amalgamated Journal* that aging workers "have all worked hard and have not got wages enough for their work," while RD Scrom, a steelworker in Kansas City, Missouri, criticized the ways industry denied men long-term economic stability. He argued that at the age of 55, 30 men in 100 were "dependent"; ten years later, 54 men would be dependent. Based on his math, Scrom concluded that a man had the "odds against him" as he aged in industry.[12] Despite a lifetime of hard work, "very few of us ever arrive at that period of our lives," Scrom lamented, "that we can retire from the daily grind."[13] A man could not expect to be "independent in his declining years after long years of servitude to his master 'Industry.'"[14]

Working-class men and women worried extensively about their savings during the 1920s, as they told Robert S. Lynd and Helen Merrell Lynd during the interviews for their book, *Middletown: A Study in American Culture* (1929). In addition to the problem of low wages, high prices and housing costs made it difficult for working families to accrue the assets that would sustain them in later life.[15] On average, industrial workers of the 1920s made less than $2,000 annually, which greatly hindered working class families' ability to acquire substantial savings.[16] A woman in Muncie, Indiana, whose husband was a forty-six year old machinist noted, "I worry about what we'll do when he gets older and isn't wanted at the factories and I am unable to go to work . . . we can't seem to save any money for that time." Another wife, whose husband was a pattern maker, told the Lynds that her household was "not saving a penny, but we are saving [for] our boys." This wife and husband could not save for themselves; they spent a large portion of their net worth on their sons' education.[17]

Chronic sickness undermined many older men's ability to work. In New York City during the 1910s, for example, social workers visited an aging man who battled asthma; moreover, now that he was getting older, his body was failing him. Earlier, he could secure work as a mason and a plasterer, but no longer. "It is pathetic," a social worker wrote, "to see his various signs advertising his trade, because of course [*sic*] he can't be very competent now because of his failing strength and poor breathing, and, besides, the present-day demand is for younger men, who will work quickly."[18] During the 1920s, a survey of men's employability in Massachusetts revealed that illness constituted the main reason why aging men often could not work. Of 2,195 men surveyed over age 65, the state noted that "chronic illness," rheumatism, and "old age," among other problems, sidelined the majority. Of those men who no longer sought work, "old age" was cited as the main reason for their retirement.[19]

Illness and disease menaced savings. Working-class men and women could lose every penny if they became ill; expensive doctor and pharmacist bills destroyed fragile working-class bank accounts. Social provision expert Abraham Epstein concluded this was a common problem, if not often discussed: "Even if a workman is fortunate enough to receive a fairly high wage, and by economy and self-denial succeeds in setting aside a small part of his earnings, it not infrequently happens that serious illness besets the family and the entire savings are wiped out after the payment of the doctor and druggist's bills."[20]

Unemployment was the overriding reason why working-class men of the 1920s could not save for the rainy days of their later years. Studies during the 1920s revealed substantial unemployment throughout the Jazz Age. Unemployment sometimes reached 10 percent during the decade, and in 1924–1925 unemployment reached 13 percent nationally.[21] In Muncie, Indiana, only 38 percent of households worked steadily for the first 8 months of 1924. Technological and seasonal unemployment were key causes of worker suffering. Between 1920 and 1929, technological change eliminated over 3 million jobs in the United States, and over 1 million unemployed workers were not reabsorbed into the industrial economy.[22] Anecdotal evidence also indicates that working people were deeply concerned with unemployment in what were supposed to be prosperous times. Abraham Epstein wrote about a man in New York who could not find a new job after a layoff—even after he repeatedly sought assistance at an employment agency. The agency could not place the man in a new post.[23]

Working men and women of the 1920s did not have a lot of money in the bank as they approached old age. At the age of 65, a man in the 1920s might live 10 more years. He would need an estimated $8,000 in assets to cover his most basic expenses for the remainder of his life. However, studies showed that most men did not have the assets needed to maintain a subsistence income for such a long period. Studies conducted by the Massachusetts Commission on Pensions and the pro-business National Civic Federation discovered, respectively, that 59.2 and 52.4 percent of the persons they studied owned personal property valued at less than $5,000.[24] Most older working-class men would not have the means to live on if they could not find work, secure a pension, rely on children, or depend on charity. Eventually, retired men and women would surely confront the end of their savings and assets.

Working-class men and women of the 1920s did not want to rely on their children; aging parents worried extensively about becoming dependent on those who had once been their dependents. Parents *and* children struggled to get by in the mass consumer economy of the decade, and older parents did not want to burden younger families' budgets with extra mouths to feed and clothe. "We can't expect our children to support us," a working-class wife in Muncie told the Lynds.[25] Men and women wanted to maintain their own homes. For men, this was paramount, as an independent household was an important emblem of adult manhood. For instance, social workers in 1920s New York City wanted a poor older couple to move in with their children. The pair sternly refused. According to *The Survey*, the couple "would be better off in the homes of their children, but the man's aversion to confinement and a woman's love for things domestic are holding them to their own small home, where they can feel responsibility in at least one aspect of their seemingly useless lives."[26] The man and woman wanted to live on their own, poor or not.

Aging men and women's demands for independence reflected broader changes in attitudes about family during the late-nineteenth and early-twentieth centuries. Instead of collecting extended families living under a single roof, men and women now embraced the smaller size and greater independence of the nuclear family unit. The historian SJ Kleinberg points out that aged parents often "did not reside with their children" at the turn-of-the-twentieth century. In Pittsburgh, for example, one struggling older couple, descending into destitution and poverty, stubbornly clung to their own home. Ultimately, however, they lost the house and their independence as a result, and the older man was forced to enter a charity hospital.[27] Depending on sons and daughters for support robbed older men of their status as patriarchs and heads-of-households; aging men insisted on maintaining their own homes, even in the face of unemployment, physical decline, and sickness. Their spouses, too, surely struggled with the loss of the home as the site that defined so much of their sense of womanhood. For working-class sons and daughters, the addition of poor aged parents to their households would have added a new burden to the family budget, not to mention other significant matters such as personal privacy, space, the allocation of household chores, etc. During the 1920s, combining families in one residence might have been unattractive to both the older and younger generation for several reasons, as moving in with children implied the addition of new personal and financial burdens on the younger generation's family in a time of declining savings and wages.

INDUSTRIAL PENSIONS?

Pensions from the employers of labor offered another possible avenue to subsistence and independence in old age. These monthly checks from former employers offered a source of income when working men were no longer wanted because of their advancing years and slowing bodies, and working men and women enthusiastically endorsed the concept. But would working-class men and their spouses receive them?

Before the years of the Great Depression, railroads, the steel industry, public utilities, and oil offered the majority of industrial pensions in the United States.[28] The American Express Company established the first private company pension system in 1875, which generously gave its retired workers half-pay after the age of sixty. In 1884, the first year of the Great Upheaval, the Baltimore & Ohio (B&O) railroad line established a pension policy. Several other firms followed suit; however, only 12 company pension programs existed in the US in 1900.[29] The institution of pensions occurred mostly during the height of the Progressive Era, the years between 1911 and 1920, when industry pension scholar Murray Webb Latimer counted 227. During the 1920s, however, the expansion of company pensions slowed considerably; and most men and women would not work at a pensioning firm. After 1929, pensioning employers began to more quickly dump their pension obligations to retirees—10 percent of the pension plans in 1929 had been discontinued, suspended, or closed to new applicants by 1932.[30] Workers in agriculture and domestic service, for instance, never saw a workplace pension, while other workers, such as autoworkers, would not secure pensions until the late 1940s and 1950s. In 1927, just 16 percent of the men employed in manufacturing, mining, office work, and transportation could expect a pension when they retired. Overall, in 1927 only 100,000 "dependent aged" men and women received a pension out of an estimated 1.8 million persons over the age of 65.[31]

Furthermore, industrial pension systems created problems that went far beyond their limited coverage. While pension programs could be interpreted as an example of employer altruism on behalf of the working class who depended on them, these pensions functioned as part of employers' efforts to regulate and control early-twentieth century industrial workplaces. In this era of implementing mass production work processes and the steady assault on workers' control in the factory, mine, and mill, managers used pension plans to influence the tone of labor-management relations, offset industrial unionism, and remove outmoded (older) men. As the management of the Pennsylvania Railroad put it, "The pension system permits the company to get rid humanely of any drones who encumber the service and to keep the entire staff constantly fresh."[32] Early in the twentieth century, during the 1900s and 1910s, several major steel and coal firms instituted pension plans that were intended to help managers cultivate an enhanced degree of cooperation on the shop floors of their operations. A manager in the steel industry told pension scholar Gorton James that his company used pensions to gain greater influence over workers' actions. If workers complained, caused trouble, or talked about unionization, they jeopardized their pensions and their economic futures. The manager noted he "could not get away with" his polices toward labor without the "aid" of the pension.[33] To protect their pensions, working men held their tongues, often to their own frustration. Veteran laborers who worked for the Colorado Fuel and Iron Company's coal mining division insisted the company "has put a rope around our necks. We are now over forty-five and we can't say anything."[34] Some firms even used pensions to create a reserve army of workers and even strikebreakers, imposing stipulations that the company could recall pensioned men if they needed. During a 1925 walk-out on the Western Maryland Railroad, management tried to break the strike by calling its pensioners back to work. However, the men refused and the company took their pensions away. The Brotherhood of Locomotive Engineers thanked the retirees for denying the company's orders by taking over the payment of the pension funds to the men.[35]

Gorton James as well as other observers pointed out that companies who featured a pension program did not often pay benefits to qualified workmen. While humane treatment of the aged and rewarding long years of service represented the pleasant public face of corporate pensions, many firms never delivered on their promises to workers. At pensioning companies, working men expected to receive their benefits once they reached, roughly, the age of sixty-five. This proved to be a privilege that could be secured only with significant difficulty. For example, rules regarding length of service limited many workers' eligibility. Layoffs, strikes, seasonal unemployment, and technological unemployment were common, and they could rob an older man of the working time needed to collect his benefits.[36] If a worker lost his job before he had completed the designated (and long) period of employment, he would receive nothing—no matter how close to meeting the requirements. "The worker," as James argued, "does not receive a penny" even if he fulfilled "95 percent of the time required."[37] Another observer of industry sarcastically noted that a working man would receive his pension

> [i]f you remain with this company throughout your productive lifetime; if you do not die before the retirement age; if you are not discharged, or laid off for an extended period; if you are not refused a pension as a matter of discipline; if the company is in business; and if the company does not decide to abandon the plan, you receive a pension at the age of _____ [sic], subject to the contingency of its discontinuance or reduction after it has been entered upon.[38]

Regulations often mandated at least 20 years of uninterrupted service, and by 1930 only 3.4 percent of working-class men in the United States lasted 20 years with a pensioning firm.[39]

For instance, working men in the steel industry lamented that so few of them ever received their pensions. At US Steel, the largest American steel company, unskilled and semiskilled workers constituted 75 percent of the men on the payroll, but only 20 percent of these workers received pension benefits.[40] Also, the number of pensions at the firm declined after 1915. US Steel revised its policies; too many men were qualifying for eligibility. In 1915, 1.6 percent of the employees collected pensions; and this very small number would continue to decline. By 1919, only 1.2 percent of the workers at US Steel received benefits.[41] Earlier, US Steel allowed workers to collect their pensions with 20 years of seniority and the age of 60, but in 1915 the company raised the age to 65 and increased the service requirement to 25 years.[42] As a result, men would have to hold on even longer—5 years—to be eligible for their pension benefit. It became so unusual for older working-class men to receive their pensions that individual retirements sometimes made the pages of the *Amalgamated Journal*. In 1924, for instance, James Sayers, a "ruffer" with over forty-five years of experience in Canadian and American steel mills, received a rare pension from the Steel Company of Canada in Hamilton, Ontario.[43]

Industrial employers of the 1910s and 1920s regarded their pension programs as benevolent "gifts," and as a result, pensioning employers did not recognize any contractual obligation towards employees and retirees to provide or guarantee these benefits in perpetuity. Pensions could be discontinued at any time, a principle that would be upheld in court. When the owners of the Morris & Co. meatpacking firm in Chicago sold their enterprise to the Armour company in 1923, the firm's 398 pensioners were abruptly and summarily dropped. With the sale, Morris & Co. discontinued its pension, originally established in 1909. Since the retirees had not worked for Armour, the company did not assume any responsibility to pay benefits to the Morris & Co. retirees. Would Morris & Co. somehow sustain a pension fund for the 398 retirees? No. In fact, Morris managers nearly liquidated the pension fund of several hundred thousand dollars, as they paid back other workers' contributions to the fund.[44]

Faced with ruin, 24 pensioners sued Morris & Co. for the creation of a $7 million dollar fund that would sustain the pensions of the nearly 400 retirees. In the lawsuit, they also alleged the Morris company was guilty of a "conspiracy" to rob the pensioners of moneys that had been legally promised to them. The litigants met with disaster at each phase of the lawsuit. In 1924, the Circuit Court of Cook County, Illinois, ruled that "pensions were gifts," not a deferred wage, as Judge Ira D. Ryner stated in his ruling. "The complainants have failed to prove any implied obligation or understanding," the judge declared, "and there is no documentary evidence showing a contract of any kind."[45] Subsequent rulings in the Illinois appellate court (1926) and the Supreme Court of Illinois (1928) affirmed Ryner's verdict. The litigants tried to argue that Armour had an obligation to continue the pension since they purchased the Morris & Co. firm and thus its financial obligations. An "implied contract" was thereby in place. The state supreme court rejected the argument. The court ruled that no contract, implied or otherwise, existed; the companies could abandon their pension programs at any time without violating any contractual arrangements. Pensions had no legal basis.[46]

For working-class men who actually received the "gift" of a pension from their employer, the amount of money was very small during the early twentieth century. At US Steel, retiring men received, on average, 25 percent of their monthly earnings. A veteran steelworker who received 60 dollars per month in wages walked out the door upon retirement with an income of 15 dollars per month.[47] At another company, working men who earned over 83 dollars per month retired with a pension of 25 dollars.[48] While company pensions provided *some* form of monetary support to men in old age, they surely forced retired men and women to implement major changes in their living standards. An older couple on a pension might very likely need to give up their house (if they owned one) and dramatically reduce expenditures.

Despite the problems and challenges that accompanied company pension plans, men appreciated the pension concept. They clearly (and dearly) valued the importance of financial support in later life. As early as the 1910s, historian James D. Rose argues that men at the US Steel facility in Duquesne, Pennsylvania, "expected to retire" on their company pensions.[49] In 1929, steelworker John A. Powell wrote that he had "the right to expect from my employer, economic security" when he could no longer work in old age.[50] Because of difficult rules, however, men struggled to secure these pensions. When problems arose on the job, quitting or striking was too risky for many steelworkers. Instead, some men tried to enhance their work situation without walking out. For instance, Andy Chervenak who worked for US Steel in Duquesne transferred from the open hearth to the conditioning department. Other men transferred to different mills in the US Steel system. William J. Smith worked in Duquesne, Homestead, and Clairton between 1913 and 1931 to protect his pension.[51] Men wanted their benefits, despite the imperfections. They tried to protect them, even by taking the matter to court.

THE POORHOUSE?

Institutionalization provided another means of possible support for aging working-class men and women during the early twentieth century. However, state-run institutions, known as "poorhouses," "poor farms," and "alms-houses," were the most problematic and undesirable source of support for older Americans. Only after all other means had been exhausted or were completely unavailable might an older man or woman of the 1920s seek residence at a state-run poorhouse or poor farm. While the number of poorhouse residents increased during the 1920s, especially among older working-class men, the actual number of aging men and women who resided in state-run institutions was very small. By 1925, over 2,183 state-run institutions throughout the United States served an "inmate" population of only 85,889 men and women, according to the US Bureau of Labor Statistics and the Department of Labor.[52] The state institutions were generally under-funded, poorly staffed, and offered few services or comforts to residents. As a cultural symbol, the poorhouse encapsulated central themes in early-twentieth century discourses on aging, gender, and work: the destruction of marriage and family; the unmanliness of dependence; the degradation of femininity; and the failure of industry to provide men and women with adequate funds for old age after a lifetime of hard work and service. These "houses" were not homes; they seemed to collect the human scrap of industrial society.

Throughout the 1920s, numerous workers, authors, and politicians used the negative symbolism of the poorhouse to attack industrial employers' disregard for aging working men and the absence of reliable and adequate financial support for the aged in the twentieth-century United States. Pension advocates frequently condemned poorhouses as places of "degradation" and "cruelty," dismissing them as "antiquated"; for example, James M. Lynch, president of the International Typographical Union, wrote in 1925 that poorhouses brought "human grief, humiliation and degradation" to respectable working-class men and women.[53] In 1926, steelworker Hugo the Third complained that craft unions, then in decline, coldly "allow our old men to go to the county home, commonly called the poorhouse."[54] The US Bureau of Labor Statistics lamented the "dilapidation, inadequacy, and even indecency" found in state-run institutions; here was "no sadder chapter in American social history than the callous neglect in dehumanized poorhouses."[55] During his campaign for governor of New York state, Franklin D. Roosevelt noted, "No greater tragedy exists in our civilization than the plight of the aged, worn-out worker who after a life of ceaseless effort and useful productivity must look forward for his declining years to a dismal poorhouse."[56]

A lengthy history of institutional coercion aimed at the working poor, and the degradation that accompanied this form of incarceration, fueled early-twentieth century working people's negative associations with the poorhouse. During the seventeenth century, British elites built "workhouses" where impoverished men and women would be forcibly detained and instructed in discipline and proper attitudes towards productive labor. Sir Matthew Hale argued in the 1600s that new workhouses would forcefully introduce destitute men and women "and their children after them [to] a Regular, Orderly and Industrious course of life which will be as natural to them as now Idleness, and Begging, and Thieving is."[57] In early modern England, then colonial America, and subsequently the United States, institutionalization meant detainment, forced labor, and elite disdain, as well as failure, loss, and isolation.

During the eighteenth century, elite contempt for the poor intensified as the Atlantic economy brought periods of both economic expansion and contraction to commercial port cities. In urban areas, where working-class people depended on wages to pay for accommodations, food, and firewood, frequent economic downturns, fires, and epidemics undermined many urban dwellers' fragile subsistence. In response to intensifying periods of poverty and a growing poor population, Anglo colonial authorities built new and larger workhouses. These facilities would allow elites to centralize, monitor, and better manage the legions of urban poor. There, authorities hoped to reform the poor's habits, presuming their ill fortunes resulted from individual failings and poor morals. In 1730s Boston, for instance, poor men and women who sought help from the local workhouse were examined by a nurse, labored according to a strict daily schedule, and were compelled to attend church services twice every Sunday. If not, they were "punifhed" [sic] with reduced rations and even solitary confinement. In eighteenth-century Philadelphia, civic-minded gentlemen built the Bettering House in 1766 to not only provide relief to the city's expanding poor population, but also to compel the working poor to improve upon and reform their questionable work ethic. In New York City, Philadelphia, and Charleston, elites obliged poor men and women to wear insignia on rough-hewn patches, such as "N:Y," on their clothes, deliberately marking them with conspicuous badges of inferiority.[58]

While the "indoor relief" of institutionalization never fully replaced "outdoor relief" for the poor, aged, and infirm, nineteenth-century elites emphasized that poorhouses, almshouses, and poor farms were a more efficient and cost-effective way to deal with impoverished older men and women, building on the precedents of the eighteenth century. Genteel men and women argued that outdoor relief only encouraged laziness among the poor; and it was also regarded as a waste of money. During 1822, the New York Secretary of State, John Yates, submitted a report (the Yates Report) to the state's legislature, where he argued that putting money in the hands of paupers only encouraged them to "relax individual exertion" and turned them away from the "desire of honest independence."[59] The poor were louts and beggars. In response, the Yates report led to the creation of the county-administered poorhouse system in New York state in 1824. Eleven years later, in 1835, with some exceptions, each county in New York operated poorhouses.[60] To keep the impoverished under strict control, institutions became common during the nineteenth century and into the twentieth, even as many middle-class reformers criticized the conditions found within them. There were 2,183 poorhouses in the US by the early 1900s. The "specter of the poorhouse" and widening anxieties about poverty led to demands for Civil War veterans pensions and pensions for single mothers, contributing to the idea that pensions were the antidote to the degradation of institutionalization.[61]

Aging working men of the early-twentieth century despised poorhouses as institutions and symbols of poverty, building on these earlier discourses that emphasized the negative connotations of institutionalization. Respectable working-class men of the 1920s believed that institutionalization collapsed gender and class distinctions into an indiscernible lump at the very bottom of society, where hard-working men—once able to maintain their manly independence as workers and breadwinners—were now thrown onto a scrap pile with the sick, the disabled, the infirm, and the forgotten. It was known that state institutions housed, in addition to the aged: "Paupers, insane, idiots, feeble-minded, blind, deaf mutes, drunkards, drug addicts, sufferers from chronic diseases, criminals, epileptics, children, prostitutes, mothers of illegitimate children."[62] Abraham Epstein described poorhouses as, put simply, "far from inviting."[63]

In the 1920s, the poorhouse came to be viewed as a powerful symbol of male anxiety since men dominated the expanding poorhouse population of the decade. Government surveys conducted in Pennsylvania, Massachusetts, and Indiana showed that the majority of poorhouse residents were older working-class males. The 1923 Federal Census of Paupers found 2 men for every 1 woman in their sample of poorhouses. In Massachusetts, 2/3 of almshouse "inmates" were men; furthermore, of the 2,798 men in Massachusetts' institutions, over 2.108 (77.5 percent) worked previously in manufacturing occupations. The census for paupers reported similar proportions for the states of Indiana and Pennsylvania, concluding that 75 percent of poorhouse "inmates" there were men.[64] The poorhouse encapsulated male vulnerability in industrial America; as the census suggested, more and more aging working-class men seemed destined to spend their final years behind the gray walls of institutions, having lost the status and personal independence they had tried to build over the course of a life spent in the service of industry. "Thus after a lifetime of toil in a modern factory," Abraham Epstein wrote, "with physical vigor gone, children and relatives either scattered or dead, the aged wage-earner . . . can hardly escape falling dependent" on the state for support.[65]

Poorhouse residents' discussions of actual conditions lent considerable authenticity to social provision experts' fault-finding statements. The rules, regulations, and living conditions found in the state-run poorhouses offended older men's sensibilities in numerous ways: even in old age, men wanted to be paid for their labor; they wanted to maintain their own homes; and many wanted the companionship afforded by women. Older working-class men wanted to be independent, despite advancing years, physical limitations, and/ or declining mental faculties; poorhouses precluded autonomy in every way. In addition, administrators ran the homes with a combination of stern discipline and benign neglect. Poorhouses were uncomfortable and inhospitable places where no working man wanted to live.

In a rare inmate autobiography, *Poorhouse Sweeney* (1927), quick-witted resident Ed Sweeney told of the rules, personalities, work routines, social relations, tensions, and even odors that dominated daily life in the poorhouse. He devoted many pages to critiquing the practices and attitudes of administrators, telling readers, for instance, how disinterested administrators ignored inmates' complaints about living conditions, rules, and provisions. In addition to providing tasteless meals and uncomfortable clothing, poorhouse managers did their best to restrict inmate sociability. They kept men and women in separate wings of the institution, even forbidding the men from fraternizing with the hired women who worked on the grounds. While Sweeney was sympathetic to others, he generally disliked his fellow inmates. He frequently characterized them as "nuts": grumpy, irritable, hostile, lustful, deranged, and inclined to probe into others' affairs. He most hated the lack of privacy; poorhouse inmates harassed each other at all times of the day. For Sweeney, and presumably other inmates, there seemed to be no escape from these daily hassles and irritations; everyone shared meals, activities, and rooms. "I sometimes would go upstair [sic] to the room where I sleep to read in peace," he wrote, "but as three others sleep in their I couldn't consider it private. I would just about get set when some simp would stick in."[66] Also, offensive odors lingered throughout the homes, which could make the bedrooms smell "worse than a monkey cage."[67]

Poorhouses were very much places of work, despite their association with the end of men's working lives. Behind the walls of the institution, Ed Sweeney described busy, unpaid work routines assigned to those who were anywhere near able-bodied. The schedule of chores was so intense that Sweeney sarcastically remarked that his poorhouse closely resembled a "plantation."[68] Though he struggled to walk, he worked daily in the kitchen, carried food to those who were confined to their beds, prepared the dining room each day for meals, cleaned laundry, swept floors, and "act[ed] as a chambermaid for ten fellows." In addition, he cut hair for the men. Angered by the lack of pay for his barber services, however, Sweeney launched a one-man "strike" in protest. But the lack of interest from either the administrators or his fellow inmates forced him to abandon his cause. Everyone simply ignored him. Reflecting on his unsuccessful strike experience, Sweeney concluded:

> It wasn't the money I wanted but the relief of getting out of bondage. I was willing to do anything thing for any one through sympathy, but I didn't like the idea that I was a slave or in bondage to the boss and his hired girls and man and also to a bunch of husky idiots and brazing degenerates.[69]

One reviewer of the book praised Ed "Poorhouse" Sweeney's unique, though intensely acerbic, insights into the state poorhouse system, labeling him a "*sans-coulotte*" and a bold, insurgent voice for the "lowest substratum of the social order."[70]

Because of the degraded conditions associated with the poorhouse, the vulnerability of older men, and women, signaled to many the decline of the family in industrial America. The majority of poorhouse residents were widowed and/or without children who could give them assistance. According to the 1923 census report on paupers, 53.7 percent of the male poorhouse population was unmarried. The majority of women in institutions were also single (meaning never married), numbering 42.1 percent. Men and women who went to the poorhouse did not, by and large, have relatives who could help them. As the 1919 report from the Pennsylvania Old Age Pension Commission noted, "Having no children of their own, their parents dead, and in many cases, with few relatives to be called upon, these paupers seek the institution as the last resort for shelter and nourishment."[71] The majority of widows in poorhouses were spouses of men who once worked in industry. Of 843 widows in Massachusetts poorhouses, 540 (83.5 percent) had been married to industrial workers.[72] Despite widespread recognition that widowhood hastened many aging men and women to the poorhouse, a 1922 editorial in the *New York Times* insisted that "marriage is pretty good insurance against a poorhouse old age."[73]

Institutionalization also broke up older married couples as a result of sex segregation at most homes. How could the state so coldly force older men and women into degraded and inadequate poorhouses—and then separate them from one another? The only comfort and support they had left? In Pennsylvania, the chairman of the Pennsylvania Old Age Pension Commission, John H. Maurer, visited a poor farm in Berkshire County. In the *American Labor Legislation Review*, Maurer wrote about an encounter with a poor older couple seeking admittance. He described to the reform community a dramatic story of the state's insensitivity towards the family and gender sensibilities of everyday men and women. The husband and wife, whose names were John and Mary, told the superintendent they "have a permit to enter the poor farm." After making introductions, the administrator told John, "You go to the building over there, and Mary, you go to that building over there." John was shocked. "What!" he cried. "After living together under the same roof for fifty years are we now to going to be separated?" The superintendent coolly told them, "Those are the rules. We cannot mix up the sexes in these institutions."[74] Maurer reconstructed the incident as a tragic example of how state poorhouses degraded the sanctity of the family. In a 1927 letter to the *New York Times*, a man argued that it "is doubtful if the separation of death is more trying, or even as trying, as the compulsory separation on entering the poorhouse." Another man concurred: "I can conceive of no sadder fate than that of the old couple who have faced life's problems together, and who have known no greater happiness than the joy of their mutual companionship, being forced to separate at the time when they have no one but each other: the man to wither away in an institution for men and the woman to grieve out her heart in a home for women."[75] "To tear a veteran of industry away from wife or children," John B. Andrews noted, "after a lifetime of honest toil and commit him to the uncertain care of strangers in a strange place is so inhuman an aspect of our industrial civilization that it is certain to be everywhere remedied."[76]

Anxieties about the devastation of womanhood shaped another important gender component of poorhouse critiques. The poverty of older women provided powerful ammunition for reformers and critics to use against employers and politicians who discriminated against aging men in the labor market and refused to support company or state pension programs. How could employers deny older men employment or a pension, thus stealing bread from the mouths of aging fathers *and mothers*? How could state politicians not endorse pension programs that would provide aging men and women with the means to retain their independence, respectability, and dignity in the twilight years of their lives?

Working-class women's troubles with isolation, abandonment, and poverty in their later years sparked widespread unease, even contributing to discussions of the subject in early motion pictures. In 1920, director Harry Millarde screened his new film, *Over the Hill to the Poorhouse*, at the Astor Theatre in New York City. Will Carleton's 1869 poem inspired the film, which explored an aging women's struggle to avoid the poorhouse as her children, one by one, abandoned her. In the poem, a 70-year old woman, "only a trifle gray," confronts the fact that her husband is dead, her children have moved away, and now, without support, she is to be remanded to the local poorhouse. She recalls her life story, which included youthful beauty and a warm courtship, a marriage to a hard-working man, John, and the happy births of 12 children. However, the sons and daughters grew up and did not want to look after the devoted mother who lovingly cared for them for so many years. Even her youngest son Charley, who had remained close to home throughout his life, turned on his poor mother; he took mother to the poorhouse "an' put me on the town." The poem, and the film adaptation, called attention to the ways old age jeopardized respectable womanhood. Husbands lost jobs and died, while children—once the "blessed little ones"—grew up, found families of their own, and forgot about the old mothers who gave life and love to them. While the film version of this sad tale updated the conclusion to reflect the audience's desire for a happy ending, a *New York Times* reviewer noted the film's "assault upon the emotions is undisguised and sweeping." "It is ruthless in its mass attack," the writer noted.[77]

As Americans of the 1920s considered the degraded state of poorhouses and the vulnerability of older men and women in industrial America, newspapers began to report often of suicides among aged couples. These suicides were often subtly presented as older men and women's condemnations of poorhouses. In 1927, for example, a New Jersey woman discovered that her neighbors (a sickly couple in their eighties, Mr. and Mrs. Patrick O'Rourke) had committed suicide. When she went to check on the couple, as she did each morning, they did not open the door. The New Jersey woman could see their figures through the window: the husband sat still in his chair, while his eighty-six year-old spouse rested on the couch. Despite repeated knocking, neither person moved. The woman ran to find a policeman. After battering their way in, the police discovered that the couple had turned on the gas in the oven, which filled their home with poison and killed them. The house was in disarray, since neither Mr. nor Mrs. O'Rourke could handle the housework. Earlier, the couple's niece had visited them and suggested that aunt and uncle should move into the nearby Arthy Pitney Home for the Aged. The older couple, however, "stubbornly refused." The police assumed the couple's suicide was their response to the threat of "being sent to an old persons' home."[78]

Suicide, however, was the most extreme way that older men and women resisted institutionalization. Most simply tried to avoid the poorhouse in whatever ways they could. In a 1923 study of homelessness in Chicago, sociologist Nels Anderson noted that many older men refused to enter institutions. "Many old men in the tramp class are not able to work and are too independent to go to the almshouse," he wrote, after working and living in the "hobo world" himself. However, "It is pitiable," Anderson noted, "to see an old man tottering along the streets living a hand-to-mouth existence."[79] Throughout Jack Conroy's novel *The Disinherited*, the aging Bun Grady struggled to remain afloat and independent. Despite declining job opportunities and worsening health, Grady pieced together his subsistence with episodic factory work and the charity of rescue missions. While he stayed at missions and accepted meals from charity groups, Grady did not talk about poorhouses. Conroy does not address the matter directly, but perhaps Grady might have disliked the idea or did not know where he could find an institution.[80] Conroy's novel implies the poorhouse was not an option.

Impoverished older working-class men of the 1920s struggled to reconstruct their notions of manly independence amidst disability, injury, declining health, permanent layoff, and the specter of the poorhouse. They stubbornly refused to seek the aid of the feared state institutions. During the late 1920s, for instance, Al Carr, Bob Critchlow, and Bill Lewis lived together in a small shanty along the Monongahela River just north of downtown Pittsburgh. The men were former Western Pennsylvania steelworkers who could no longer work in the mills due to repeated injuries and hiring age limits. Al Carr was once a man of "iron biceps," who would have "spat out his lager in laughter if he had been told he would give up steel rolling." Over his career, however, a series of events pushed him toward poverty and dependency. Carr lost his wife, his eleven children married and moved away, and he became "unable to operate a machine" because of a serious injury to his hands.[81] Permanent layoff and old age poverty threatened breadwinner status and personal independence as bases of his manhood.

However, Al Carr and his friends reconstructed their manhood, economically and symbolically, by working odd jobs where possible, dredging scrap iron, and building their own residence along the river. The *Pittsburgh Post-Gazette* sketched their journey from the unmanliness of poverty to a patchwork brand of manhood. As a result of their endeavors, the paper suggested, they were now urban pioneers and rugged individualists—scratching a life out of the hostile urban wilderness. "Broke, unable to moil [*sic*] as in the roistering days of the past," the *Post-Gazette* noted, "Carr, Lewis and Critchlow built their home of flotsam beside the railroad tracks where fuel was handy, in a spot in view of the Homestead mills."[82] Once devastated, the aging males were now independent. They had patched over their battered masculinities, even though they lived so close to the steel mills that had once defined their identities as working men.

During the 1920s, workers', social reformers', and journalists' discussions of the poorhouse evoked working-class men's uncertainties about the foundations of manhood and gender in their later years. As working-class men faced their future, they worried that the degraded poorhouse lie coldly in wait for them. Institutionalization loomed over the fragile careers of working men, waiting for them to succumb to hiring age limits and permanent layoff. Citing a New Jersey newspaper, Epstein discussed an aging man, Jacob, who fell ill because of intense anxiety about his darkening future. Confronted with no job, savings, or relatives, the man who lived with his aging brother in Camden was about to be sent to the Blackwood, New Jersey, poorhouse. Jacob was "heartbroken because he had to go to the almshouse," becoming very sick. He soon died. "As age crept upon them," the newspaper reported, "they found themselves unable to obtain work, but they eked out their slender savings until the final penny was gone." Reduced to pauper status, the specter of institutionalization loomed over them. After Jacob died, "His brother went to the almshouse alone."[83] In 1929, an illustration in the *American Labor Legislation Review* depicted an older man in his worker overalls, beaten and standing with his shoulders slumped in front of the lengthening, ominous shadow of the poorhouse. It threatened to overcome him, approaching his heavy, planted feet. Unless he received immediate help, in the form of a pension from the state, he would not be able to hold out for much longer.[84]

PRIVATE OLD AGE HOMES?

In addition to the despised state institutions, a variety of private organizations operated old age homes. Private home operators tried to make the home concept more acceptable to aging men and women. They wanted the public to see their institutions as *homes*—not impersonal and inhumane prisons or hospitals where the destitute went to die. During the 1920s, old age homes operated by private, nationality, fraternal, and religious organizations, and unions received some attention in the labor press. Reformers, workers, and unionists all wanted alternatives to state poorhouses. Men and women, who struggled for many years to stay afloat in industrial society, did not want to live in degraded poorhouses. Men wanted to retain roles as patriarchs, living in their own residences with their partners. Organizations thus tried to soften the old age home image by emphasizing themes of family and familiar home settings. For a variety of reasons, however, private organizations did not resolve the problems of aging and gender for older Americans. Because of small budgets and limited facilities, the limited populations they served, and the awkward relationships that developed among home staff and residents (dubbed "inmates"), private old age homes could not meaningfully sustain respectable working-class gender ideals in the terrain of later life. Behind the veil of manicured grounds, rocking chairs, and lace curtains, dependence replaced independence in older men's lives.

The private organizations that operated old age homes targeted very specific populations—generally their own members or clients. Fraternal homes, for instance, catered to dues-paying, senior members of a particular order, such as the Knights of Pythias, the Masons, and the Odd Fellows. Exclusivity defined the private old age home of the 1920s. Many of the religious homes cared for aged ministers, their wives, and/or widows. The Baptists, Congregationalists, and Episcopalians, organized numerous homes for older ministers and their spouses.[85] The craft union old age homes did not provide support to the majority of workers, focusing instead on the "tried and true men of organized labor."[86] These characteristically small institutions mirrored craft jurisdictions, excluding unskilled workers from the working-class masses. Furthermore, union homes also placed specific requirements on which men could join. For example, the United Brotherhood of Carpenters stipulated thirty years of membership and sixty-five years of age as prerequisites.[87] If a working man joined the union late or experienced trouble in his early sixties, he would not be eligible for home residence. Finally, many aged men and women often could not enter private homes due to lengthy waiting lists.[88]

To gain admittance to private old age homes, older men's need had to conform to very specific sets of criteria; otherwise, they would not be helped. Private home administrators deliberately excluded certain applicants in order to limit the number of residents in their care. While administrators professed their desire to help the "deserving" poor; they did not want to assist those who needed *too much* help. For instance, one home preferred applicants who "have respectably sustained a struggle with disease or misfortune, till such a refuge as the home will be appreciated and enjoyed by them."[89] At fraternal organization homes, "Almost without exception it is required that the applicant be of good moral character, of temperate habits." In addition to policing applicants' morals and economic backgrounds, home administrators worried about potential residents' health situations. It was expensive, after all, to provide constant care to "inmates" who suffered from dementia, chronic illness, or immobility. Many fraternal homes thus favored applicants who were "free from mental, infectious, or contagious diseases."[90] At the Knights of Pythias' old age home in Illinois, "Persons unable to dress and care for themselves are usually specifically excluded."[91]

As administrators made their decisions regarding admittance, they conducted an extensive screening process to gain detailed information about the applicants. Managers of homes asked older men detailed questions about their health and medical history, personal habits, employment background, and asked them to "submit references."[92] For older working-class men of the 1920s, this surely would have been an eerie reminder of awkward and tense encounters with hiring managers from the factory. Once used to exclude them from the assembly line as they reached their later years, now a new manager was using interviews, background checks, and medical exams to exclude them—from the old age home. Men might have bristled when confronted with a barrage of medical exams, questions about morals, probing inquiries into their health, and questions regarding their work experiences.[93] If a man mentioned to an old age home administrator about quitting a job many years ago, did he jeopardize his chance to enter the home as a resident? For some aging men, these interviews and examinations must have reminded them of earlier interviews and work experiences at Colorado Fuel and Iron, the steel mills of the Midwest, or the automobile factories of Detroit.

Most of the private old age homes admitted married couples and widows, a response to public criticism of the state institutions' treatment of aging men and women. In nationality group homes, the US Bureau of Labor Statistics noted that "married couples are accepted." Most fraternal homes featured similar policies. "In the majority of cases," wives were admitted with husbands. In homes operated by religious groups, however, homes for widows were the most prominent. Overall, most homes "admit not only individuals of either sex but also take in married couples."[94] Maintaining the family was a major concern. As the officials at the Scottish Old People's Home in Riverside, Illinois, argued, "The separation of aged married couples is one of the tragedies of life."[95] (But to live in the Riverside home both husband and wife needed to meet rigid health and admittance criteria.) It was more common for men and women to apply for admittance if they were widowed and alone.

Most private old age homes asked applicants to donate their property and/ or pay an admittance fee; administrators, in turn, used the capital to fund the facilities. Fraternal orders' homes typically asked aged men to relinquish their property holdings, avoiding cash fees. At least forty fraternal homes required property donations. On the other hand, benevolent organizations and nationality groups required cash fees. Fees varied widely. The Bureau of Labor Statistics found the lowest fee was $70, while the highest reached $5,076.[96] These requirements must have frustrated men seeking entry. Men, who valued their careers as breadwinners, must have resented giving up the assets they had built up throughout their lives. For poorer men, property requirements and fees would have been a more immediate worry. If a home asked a poor man for a $300 fee, how could he pay it? What if he owned no property? Giving up one's assets would have rankled aged men; they surely valued whatever estates they possessed. And for poor men, they would have lacked the assets to pay the homes' stipulated fees or make the required donations anyway.

Many of the old age homes maintained minimum age entry requirements, something many working-class men would have remembered from their days in the factory. The minimum age requirement might have been a nagging reminder of a serious reality in working-class life: age could keep men out of the places they needed to be everyday. In the private old age homes of the 1920s, each type of institution frequently obliged applicants to meet age requirements. Some homes went as low as 50, while most only accepted applicants at 60, 65, or 70.[97] If a home's age requirement was 65 or 70, a struggling man in his early 60s would have been denied support because he failed to meet the age criteria.

Like state-run institutions, many of the private homes extracted various forms of labor from residents. Home administrators believed that occupied hands and minds would help older men and women remain as mentally sharp and active as possible; work would prevent senility, offset physical decline, and promote intellectual engagement.[98] Good health for residents was not the only objective, however. Efficiency also mattered to administrators. A healthier population would be easier to care for. To promote activity among the "inmates," residents were first required to maintain their rooms: to keep them, as the operators of the Railroad Employees of America home put it, "neat and tidy when his physical condition will permit, attending to it the first thing in the morning."[99] For retired men, however, this may have been somewhat unfamiliar and unmanly. Did these aging men, probably widowed, once have spouses who previously completed domestic labor? To be obligated to work in a domestic capacity may have been uncomfortable and unwelcome.

In addition to taking care of one's room, some organizations required men and women to complete a range of other tasks. Residents helped in kitchens, set tables, washed dishes, worked in gardens, tended animals, and completed maintenance chores. Various old age homes employed a gender division of labor. "Usually, where tasks are assigned," the US Bureau of Labor Statistics noted, "the attempt is made to make use of the aptitudes . . . of the residents. This is especially apt to be the case with the male members of the home family." If a man made shoes previously, his home would put him to work fixing shoes. If another older man had been a carpenter, administrators would ask him to help with maintenance and repairs. The administrators of various old age homes believed older men would be happiest if they could somehow revisit their previous identities as workers. Administrators asked older men to put up shelving, fix doors, make tables and chairs, paint walls, and maintain machinery, as well as work in gardens, guard stockrooms, maintain lawns, and take care of livestock. Women, on the other hand, washed dishes, cooked, swept floors, cared for plants, sewed, dusted, and set tables for meals.[100]

Often, however, homes did not uphold boundaries between "men's" and "women's" work. At one fraternal organization home, older men could be seen "firing the boilers and keeping the basements clean"; they also completed "carpenter work and painting." However, men also prepared "fruits for canning and vegetables for the tables . . . mending and darning and making of all new material into sheets, pillow cases, table linen, etc., assisting in office errands for hospital, washing of dishes and dining room work, cleaning of parlors very day, washing windows, etc." These men did not enjoy what they viewed as women's work. The home matron noted, "these are not our happy and contented residents."[101]

Aging men might have bristled at the feminine image of private old age homes. Women were in the majority at many private facilities, particularly in religious institutions. For men, the extensive rules not only signaled the end of their independence, but the large numbers of women might have verified worries about feminization in old age. Only a minority of private facilities were dedicated to older men's care. In the US Bureau of Labor Statistics' sample of 350 homes, researchers found that 195 only admitted women, while 22 only accepted male residents. "In general," the *Monthly Labor Review* reported, "old ladies seem to be better provided for, in the way of homes for their declining years, than do men."[102]

If aging men went to a private old age home, or even a state-run institution, they had to accept a new mother figure into their lives. A "home matron" managed day-to-day functions. Matrons oversaw all activities, tended to residents' general welfare, supervised meal preparations, and saw to the overall maintenance and cleanliness of the facility. Matrons were in charge. "It should be remembered," the US Bureau of Labor Statistics noted, "that the old people are, for all practical purposes, in the power of the matron." The matron's position of power might have been difficult for aging men to accept. As the *Monthly Labor Review* noted, "Some of the old people are subject to delusions of persecution, and fancy all sorts of wrongs and neglect."[103] The older residents of one private home were reportedly very "fearful" of their matron.[104] Men probably resented submission to this strange woman who now governed their lives. They would now be children again, subject to a mother's authority and discipline. Confined to a county-run institution, Ed Sweeney noted that the home matron frequently threatened the residents with corporal punishment if they annoyed her. Whenever the men made too much noise, for instance, she threatened to "kick" the offenders in the "seat."[105]

The overarching reason why the old age homes would not sufficiently provide economic support to older men and women is because they served very limited populations. Of the different types of homes the *Monthly Labor Review* identified, there were only 1,200—this included 200 or more of the highly criticized state poorhouses, as well as a small number of homes for soldiers and state employees. Of this number, the five key alternatives (the nationality, union, fraternal, religious, and private homes) constituted the majority. Most of the homes catered to their client populations. According to the Bureau of Labor Statistics, only 80,000 men and women were served by private homes. Religious homes (especially Roman Catholic) and private homes made up the majority of the groups who offered old age homes. There were 475 religious homes and 350 private homes in the US. Fraternal organizations operated 111 homes, nationality groups' homes ran 39 homes, and trade unions offered only 5 homes (centered in the carpenters', printers', and railroad workers' organizations).[106]

The realities of life inside old age homes, as well as their reputation, led older men and women to view institutionalization as a last resort. Rigid rules and authority figures who intruded on personal and financial independence and the stigma of institutionalization would have been worrisome for aging working-class men. Institutionalization in a private facility, despite the attempts to challenge the stigmas attached to state homes, was still an unpopular solution to older men and women's problems with economic support. Working-class men and their partners wanted to maintain their own residences with their own funds, and institutionalization was pursued only when all other resources had been exhausted or denied.

The various avenues of support—from savings to industrial pensions to institutionalization—could not promise to sustain manhood in old age. Private old age homes and poorhouses bore the stigmas of unmanliness, as grim conditions, a lack of personal freedoms, and house matrons, for example, symbolized male dependence and submission. Private old age homes, moreover, only served very specific populations. Industrial wages failed to provide the savings needed, and unemployment, strikes, and firings liquidated working men's savings. Even if they worked in a pensioning industry, most men would not receive benefits; the likelihood of receiving a pension was slim. Furthermore, reliance on children was unacceptable to aging parents. Sons and daughters had their own families; aging parents, especially if they were poor, would be extra burdens on already-lean working-class budgets. Older men and women wanted their own homes and households. The state pension idea offered the most promise: pensions could protect a man's independence, uphold the integrity of a life spent at labor, and help to protect and ensure the stability of his family and personal household.

ABRAHAM EPSTEIN AND THE
GENDER POLITICS OF PENSION POLITICS

The writings of the social provision expert Abraham Epstein not only reflected but also very much defined the ideas about manhood, womanhood, and family that fueled public discussions of old-age poverty and state pension demands during the 1920s. Epstein researched and wrote the decade's most influential studies of age discrimination, old-age poverty, and pensions. In *Facing Old Age*, published in 1922, Epstein insisted that ageism and permanent layoff were rampant problems in industrial America that created old-age poverty and the loss of respectable working-class manhood; that poorhouses and other means of potential support were unacceptable because they were synonymous with dependency; and that only pensions from the state could allow older men to maintain their independence and status as patriarchs. Ann Shola Orloff argues that "Welfare capitalism and private charity were widely preferred to public relief by many social reformers through the 1920s," but the content of Epstein's work indicates that social reformers generally agreed that the state, not private institutions, would best alleviate older men and women's struggles in the interwar economy.[107]

Epstein was an up-and-coming intellectual and activist of the late 1910s and 1920s. He emigrated from Russia to the United States in 1910 at the age of 18, and despite the fact that English was not his first language, quickly earned an undergraduate degree in economics at the University of Pittsburgh in 1917. Epstein also naturalized as a United States citizen in 1917 and stayed in Pittsburgh for another year, completing an MA at Pitt and publishing his thesis, *The Negro Migrant in Pittsburgh*. Harvard University, the University of Minnesota, and Clark University offered him fellowships for additional study, but Epstein turned them down. Instead, he accepted a position as the research director for the Pennsylvania Old Age Pension Commission, who, as a result of Epstein's substantial help, published a major study of Pennsylvania's state poorhouses in 1919. Later, he organized the Workers Education Bureau of America in 1920 and served as its first secretary-treasurer, as well as organized the American Association for Old Age Security (later the American Association for Social Security) in 1927 and served as executive secretary. As a result of his prolific writing and organizing efforts, Epstein quickly gained respect as an authority on social provision and pension politics. He lectured throughout the United States and cultivated working relationships with numerous lobbyists, academics, and politicians, including Jane Addams of Hull House and Franklin Delano Roosevelt. He published numerous articles and books during the 1920s and into 1930s. In 1929, the *New York Times* described Epstein, then enrolled in graduate studies at Columbia University, as a "leader in the fight" to create state pensions for aging working-class men and women. As historian Roy Lubove argued, Epstein "contributed more to the old age pension movement than any single individual."[108]

Epstein highlighted old age as a time of personal, social, and financial collapse—a period when manhood and family could too easily crumble under the weight of permanent layoff, evaporating savings, and the absence of important safety nets such as state and industrial pensions. Old age was a fragile space where the gender and class foundations of working-class respectability were besieged by an industrial system that had no regard for laborers' long-term needs. "In spite of superior wealth and accumulation of goods," he wrote, "our national conscience is not in the least disturbed when the former creators of our wealth [working-class men] are forced to drag out their final days, physically exhausted, friendless and destitute, in the wretched confines of a poorhouse, or to receive some other degrading and humiliating form of pauper relief."[109] Epstein worried that men's long-term need for employment depended on the whims of employers who craved only speedy production. "After a certain age has been attained," he reminded readers, "although the worker may be still be able to do fair work, if he is no longer able to maintain his former speed, he is likely to be eliminated."[110]

Facing Old Age dominated the field of social provision and old-age poverty during the early 1920s, but Abraham Epstein was not the first to examine these themes. He leaned heavily on the work of earlier scholars such as Edward Devine, Lee Welling Squier, and Isaac Max Rubinow. Devine and Squier, who published books that examined old age dependency during the 1900s and 1910s, recognized that discrimination, the lack of savings, and the absence of state pensions contributed to a state of constant vulnerability for older working men. Just as Epstein would write later in the 1920s, Devine and Squier noted that permanent layoff and unemployment were working men's most prevalent "misfortunes." Because so many men would not enjoy steady work at a high wage, older working men could not "provide for old age." Squier worried that legions of veteran workmen were consistently "compelled to change occupation with decreasing opportunities for saving against the demands of old age."[111]

Isaac M. Rubinow, an older acquaintance of Epstein, wrote about "The Old Man's Problem in Modern Industry" in his 1913 study, *Social Insurance*. Like Epstein, Rubinow emigrated from Russia (he grew up in Grodno) during his late teens, arriving in the United States in 1893. The young Russian received a medical degree from the New York University medical school in 1898, but quickly abandoned medicine to study political science at Columbia. After briefly practicing medicine in poor New York City communities, Rubinow became convinced that the study of social provision was a more meaningful way to address social inequality and the problems of the poor.[112] The human dimensions of social injustice (from old-age poverty to anti-Semitism) very much informed his scholarship and his activism. Rubinow argued, as Epstein would later, that "modern civilization on its industrial side has created the very grave problem of superannuation—the problem of the jobless, income-less, and propertyless old man."[113] Epstein's work fit within a broader trajectory of social reformers' writings on old-age poverty and age discrimination during the early twentieth century, but his timing (two of his most important books appeared during the 1920s) brought his voice to the forefront.

Facing Old Age centered on men's struggles with age in industry, but Epstein did not ignore older women or their troubles. His book was typical of those who wrote about aging working-class men and women during the interwar years. Epstein envisioned women in the role of the vulnerable and dependent, though respectable, housewife. Women experienced a distinct form of suffering, he argued, because employers discriminated against their aging husbands and jeopardized not only men's livelihoods but also women's subsistence and respectability. Women, he implied, were defenseless against the ageism that menaced working-class men's careers. Epstein's goal was to evoke sympathy and outrage. Age discrimination undermined the sanctity of the patriarchal working-class family: because of their delicate economic situation, Epstein described how men and women bore fewer children and could not count on dependents for support when they reached their twilight years. "With increasing rapidity," Epstein warned, "home-ties and family solidarity are being broken."[114]

Working-class women figure awkwardly in *Facing Old Age*. While Epstein often discussed "men and women," he would not situate them on the equal plane of wage-worker status. In one sentence he might write, "Today, most men and women are dependent upon their daily toil for their daily bread"; however, later he would describe how "the wage-earner is confronted with the fact of being compelled to discontinue work . . . because *he* is unable to maintain the pace necessary in modern production."[115] Old-age poverty concerned Epstein because it first menaced working men's identities as breadwinners and laborers. In *Facing Old Age*, Epstein returns again and again to men as the central figures in his analysis.

The reception of *The Challenge of the Aged*, a new study published in 1928, illustrated how Epstein was the leading figure in the area of state pension advocacy. As a way of acknowledging the importance of her colleague's work, Jane Addams wrote a special introduction for the book.[116] Also at this time, Franklin D. Roosevelt consulted with Epstein regarding pension legislation in New York state.[117] Epstein, in fact, dedicated the new book to Roosevelt. It was also very likely that Eleanor Roosevelt, an important political figure in her own right, knew a great deal about Epstein's work. Epstein passionately pointed toward state pensions as the way to enduringly resolve the gender and economic insecurities of older men and women, and influential politicians and reformers agreed with him. Pensions, as the new book insisted, insured that "the independence of the veteran or his widow is maintained."[118] Further underscoring his pre-eminence, working people themselves knew Epstein's work. In the *New York Times*, Epstein referred to letters he received from jobless older men.[119]

While reformers, scholars, and workers often discussed the problems of gender and poverty in later life, Abraham Epstein's influential 1920s writings laid the groundwork for the ways Americans thought about state pensions, social provision, and old-age poverty throughout the interwar period. Government pensions were envisioned as ways to reconcile respectable gender ideals and the problem of old age in industrial America. Men wanted ways to maintain independence and breadwinner status as foundations of manhood; they wanted the possibility to maintain these ideals they had embraced throughout their careers.

STATE PENSIONS: "THE ONLY PRACTICAL REMEDY"

Because of the urgency social provision experts attached to "the problem of the old man," Americans increasingly believed that older working-class men could not resolve this problem on their own. During the 1920s, older working-class men and women moved working people more generally away from "voluntarism," from the idea that labor would independently resolve their troubles without the aid of the state.[120] Instead, the working class of the 1920s endorsed the creation of a new American welfare state. After a decade of urgent discussion about old age poverty, more and more men and women (younger and older) viewed state pensions as the principle way to resolve older people's troubles. To preserve the gender foundations of working-class respectability in old age, men and women embraced an active state that would provide them with economic support.

A flurry of books, articles, lobbying, and organizing insured that pensions remained a prominent topic of public discussion. At the 1924 Pennsylvania Conference on Old Age Assistance, for example, Isaac Max Rubinow (then director of the Jewish Welfare Society of Philadelphia), Thomas Kennedy (District No. 7 president of the United Mine Workers of America), John F. O'Toole (Pennsylvania FOE), and John B. Andrews (AALL) agreed that the individual states needed to push pensions through their legislatures.[121] The Fraternal Order of Eagles (FOE), which claimed nearly half a million members by 1923, lobbied extensively on behalf of state old age pensions for aging working-class men. In addition to organizing 2,100 clubs throughout the US, the Eagles forwarded letters and petitions to politicians and sent letters to newspapers. "Perhaps no social cause in the United States ever had more effective championship," argued Frank E. Hering, the chairman of the FOE pension commission.[122] By the decade's end, influential politicians such as Governor Franklin D. Roosevelt of New York supported state pensions. Even the anti-welfare state AFL embraced state pensions, passing a resolution in favor of pensions at its 1929 Toronto convention.[123]

While the number of state pension programs in the US remained very small throughout the 1920s, comprising no more than a "symbolic success" for state pension advocates and reformers, this intense public conversation about the fate of older men and their spouses helped to transform men and women's thinking about the role of the state in American society; due to the injustices created by industrialization in the new era of mass production, state intervention seemed both logical and immediately necessary.[124] Thus, workers' and reformers' demands for state pensions during the 1920s laid the cultural groundwork for the future American welfare state, as it compelled men and women to consider what would be necessary to systematically guarantee the preservation of gender ideals in old age.

True, pensions from the state did exist previously in various forms; but state pension advocates of the 1920s were proposing a dramatic expansion of social entitlements. In the late nineteenth century, the federal government offered pensions to the veterans of the Civil War. The veterans' pension was the broadest entitlement of the time, promising benefits initially to any aging veteran of the War Between the States and ultimately to all military veterans who were no longer able to work for themselves—regardless of whether or not they were veterans of combat or if they had been wounded or disabled in the service. The program also allowed for veterans' dependents to collect benefits. During the years between 1867 and 1912, expenses for the program increased from $21 million per year to an enormous $153 million. Pensions for military veterans comprised "one large, important social insurance scheme," as the historian Michael B. Katz wrote, as the federal government devoted a gigantic 18 percent of its budget towards the maintenance of the pension program.[125]

Despite the broad net cast over the military's veterans by the pension plan, the program was still a limited social entitlement, focusing on the finite population of veterans. Until the 1920s, discussions of pensions from the state to help needy populations continued to focus on specific groups rather than the population writ large. During the 1910s, as the Progressive Era reached its height, pensions for needy mothers became another form of social entitlement promised by the government. Organized at the state level, mothers' pensions offered single women with dependents the opportunity to keep families together by augmenting their capacity to pay bills and meet their expenses. The pensions also allowed women to be closer to children, spending a greater amount of time at home rather than the shop or factory. In 1911, Illinois and

Missouri were the first states to pass mothers' pension programs, and the number would increase to 39 states by the year 1919. By 1931, there were 200,000 children in each state (minus South Carolina and Georgia) who were aided by state mothers' pensions.[126]

State pension advocacy during the 1920s widened the terrain of possible social entitlements: advocating pension funds for aging men and women who could no longer work or support themselves. However, the state-by-state approach to pension politics hindered the growth and success of state pensions. Organized at the state and county levels, limited funds and political resistance hindered the growth of a welfare state.

The state pensions of the 1920s (those proposed and on the books) were beleaguered by limitations of funds, requirements, and even political will. First, pension legislation languished in state legislatures. And even where they passed, some state courts declared them unconstitutional, sending the process back to the state legislatures for further debate. Second, no states with pensions were actually obligated to fund them during the 1920s. Third, those states that did fund their pensions typically did not provide adequate benefits. In 1923, only four state pensions existed. The Alaska territory pensioned aged men and women in 1906, and Montana and Pennsylvania followed suit in 1923. Nevada was next, authorizing state pension provisions in 1925. These early pensions were laden with residency, property, and age requirements. In Montana and Pennsylvania, applicants needed to be 70 years old and 15-year residents. To receive a dollar per day, applicants could not be "beggars," have prison records (for the past 15 years), have children who could care for them, could not own more than $3,000 in property (Pennsylvania), or earn more than $300 in income (Montana).[127] Pennsylvania's state pension plan, however, never materialized. The Dauphin County court deemed the state pension unconstitutional in 1924, affirming their decision in 1925. Pennsylvania, the court ruled, could not allocate state moneys for the maintenance of *private* groups or individuals.[128]

After 1924, the number of state pension laws grew slowly until the Great Depression, when the number of pensions began to increase more significantly. Between 1924 and 1929, pension plans appeared in Wisconsin (1925), Kentucky (1926), Colorado (1927), Maryland (1927), California (1929), Minnesota (1929), Utah (1929), and Wyoming (1929). Still, only eleven states featured pensions by 1929.[129] And the most industrialized states—New Jersey, Illinois, Michigan, and Ohio—did not pass pension laws. State pensions did not take hold in the industrial heartland during the 1920s, despite reformers' focus on the most industrialized states.[130]

Pension programs of the 1920s barely reached anyone. Of a total 738 counties covered by state pension laws, only 293 actually paid any benefits during the decade; and these programs only served 102,527 older Americans.[131] In terms of legislative success, the state pension movement achieved disappointing results until the early years of the depression, when Massachusetts and New York passed state pension legislation in 1930, followed by New Jersey, West Virginia, Delaware, Idaho, and New Hampshire in 1931.[132]

Why were states so slow to pass state pension laws? Abraham Epstein blamed "greedy interests" and "propaganda"—especially the pro-business, anti-labor National Civic Federation—as the primary obstacles to state pension legislation.[133] When Pennsylvania first passed its pension plan in 1923, the Pennsylvania State Chamber of Commerce responded by denouncing the law as "un-American and socialistic." Clearly utilizing the recent anti-Communist furor of the 1919 Steel Strike period and the Red Scare to its advantage, the organization denounced pension support for aging men and women as "an entering wedge of communistic propaganda in Pennsylvania."[134] In reality, however, state politicians' worries about high costs hampered pension legislation the most. In 1928, for instance, the New York state pension plan was initially voted down. Politicians in the Albany legislature argued that old age pensions were "too costly" of a burden to put on state resources.[135] Despite politicians' reservations, New York's pension was finally authorized during the first full year of the Great Depression, 1930.

The government pension idea certainly took hold among working-class men and women. In "Middletown," a woman noted that her working-class husband "hopes and prays they get the state pension through pretty soon."[136] In 1927 Alex Flowers, a steelworker from Pennsylvania, reminded Amalgamated Association members that "it is impossible to lay anything by for old age." The Amalgamated, he argued, should "insist the cause be put before the public for vote."[137] Steel industry scholar Horace B. Davis agreed. "For all steel workers," he argued, "there is only one satisfactory kind of pension—a steady money pension guaranteed by the government."[138] "The only practical remedy" for old age poverty, a man from New York City wrote, "is a national pension."[139] Men and women appreciated the pension idea and they wanted the states, and ultimately the federal government, to implement them.

Since men so greatly valued the male breadwinner ideal, patriarchal status, and personal independence, working men and women, reformers, and politicians believed that state old age pensions would provide the best form of support in later life. Old age homes (state and private), savings, industrial pensions, reliance on children would not suffice; they were too unreliable or inconsistent with the cherished ideals of manhood and family. While state pension legislation languished in legislatures until the onset of the Great Depression, the popularity of the state pension idea had certainly taken hold.

Among working people, reformers, and politicians, many concluded that state pensions were the best solution to worries about gender in old age. As Abraham Epstein put it in a letter to the *New York Times* in the summer of 1929, "The burden of responsibility for the old age and dependents of the workers must first be removed from the individual corporation and placed in the hands of the State or the nation where it properly belongs."[140] Only the state, the argument went, could guarantee respectable working-class manhood in old age.

In the next decade, older working men's problems would only worsen. The collapse of the industrial economy and staggering rates of unemployment, combined with employers' worsening preferences for younger workers, further undermined aging workers' precarious position in the labor market. Social Security and the welfare state emerged in response to older working men's struggles during the interwar years, but aging workers' struggles to secure and sustain manhood would take them elsewhere as well: to new labor unions and other organizations for working people, as well as the pension schemes and panaceas of the consumer marketplace.

NOTES

1. Sam T. Baker, "The Reward for Faithful Service," *Amalgamated Journal*, 4 November 1926, 21.

2. Ibid.

3. On maternalism and social welfare, see Theda Skocpol, *Protecting Soldiers and Mothers: The Political Origins of Social Policy in the United States* (Cambridge, MA: Harvard University Press, 1992); Joanne L. Goodwin, "'Employable Mothers' and 'Suitable Work': A Re-Evaluation of Welfare and Wage-Earning for Women in the Twentieth-Century United States," *Journal of Social History* 29:2 (1995): esp. 253; and Joanne L. Goodwin, *Gender and the Politics of Welfare Reform: Mothers' Pensions in Chicago, 1911–1929* (Chicago: University of Chicago Press, 1997). Gwendolyn Mink takes the maternalist reformers of the early-twentieth century to task in *The Wages of Motherhood: Inequality in the Welfare State, 1917–1942* (Ithaca: Cornell University Press, 1995). For another look at this shift with a focus on delinquent male breadwinners, see Michael Willrich, "Home Slackers: Men, the State, and Welfare in Modern America," *Journal of American History* 87:2 (2000): 460–489.

4. Ann Shola Orloff, *The Politics of Pensions: A Comparative Analysis of Britain, Canada, and the United States, 1880–1940* (Madison: University of Wisconsin Press, 1993), 280.

5. "A Man's Home Called Best Old-Age Pension," *New York Times*, 7 April 1929, 22.

6. On unemployment and working-class poverty during the 1920s, see Alexander Keyssar, *Out of Work: The First Century of Unemployment in Massachusetts* (New York: Cambridge University Press, 1986); and Susan Porter Benson, *Household Ac-*

counts: Working-Class Family Economics in the Interwar United States, afterword by David Montgomery (Ithaca: Cornell University Press, 2007).

7. John R. Commons and John B. Andrews, *Principles of Labor Legislation* (New York: Harper & Brothers Publishers, 1916), 398.

8. Bill G. Boswell, Report of Washington Lodge, No. 5, PA, *Amalgamated Journal*, 17 April 1919, 17.

9. Fred Caswell, Report of Altoona Lodge No. 104, PA, Amalgamated Journal, 9 October 1924, 18.

10. David Hackett Fischer, *Growing Old in America* (New York: Oxford University Press, 1977), 162.

11. Otto P. Deluse, "Old Age Pensions," *Chicago Daily Tribune*, 15 July 1925, 8. On the FOE and pension politics during the 1920s, see Jill Quadagno, *The Transformation of Old Age Security: Class and Politics in the American Welfare State* (Chicago: University of Chicago Press, 1988), 66–72; and Orloff, *Politics of Pensions*, 281–282.

12. JG Hansell, Report of Knoxville No. 1, TN, *Amalgamated Journal*, 5 December 1918, 3; RD Scrom, Report of Blue Valley Lodge, No. 2, MO, *Amalgamated Journal*, 12 January 1928, 11.

13. RD Scrom, Report of Blue Valley Lodge, No. 2, MO, *Amalgamated Journal*, 12 March 1925, 11.

14. Scrom, Report of Blue Valley Lodge (1928), 11.

15. Frank E. Hering, "Awakening Interest in Old Age Protection," *American Labor Legislation Review*, June 1923, 140; Abraham Epstein, "Old Age Pensions," *American Labor Legislation Review*, December 1922, 225; "Worker Paying for Old-Age Relief," *New York Times*, 19 September 1929, 14.

16. Deluse, "Old Age Pensions," 8.

17. Robert S. Lynd and Helen Merrell Lynd, *Middletown: A Study in American Culture* (New York: Harcourt, Brace & World, 1929), 34–35.

18. Mabel Louise Nassau, *Old Age Poverty in Greenwich Village* (New York: Fleming H. Revell Company, 1915), 29.

19. "Extent, Distribution, and Causes of Old Age Dependency," *Monthly Labor Review*, April 1930, 14–15.

20. Abraham Epstein, *Facing Old Age: A Study of Old Age Dependency in the United States and Old Age Pensions* (New York: Alfred A. Knopf, 1922), 142.

21. Irving Bernstein, *The Lean Years: A History of the American Worker, 1920–1933* (Boston: Houghton-Mifflin, 1960), 59.

22. Ibid., 60.

23. Epstein, "Old Age Pensions," 18.

24. Harry A. Millis and Royal E. Montgomery, "The Problem of the Industrially Old Worker," in *Labor's Risks and Social Insurance* (New York: McGraw-Hill Book Company, 1938), 360–361.

25. Lynd and Lynd, *Middletown*, 34. See also "Worker Paying for Old-Age Relief," 14.

26. Sonia Kay and Irma Rittenhouse, "Why Are the Aged Poor?" *Survey*, 1 September 1930, 471.

27. SJ Kleinberg, *The Shadow of the Mills: Working-Class Families in Pittsburgh, 1870–1907* (Pittsburgh: University of Pittsburgh Press, 1989), 251, 252.

28. Quadagno, *Transformation of Old Age Security*, 79, 81–82; Jennifer Klein, *For All These Rights: Business, Labor, and the Shaping of America's Public-Private Welfare State* (Princeton: Princeton University Press, 2003), 57–63; Steven A. Sass, *The Promise of Private Pensions: The First Hundred Years* (Cambridge: Harvard University Press, 1997).

29. Fischer, *Growing Old in America*, 165–166.

30. Murray Webb Latimer, *Industrial Pensions in the United States and Canada* (New York: Industrial Relations Counselors, 1932), 41–42; Quadagno, *Transformation of Old Age Security*, 104.

31. "Problem of Old-Age Pensions in Industry," *Monthly Labor Review*, March 1927, 518.

32. Quoted in Quadagno, *Transformation of Old Age Security*, 87.

33. Gorton James, "The Problem of the Old Man," *Survey*, 16 September 1921, 673, 674; Quadagno, *Transformation of Old Age Security*, 83–85; Klein, *For All These Rights*, 61.

34. Ben M. Selekman and Mary Van Kleeck, *Employes' Representation in Coal Mines: A Study of the Industrial Representation Plan of the Colorado Fuel and Iron Company* (New York: Russell Sage Foundation, 1924), 198–199.

35. Quadagno, *Transformation of Old Age Security*, 85.

36. James, "Problem of the Old Man," 673–674; Klein, *For All These Rights*, 59.

37. James, "Problem of the Old Man," 673; Quadagno, *Transformation of Old Age Security*, 86.

38. Quoted in Cohen, *Making a New Deal*, 195.

39. Statistic reported in Millis and Montgomery, "Problem of the Industrially Old Worker," 370. On workers' struggles with length of service requirements, see Quadagno, *Transformation of Old Age Security*, 87.

40. Klein, *For All These Rights*, 59.

41. Jonathan Rees, "Managing the Mills: Labor Policy in the American Steel Industry, 1892–1937" (PhD diss., University of Wisconsin at Madison, 1997), 174.

42. Ibid., 173.

43. See "James Sayers Retired After 45 Years' Service," *Amalgamated Journal*, 25 September 1924, 5.

44. "Employes Lose Morris & Co. Pension Fight," *Chicago Daily Tribune*, 22 March 1925, 6; "Decision of State Supreme Court in Morris & Co. Pension Plan," *Monthly Labor Review*, September 1928, 506–507. On pensions as gifts, see Quadagno, *Transformation of Old Age Security*, 79.

45. "Morris Pension Plan Defined in Court Case," *Chicago Daily Tribune*, 4 July 1924, 7.

46. "Decision of State Supreme Court," 506–507.

47. Charles A. Gulick, *Labor Policy of the United States Steel Corporation* (New York: Longmans, Green & Co., 1924), 177.

48. A W MacDonald, "The Problem of Pensions," *Personnel*, May 1929, 15.

49. James D. Rose, *Duquesne and the Rise of Steel Unionism* (Urbana: University of Illinois Press, 2001), 31.

50. John A. Powell, "Through the Eyes of the Worker," *Amalgamated Journal*, 26 September 1929, 3.

51. Rose, *Duquesne*, 50.

52. See "Shameful Waste and Inhumanity of American Poorhouses," *American Labor Legislation Review*, December 1925, 360. On men's prominence in state institutions, see Abraham Epstein, *The Challenge of the Aged* (New York: Vanguard Press, 1928), 37–38.

53. Deluse, "Old Age Pensions," 8; "Pensions are Superior to Poorhouses," *American Labor Legislation Review*, September 1925, 263.

54. Hugo the Third, Report of Crescent Lodge No. 8, WV, *Amalgamated Journal*, 7 October 1926, 20.

55. Quoted in Roy Lubove, *The Struggle for Social Security, 1900–1935* (Cambridge: Harvard University Press, 1968), 133–134.

56. Franklin Delano Roosevelt quoted in Abraham Epstein, "Facing Old Age," *Commonweal*, 11 December 1929, 163; see also "Governor Roosevelt of New York Sends Special Message to the Legislature on Provision for Old Age," *American Labor Legislation Review*, March 1929, 54.

57. Quoted in Edmund S. Morgan, *American Slavery, American Freedom: The Ordeal of Colonial Virginia* (New York: WW Norton & Company, 1975), 322.

58. See "Rules Relating to the Poor," *Boston News Gazette*, March 1738; as well as Gary Nash, "Poverty and Poor Relief in Pre-Revolutionary Philadelphia," *William and Mary Quarterly* 33:1 (1976): 15–16; and Gary Nash, "Poverty and Politics in Early American History," in *Down and Out in Early America*, ed. Billy Smith (University Park, PA: Pennsylvania State University Press, 2004), 15.

59. David Wagner, The *Poorhouse: America's Forgotten Institution* (Lanham, MD: Rowman & Littlefield Publishers, Inc., 2005), 9.

60. Joan Underhill Hannon, "The Generosity of Antebellum Poor Relief," *Journal of Economic History* 44:3 (1984): 810.

61. Wagner, *Poorhouse*, 3, 10; Skocpol, *Protecting Soldiers and Mothers*.

62. "Poorhouses: 'The Shame of the States,'" *American Labor Legislation Review*, September 1926, 244.

63. "Official Report Tells Why Old Age Pensions Are Needed," *American Labor Legislation Review*, September 1925, 265; Epstein, *Facing Old Age*, 53.

64. Massachusetts Commission on Pensions, *Report on Old Age Pensions* (Boston: Commission on Pensions, 1925), 87 (Table 9); Epstein, *Challenge of the Aged*, 37–38, 45–46.

65. Epstein, *Challenged of the Aged*, 59.

66. Ed Sweeney, *Poorhouse Sweeney: Life in a County Poorhouse* (New York: Boni & Liveright, 1927), 37.

67. Ibid., 55.

68. Ibid., 37.

69. Ibid., 74.

70. See Katharine Jocher, "Book Lists," *Social Forces*, December 1927, 330.

71. Quoted in Epstein, *Challenge of the Aged*, 39–40.

72. Massachusetts Commission on Pensions, *Report on Old Age Pensions*, 89.
73. "Fewer Go To the Poorhouse," *New York Times*, 21 May 1922, 91.
74. "The Tragedy of Old Age," *American Labor Legislation Review*, December 1923, 261.
75. John Gray, "National Old Age Pensions," *New York Times*, 29 May 1927, 12; George W. Wickersham, "A Home for the Aged," *New York Times*, 1 December 1928, 10.
76. "Old Age Pension Legislation Found Economical and Humane," *American Labor Legislation Review*, December 1924, 287.
77. "The Screen," *New York Times*, 18 September 1920, 21; the text of Will Carleton's poem can be found at: http://news.minnesota.publicradio.org/features/200207/29_gundersond_poorfarm-m/poem.shtml.
78. "Aged Couple Die To Escape Charity," *New York Times*, 27 May 1927, 25. For other examples, see "Hangs Herself Amid Rejected Stories," *New York Times*, 21 September 1922, 16; "Told By Mail of Suicides," *New York Times*, 28 August 1929, 16; "Tells of Problems In Aiding the Aged," *New York Times*, 6 December 1929, 25. For another historical perspective of suicide during the 1920s, see Kathleen W. Jones, "When a Young Woman Dies: Gender, Youth, and Suicide in the Jazz Age," in *Death and Dying: Inter-Disciplinary Perspectives*, Asa Kasher, ed. (London: Rodopi Press, 2007): 135–152.
79. Nels Anderson, *The Hobo: The Sociology of the Homeless Man* (Chicago: University of Chicago Press, 1923), 69. On Nels Anderson and his experiences with homeless men, see Frank Tobias Higbie, *Indispensable Outcasts: Hobo Workers and Community in the American Midwest, 1880–1930* (Urbana: University of Illinois Press, 2003), 74.
80. Jack Conroy, *The Disinherited: A Novel of the 1930s*, introduction by Douglas Wixson (1933; repr., Columbia: University of Missouri Press, 1991), 106, 134–139, 146–149, 187.
81. "Old-Timers of Steel Mills Are River Beachcombers," *Pittsburgh Post-Gazette*, 26 June 1929, 17.
82. See "Old-Timers of Steel Mills," 17; and Horace B. Davis, *Labor and Steel* (New York: International Publishers, 1933), 14. On manliness and the frontier idea, begin with Kimmel, *Manhood in America*, 148–155.
83. Epstein, *Facing Old Age*, 52.
84. "A Real Haunted House," *American Labor Legislation Review*, June 1929, 153.
85. "Homes for the Aged, Maintained by Religious Organizations," *Monthly Labor Review*, March 1929, 16–17.
86. Thomas G. Gillis, Report of West Pittsburgh Lodge No. 70, PA, *Amalgamated Journal*, 8 November 1928, 21.
87. "Trade-Union Old-age Pensions and Homes for the Aged and Tubercular," *Monthly Labor Review*, February 1928, 7.
88. Wickersham, "Home for the Aged," 10.
89. "Private Benevolent Homes for the Aged," *Monthly Labor Review*, April 1929, 10.
90. "Homes for the Aged, Operated by Fraternal Organizations," *Monthly Labor Review*, March 1929, 4.

91. "Homes for the Aged, Operated by Fraternal Organizations," 4.

92. "Private Benevolent Homes for the Aged," *Monthly Labor Review*, April 1929, 9.

93. "Homes for the Aged, Maintained by Religious Organizations," *Monthly Labor Review*, March 1929, 15;

94. "Old People's Homes Maintained by Nationality Groups," *Monthly Labor Review*, April 1929, 4; "Homes for the Aged, Operated by Fraternal Organizations," 4; "Homes for the Aged, Maintained by Religious Organizations," 17.

95. "Old People's Homes Maintained by Nationality Groups," 4.

96. "Homes for the Aged, Operated by Fraternal Organizations," 7; "Private Benevolent Homes for the Aged," 10; "Old People's Homes Maintained by Nationality Groups," 4.

97. "Private Benevolent Homes for the Aged," 19; "Old People's Homes Maintained by Nationality Groups," 4; "Homes for the Aged, Operated by Fraternal Organizations," 4; "Homes for the Aged, Maintained by Religious Organizations," 17; "Trade-Union Old-Age Pensions and Homes for the Aged and Tubercular," 7.

98. "Problem of Idleness in Old People's Homes," *Monthly Labor Review*, December 1929, 13.

99. "Trade-Union Old-Age Pensions and Homes for the Aged and Tubercular," 17.

100. "Problem of Idleness in Old People's Homes," 15, 16; "Homes for the Aged, Maintained by Religious Organizations," 21.

101. "Homes for the Aged, Operated by Fraternal Organizations," 8.

102. "Private Benevolent Homes for the Aged," 10.

103. "Administration and Conditions of Old People's Homes," *Monthly Labor Review*, July 1929, 16–17.

104. Ibid., 17.

105. Sweeney, *Poorhouse Sweeney*, 54, 59.

106. "Administration and Conditions of Old People's Homes," 1; "Care of the Aged in the United States," *Monthly Labor Review*, March 1929, 1; "Old People's Homes Maintained by Nationality Groups," 1–2; "Private Benevolent Homes for the Aged," 7–8; "Trade-Union Old-Age Pensions and Homes for the Aged and Tubercular," 7, 13, 15, 19; "Homes for the Aged, Operated by Fraternal Organizations," 3, 5; "Homes for the Aged, Maintained by Religious Organizations," 12, 13.

107. Orloff, *Politics of Pensions*, 269.

108. See Louis Leotta, "Abraham Epstein and the Movement for Old Age Security," *Labor History* 16:3 (1975): 360–373; Pierre Epstein, *Abraham Epstein: The Forgotten Father of Social Security* (Columbia, MO: University of Missouri Press, 2007); "Tells of Problems in Aiding the Aged," *New York Times*, 6 December 1929, 25; Lubove, *Struggle for Social Security*, 138–139, 143; Fischer, *Growing Old in America*, 173; and "Abraham Epstein Is Dead Here at 50," *New York Times*, 3 May 1942, 53.

109. Epstein, *Facing Old Age*, 1.

110. Ibid., 3, 4.

111. Devine, *Misery and Its Causes*; Lee Welling Squier, *Old Age Dependency in the United States: A Complete Survey of the Pension Movement* (New York: The Macmillan Company, 1912), 35.

112. Fischer, *Growing Old in America*, 172. On Rubinow's background and career, see "Dr. Isaac Rubinow, Social Expert, Dies," *New York Times*, 3 September 1936, 21.

113. Rubinow, *Social Insurance*, 301–302.

114. Epstein, *Facing Old Age*, 6.

115. Ibid., 2, 6. Emphasis mine.

116. See Jane Addams, "Introduction," in Epstein, *Challenge of the Aged*, xi.

117. Leotta, "Abraham Epstein," 368–369; Klein, *For All These Rights*, 80.

118. Epstein, *Challenge of the Aged*, 229.

119. Abraham Epstein, "Old Age Pensions," *New York Times*, 13 February 1928, 18.

120. Lubove, *Struggle for Social Security*, 116–117. See also Quadagno, *Transformation of Old Age Security*, 53, 63.

121. "Old Age Pension Legislation Found Economical and Humane," *American Labor Legislation Review*, December 1924, 286.

122. Hering, "Awakening Interest," 144.

123. "Modern Retirement," *Amalgamated Journal*, 7 November 1929, 19; Bernstein, *Lean Years*, 238.

124. See Orloff, *Politics of Pensions*, 269. Joanne L. Goodwin reaches a similar conclusion regarding women reformers' turn towards the state before the New Deal era. See Goodwin, *Gender and the Politics of Welfare Reform*, 6–7.

125. Michael B. Katz, *In the Shadow of the Poorhouse: A Social History of Welfare in America* (1986; repr., New York: BasicBooks, 1996), 207.

126. Ibid., 133.

127. "Legislative Action on Old-Age Pensions, 1923," *Monthly Labor Review*, November 1923, 182.

128. Abraham Epstein, "Present Status of Old-Age Pension Legislation in the United States," *Monthly Labor Review*, October 1924, 31; "Old Age Pension Law of Pennsylvania Held Unconstitutional," *Monthly Labor Review*, May 1925, 199.

129. "Experience Under State Old-Age Pension Laws in 1932," *Monthly Labor Review*, August 1933, 253; Bernstein, *Lean Years*, 238.

130. See also Orloff, *Politics of Pensions*, 69; and Quadagno, *Transformation of Old Age Security*, 51.

131. "Experience Under State Old-Age Pension Laws," 253.

132. Ibid.

133. Abraham Epstein, "Old Age Pensions," *American Labor Legislation Review*, December 1922, 227.

134. Fischer, *Growing Old in America*, 174.

135. Leotta, "Abraham Epstein," 368.

136. Lynd and Lynd, *Middletown*, 34.

137. Alex Flowers, Report of Chartiers Valley, No. 71, PA, *Amalgamated Journal*, 28 April 1927, 17.

138. Davis, *Labor and Steel*, 14.

139. Gray, "National Old Age Pensions, 12.

140. Abraham Epstein, "The Middle-Age Deadline," *New York Times*, 28 July 1929, 53.

Chapter Three

Older Men and the Boundaries of Manhood during the 1930s

The man appears bewildered and humiliated. It is as if the ground had gone out from under his feet.

—Mirra Komarovsky, sociologist, 1940[1]

In her study of unemployed men and family life during the Great Depression, Mirra Komarovsky documented how persistent unemployment had shattered the underpinnings of working-class manhood. With so many men out of work for protracted periods of time, the sociologist found extensive patterns of gender inversion in American households. Many women assumed control of family finances, losing respect for troubled husbands. Children ignored their fathers—traditionally the authority figures within the home. Men felt isolated and depressed, she pointed out, unused to remaining within domestic space during daylight hours. Male anxiety permeated American culture. As historians have noted, men responded to their plight by voicing opposition to women's employment, and they openly worried about adolescent sons' sexual choices.[2] The period witnessed what some historians describe as a "crisis" of masculinity, as the expression of manhood through work, bread-winning, and patriarchy seemed to be wiped away by constant joblessness. "He experiences a sense of deep frustration," Komarovsky noted, "because in his own estimation he fails to fulfill what is the central duty of his life, the very touchstone of his manhood—the role of family provider."[3]

Komarovsky's analysis of depression-era unemployment points to a common assumption, then and now, about the relationship between joblessness and manliness: that unemployment signals the loss of masculinity and a subsequent male identity "crisis," as men lose their ties to productive labor and the male breadwinner ideal—key foundations of male identity in indus-

98

trialized society. Since the antebellum period, males needed to demonstrate enduring economic success in order to claim the mantle of manhood; they needed to embody the productive ideals of "heroic artisans" or "self-made men." As Komarovsky and later William Serrin suggested, joblessness consigned men to feminized roles and spaces, confining them to the home where their most important daily activity was picking up children from school. They no longer fulfilled the ascribed adult male roles of breadwinner and wage-earner. Discussions of a "crisis" of manhood, rooted in chronic depression-era joblessness, are a major theme in the gender and labor history of the 1930s. For aging working-class men, this crisis should have been especially acute, given their highly disadvantaged status in an industrial economy that openly favored the young, agile, and brawny. As a working-class man reported to sociologist E. Wight Bakke, "This world is no place for men over forty-five."[4]

However, unemployment did not necessarily mean the end of manhood, as aging men's actions demonstrated. In order to maintain their sense of manliness in a decade that was dominated by rampant joblessness and discrimination against older men, aging men of the Great Depression directly challenged the prevalent assumption that joblessness meant the end of manhood. Since they faced the unrelenting danger of permanent layoff, older men first looked for ways to sustain manhood during the time when they *could* work, supporting industrial unions that endorsed seniority clauses, for example. They even embraced a consumer culture of advice literature and health products that aimed to help aging workers retain the physical and mental acuity needed to survive and thrive in a youth-driven labor market. As they looked beyond their working lives, at permanent layoff, at superannuation, aging men struggled to retain connections between manhood and their notions of work. Older men embraced the New Deal welfare state, which promised new economic foundations for the male breadwinner ideal once these veteran men could no longer acquire or sustain gainful employment on their own. Still, other jobless veteran men organized clubs and organizations that fought directly against the rampant ageism of the interwar years, challenging the widespread idea that advancing years meant decreasing job opportunities and employability.

Komarovsky's focus on isolated, jobless men, consigned to domestic spaces, led her to overlook the activity among older men that challenged the presumably fundamental connections between joblessness and the loss of manhood. Aging men blurred the boundaries between the feminized connotations of joblessness and the manliness of paid employment by searching for new ways to work in their later years.

This chapter examines how older blue-collar and white-collar men of the 1930s struggled to secure new foundations for manhood in an era when paid employment proved to be more elusive than at any point in the early-twentieth century. The first section examines how the New Deal welfare state, created during Roosevelt's Second New Deal (particularly the Social Security Act and the Works Progress Administration), promised aging males paths to manhood during times of joblessness by honoring, however poorly, the concept of the male breadwinner ideal. The second section examines organizations known as Forty Plus Clubs, which were organizations for middle-aged white-collar workers that directly challenged joblessness as a marker of feminization by struggling to place unemployed workers in new jobs and recreating the demands, pressures, and routines of the white-collar office within the clubs' culture. The third section explores how blue-collar working men struggled to solidify manhood in the workplace by supporting new industrial unions and contractual seniority clauses. Lastly, responding to blue- and white-collar anxieties about aging during the depression, a very active consumer marketplace offered solutions aimed at alleviating the physical effects of growing old and thus preserving aging males' toehold in the volatile labor market of the 1930s.

THE SECOND NEW DEAL

In conversations with Secretary of Labor Frances Perkins and other members of his cabinet, President Franklin D. Roosevelt discussed his hope that any new federal system of social assistance for the aged and disabled would uphold the principle of "cradle to the grave" coverage. Roosevelt said, "I see no reason why every child, from the day his born, shouldn't be a member of the social security system. When he begins to grow up, he should know he will have old-age benefits direct from the insurance system to which he will belong all his life. If he is out of work, he gets a benefit. If he is sick or crippled, he gets a benefit . . . . I don't see why not. Cradle to the grave—from the cradle to the grave they ought to be in a social insurance system."[5]

Roosevelt's discussion of "cradle to grave" Social Security coverage emphasized continuity in social and economic security and living standards throughout the human life cycle. From birth to adulthood, and from adulthood into old age, he implied that men, for example, should be able to count on some reliable form of assistance when confronted with the inability to work and earn. The president did not want unemployment, permanent layoff, or disability to mean the abrupt end of a man's personal independence and status.

Franklin D. Roosevelt's principle of "cradle to grave" social security challenged the idea that joblessness would mean the end of manhood. Men worked all their lives to secure careers, build households, and live independently. When faced with old age or disability, Roosevelt imagined a form of social insurance that preserved, in some form, the economic foundations of manhood when work was no longer possible for men. Roosevelt's notion of Social Security opened the door for manhood to exist without work.

However, the 1935 Social Security Act's old-age provisions did not offer a secure path to manhood in later life. Pension checks for superannuated men would not arrive in the mail until 1940, which forced many men to continue looking for other ways to sustain themselves and their families during the depression decade. While Roosevelt's Social Security program promised to uphold the male breadwinner ideal as the basis for manhood at a moment in the life cycle when many men could no longer work, it could not ultimately make good on this promise. Elaborate rules for eligibility, formulas for payments that favored younger men, and proportionally fewer earnings in retirement actually threatened the economic foundations of manhood in old age. As the depression dragged on, men would have to rely on other New Deal programs to secure an income and a foothold in the bruising labor market. The working class embraced the New Deal, but it was the job programs of the WPA (Works Progress Administration) that made it possible for unemployed older working-class men to earn.

As historians have long pointed out, the economic and social dislocations that accompanied the Great Depression were extensive. In 1930, 16 percent of workers in the United States were unemployed; by late 1932–early 1933, the number had climbed to 25 percent. These numbers remained high throughout the 1930s.[6] At the local level, numbers looked even worse. In Chicago, for instance, 50 percent of men working in 1927 were not employed in 1933, and those who did work received only 25 percent of what they earned previously.[7] The depression appeared to undermine working-class manhood on a broad scale. "With nearly one in four men out of work," sociologist Michael Kimmel concluded, "the workplace could no longer be considered a reliable arena for the demonstration and proof of one's manhood."[8] This was especially worrisome for older working-class men, whose ties to the industrial workplace had been deteriorating since the turn of the century. As a jobless man quipped to Mirra Komarovsky, "What is a man supposed to do? Go to the kitchen and turn on the gas?"[9]

As if to answer the man's question, working-class men and women increasingly turned towards the state for assistance during the 1930s, building on the worker turn towards the welfare state initially begun by public discussions of old-age insurance, pensions, and manhood during the previous decade. Self-reliance and voluntarism had failed to protect Americans from the ravages of unfettered *laissez-faire* economics during the Jazz Age and the ravages of massive unemployment during the opening years of the depression. Individual effort alone could not produce sorely needed jobs for the young and old, nor could worker savings sustain families in the long term from capitalism's cycles of boom and bust.

As a result, men and women now viewed the state as a vital agent in society and the economy, questioning long-standing assumptions that the economy functioned best with minimal government intervention and oversight. Working men and women increasingly wanted the federal government to supervise the workings of the economy and bring democracy to the workplace, protect the legality of unionization, and provide assistance and subsistence during times of unemployment, disability, and old age. "Millions want the aged cared for," an editorial proclaimed in a 1936 labor newspaper.[10] Indicative of their changing attitudes toward government and the economy, many Americans supported new federal programs such as the National Industrial Recovery Act (NIRA), the Federal Emergency Relief Administration (FERA), the Agricultural Adjustment Act (AAA), the Civilian Conservation Corps (CCC), the Works Progress Administration (WPA), the National Labor Relations Act (called the Wagner Act), and especially the Social Security Act—the centerpiece of the New Deal.[11]

Building upon the state pension ideologies established during the 1920s, politicians and reformers believed the 1935 Social Security Act would sustain the ebbing masculinity of the oldest male breadwinners at the time of life when they could no longer work.[12] As the Roosevelt Administration pointed out, ongoing problems such as age discrimination in industry, technological change, and rampant unemployment underscored the need for decisive state intervention on older working men's behalf. When Roosevelt signed the Social Security Act into law during the spring of 1935, he acknowledged that "the civilization of the past hundred years, with its startling industrial changes, has tended more and more to make life insecure." Worries about the long-term sustainability of manhood over the life course were thus a major catalyst for social provision during the interwar period. "Today a hope of many years' standing is in large part fulfilled," the president announced. "Young people have come to wonder what would be their lot in old age. The man with a job has wondered how long the job would last . . . . we have tried to frame a law which will give some measure of protection to the average citizen and to his family against poverty-ridden old age."[13]

Building on the President's argument, new Social Security Board Chairman John G. Winant summarized how older working-class men's troubles made Social Security a necessary program. His assessment harkened back to the 1910s–1920s writings of Abraham Epstein and Isaac Max Rubinow. "The worker is no longer a free agent," Winant argued. In an industrial society, working men depended on their employers' wages for entirety of their livelihood; however, employers could not (or would not) provide adequate wages with any regularity. Winant continued, "He [the working man] counts for little against the gigantic and impersonal forces that surround him, the fierce play of industrial competition, the might and speed of machines that dwarf his single manpower into insignificance." As the Great Depression emphasized with frightening seriousness, working-class men lived at the mercy of industrial cycles of expansion and contraction and employers' arbitrary hiring and firing policies and biases. Industry could not provide men with the security they needed. "His working life," said Winant, "is liable to be hedged about by insecurity and his future clouded with uncertainty and fear. For him social insurance is a real and pressing necessity."[14]

Even the most outspoken critics of the White House echoed the president's language. For example, the Townsend Movement of the mid-to-late 1930s grounded its demands for old-age pensions in frequent rhetoric about the need to honor manhood. The Townsend Movement was the brainchild of Dr. Francis Everett Townsend, a struggling former medical doctor who lived in Long Beach, California. Inspired by the sight of poor women and men on the streets of Long Beach, Townsend devised a plan whereby the federal government would pay each 60 year-old man and woman 200 dollars per month. Each recipient would be required to spend the entire sum within the month, thus contributing to the overall economic recovery. To receive the funds, however, each man and woman would have to retire fully from the labor market. Their retirement would, in turn, create job opportunities for young unemployed workers, who themselves were struggling with joblessness.[15] In the *Modern Crusader*, a Townsend publication, a poet wrote, "Legislators 'agin' [*sic*] the Townsend plan,/Will find it hard work/When they try to shirk/The goal it brings to the working man."[16] The movement became wildly popular; by 1936, the Townsend Movement boasted a huge membership of between 1.5 and 2 million men and women.[17] The Townsend Movement framed itself as a group primarily for men of different social classes, despite the popularity of the plan among both women and men. However, the promise of a guaranteed $200 every month surely appealed to disaffected factory workers, shopkeepers, salesmen, and executives alike. In the *New York Times*, reporter Duncan Aikman noted that farmers, small business owners, and laborers of "the old Yankee stock" constituted the core of the "Townsend soldiers."[18] The Townsendite warriors were the everymen of modern America, concerned about the present and future of manhood. "Mr. X is over 60. He has a wife about the same age. Most likely Mr. X is a farmer, small-town storekeeper, clerk, or mechanic," Russell Porter wrote in the *New York Times Magazine*. "He has been thrifty and industrious all his life, but the depression caught him at a bad age. He lost his job, his home, or his savings, and he did not have the strength or wit of a younger man to regain them."[19] "I am 57 years old and have helped to make the country what it is," another Townsend man wrote to the *Modern Crusader*. "I think the world owes us [older men and their families] a living."[20]

Social Security proponents, however, wanted to make sure the program promoted a "distinctly American" vision of social provision. The American Federation of Labor, for instance, charged that government programs (such as unemployment insurance) too closely resembled European "handouts," forcing the noble working man into a state of "cowardly submission," as historian Alice Kessler-Harris points out.[21] Politicians in Washington, DC, also wanted to respond to persistent demands for pensions from hundreds of thousands of Dr. Townsend's supporters and weaken the broad appeal of the Townsend movement.[22] To achieve real "security," the Social Security Board argued in 1936 that America's version of support actually began with individual working men and their own efforts in the labor market. Then, once work was no longer available or possible, the state would provide the superannuated worker with funds that "he" himself had contributed to his own support. "It grants him an opportunity and imposes upon him the obligation to find security for himself," the Board proclaimed. "It [Social Security] recognizes work and a wage as the best security which the worker can find for himself."[23] Politicians stressed that Social Security built upon the aging working man's personal earnings, created as a result of his own labor; taxes levied on workers' wages greatly funded the new program. "The worker's living comes from his job," the Social Security Board concluded. "[Y]et his life is likely to outlast the skills which he can market."[24] When this moment came, Social Security would help older men retain the manhood they had already earned.

Craft unions supported Social Security. Since the 1920s, craft unionists, including those who were affiliated with the conservative American Federation of Labor (AFL), believed that pensions from the state were needed to uphold the male breadwinner ideal in later life, especially since employer ageism often barred so many older men from the factory floor. In 1938, an article in the *American Federationist* endorsed Social Security because the program promised some form of income to men who had no other family or friends to depend on, provided relief to older men and women who lived with struggling sons and daughters, and promised young men a pension when they reached the age of sixty-five.[25]

The men who *belonged* to craft unions, however, worried that Social Security would not provide the solution they had long hoped for. During the early 1930s, men in the Amalgamated Association (AA) praised the expansion of state pension programs; they liked state pensions and were eager for a larger program from the federal government. "If the old timers can hang on until the old age pension gets functioning, there'll be a change in our looks and features," a steelworker from Youngstown, Ohio, remarked in 1933.[26] Working men worried that Social Security's overall starting age—sixty-five years old—did little to help middle-aged men. "The age at which the pension starts is too high," George Smith, who possibly experienced discrimination in his past, noted in 1936. "What is one to do who at 55 is out of a job because he is considered too old and must wait 10 years for his pension to start?"[27] Townsend Movement followers agreed; Social Security might give aid to the oldest, but not those who were simply *older*. "He [a 45-year old working man] complains that New Deal social security means little," the *New York Times* reported of the Townsendites' views. "If he is employed he would have to work 20 years before he could receive substantial insurance payments."[28] Men in their forties and fifties faced a difficult predicament. As Secretary of Labor Frances Perkins noted of these men, "Probably they had worked since they were about nineteen"; however, "[t]hey were fifteen to twenty years short of retirement age. When they retired, they and their employers would have paid less than half the premium required to build them a decent, normal retirement allowance."[29] In addition, over time younger men would ultimately also qualify for higher Social Security payments than their older co-workers because young men would put more time (and dollars) into the system.[30] Younger working men, with their significantly longer years of working and contributing to the system, would find significantly greater financial rewards when they began collecting Social Security benefits than their older, already retired counterparts.

Social Security was popular, despite its flaws. More than 1 million men and women received some form of emergency old-age assistance from the Social Security Board between 1936 and 1938, so many would have been familiar with the new program.[31] Gallup polls from the late 1930s indicated that men and women agreed that old age pensions and other forms of assistance for the aged were necessary, and they approved of the program. During 1938 and 1939, over 90 percent of Americans "believed" in government old-age pensions; but most Americans (79 percent, as reported in September 1938) believed that old-age pensions should be reserved for only those who were most in need. Also, a majority of Americans approved of the Social Security tax on wages to fund the program: a January 1938 poll showed that 73 percent agreed that it was best for workers' themselves to pay for the program; and 85 percent agreed that employers should not pay the entire amount of the Social Security tax.[32]

Despite Social Security's possibilities and popularity, the new program could not resolve the fundamental economic uncertainties that rested at the center of gender uncertainty in later life. First, Social Security payments for retired men and women would not commence until the beginning of the next decade, in 1940. (The Roosevelt Administration amended the original 1942 starting date.) Second, the program's bias towards men in industry slighted men who worked in other sectors of the economy. Social Security favored men in heavily industrialized states such as New York, Pennsylvania, Illinois, Ohio, California, Michigan, Massachusetts, and New Jersey. Men in other states, such as African-American men in the South, who despite the Great Migration of the 1910s and 1920s, worked predominantly in agricultural occupations, were generally excluded. Over 92 percent of eligible men were white.[33] Unless men worked in the industrial regions of the Midwest and Northeast, they probably would not qualify for a pension. While some working women qualified for Social Security benefits, men received the lion's share of the government's assistance. Of 30.2 million eligible workers in 1938, 72.5 percent (21.9 million) were men; 27.5 percent (8.3 million) were women.[34]

In addition, Social Security's "gendered imagination," which favored the male industrial worker, actually worked *against* the interests of aging men in industrial jobs. In order to receive pension funds, older men would need to navigate a labyrinth of rules. First, men had to be 65 years old. Second, men would need to earn annually, beginning in January 1936, a large sum of $2,000 or more before they reached their 65th birthday. Third, he would need to have earned wages on 5 different days prior to his 65th birthday. (However, these workdays needed to be from 5 different years.[35]) This would have been problematic for men during the Great Depression, especially since older men were more likely than young men to be out of work. Men in their 40s, 50s, and 60s were struggling to secure work of any kind. If a man had been out of work throughout the depression years, he would be deemed ineligible for Social Security when the program would start paying benefits in 1940.

For those who were eligible, Social Security failed to provide earnings comparable to those found in employment. Factory wages paid out far more than funds from the federal government. Once a man reached his 65th birthday, he would collect—at most—85 dollars each month. If a man worked steadily and earned a substantial sum (such as 200 dollars per month), this would be a heavy loss of income.[36] Even after the 1939 amendments to the Social Security Act, which increased benefits and broadened eligibility, retirement on Social Security represented a major monetary step backward. If worker Joe Johnson earned $50 every month between 1936 and 1939 and retired in 1939, he would receive only 20 dollars per month. He could receive 10 more dollars, but he needed to wait for his younger wife to formally retire—at 65. These provisos were improvements over what he would have earned under the original Social Security Act. Then, Joe would have received a single lump sum of only 63 dollars.[37] As the January 1, 1940, the starting date for Social Security retirement benefits approached, the *New York Times* reported in late 1939 that men who earned $100 per month on the job would receive a monthly sum of $25.75 when they retired and began collecting benefits.[38] The Social Security Board estimated that a total of $114 million would be paid to 912,000 Americans by the end of 1940.[39] (This number equaled less than 10 percent of the 9 million Americans who were 65 years old and older in the US in 1940.[40]) "That is regarded as the modest beginning of a system," the *New York Times* noted, "that is expected to grow in the number of beneficiaries and the amount of benefits. Whether it will encompass every aged person in the land remains to be seen."[41]

Under Social Security guidelines, the specific occupations of working-class men would greatly determine the social and economic status of men in retirement. Frances Perkins lamented that a "flat rate" was not applied to Social Security benefits, which would have guaranteed the "the same amount to everyone."[42] Instead, stratification within the working class would be sustained in later life, as working men would retire with Social Security benefits that had been directly shaped by the contributions they were able to make as workers. Perkins suggested that uniform benefits challenged "the typical American attitude that a man works hard, becomes highly skilled, and earns high wages 'deserves' more in retirement than one who had not become a skilled worker."[43] Under Social Security rules, men who had earned the higher wages of skilled laborers would retire with larger benefits and greater financial security, while unskilled working-class men, who earned lower wages during their careers, would end their life-long labors with fewer benefits and fewer assets. Men at these higher economic levels surely supported the continuation of their privileged status into retirement, thus helping to insure the continuation of their social and economic position. However, Social Security could not consistently provide working-class men with stronger or enhanced economic foundations for continued identities as providers. In retirement, manhood would be grounded in unequal Social Security benefits, creating the possibilities for new uncertainties about male identity in later life. Since Social Security payments did not begin until 1940, and the apparatus of rules hindered the number of men who were eligible, the Works Progress Administration became a crucial program where older men could better utilize the state for assistance. The agency created public works projects and gave relief (in the form of paid work) to unemployed men. While younger and older men worked for the WPA, it was easier for younger men to find jobs, forcing aging men to depend on public works to a greater extent. In 1939, more than half of the 167,000 men on the WPA in New York City, for instance, were over the age of 40.[44] Nationally, the *New York Times* cited a WPA report which "shows clearly that larger proportions of the older workers have been employed on WPA for long periods." According to government statistics, more than ⅕ of the men who had worked for 3 years or more were 40 years old and older (21.8 percent), while only ⅛ were younger than 40 (12.1 percent).[45]

The older working-class man was heavily represented among the unemployed population. In a 1934 state of Massachusetts study of unemployment, researchers discovered that the state's unemployed were disproportionally older—while the average number of unemployed in Massachusetts was 25 percent, the percentage of older men (ages 60–69) out of work was substantially higher at 29 percent. In Philadelphia, a 1931 survey disclosed that 34.4 percent of employable men over age 66 were out of work, while only 22.9 percent of men between 26 to 55 years old were unemployed. In Detroit, an estimated 12 percent of men between the ages of 25 and 40 were out of work; for men over 40, however, the number was twice as large.[46] Available data is incomplete, but a variety of sources indicate that the percentage of firms with age limits ranged from roughly 30 percent to over 40 percent by the 1930s.[47] While traveling throughout the United States during 1934, Lorena Hickok wrote to Harry L. Hopkins in Washington, DC, that older working-class men constituted "A WHOLE STRANDED GENERATION."[48] With a more moderate and somber tone, Hopkins himself concluded that the typical unemployed worker was an aging working-class man. "[H]e had been more often than not an unskilled or semi-skilled worker in the manufacturing or mechanical industries," Hopkins wrote. "He had had some ten years' experience at what he considered to be his usual occupation." Hopkins worried most about the oldest men. Men in their sixties and seventies, who "through hardship, discouragement and sickness as well as advancing years, [have] gone into an occupational oblivion from which they will never be rescued by private industry."[49]

After 1935, many aging men relied on the WPA as a way to retain a foothold in the labor market. "The work relief rolls," as Louis Stark observed of the WPA, "are heavily weighted with unskilled workers, white collar workers, housewives, men above 40 years of age, new and untrained workers with slight experience, and agricultural laborers."[50] In 1937, Secretary of Labor Frances Perkins expressed her opinion that older men always seemed to work harder and outperform the younger men who worked alongside them. Grades of "excellent" work usually went to men over the age of 47, while the grade of "inferior" typically went to men under the age of 41. "In general," Perkins remarked, "[t]he older men tended to produce more than the younger men."[51] Aware that older working-class men desperately needed jobs in this era before monthly Social Security checks, Perkins challenged the prevailing reality in employer hiring practices by arguing for expanded employment opportunities for aging men and an end to hiring age limits in industry.[52] In her view, WPA public works had given these old men a much needed opportunity—and they had made the most of the government's assistance. Employers in the private sector needed to reverse course and do the same.

Despite Perkins' sanguine assessment of older men in the WPA ranks, many aging males could not manage the labor demands placed upon them by Uncle Sam. Harry Hopkins, the director of the WPA, received letters from aged men who were stunned that the government would ask men in their 60s to work as strenuously as men in their 20s and 30s. A working-class man in Michigan wrote to Hopkins in 1936, telling the Roosevelt Administration to pension rather than employ these old-timers:

> Do you think that a man of the age of 60 or 70 years old can do the work that a man can do at the age of 25 he can not he would collapse. When old age creaps upon you. you come incontact with all kinds alments akes pains nerviness sleepless and sightless. There is know 60 per cent of the WPA workers over 60 years old. The younger class seems to forget the for-fathers. [sic] [53]

The federal government tried to expand work opportunities for aging working men, but for some of these oldest laborers the available jobs were simply too harsh for their aging bodies. An older man in Milwaukee wrote to the United Electrical Workers union (UE) to say that he could no longer afford his subscription to the union's newspaper because he was "too crippled" to continue his job with the WPA.[54] Pensions for many of them proved to be the ideal form of "social security." In fact, the man in Michigan told Hopkins that the Townsend Plan, in his opinion, was the best pension scheme for the aged.

While the Roosevelt Administration envisioned New Deal programs as ways to give aid to struggling male breadwinners, the success of their efforts to uphold manhood throughout the male life cycle varied widely within, and across, various programs. Both Social Security and the Works Progress Administration favored male (and usually white) breadwinners, but the WPA most effectively provided economic aid (and financial reinforcement of the ebbing male breadwinner ideal) to older unemployed men during the 1930s. The welfare state proved to be an uncertain vehicle for the preservation of manhood, even as Social Security opened up the possibilities for aging males to remain "men" without employment. Social Security was intended to protect men from the horrors of growing old during an era of rampant employer ageism and industrial recession; but as historians have pointed out, the program would actually widen job opportunities for younger men in the labor market (as older men retired from work) and legitimated the compulsory retirement of older working-class men.[55] The program favored young men; they had greater opportunities to work during the 1930s and would thus pay more into the Social Security system throughout their lives. Aging men needed to look beyond Social Security for social security. As a 1938 byline in the *New York Times* put it, "Industry Has Created a Problem for Which Social Security Has Not Found the Answer."[56]

FORTY PLUS CLUBS

The Roosevelt White House and the Social Security Board were not the only depression-era institutions to challenge the idea that employment was a prerequisite for manhood. In the late 1930s, aging male office workers and professionals formed new organizations called Forty Plus Clubs to combat unemployment and hiring age limits. The group's unique activities and organizational culture emphasized the creation of social and professional continuity between employment and unemployment, challenging the idea that joblessness meant feminization and the loss of manhood. The members of Forty Plus did not experience a "crisis" of manhood per se because they were very much able to mobilize and secure new white-collar jobs, while the culture and activities of the organization recreated and continued the environment, routines, and social practices of the white-collar office. Forty Plus Clubs provided unemployed white-collar men with a workable foundation for manhood. White-collar men of Forty Plus were able to blur the presumably stark divide between employment and unemployment, challenging the rupture that defined the decade's "crisis" of masculinity. Still in existence today, the Forty Plus Clubs' message to the unemployed remains the same: "job searching is not joblessness; it is a job in itself and should be structured to resemble one."[57]

Forty Plus Clubs were the brainchild of Roland Darling, a struggling advertising man and former newspaper editor from New England. When he lived in Bar Harbor, Maine, during the early 1930s, he knew many hotel workers who were struggling. He helped them organize a self-help group that "worked well enough," and some of the men found work. After relocating to Boston in 1938, he met many more unemployed men, "all desperately in need of work." However, despite the group's origins in the service work economy, it was respectable white-collar men's rapid downward mobility that most alarmed and inspired Darling. "Here were men," he noted, "whose previous measure of success had led them to acquire homes, encourage their children to expect college educations, and in general set up standards of living which were now going to smash."[58] Darling wanted to form a new organization that would combat managerial biases against veteran white-collar job-seekers and help these once-respectable men find jobs. Aging male office workers, like blue-collar factory workers, often heard hiring managers tell them: "We make 40 our deadline in taking on new people."[59]

In a study of office workers during the 1930s, historian Clark Davis argues: "White-collar unemployment attracted considerable attention, for it seemed a new problem and one that aroused many status anxieties."[60] Male office workers in their forties and fifties constituted a major element of the unemployed ranks, as observers and workers themselves often pointed out. For example, in Tulsa, Oklahoma, a struggling executive in the oil industry, approaching the age of forty, wrote to President Franklin D. Roosevelt about his troubles finding a new position. He worried that when his old job would be refilled "it will be with a younger man." In 1938, an unemployed salesman in Minneapolis complained that "none" of the offices in his city would hire a 40-year-old man, and some companies even refused to hire men over 35.[61] Before the hard times of the 1930s, white-collar men enjoyed status and privilege. However, although unemployment rates for white-collar workers were lower than for industrial workers, the new problem of white-collar unemployment began to push them downward. Statistics showed that while the national unemployment rate reached 15 percent in 1937, the number of white-collar men that were out of work reached a significant 8.8 percent.[62] In addition to letters from former industrial workers and farmers, the "majority" of letters sent to the National Recovery Administration (NRA) in Los Angeles were from jobless male office workers. "Please, please give this consideration," an unemployed executive wrote, "what I want is a job and I will not fall down on you no matter what it is." A relief worker was shocked by the condition of white-collar men. He met many dethroned executives, "able-bodied, well-educated men of the finest sort who came into his office and simply cried because they could not find a job."[63]

In response to fears such as these, Roland Darling organized the first Forty Plus Club in Boston, which he called "Forty Plus of New England."[64] The group started small, featuring only 13 members, and the organization went to "work" immediately; five found new jobs during the first summer. Within the next few months, over 100 men joined. Soon after, anxious executives in other cities formed their own. In addition to other clubs in New England (such as Hartford, Connecticut, and Springfield, Massachusetts), unemployed professionals started organizations in Buffalo, Detroit, Chicago, Cincinnati, Cleveland, New York City, Philadelphia, Kansas City, Missouri, Los Angeles, Pittsburgh, Milwaukee, and Syracuse. In the South, clubs appeared in Miami, Greenville, South Carolina, Tulsa, and Savannah. The group was also international; men in Montreal, Toronto, and London, England, formed Forty Plus Clubs.[65]

Darling envisioned the Forty Plus Clubs as practical, rather than political, organizations. The members aggressively used their professional skills as administrators, advertisers, and negotiators to locate jobs for members. The men came together to "sell" one another. Members of Forty Plus contacted business managers in various fields to convince them to fill vacancies with members; some "salesmen" claimed to meet with as many as 200 employers every week. Forty Plus members circulated "rosters" of men, which highlighted their skills and experience. In an effort to protect older men from discrimination, Forty Plus leaders concealed names and ages. The clubs hoped to see veteran job-seekers get hired (or even denied employment) based on their qualifications and experience, rather than age.[66]

Even though Forty Plus Club members were technically unemployed workers, their "sales" activities allowed them to obscure and conceal their true social and economic status, taking on instead the professional identity of a working salesman. The problem of unemployment only factored into their "work" when they pitched the resumes of Forty Plus members to potential employers. Whether the commodity to be marketed and sold was paper, machinery, or unemployed veteran executives, the Forty Plus Club salesmen negotiated with managers, tried to charm, won over employers (or failed to do so), and made deals. As an editorial noted in the *Washington Post*, "They go out and call on employers and persuade them" not to buy life insurance or encyclopedias, but "to give older men a chance."[67]

Commentators emphasized that it was very advantageous for men to help other men via Forty Plus. Rather go in to a job interview alone, men benefited from the institutional support and recognition of the club, its identity, and its purpose. Employers were not dealing with one man; they were dealing with many. Forty Plus Clubs also gave middle-aged men a feeling of security and confidence that had eluded them throughout most of the depression decade. "Members found that selling another man to an employer, instead of yourself, has many advantages," author Ray Giles observed. "It kills off the nervousness, the over-anxiety, the apologetic attitude or the artificial boldness which afflicts men trying to get a badly needed job."[68]

Male professionals celebrated Forty Plus. They were places where white-collar men—salesmen, bankers, managers, professors—could affirm their notions of manhood. "Association and mutual helpfulness," Ray Giles wrote, "gave them the priceless grit to go on making call after call, in spite of discouragement. Their . . . tasks kept them busy everyday, and that helped sustain morale and self-respect." He continued, "The club is hard-boiled, [and] makes no pleas for sympathy."[69] In a 1941 letter to the *New York Times*, probable member Lucien Dix celebrated their honorable efforts to reclaim jobs in the professional world. The Forty Plus Clubs' members were not burned out "forgotten men," aging men with sagging shoulders, sullen demeanors, and tired bodies; they were not the men who languished in breadlines or sold apples on corners. Rather, the men of Forty Plus were "unusually attractive," vigorously collaborating "in a voluntary association." They were, indeed, men. In fact, Dix argued that the Forty Plus Clubs' struggle was comparable to English soldiers' heroic war against Nazi Germany on the Continent: "I see in these men mutually striving with courage and patience for victory over the depression their brethren of Britain facing as gallantly a much more evil foe."[70]

Forty Plus Clubs certainly were places where struggling staffers and professionals could feel manly again. The depression, as observers liked to point out, may have bloodied the members of Forty Plus, but they were unbowed.[71] Every club designated tasks for their members that gave them an expressly renewed sense of purpose. "These men don't sit around and twiddle their thumbs and complain," the *Washington Post* observed in 1939. "No, indeed. They go into action."[72] They did not want to think of themselves as unemployed or to be viewed as such; the men of Forty Plus were working at a new white-collar job (albeit without a salary). Everyday, in addition to meeting with managers about job openings and placements, members wrote and revised resumes and cover letters for out-of-work white-collar workers and gave speeches to community groups about the Forty Plus Clubs' program.[73] The clubs did their best to reconstruct the high-stakes, goal-oriented atmosphere of the office. A lack of productivity or dereliction of duty was not tolerated. If a member skipped meetings or failed to execute his assigned tasks, then he would be summarily "dismissed" and replaced.[74] He would be fired—just like any other worker who failed on the job.

The leaders of Forty Plus envisioned their organization as a place where manly work was done. Even though they called their group a "club," they did not want their organization to be viewed as a social or recreational site. Forty Plus was about work—not play; it was a "job-getting club."[75] In a 1938 article in *Reader's Digest*, Ray Giles noted, "Strictly taboo are social gossip, religious arguments, [and] off-color stories."[76] Unemployed executives and professionals wanted Forty Plus to be a place where men completed "productive" work. As unemployed men in the midst of a depression, the members shied away from any associations between themselves and any non-work related activity. Forty Plus wanted no part of merriment, fun, or frivolity.

Forty Plus Clubs of the late 1930s and early 1940s catered exclusively to men. Club members and the journalists who wrote about the group were careful to point out that women were absent from the ranks. Forty Plus was a stronghold of manhood: there were no women to compete with men, nor did men share the club space with women. A newspaper reporter for the *Los Angeles*

Times visited the Southern California club and observed, "Though the office is filled all day with workers, not one of them is a woman."[77] By excluding women, Forty Plus Clubs guaranteed a solidly male space amidst a broader pattern of uneasiness about manhood and feminization during the 1930s.

Despite men's preeminence, Forty Plus was never completely free from the feminine connotations of work activities that were traditionally associated with women. In the early-twentieth century office, assumptions about gender defined the range of acceptable work activities for men and women, as well as corporate hierarchies themselves.[78] While men dominated the leadership positions within corporations, women worked in clerical jobs. Women typed, filed, and shuffled paper for the men they worked for. However, since women could not participate, the male membership of Forty Plus was responsible for its own secretarial work. "Men do all the typewriting and telephone answering," as the *Los Angeles Times* pointed out.[79] The unemployed men in the Forty Plus Clubs could not perfectly recreate the environment of the male-dominated office, where they once gave orders to female subordinates. Rather, these executives now had to manage clerical tasks on their own.

White-collar men also paid careful attention to their attire and personal appearance to affirm white-collar manhood. The white-collar dress code of dark suits and ties provided a convenient and immediate way to affirm the professional identities of white-collar men, even in unemployment. The look of the suit visually obscured Forty Plus members' actual status as unemployed workers, especially since it was common for white-collar men to wear their suits both in and outside of the workplace.[80] Despite the lack of formal employment, business suits provided the men of Forty Plus with a way to challenge the idea that unemployment was the end of manhood.

Available photos of the organization in action pointed to the importance of physical appearance in the organization's culture. In a 1940 *Los Angeles Times* photo, for example, the photographer was careful to represent Forty Plus Club members in a scene reminiscent of their earlier days as busy executives. Instead of depicting unemployed men who were actually battling to find jobs, the photo shows hard-working veteran executives, clad in suits and ties, engaged in what looks like company business. We see two groups of men in conference, examining what could have been memos, contracts, reports, or orders to be given to subordinates. The members' dress, postures, and actions suggest they were worthy of calling themselves "men."[81] Unemployment had not destroyed their manhood.

The 1940 photo of the productive men in Forty Plus differed greatly from other depression-era photographs of the unemployed. The members of Forty Plus avoided associations with discussions of the industrial or rural working classes, unionization, the New Deal, or the poor. While the *Los*

Angeles Times framed the men of Forty Plus as authentic working white-collar executives, the federal government's Farm Security Administration (FSA) photographers, for example, framed the unemployed man as a shattered victim of chronic joblessness. Most famously, Dorothea Lange's images of migrant "Okies" in California became synonymous with the human devastation of the depression. As the historian Linda Gordon wrote about Lange's photography, viewers typically saw former working men who had been robbed of their identities as workers, breadwinners, and patriarchs by drought, employer disinterest, and extensive mechanization. Lange typically suggested that unemployed men were "dejected": Their expressions indicated sadness and isolation, while their bodies showed signs of fatigue, hunger, dirt, grime, and old age. Photos showed struggling men's hands jammed into the pockets of their overalls, no longer used to labor with farming implements in the fields. Wholly inactive, they now leaned back against dusty buildings in the center of their hometowns and did nothing. After so many years without steady work, there was little reason why men should have hope or take action: "Everywhere are idle groups of men in conversation . . . The men appear by the sides of the empty, silent main streets. They are all thin . . . Many attend morning movies because there is nothing else to do."[82] The photographers who documented the men of Forty Plus, on the other hand, were careful to establish symbolic distance between their subjects and the depressed men of the westward Okie migration. Carefully calling attention to the Forty Plus members' professional dress and deportment allowed the members of the organization to avoid the stigmas and associations that surrounded the struggling men in the FSA photographs.

While they were limited in scope, Forty Plus Clubs enjoyed real success. Across the United States, the groups placed significant numbers of members in new positions. In 1939 alone, Forty Plus of Chicago placed 115 middle-aged executives into new jobs. In Kansas City, Missouri, 45 members moved on to new positions. In Pittsburgh, 41 of 175 executives found full-time work. Between 1938 and 1941, the Forty Plus Club in New York City found work for 275 businessmen, boasting in 1941 that it reached a "low water mark." Due to its success, only 70 men were on the active membership list. An estimated 60 percent of the first cohort who joined the Los Angeles club found employment in the first year, 1939.[83]

In addition to the popular Forty Plus Clubs, numerous smaller organizations appeared in New York City, Boston, and other cities. To combat what newspapers called "Fortyphobia," aging professional men drew on Forty Plus's model of organization and formed a variety of groups such as "Life Begins at 40 Leagues," "The Job Hunters League," and "The Foundation for Americans of Mature Age," among other organizations.[84]

Despite their popularity between 1938 and 1942, increasing prosperity during World War II and the widening of white-collar employment opportunities
after the war halted the growth of Forty Plus. The clubs became redundant,
as younger and older men in white-collar jobs enjoyed rising incomes, expanding benefits, and increasing employment stability. Companies such as
General Electric (GE), General Motors (GM), and AT&T symbolized long-
term job stability and white-collar opportunity during the late 1940s, 1950s,
and 1960s.[85] The economic foundations of white-collar manhood would be
solidified in postwar America; executives would no longer need the sanctuary
provided by the Forty Plus Clubs.

During the late 1930s and early 1940s, the Forty Plus Clubs most directly
challenged the assumptions of observers such as Mirra Komarovsky who assumed that joblessness meant the end of manhood. Faced with rampant age
discrimination in the labor market, the Clubs struggled to wrench manliness
from chronic joblessness. They employed a vigorous regimen of salesman-
ship and coordination to place members in new jobs, while the organizational
culture of Forty Plus deliberately reconstructed the productive, manly world
of the white-collar office. While Social Security opened up new possibilities
for aging men to retain masculinity by earning an income in a time of life
when they could no longer work, Forty Plus secured masculinity by pursuing
various forms of labor in the context of joblessness.

INDUSTRIAL UNIONISM

The Great Depression forced jobless men to think about themselves and their
relationships to others in ways that were not dependent on employment. Social Security and the Forty Plus Clubs, for example, created new social and
cultural spaces where manhood could exist without employment. Social Security would allow some superannuated men to retain some of their favored
identities as breadwinners in old age, while Forty Plus Clubs challenged the
idea that joblessness was synonymous with the loss of manliness.

The resurgence of the labor movement, however, helped to sustain the
workplace as the principal site where most men would hope to secure their
manhood. The revival of organized labor led to new and sustained challenges
against employer discrimination; and new seniority clauses in union contracts
promised to sustain the employment of older men into their later years—ensuring that productive work would remain the main activity that defined male
identities. And union-won seniority provisions reinforced the importance of
the workplace as the foundation of working-class manhood further into the

realm of later life. In unionized basic industries, seniority protections would calm many men's fears of "old age at forty."

For the aging working-class men who managed to remain employed during the depression, they had to struggle to remain on the job. Employment certainly became more and more precarious for veteran men during the depression decade, especially since managers increased line speeds to maximize workers' output during the limited number of hours they would be paid to work and sought ways to trim redundant men from the payroll.[86] Speedup led to unemployment: it robbed men of steady work, as employers overloaded them with production orders for only short, intense periods of time. Sociologist E. Wight Bakke spoke with a working man in New Haven, Connecticut, who told him that his boss used speedy young workers to set piece rates—as a result, veteran men were struggling to maintain the required speed of work. The worker told Bakke about an aging man named George who lost the foot race with his fellow laborers and was fired. The factory foreman soon told George "he has been falling behind in production so they will have to let him go till work picks up." Bakke's interview subject told him, "Well maybe work picks up . . . , but usually it doesn't. The shop takes on new blood and the old fellow is on his uppers."[87] During the 1933 Briggs auto body strike in Detroit, leaders called attention to aging men's problems with speed. "The men," strikers asserted, "are forced by the threat of dismissal to work so fast at heavy labor that the older men are unable to work the full number of hours that they are expected to and are sent home because of this fact."[88]

Aging men of the 1930s viewed young workers with tremendous unease. Clarence Lischer, who worked in Flint, Michigan, at Fisher Body No. 1, recalled a young worker who could complete his job with terrific speed. When he finished his task, the teenager (dubbed a "speed demon") had ample time to relax. Lischer disliked the lad, saying "well that don't look good you know." These "pushers" could easily "foul things up." Older men in Flint often "reminded" their young counterparts to work at a moderate pace: protecting not only the veteran men's jobs but their own as well.[89] When an "enthusiastic boy" went to work in the screw machine department of "a large manufacturing plant," his older colleagues told him, "Well, don't work so damn fast . . . it's healthier." In order to protect all of their jobs, older working men knew it was best for the entire department to work as slowly as possible. Otherwise, management would lower the wage, intensify the pace, and layoff the old-timers.[90]

Numerous unionists who worked with the Committee of Industrial Organization (CIO) envisioned strong and active industrial unions as vital and necessary ways protect the social and economic foundations of working-class manhood from the many troubles that accompanied growing old in industries that were increasingly driven by mass production managerial philosophies and assembly line technology. "The system puts a premium on youth," CIO supporter J. Raymond Walsh argued. "Life in the industry ends before fifty. The companies deny having such a policy of discharge, but the fact is clear to anyone who stands at a factory gate." Walsh asserted that men were powerless against employers' demands for youth. Walsh lamented, "Having done their ten-fifteen-or twenty-year stint for the industry they are pushed out, industrially aged, while still in middle life. The individual worker has no means of combating this scrapping."[91] Only "industrial unionism in action" could help these aging men. As a member of the Steel Workers Organizing Committee (SWOC) told an audience at the Duquesne Light plant in Springdale, Pennsylvania, "They don't scrap the older men at our works" because the SWOC vigorously looked after their needs for long-term ties to the workplace.[92] If manhood would be preserved, men needed active, vigilant guardians.

Between 1933 and 1937, the ascendency of the New Deal in American politics and culture afforded working people new opportunities to press for rights in the economy and the workplace, and offered organized labor an unprecedented degree of legitimacy and importance. During the Great Depression, as the industrial economy collapsed and worker unrest increased, many Americans concluded that the resolution of the "labor question"—the interrelated problems of labor unrest and worker poverty—was an important step toward ending the Great Depression and bringing about economic recovery. President Franklin D. Roosevelt and members of his cabinet endorsed the idea that industrial capitalism could not function properly without fairness and oversight in the market and the workplace. Before the New Deal, in the unregulated economy of the 1920s, employers had not been accountable for their business actions, and their unfettered pursuit of profit (often at the expense of workers' civil liberties) created an unstable economy and hastened the onset of the Great Depression. In response, Roosevelt's New Deal legislation promoted "industrial democracy": the idea that equitable relations among workers and employers, union organization and collective bargaining, and government regulation in the workplace would create a more stable and democratic capitalism that would benefit a majority of Americans. For working people and leaders of organized labor, who had struggled for decades against erratic wages, company spies, the arbitrary powers wielded by foremen, strikebreaking, and employer demands for "efficiency," the regulatory state ushered in by the New Deal offered a path to citizenship, the rule of law, and social justice.[93]

The populism of the New Deal and the growth of organized labor were interconnected. Workers needed greater power in their places of work if they were to stay on the job and off the picket line. Also, they needed the power to bargain for higher wages that would, it was hoped, bring about the end of "underconsumption" and the Great Depression. The 1935 Wagner Act proved to be labor's "Magna Carta." The bold law imposed standards of equity and fairness in the workplace, as the federal government created the new National Labor Relations Board (NLRB) to administer the formation of a more balanced framework for labor relations. The Wagner Act and the NLRB protected workers' right to strike, organize unions, and vote for independent union representation. The Wagner Act also banned several "unfair labor practices" that had been veritable standards of industry, such as company-controlled unions, the creation of blacklists, the firing of workers who joined or organized unions, and industrial espionage. The NLRB also adjudicated labor disputes and workers' grievances. The Board was responsible for bringing democracy to labor relations, institutionalizing government oversight in the capitalist economy and ensuring workers' civil liberties on the job.[94]

The labor-friendly political climate, as reflected in the passage of the Wagner Act and the creation of the NLRB, helped spur the growth and institutionalization of organized labor. The growing power of labor, in turn, pushed further the changes that were made possible by New Deal labor legislation. The New Deal era transformed the politics of the labor movement, as a new generation of industrial unionists wanted to take full advantage of the labor-friendly tone in Washington, DC, to organize workers along industry-wide lines, regardless of craft or skill. The labor movement became more militant during the 1930s, challenging the conservative AFL who had long dominated organized labor and insisted that workers should be organized according to craft. In the autumn of 1935, industrial unionists such John L. Lewis of the United Mine Workers and Sidney Hillman of the Amalgamated Clothing Workers created the Committee of Industrial Organization (CIO) to build mass unions of workers that could effectively challenge employer power. In contrast to the exclusivity of the AFL, the CIO was an inclusive grassroots organization that derived its energy from the large mass of unorganized unskilled workers (including immigrants, women, African Americans, and Latinos) and energetic young organizers with Communist and Socialist credentials. Following the creation of the CIO, the organizing efforts of Walter and Roy Reuther of the United Automobile Workers (UAW), Mike Quill of the Transport Workers Union of America (TWU), and Harry R. Bridges of the International Longshore and Warehouse Union (ILWU), among others, typified the energy offered to the industrial union movement by Left-leaning activists.[95]

The growth of the labor movement, the state's expanded support for labor through the Wagner Act, and the reelection of President Roosevelt with overwhelming working-class support in 1936 emboldened working people to push forward their demands for industrial democracy. In 1936–37, a new period of strike activity and union organizing feverishly swept through workplaces, both large and small. As CIO organizers in Michigan noted in 1936, working people wanted now more than ever to "get a New Deal in the shop."[96] The new industrial union movement won its first major contest at the factories of General Motors in Flint. GM was the largest and most powerful company in the US; and the petty tyranny wielded by foremen, relentless assembly line speed-up, and aggressively anti-union practices (especially its widespread use of labor spies) had made the company, by the 1930s, a focal point of worker discontent. On December 30, 1936, working men and UAW activists at the massive Fisher Body One plant launched a "sit-down" strike, seizing control of the factory. By sitting down inside the plant, the strikers could shut down production and better protect themselves from strikebreakers and police. The sit-down strike in Flint sparked rebellion throughout the GM system. Beginning in early January, sit-down strikes erupted at Fisher Body in Cleveland, the Guide Lamp plant in Anderson, Indiana, the Chevrolet facility in Toledo, the Cadillac plant in Detroit, and the Chevrolet and Fisher Body factories in Janesville, Wisconsin.[97]

The successful sit-downs at GM sparked a massive strike wave that lasted into the spring of 1937. According to the US Bureau of Labor Statistics, there were at least 477 sit-down strikes that year. In Flint, Detroit, and beyond, more than 398,117 men and women in the United States went on strike.[98] Workers' demands for a New Deal extended beyond the largest factories of manufacturing industries into the confined spaces of small businesses, underlining the far-reaching impact of the sit-down movement and the intensity of workers' demands for justice in their workplaces and communities. In February 1937, 10 bakers at the Brownie Pie Shop in Los Angeles abruptly sat down for a 25 percent wage increase. On March 13, 38 workers at the Hamilton Hotel in Washington, DC (including 22 chambermaids), launched a sit-down strike for better wages that ended a few minutes later when managers capitulated. (The success of this protest inspired a sit-down strike among valets in the hotel's parking lot later that day.) Also in March, a group of 30 women laundry workers sat down on the job in Hilo, Hawaii, demanding an hourly wage increase of 3–5 cents from their employers; and 75 women who worked at the Roberts Dress Company in Baltimore launched a sit-down strike to demand recognition of the International Ladies Garment Workers Union (ILGWU). Henry Frank, a Milwaukee tailor who worked alone in a single-employee shop, sat down at his workbench for better hours and wages in the spring of 1937. His boss gave up after three hours.[99]

The upsurge of labor militancy during the sit-down era created new opportunities for working-class men to reinforce the importance of the workplace as the site that fundamentally determined male identity. Working men and unionists of the 1930s were particularly concerned with the problem of protecting work and breadwinner status over the long term, sustaining manhood into the uncertain space that was old age. Frequent and widespread demands for seniority principles underlined the importance of older working men's struggles to the organizing efforts and gender politics of men in the CIO; and working-class men viewed CIO gains as ways to better protect their claims to manliness.[100] To best protect working-class manhood from the constant threat of discrimination and permanent layoff, the unions of the CIO insisted that working men needed seniority clauses as a shield from industrial practice.[101] Industry reformers Clinton S. Golden and Harold J. Ruttenberg argued that seniority was the only way "to eliminate favoritism and discrimination among a group of workers" by giving "workers prior claim to a job over others with fewer years of continuous service."[102]

Years of employer discrimination against older men made seniority a key demand. Throughout the years before the arrival of the CIO, steelworkers complained that employers often hired a group of men only to lay off the oldest when work slowed down again.[103] Aging laborers had perceptibly fewer chances in the labor market. "Even if conditions would improve," a steelworker noted of the 1930s, "many mill men would still be idle, because of their age."[104] An out-of-work steelworker in New Castle, Pennsylvania, complained that if his mill ever started up again, managers surely would only take back young men. He lamented, "They won't call me back to work at the strip mill, I'm too old." However, he held out hope for the younger men. "Maybe my two boys . . . will be called," he remarked.[105]

Men typically agreed that workers with the most years of service should receive "the breaks"; and many believed their situations had improved as a result of new seniority clauses in their contracts.[106] Before the Steel Workers Organizing Committee (SWOC) and the CIO, men of steel, for example, lived entirely at the mercy of employer hiring, firing, and promotion policies. After SWOC forced the US Steel firm to recognize the CIO, and won the April 1937 strike in Aliquippa, Pennsylvania, men won greater job stability and a political voice in the factory and community.[107] Seniority clauses would thereby allow men to protect their status as workers over the long term. Clinton S. Golden and Harold J. Ruttenberg described how steelworkers, because of seniority, were no longer "wantonly" tossed aside when they were "too old to work."[108] Men went to surprising lengths to bring seniority to their workplaces. Working men and the independent Progressive Steel Workers' union at the Wisconsin Steel plant in Chicago promised not to strike in exchange for contractual seniority clauses. The men at Wisconsin Steel received "full recognition of seniority" from management in exchange for a pledge that the workers "would refrain from sitdown strikes under all circumstances."[109] More than anything else, the men at Wisconsin Steel wanted greater certainty about their futures as they aged in the mill. They were even willing to set aside the most potent political weapon of the sit-down era (the strike) in exchange for this very fundamental demand of seniority.

CIO unionists made the long-term defense of working-class manhood a foundation of their organizational culture. The United Automobile Workers (UAW) argued that only unionization and seniority could reign in managers' actions and protect working men's jobs in industries that historically drew energy from youth and brawn. "The UAW-CIO is the only true friend the old men have," stewards insisted at Packard Motor Company in 1939. "Three long years of militant, progressive unionism is the best insurance that the cause of the old men is in capable hands. Seniority protection and humane conditions of work are twin-pillars of the UAW." To combat permanent layoff at forty and the end of paid employment as the foundation of working-class manhood, the UAW insisted that only a strong union could ensure the preservation of a man's identity as a worker and provider into later life. The UAW was established on "the protection of the autoworker in his declining years."[110] For the next fifty years, veterans of the sit-down strikes in Flint and Detroit argued that "job security for older workers" was one of the most important achievements brought about by unions.[111]

Seniority clauses promised improved job stability in the long-term to older men, but did so at the expense of young men's nascent careers. Seniority clauses stipulated that the most recently hired (and probably younger) workers would be laid off first, thus protecting the employment of veteran men. The US Department of Labor worried that seniority clauses would transform depression-era unemployment into a social problem that primarily attacked the youngest members of the labor market. "When lay-offs are based on length of service, the impact of unemployment falls entirely on the younger workers," the *Monthly Labor Review* noted in 1938.[112] An editorial in the *New York Times* complained that "seniority increases the security of the older workers," but "does this at the expense of the younger workers."[113] In the auto factories of Detroit, where seniority clauses swept through the entire industry in the late 1930s, younger men often found themselves at the bottom of seniority lists and more vulnerable to layoff. As Louis Stark noted in an article about ""strike-tired" autoworkers:

The young employe [sic] holds that this system [seniority] tends to freeze the older men in their jobs. He sees the motor industry as the creation of young men, but finds himself close to the bottom of the seniority list if he has been at work in a plant only a few years. He feels full of energy and sees no reason why his future should be founded by a seniority system which tend to raise the average age of workers higher and higher as the years pass.[114]

CIO unions, too, worried about the possible impact of seniority on the future of unionism in mass production industry. "The seniority system would tend to keep them [future young worker-members] out," Louis Stark wrote. "Thus there is created a possible reservoir of non-union men."[115] Seniority clauses might, he feared, ultimately transform young men into a new reserve army of anti-union unemployed men.

Employers used young working men's anxieties about seniority to argue against the CIO revolution that was transforming the rules of American workplaces. As a result of unionization and seniority provisions, managers argued again and again in business periodicals and trade journals that companies became "feudal" bastions for the old, overprivileged, and outmoded.[116] Industry as a whole, managers claimed, would become stale, listless, and lifeless if aging men (and union protections) predominated in the factory. In the *Personnel Journal*, a writer in 1939 described seniority as a "curse" on industrial managers, as seniority clauses "disillusioned" young men and made it possible for older men to "bump" their co-workers out of their jobs in order to selfishly protect themselves.[117] Managers complained that seniority clauses prevented them from "weed[ing] out" the "less efficient" veteran workers, leading to "oversupplied" factories that were less able to compete in the marketplace.[118] Subtly, anti-union voices suggested that the growing labor movement and contractual seniority would ultimately jeopardize the competitiveness of the American manufacturing economy. As Frederick H. Harbison of the University of Chicago argued in 1940: "Many employers have complained that seniority . . . dampens the initiative and incentive of younger employees, and results in stagnation and impaired efficiency of the working force as a whole." Seniority, he claimed, had become a "headache" in mass production industry that even unions could no longer tolerate.[119]

The rise of the CIO during the 1930s proved to be a major moment in the history of older workers in the United States. Union-won seniority provisions challenged prevalent early-twentieth century attitudes toward older laborers by empowering these veterans. In industries where seniority principles could be implemented, aging men could depend on the workplace to sustain them and their notions of manliness well into their later years—a kind of social security that had not existed previously in industry. The labor militancy of the 1930s and the growth of the Committee of Industrial Organization, SWOC, and the UAW, and other industrial unions, created new possibilities for aging working-class men to remain *working men* even as their hair grayed and bodies aged. By doing so, seniority clauses played a significant role in ensuring that work would remain the basis of working male identity.

THE CONSUMER MARKETPLACE

Sociologist Mirra Komarovsky argued that the economic collapse of the depression decade fostered intense male malaise, as prolonged unemployment seemed to undermine the gender foundations of work, employment, and domesticity that defined American society. However, as the actions of Forty Plus Clubs, CIO unionists, and policy makers showed, there were ways for older men to reclaim a sense of manhood. Even as managers discounted the employment of older men, CIO unions and Forty Plus Clubs mobilized members to challenge ageism, while the WPA and Social Security programs promised to employ struggling older job-seekers on public works jobs and to honor older men's dignity after their life-long labors by offering them a small pension when they could no longer find employment.

In addition, aging men themselves looked to the twentieth-century arena of mass consumption for new ways to strengthen their bodies and improve their physical and emotional health in later life, thereby bolstering their employability and longevity on the job during their later years.[120] During the Great Depression, older men became a key buying demographic, as suggested by the Herculean attempts of corporations, insurance companies, and health advice providers to tap into, and shape, this burgeoning market of anxious consumers. Sellers knew well the anxieties of older men in the depression-era labor market, and they actively tried to market various products—from pension savings plans, to books about health and longevity, to food products—to these desperate consumers. For aging men, consumerism became an everyday way to do something to challenge the idea that growing old would lead to the end of manhood. Older men looked to new forms of health advice, dieting, exercise, and savings programs to strengthen their bodies so they might remain attractive to potential employers as well as remain energetic and healthy enough to stay at work. A vigorous, energetic working body and a bank account filled with earned assets were regarded as older men's surest protection from old-age poverty, dependency, and the poorhouse.

Medical experts in the consumer marketplace continually reminded men that healthy bodies were the principal tools they needed to secure jobs and remain employed. During the 1930s, experts in the health sciences worried that older men's health was too fragile—especially since the onset of the economic crisis—and thus threatened the ability to work. Against the backdrop of a frightening economic crisis, health and medical experts renewed their interest in the aging male body's limitations.[121] Vulnerable bodies, for instance, stood in the way of work and, ultimately, economic survival. The Great Depression left no man unscathed: factory workers, artists, executives, and farmers all faced the realities of personal disaster and declining health. Some observers highlighted references to sexual impotence to underscore the most dire personal outcomes of unemployment. One middle-aged man was emotionally devastated by his struggles with joblessness which also led to sexual problems. "It is awful to be discarded at 40," the downtrodden man told Mirra Komarovsky. "A man is not a man without work." Marginalized in the labor market, he also felt marginal in the bedroom. The man believed he and his spouse "were too old" for sexual intercourse; "It is possible that his failure" in the labor market, Komarovsky noted, contributed to his anxieties about sex.[122]

Medical experts emphasized programs of health and wellness for aging males (especially for men like themselves who worked in corporate offices). The heart became a popular topic in medical literature; to remain employable, experts urged older men to take good care of their hearts. Aging men needed their blood to flow strongly and freely. If not, their bodies quickly declined and died. Arteriosclerosis, one doctor insisted, "might be defined as the essential element in the process that makes people grow old." A weak heart could not deliver blood to a man's hair, skin, and brain. As a result, arteriosclerosis led to gray hair, wrinkled skin, and senility. Aging men needed to be careful. If not, death would surely claim them: "At the beginning a man will not admit to himself that his virility is impaired; he will continue to brag about his great strength when he is trying to hide the fact that his strength is not what it used to be. He refused to attach any importance to a slight tightness in his chest on climbing stairs, or a feeling of breathlessness when he goes out into the cold air."[123]

The pharmaceutical industry begged aging men to see their doctors. Even if a middle-aged man's health was good today, experts warned him that tomorrow could be very different. In a series of advertisements, the ER Squibb & Sons Company talked about aging men who were, at least today, enjoying fair health. "Like most men at fifty," an advertisement stated, "you feel that you're right at the top of your swing. You want to go on getting the most out of life—from healthy sport, from business, from pleasant companionship." But diabetes, heart trouble, kidney trouble, and high blood pressure drove men to the grave. Men needed to avoid taking chances; life was too precarious in this modern age. Aging men, ER Squibb & Sons argued, needed to have regular medical check-ups. If an older man stayed healthy, he could remain employed; and someday, when the depression ended, he might be able to resume a pleasant life enjoying golf, climbing, and travel in his leisure moments.[124]

To prevent catastrophes, experts in the health sciences reminded men that good health began in youth. Instead of trying to become healthier in later life, when it might be too late, experts reminded men that they should begin taking care of health and wellness as soon as possible. Samuel Morrison lamented that the age of 40 marked a serious moment in men's health history. After 40, diseases became more serious, more frequent, and more difficult to control. "Youth seems to be invulnerable," he wrote. But after 40, "the accumulation of repeated mild illnesses begins to present symptoms which are more disturbing, less intermittent, and for the first time very significant as far as the host's general health is concerned." Morrison reminded young males that as men aged, their ability to fight off "cells, bacteria, toxins, and other destructive agents" sorely declined. To protect themselves as they aged, young men needed to listen to their doctors, stay away from alcohol and fatty foods, avoid smoking, eat slowly, and stay active. "Consistent care in youth, adolescence and maturity up to 40 will make it unnecessary to treat old age during middle life," Samuel Morrison cautioned.[125] Experts worried greatly about men's health, especially since the Great Depression menaced in the background.

To remain vital to the companies they worked for, experts advised older men to maintain good health and tidy appearances. Diet, weight, and dress were just as important, if not more so, for the older man than the young man. In the midst of a depression, men needed to be ready for a frantic struggle to remain employed. Men might expect to slow down in later life, but they could ill-afford to appear sickly, slow, or rumpled. To protect their jobs, the magazine *Hygeia* reminded readers to stay fit, youthful, and attractive. "The man of advancing years must guard against increasing weight," a 1933 article noted. "Neatness and cleanliness are just as important in the later years of life as in the courting days," the essay continued. "[U]ntidiness must be guarded against by all." No employer, the writer implied, wanted to keep a sloppy ne'er-do-well on the payroll. Finally, *Hygeia* urged men to modify their diets: "The diet must be adjusted, of course, to the needs of the individual." Stay away from fat: too much fatty food, cigarettes, and coffee damaged the man's body, accelerating aging. Sick old men would not be able to remain vigorous and ready for the depression's many "hazards."[126]

Numerous companies promised to help older men look more attractive and more youthful. Perhaps playing upon men's worries about looking "old," the Shick Shaver firm argued that its new electric razors helped aging men look more "natural." Shick told consumers in 1937 that conventional straight razors left an aging man's face "tough, calloused and scaly." As a result, a middle-aged man looked much older than his actual age. The electric razor, however, would correct this artificial aging. "Continuous use of a Shick

Shaver," a 1937 advertisement proclaimed, "gets rid of most of this old skin." Shick argued that its product erased the look of aging from men's faces "and a new, more youthful skin takes its place."[127] Since so many older men were struggling at work, the Shick Shaver company possibly hoped they could play upon older workers' anxieties to sell their razors.

During the mid-1930s, popular magazines advertised a steady procession of advice books and diets that promised to invigorate aging men's health. Advice authors promised that their lessons on life and health would help older men remain physically vigorous, mentally sharp, and professionally competitive. Anxious men might have been drawn to advertisements in *Newsweek* for Robert G. Jackson's *How To Always Be Well*, a book originally published in 1927. The seventy-six year-old Jackson appealed to aging men who felt as though the Great Depression had sapped them of their manly strength:

> If you're like most people you probably feel that the last five depression years have taken at least ten off your life. You've probably been going at a terrific pace and under a terrific tension, mentally and physically . . . seemingly butting your head against a stone wall. You've probably lost much of your pep and vim—tire easily—have to drive yourself to keep going—and feel twice your actual age. If you're forty or over life may have lost all of its zest. You may even feel that Old Man Depression has taken so much out of you that you'll never regain the ground you've lost.[128]

Jackson promised older men that his blend of positive thinking, diet, exercise, and limited rest could help aging workers regain their vim and vigor. He emphasized how he had saved himself from the loss of manhood. Jackson claimed he was near death at fifty, struggling with a "worn-out" heart, glaucoma, high blood pressure, and nagging arthritis. With hard work and stern dedication to a strict health regimen, Jackson boasted he remade himself into a model of male perfection—even in his 60s and 70s. An insurance company, he claimed, rated his rebuilt body as better than a 35 year-old. He walked 10 miles every day, slept naked with the windows open (even in cold weather), exercised while laying naked in his bed every morning, and exercised again as he stood in the bathroom. He willed himself to stay active, making no allowances for tiredness or illness: lecturing, touring, and writing without let-up. Jackson claimed to never take vacations; he never tired. Jackson presented himself as the kind of man who could survive the worst of the Great Depression and defy the advance of age and time. He was tough, healthy, and smart. He could surely survive the mere loss of a job or whatever else "Old Man Depression" might throw at him, including tiredness, sadness, or stress. Robert G. Jackson's ads boldly proclaimed to readers: "Today, at 76, Dr. Jackson has a 35 year old body and repeatedly demonstrates that he can do anything the average 22 year old can do and do it better . . . . Today, he can run up five flights of stairs without even breathing hard. His philosophy can bring you like benefits just as it has brought them to thousands."[129]

If aging men could not afford Jackson's book, or if they did not like to read, they could always eat Fleischmann's Yeast. In 1938, the makers of Fleischmann's Yeast insisted that digestion problems exacerbated the "feeling of age." As men and women aged, their "gastric juices" weakened, hindering the process of digestion. As a result, older men felt ill—thus weakening their daily on-the-job performance. Fleischmann's insisted that its product hastened proper digestion and introduced much-needed vitamins into a man's diet. The company urged its customers to eat yeast three times each day. Fleischmann's claimed its yeast helped men and women fight off colds and increase their overall vitality.

To authenticate their claims about yeast, Fleischmann's brought forward happy customers to speak to aging consumers directly. Harry Halbert, a man who worked in real estate, testified, "I don't need to tell anyone what the depression did to the real estate and building business. It did its worst to me!" He felt weak and sick during his bout with unemployment, but a friend urged him to try Fleischmann's Yeast: "Soon my appetite picked up, and I'd wake up in the morning feeling fresh and rested. After a few months, I felt up to putting the pieces of my business life together again and I'd got a job back in my old business."[130] A man who worked in advertising boasted of similar results. After eating the yeast, Eddy McLaughlin noted, "With my new health I feel a whole lot better about my job, too."[131] Thanks to Fleischmann's miracle food, numerous men claimed that the product eased their nerves and helped them feel healthy again—able to work and compete during these lean years of the depression.

Other arbiters of advice simply pitched ideas to anxious older men. Focusing on the white-collar office, some advice writers warned aging men to adapt to workplace pressures any way they could; older men needed to work much harder and *smarter* than their young counterparts. Older men needed to be extra careful with their energy level at work: prepare during slack times to work rigorously in peak times; give up demands for perfection; enlist other workers to help with work that may be physically difficult; copy the methods of younger men; be willing to improve upon skills; and avoid the loss of mental "energy" by worrying needlessly. But most importantly, aging men needed to avoid singling themselves out as outmoded workers. With care, the older male office worker would ideally enhance his expertise and efficiency; if he kept moving, the rolling stone would gather no moss.[132]

Other advice writers told aging men to think about layoffs not as a period of joblessness, but as a chance to "try" new career paths. If a man lost his job, writers insisted that he simply needed to try something else. Walter B. Pitkin, a professor of journalism at Columbia University, wrote in 1937 that, despite the depression, there *were* other jobs. Older men, however, needed to be creative to find them. "Most people," Pitkin claimed, "when left to their own devices, mill around in a tiny corral like penned steers. . . . Instead of getting out and sniffing new terrains they sit at home, read the same papers, think in the same old rut. If they were wise, they'd 'wake up and live,' get out and look for the unusual jobs that can be done." Aging men needed to stop looking for work in high-powered job sectors; government, the military, politics, and corporate work were no longer ideal settings for dinosaurs, Pitkin suggested. Instead, he noted that aging men could probably find their best opportunities as gardeners, watchmen, crane operators, truck drivers, cashiers, chippers, tour guides, and teachers.[133] White-collar working men in particular, he suggested, needed to lower their expectations for the future, abandon any sense of entitlement, and find the will and ability to be creative.

Life insurance companies claimed to offer solutions to older men's anxieties about savings. Companies such as Phoenix Mutual, based in Hartford, Connecticut, promised older men in offices and factories that its pension programs insured a stable economic existence in later life.[134] Insurance companies hoped to profit from the popularity of the Townsend Movement. If a man was willing to devote a certain amount of money from his pay every month to a Phoenix Mutual Retirement Income Plan, then Phoenix Mutual promised 200 dollars each month (the amount Dr. Francis Townsend hoped to secure for aging men and women) beginning at age 55.[135] A 1935 advertisement in *Newsweek* promised, "If you want to retire someday, and are willing to lay aside a portion of your income every month, you can have freedom from money worries."[136] (To learn more details about the Phoenix Mutual pension scheme, would-be consumers needed to send the magazine clipping back to the company.) For anxious working men in their 40s, 50s, and 60s, the Phoenix Mutual scheme would have been too good to be true. Phoenix Mutual promised a financially stable old age, despite the depression.

Phoenix Mutual denied there was a depression in the economy. "It makes no difference if you're carefully laid plans for saving have been upset during the past few years," advertisements claimed. "It makes no difference if you are worth half as much today as you were then. Now, by following a simple, definite Retirement Income Plan, you can arrange to quit work forever fifteen years from today with an income guaranteed to you for life." Phoenix Mutual insisted they offered an "investment that pays, depression or no depression."[137] (None of its ads in *Newsweek* specified how much savings a man had to devote to the plan.) The company offered men way to escape from clutches of the economic crisis: In 1936, a man exclaimed that he "didn't dream [he] would ever have enough money to retire." But Phoenix Mutual told the young worker he certainly would. By joining the program, Phoenix Mutual promised the man the good life in old age—despite the menacing depression of his present.[138]

To sell its pension scheme, Phoenix Mutual promised lavish retirement lifestyles, worry-free utopias that were beyond the menace of depression-era old-age poverty. With Phoenix Mutual behind them, men could enjoy the full fruits of their life-long labors and wise investments. Throughout the 1930s, advertisements showed retired men who enjoyed the good life: cruises, restaurants, golf, seaside relaxation, campfires, and suburban homes. The retired man, comfortable with a small fortune in the bank, coolly smoked his pipe with a contented smile on his face. Phoenix Mutual offered anxious older men a better future—which they clearly believed would resonate. They claimed investors lived very well. "For me, life really began at 55 when I got my first retirement check," one caption read. "I have no cares or worries," an older man proclaimed. "I'm just taking life easy."[139] Another ad discussed three young men who all wanted to become rich. One man was saving every penny he earned, the second foolishly invested his money in the stock market. The third young man defined wealth as: "I want security as long as I live. I want an independent income of my own. I want to be able to retire when I'm 55 and take life easy—forget money worries and business troubles . . . That's what I call being rich."[140] Men of the 1930s surely would have leapt at the chance to "take life easy" and be "rich." By 1935, Americans who invested in retirement and life insurance policies helped Phoenix Mutual acquire "all-time high" assets worth $195 million.[141]

The ads and health discussions in health journals and popular magazines provide an evocative view of Americans' responses to depression-era anxieties. While many working men and women turned towards the New Deal welfare state and labor organizing to tackle their struggles with poverty and joblessness, companies and advertisers believed that many Americans would also look to consumerism for ready solutions to their problems. Companies promised endless quick fixes: improved health, strengthened bodies, the ability to work, fiscal stability, and increased longevity—all of which aging men would need if they were going to retain their notions of manhood during the depression.

Mirra Komarovsky's conclusion that men were "bewildered" and "humiliated" because of chronic unemployment led her, and other observers, to overlook the scope of aging working men's busy efforts to secure paths to manhood. In CIO unions, Forty Plus Clubs, the Works Progress Administration, and the consumer marketplace, older men sought ways to retain identities as workers and earners amidst the economic collapse, while Social Security and even private pension schemes promised to honor what men had tried to build during their working years: the accumulation of assets that allowed men to retain steady identities as earners and providers in later life. Older workers, union activists, policy makers, and advertisers challenged the idea that joblessness meant the end of manhood, and in the process, they often blurred the boundaries between employment and joblessness by stressing other busy endeavors. During the Great Depression, "work" came to mean something more broadly defined than employment.

Chapter 4 explores men's uncertainties about the new cultural and economic institution of retirement during the 1940s and 1950s. Mandatory postwar retirement policies generally required men to retire at age sixty-five to a pension; however, many did not want to retire since expanding employment opportunities, higher earnings, and a heightened cultural emphasis on attaining middle-class status demanded that males, young and old, become productive and successful middle-class men. As the culture of modern retirement took shape during the 1940s and 1950s, observers and retirees would import ideals of youth, affluence, and productivity into a time of life greatly characterized by aging bodies and the end of employment.

NOTES

1. Mirra Komarovsky, *The Unemployed Man and His Family—The Effect of Unemployment Upon the Status of the Man in Fifty-Nine Families* (1940; repr., New York: Octagon Books, 1973), 74. For discussions of the "crisis" of masculinity during the 1930s, see Elizabeth Faue, *Community of Suffering and Struggle: Women, Men, and the Labor Movement in Minneapolis, 1915–1945* (Chapel Hill: University of North Carolina Press, 1991), 191; Lizabeth Cohen, *Making a New Deal: Industrial Workers in Chicago, 1919–1939* (New York: Cambridge University Press, 1990), 246–249; and Lois Scharf, *To Work and To Wed: Female Employment, Feminism, and the Great Depression* (Westport, CT: Greenwood Press, 1980).

2. Alice Kessler-Harris, *Out to Work: A History of Wage-Earning Women in the United States* (New York: Oxford University Press, 1982), 250–272; Michael Kimmel, *Manhood in America: A Cultural History* (New York: Free Press, 1996), 191–221; George Chauncey, *Gay New York: Gender, Urban Culture, and the Making of the Gay Male World, 1890–1940* (New York: Free Press, 1994), 331, 334; Miriam Forman-Brunell, *Babysitter: An American History* (New York: New York University Press, 2009), 8.

3. Komarovsky, *Unemployed Man*, 74; William Serrin, *Homestead: The Glory and Tragedy of an American Steel Town* (New York: Times Books, 1992), esp. 392–398.

4. E. Wight Bakke, *The Unemployed Worker: A Study of the Task of Making a Living without a Job* (New Haven: Yale University Press, 1940), 80.

5. Frances Perkins, *The Roosevelt I Knew* (New York: Viking Press, 1946), 282–283.

6. See Alice Kessler-Harris, "Providers: Gender Ideology in the 1930s," in *Women's America: Refocusing the Past*, ed. Linda K. Kerber and Jane Sherron De Hart, 5th edition (New York: Oxford University Press, 2000), 420; idem, *Out To Work*, 250; and Kimmel, *Manhood in America*, 193.

7. Cohen, *Making a New Deal*, 217.

8. Kimmel, *Manhood in America*, 193.

9. Komarovsky, *Unemployed Man*, 119.

10. "Townsend Campaign Worth a Million," *People's Press*, 4 April 1936, 11. The *People's Press* was a publication of the United Electrical Workers (UE).

11. Despite inequalities along the lines of race, age, and gender, many Americans nonetheless favored government intervention in the economy during the interwar period. In the US, the literatures that relate to the shift towards the welfare state are voluminous. By way of an introduction to the field, see Jill Quadagno, *The Transformation of Old Age Security: Class and Politics in the American Welfare State* (Chicago: University of Chicago Press, 1988); Theda Skocpol, *Protecting Soldiers and Mothers: The Political Origins of Social Policy in the United States* (Cambridge, MA: Belknap Press, 1992); and Ann Shola Orloff, *The Politics of Pensions: A Comparative Analysis of Britain, Canada, and the United States, 1880–1940* (Madison: University of Wisconsin Press, 1994). See also additional citations in note 12.

12. On the relationships between gender ideology and the welfare state during the 1930s, see Linda Gordon, "Social Insurance and Public Assistance: The Influence of Gender in Welfare Thought in the United States, 1880–1945," *American Historical Review*, 97:1 (1992): esp. 19–22, 47–50; Gwendolyn Mink, *The Wages of Motherhood: Inequality in the Welfare State, 1917–1942* (Ithaca: Cornell University Press, 1995); Linda Gordon, *Pitied But Not Entitled: Single Mothers and the History of Welfare, 1890–1935* (New York: Free Press, 1994); Suzanne Mettler, *Dividing Citizens: Gender and Federalism in New Deal Public Policy* (Ithaca: Cornell University Press, 1998); and Alice Kessler-Harris, *In Pursuit of Equity: Women, Men, and the Quest for Economic Citizenship in 20th-Century America* (New York: Oxford University Press, 2001).

13. "Presidential Statement Upon Signing the Social Security Act, 14 August 1935," in *The Public Papers and Addresses of Franklin D. Roosevelt, with a Special Introduction and Explanatory Notes by President Roosevelt: Volume IV: The Court Disapproves, 1935* (1938; repr., New York: Random House, 1969), 324.

14. John G. Winant, "Social Security Begins," *Survey Graphic*, January 1937, 7. Similar themes can be found in Ewan Clague, "Social Work and Social Security," *Survey*, January 1937, 5–6; and Delbert Clarke, "Era of Social Security Begins for the Worker," *New York Times*, 31 December 1939, 50.

15. On the history of the Townsend Movement, see Edwin Amenta, *When Movements Matter: The Townsend Plan and the Rise of Social Security* (Princeton: Princeton University Press, 2006); and Steven B. Berg, "The Gray Crusade: The Townsend Movement, Old Age Politics, and the Development of Social Security" (PhD diss., University of Wisconsin-Madison, 1999).

16. "Crusader Comment," *Modern Crusader*, 26 October 1934, 12.

17. Herbert Harris, "Dr. Townsend's Marching Soldiers," *Reader's Digest*, April 1936, 95–96; "Townsend Talks of His Plan and Hopes," *New York Times Magazine*, 29 December 1935, 3.

18. Duncan Aikman, "Townsendism," *New York Times Magazine*, 8 March 1936, 25.

19. Russell Porter, "Looking For Utopia Along the Townsend Trail," *New York Times Magazine*, 5 February 1939, 13.

20. Berg, "Gray Crusade," 240.

21. Kessler-Harris, *In Pursuit of Equity*, 85.

22. Ibid., 130.

23. Social Security Board, "Foreword: Security for a People," in *First Annual Report of the Social Security Board* (Washington, DC: Government Printing Office, 1937), v, vi.

24. Ibid., vi.

25. "More Security For Old People," *American Federationist*, January 1938, 64–71.

26. JFC, Report of Fairview Lodge No. 40, Ohio, *Amalgamated Journal*, 14 December 1933, 11.

27. George Smith, Report of Canonsburg Lodge No. 79, PA, *Amalgamated Journal*, 17 December 1936, 20.

28. Porter, "Looking For Utopia," 13.

29. Perkins, *Roosevelt I Knew*, 293.

30. Henry E. Jackson, "Our New Social Security Act," *Review of Reviews*, October 1935, 26.

31. "Characteristics of Recipients of Old-Age Assistance," *Monthly Labor Review*, July 1939, 74.

32. See "Surveys, 1938–1939," *Public Opinion Quarterly*, October 1939, 592; and "Surveys, 1935–1938," *Public Opinion Quarterly*, July 1938, 382.

33. Federal Security Agency, *Fourth Annual Report of the Social Security Board* (Washington, DC: Government Printing Office, 1940), 24; Jill S. Quadagno, "Welfare Capitalism and the Social Security Act of 1935," *American Sociological Review* 49:5 (1984): 634. On racial inequalities in the administration of Social Security in the Jim Crow South, see Quadagno, *Transformation of Old Age Security*, 127–137.

34. Federal Security Agency, *Fourth Annual Report of the Social Security Board*, 24.

35. Jackson, "Our New Social Security Act," 26.

36. Ibid.

37. John J. Corson, "Advances in Old Age Security," *Survey Midmonthly*, September 1939, 268.

38. Luther A. Huston, "Federal Age Pensions Get Under Way," *New York Times*, 19 November 1939, E7.

39. Ibid.

40. Social Security Online, "History," http://www.ssa.gov/history/lifeexpect.html (accessed 8 July 2008).

134 Chapter Three

Chapter Three

Chapter Three

Chapter Three

41. Huston, "Federal Age Pensions," E7.

42. Perkins, *Roosevelt I Knew*, 292.

43. Ibid.

44. "Half On WPA Rolls in City Over 40 Years Old," *New York Times*, 16 February 1939, 3; Benjamin Colby, "Jobless Over 45 Handicapped," *New York Times*, 6 December 1936, 12; Blumberg, *The New Deal and the Unemployed*, 137; David M. Kennedy, *Freedom From Fear: The American People in Depression and War, 1929–1945* (New York: Oxford University Press, 1999), 252.

45. "WPA Job Duration Averaged at a Year," *New York Times*, 6 May 1939, 10.

46. Massachusetts study quoted in W. Andrew Achenbaum, *Old Age in the New Land: The American Experience since 1790* (Baltimore: Johns Hopkins University Press, 1978), 128; Philadelphia study quoted in Abraham Epstein, *Insecurity: A Challenge to America*, introduction by Frances Perkins (New York: Harrison Smith and Robert Haas, 1933), 495; Detroit statistics are found in James J. Lorence, *Organizing the Unemployed: Community and Union Activists in the Industrial Heartland* (Albany: State University of New York Press, 1996), 6. See also Robert S. Lynd and Helen Merrell Lynd, *Middletown in Transition: A Study in Cultural Conflicts* (New York: Harcourt, Brace and Company, 1937), 52.

47. "Age Limits on Employment by American Manufacturers," *Monthly Labor Review*, May 1929, 1024; "Employment of the Older Worker," *Monthly Labor Review*, March 1930, 542–543; Wolman and Peck, "Labor Groups," 811; Murray Webb Latimer, *Industrial Pensions Systems in the United States and Canada* (New York: Industrial Relations Counselors, 1932), 800. See also Lynd and Lynd, *Middletown in Transition*, 52.

48. Lorena Hickok to Harry L. Hopkins, 17 April 1934, in *One Third of A Nation: Lorena Hickok Reports on the Great Depression*, ed. Richard Lowitt and Maurine Beasley (Urbana: University of Illinois Press, 1981), 227, 233. All capitals in original. Cohen, *Making a New Deal*, 246.

49. Kennedy, *Freedom From Fear*, 165.

50. Louis Stark, "Find Many on WPA Unfit for Jobs," *New York Times*, 25 December 1936, 4.

51. "Best Workers of WPA Average 47 in Age," *New York Times*, 8 November 1937, 1.

52. "Perkins Asks Work for Those Over 45," *New York Times*, 7 September 1937, 2.

53. A tak payer [sic] to Harry L. Hopkins, 12 March 1936, in *Down and Out in the Great Depression: Letters from the Forgotten Man*, ed. Robert S. McElvaine (Chapel Hill: University of North Carolina Press, 1983), 187–188.

54. William Kirchner, letter to the editor, *People's Press*, 6 March 1937, 6.

55. See William Graebner, *A History of Retirement: The Meaning and Function of an American Institution, 1885–1978* (New Haven: Yale University Press, 1984); as well as Achenbaum, *Old Age in the New Land*, 95–102; and Kessler-Harris, *In Pursuit of Equity*, 117–118.

56. Waldemar Kaempffert, "The Man Over 40," *New York Times*, 6 March 1938, 109.

57. Barbara Ehrenreich, *Bait and Switch: The (Futile) Pursuit of the American Dream* (New York: Owl Books, 2005), 45.

58. Ray Giles, "Hired After Forty," *Reader's Digest*, December 1938, 2–3.

59. Giles, "Hired After Forty," 2; Roger W. Babson, "The Cooperative Spirit," *Washington Post*, 20 May 1940, 19.

60. Clark Davis, *Company Men: White-Collar Life and Corporate Cultures in Los Angeles, 1892–1941* (Baltimore: Johns Hopkins University Press, 1004), 199.

61. Tell T. White to Franklin D. Roosevelt, 9 September 1936, in *The People and the President: America's Conversation with FDR*, ed. Lawrence W. Levine and Cornelia R. Levine (Boston: Beacon Press, 2002), 156; James M. Mead, "Our Older People," *Vital Speeches of the Day*, 1 March 1938, 319, 320.

62. Davis, *Company Men*, 199.

63. Ibid.

64. Ray Giles, "Men Over Forty Preferred," *Reader's Digest*, March 1938, 97–100; "Forty Plus Clubs," *Monthly Labor Review*, April 1940, 804; "Urge Jobs for Men Over 40," *Business Week*, 16 July 1938, 24.

65. "Forty Plus Clubs," 805–806; "Jobless Over 40 Organize A Club," *New York Times*, 20 January 1939, 32.

66. Timothy Turner, "For Men Above Forty," *Los Angeles Times*, 11 February 1940, 15; Giles, "Hired After Forty," 4.

67. "Dale Carnegie Says," *Washington Post*, 19 March 1939, 2.

68. Giles, "Hired After Forty," 2.

69. Ibid.

70. Lucien Dix, "Forty-Plus and Still Useful," *New York Times*, 28 March 1941, 22.

71. Ibid.

72. "Dale Carnegie Says," 2.

73. Giles, "Hired After Forty," 3–4.

74. Ibid., 4.

75. Turner, "For Men Above Forty," 15.

76. Giles, "Hired After Forty," 4.

77. Turner, "For Men Above Forty," 15.

78. See Sharon Hartman Strom, *Beyond the Typewriter: Gender, Class, and the Origins of Modern American Office Work, 1900–1930* (Urbana: University of Illinois Press, 1992); and Angel Kwolek-Folland, *Engendering Business: Men and Women in the Corporate Office, 1870–1930* (Baltimore: Johns Hopkins University Press, 1994).

79. Turner, "For Men Above Forty," 15.

80. See Angel Kwolek-Folland, "Gender, Self, and Work in the Life Insurance Industry, 1880–1930," in *Work Engendered: Toward a New History of American Labor*, ed. Ava Baron (Ithaca: Cornell University Press, 1990), 184.

81. Turner, "For Men Above Forty," 15.

82. See Linda Gordon, "Dorothea Lange: The Photographer as Agricultural Sociologist," *Journal of American History* 93:3 (2006): 711–712.

83. "Forty Plus Clubs," 805; "Job Club Rejoices at Low Membership," *New York Times*, 26 January 1941, 40; "Recent Activities of New York Forty Plus Club,"

Monthly Labor Review, September 1940, 623; "Forty-Plus Gets Many Jobs," *Los Angeles Times*, 14 August 1939, 3.

84. "Fathers and Sons Engage in Job War," *New York Times*, 5 June 1938, 43; Turner, "For Men Above Forty," 15.

85. Jill Andresky Fraser, *White-Collar Sweatshop: The Deterioration of Work and Its Rewards in Corporate America* (New York: WW Norton & Company, 2001), 98–103. However, long-term security in white-collar work would once again diminish during the 1980s and 1990s. As Fraser points out, firms curtailed executive job security, creating a new white-collar employment pattern characterized by job impermanence, "downsizing," declining benefits, and decreasing salaries (Fraser, *White-Collar Sweatshop*, 9).

86. Ronald Edsforth and Robert Asher, with Raymond Boryczka, "The Speedup: The Focal Point of Workers' Grievances, 1919–1941," in *Autowork*, ed. Robert Asher and Ronald Edsforth, with Stephen Merlino (Albany: State University of New York Press, 1995), 83.

87. Bakke, *Unemployed Worker*, 79.

88. "Strikers Give Explanations of Their Actions," *Detroit News*, 29 January 1933, 2; "Crisis Comes Today In Ford Shut-Down," *New York Times*, 30 January 1933, 3.

89. Kenneth B. West, "'On the Line': Rank and File Reminiscences of Working Conditions and the General Motors Sit-Down Strike of 1936–37," *Michigan Historical Review* 12 (1986): 70.

90. Stanley B. Mathewson, *Restriction of Output Among Unorganized Workers* (New York: Viking Press, 1931), 15–16.

91. J. Raymond Walsh, *CIO: Industrial Unionism in Action* (New York: WW Norton & Company, 1937), 106; Benjamin Stolberg, *The Story of the CIO* (New York: Viking Press, 1938), 156; Irving Howe and BJ Widick, *The UAW and Walter Reuther* (New York: Random House, 1949), 23, 29, 31; Edward Levinson, *Labor on the March* (New York: Harper, 1938), 150. See also Nat Weinberg, interview by Jack W. Skeels, 20 March 1963 and 30 April 1963, transcript, 9, Reuther Library; and Morris Field, "Seniority, Major Item in Auto Contracts," *United Automobile Worker*, 26 February 1938, 6.

92. "Duquesne's Employees Hear Truth," *People's Press*, 31 October 1936, 5.

93. See Nelson Lichtenstein, *State of the Union: A Century of American Labor* (Princeton: Princeton University Press, 2002), 30–38.

94. Ibid., 36–38.

95. Ibid., 44–45.

96. Ibid., 48.

97. Ibid., 48–53.

98. "Analysis of Strikes in 1938," *Monthly Labor Review*, May 1939, 1129–1130.

99. See "Sit Down Bakery Strikers Quit Plant on Court Order," *Los Angeles Times*, 25 February 1937, 7; "Hotel Workers Win Pay Boost in Short Strike," *Washington Post*, 13 March 1937, 25; "First Sit Down Strike in Hawaii," *New York Times*, 31 March 1937, 9; "'Lovely Time' Reported in De Luxe Strike," *Washington Post*, 15 March 1937, 3; and "Milwaukee Has a Record 50 Strikes in 1937," *Chicago Daily Tribune*, 29 June 1937, 13.

100. On gender and labor militancy during the 1930s, see Faue, *Community of Suffering and Struggle*, 66–99.

101. Labor historians' interest in seniority has been sporadic. For valuable discussions of seniority, see David Montgomery and Ronald Schatz, "Facing Layoffs," in *Workers' Control in America: Studies in the History of Work, Technology, and Labor Struggles* (New York: Cambridge University Press, 1979), 140–143; Ruth Milkman, *Gender at Work: The Dynamics of Job Segregation by Sex during World War II* (Urbana: University of Illinois Press, 1987); Nancy Gabin, *Feminism in the Labor Movement: Women and the Auto Workers, 1935–1975* (Ithaca: Cornell University Press, 1990); Robert J. Norrell, "Caste in Steel: Jim Crow Careers in Birmingham, Alabama," *Journal of American History* 73:3 (1986): 675; Eric Arnesen, "'Like Banquo's Ghost, It Will Not Down': The Race Question and the American Railroad Brotherhoods, 1880–1920," *American Historical Review* 99:5 (1994): 1601; Thomas Sugrue, *The Origins of the Urban Crisis: Race and Inequality in Postwar Detroit* (Princeton: Princeton University Press, 1995), 103–104; Cohen, *Making a New Deal*, 320–321; Fine, *The Automobile Under the Blue Eagle: Labor, Management, and the Automobile Manufacturing Code* (Ann Arbor: University of Michigan Press, 1963), 222, 250–258; Nelson Lichtenstein, "Conflict Over Workers' Control: The Automobile Industry in World War II," in *Working-Class America: Essays on Labor, Community, and American Society*, ed. Michael H. Frisch and Daniel J. Walkowitz (Urbana: University of Illinois Press, 1983), 285–286.

102. Clinton S. Golden and Harold J. Ruttenberg, *The Dynamics of Industrial Democracy* (New York: Harper & Brothers Publishers, 1942), 129.

103. Michael Skertic, Report of Star of Bethlehem Lodge No. 182, PA, *Amalgamated Journal*, 6 September 1934, 17.

104. Fred Caswell, Report of Altoona Lodge No. 104, PA, *Amalgamated Journal*, 2 April 1931, 15.

105. Harold J. Ruttenberg, "The Big Morgue," *Survey Graphic*, April 1939, 267.

106. Golden and Ruttenberg, *Dynamics of Industrial Democracy*, 127, 121.

107. Kenneth Casebeer, "Aliquippa: The Company Town and Contested Power in the Construction of Law," *Buffalo Law Review* 43:3 (1995): 617–687.

108. Golden and Ruttenberg, *Dynamics of Industrial Democracy*, 121.

109. "Union Agrees to Not Sit Strike in New Contract," *Chicago Daily Tribune*, 7 October 1937, 29.

110. "Once . . . Watches and Orchids Now . . . Speed-up & Layoffs," union newspaper clipping, Packard Local 190, 14 June 1939, Box 1, Folder "Age and Employment," Joe Brown Papers (hereafter Brown Papers, Walter P. Reuther Library, Wayne State University (hereafter Reuther Library); "Packard Problem No. 1: Too Old at Forty?" union newspaper clipping, Packard Local 190, 14 June 1939, Box 1, Folder "Age and Employment," Brown Papers, Reuther Library.

111. A survey of UAW newspapers and oral histories at the Walter P. Reuther Library at Wayne State University in Detroit highlights the ongoing importance of seniority principles in the union's organizational culture. See Frank Marquart, "Plain Talk," *Voice of Local 212*, 28 March 1947, 2; "All AC Workers Should Belong to the UAW-CIO," *AC Sparkler*, 3 July 1947, 7; "General Motors, Chrysler, Briggs

Workers Observe 20th Anniversary of Sitdown Strikes," *United Automobile Worker,* March 1957, 2. See also Elmer Yenney, interview by Jack W. Skeels, 27 April 1961, transcript, 23, Reuther Library; JA Beni, interview by Jack W. Skeels, 4 March 1963, transcript, 5, Reuther Library.

112. "Seniority Provisions in Collective Agreements," *Monthly Labor Review,* December 1938, 1250.

113. "Seniority," *New York Times,* 8 September 1938, 22.

114. Louis Stark, "Events Daze Auto Workers," *New York Times,* 6 August 1939, E7.

115. Ibid.

116. The term "feudal" is used in Ibid.

117. Fred W. Cottrell, "The Seniority Curse," *Personnel Journal,* October 1939, 177–180; see also Edward S. Cowdrick, "The Riddle of Employee Seniority," *Nation's Business,* September 1939, 25.

118. Harry A. Millis and Royal E. Montgomery, *Organized Labor* (New York: McGraw-Hill Book Company, 1945), 458.

119. Frederick H. Harbison, "Seniority in Mass-Production Industries," *Journal of Political Economy* 48:6 (1940): 859, 852.

120. On consumer politics during the 1930s, see Meg Jacobs, *Pocketbook Politics: Economic Citizenship in Twentieth-Century America* (Princeton: Princeton University Press, 2005); Lizabeth Cohen, *A Consumer's Republic: The Politics of Mass Consumption in Postwar America* (New York: Vintage Books, 2003), esp. 18–61; and Lawrence B. Glickman, "The Strike in the Temple of Consumption: Consumer Activism and Twentieth-Century American Political Culture," *Journal of American History* 88 (2001): 99–128.

121. For analyses of aging and medical advice during the 1910s and 1920s, see Laura Davidow Hirshbein, "The Transformation of Old Age: Expertise, Gender, and National Identity, 1900–1950" (PhD diss., Johns Hopkins University, 2000), ch. 1–2. For analyses of gender meanings in ads for consumer products for older men and women in the present, see Toni Calasanti, "Bodacious Berry, Potency Wood and the Aging Monster: Gender and Age Relations in Anti-Aging Ads," *Social Forces* 86:1 (2007): 335–355.

122. Komarovsky, *Unemployed Man,* 133.

123. Laurence E. Hines, "Heart Disease After Middle Age," *Hygeia,* August 1935, 711–712.

124. "Following Through . . . After Fifty," *Hygeia,* July 1937, 579; "After Fifty the Hills Get Higher," *Hygeia,* May 1937, 387; "To Be Continued . . . After Fifty?" *Hygeia,* November 1937, 964; "And Life Can Begin *Again* at Fifty," *Hygeia,* December 1937, 1058.

125. Samuel Morrison, "Does Illness Begin at Forty?" *Hygeia,* January 1936, 7.

126. John R. Hamilton, "Forty—Looking Forward," *Hygeia,* August 1933, 734, 684.

127. "To A Man Who Looks Older Than He Is," *Nation's Business,* May 1937, 113.

128. "Have You Been Killing Yourself the Last 5 Years?" *Newsweek,* 22 September 1934, 5. On the theme of "masculine self-control" during the early twentieth

century, see James Gilbert, *Men in the Middle: Searching for Masculinity in the 1950s* (Chicago: University of Chicago Press, 2005), 26–27; as well as John F. Kasson, *Houdini, Tarzan, and the Perfect Man: The White Male Body and the Challenge of Modernity in America* (New York: Hill & Wang, 2001).

129. "Have You Been Killing Yourself," 5; "If You KNEW You Were Dying," *Newsweek*, 13 October 1934, 31.

130. "Life Begins at 40," *New York Times Magazine*, 13 March 1938, 16.

131. Life Begins at 40," *New York Times Magazine*, 6 March 1938, 20. See also "Life Begins at 40," *New York Times Magazine*, 20 March 1938, 16.

132. Hamilton, "Forty," 734.

133. "After 40," *Literary Digest*, 27 March 1937, 26, 27.

134. For an excellent overview of private insurance systems before the New Deal, with a focus on life insurance, see Klein, *For All These Rights*, 16–52.

135. In the *New York Times Magazine*, Phoenix Mutual published an ad alongside an article about the Townsend Movement. See *New York Times Magazine*, 8 March 1936, 25.

136. "How A Man of 40 Can Retire 15 Years from Today," *Newsweek*, 28 September 1935, 1.

137. "How a Man of 40 Can Retire In 15 Years," *Newsweek*, 26 September 1936, 1; "You Don't Have To Be Rich To Retire at 55 on $200 a Month," *Newsweek*, 2 November 1935, 1.

138. "I Earn $55 a Week. . . . And I'll Retire At 60 on $100 A Month," *Newsweek*, 21 September 1935, 1.

139. "Began at 40. . . Retired At 55," *Newsweek*, 24 October 1936, 1; "How A Man of 40 Can Retire 15 Years From Today," 1. Similar themes appeared in ads for other insurance companies. See, for example, John Hancock Mutual advertisement, *Newsweek*, 13 October 1934, 43.

140. "The Story of Three Men Who Wanted To Be Rich," *New York Times*, 12 March 1939, 123; see also "Quit Work at 55," *New York Times*, 16 February 1930, 91; "$200.00 A Month Reward," *New York Times*, 19 February 1933, 13; and "To the Man Who Wants To Be Worth $50,000 When He Retires," *New York Times*, 27 November 1938, 155.

141. "Phoenix Mutual Life Sets Record," *New York Times*, 27 January 1936, 30.

Chapter Four

Postwar Manhood and the Shock of Retirement

My legs trembled as I climbed into the car, and I drove home battered and bruised, physically half sick and emotionally stunned. When I got home, the house was empty. I collapsed on a bed and lay there, suffering.
This was retirement day.
This was it.
Now I was a retired man.

—Gifford R. Hart, retired white-collar worker, 1957[1]

When an unnamed company retired Gifford R. Hart, a long-time executive with the firm, he experienced powerful feelings of anxiety and dread. While he warmly appreciated the retirement ceremony that honored his service to the company, Hart lamented the end of the job he had valued for so long. After so many years spent at his desk, Hart drove home from work for the last time, now facing an uncertain future as a "retired man." Why did he worry about retirement? What was so alarming about this new (and increasingly common) phase of life? He was then in the throes of what scholars and writers of aging and retirement described as "retirement shock": Retirement from work created individual trauma that produced profound emotional despair, abrupt physical decline, and even death. Retirement threatened to utterly demolish male identity, the sense of manhood that he (and other men) had built up throughout the course of their working years. The aging men of the postwar years worried they might not be able to preserve their notions of identity and purpose as they transitioned from work into retirement. Hart worried to such an extent that he even needed to write a book about it. (Later generations would return to the theme of retirement shock in texts such as the film adaptation of Louis Begley's novel *About Schmidt*, which starred Oscar winners Jack Nicholson and Kathy Bates.[2])

While American men had weathered the Great Depression, won a global war against fascist tyranny, and proudly opposed Soviet expansionism, the postwar years ushered in a new era of anxiety about gender. Uneasiness about retirement rested at the center of postwar anxieties about masculinity, perhaps to a much greater degree than ambivalence about mass culture, mass consumerism, or the increased bureaucratization of American society.[3] As more and more men faced retirement at the age of sixty-five, they lamented their diminishing incomes, the end of familiar daily routines, the disruption of gender relations within marriage, the end of friendships with other men in the workplace, the onset of physical decline and death, and the loss of their socially valued status as workers, professionals, and breadwinners. World War II and the Cold War elevated the importance of service and usefulness as men's cardinal virtues, while increasing suburbanization, rising incomes, and expanding job opportunities made middle-class status a key prerequisite for postwar manhood. Men worked within a broader culture that put a heightened premium on useful service to the nation and the achievement of affluence. Postwar experts and retiring workers viewed retirement as an overriding threat to manhood, since core notions of manliness now depended on the maintenance of middle-class incomes and participation in the economically meaningful and productive activity of work.

In post-World War II discussions of the aging, retirement, and gender, the blue-collar working man largely disappeared from observers' and experts' writings, replaced with the now-ubiquitous figure of the retiring white-collar male professional. The cultural conversation about men and retirement during the 1940s and 1950s reflected, as well as reinforced, postwar notions of the United States as a generally affluent and upwardly mobile middle-class nation. When experts envisioned the retiring worker, they often assumed that white-collar office labor typified the work experiences of American men writ large. As we will see below, the self-proclaimed experts who wrote about men and retirement during the postwar years began with particular assumptions about retirees' anxieties, abilities, and assets. They imagined retiring men as professional men, struggling to transition away from meaningful careers into a presumably less-engaging and less-rewarding life of rocking chairs and park benches.

Widespread anxieties about retirement in postwar America ironically reinforced the connections between work and manhood in twentieth-century American culture. As experts, observers, and retiring men explored the uncertain terrain of the lengthening life span in postwar America, they concluded that, somehow, manhood's working foundations needed to be refashioned in the context of retirement. The new social and cultural institution of retirement became a crucial new site that truly gave rise to the idea of productive manhood in the postwar years. During the 1930s and early 1940s, Social Security and Forty Plus Clubs made it possible for aging men to envision masculinity in ways that did not depend on employment, but the social, cultural, and economic transformations of the postwar years ensured that work would now matter more than ever in working men's efforts to make sense of gender, self, and society.

This chapter details how the important connections between work and manhood intensified in postwar American culture, as evidenced by extensive conversations among retirees, intellectuals, and authors about work as the pathway to postwar success and status, the purported dangers of a life without work in old age and retirement, retiring men's deep ambivalence about their upcoming final days of work, and many men's struggles to put off retirement. As Gifford R. Hart's comment suggests, aging men did not want to exchange their desk chairs for rocking chairs.

SERVICE, USEFULNESS, AFFLUENCE: MANHOOD AFTER WORLD WAR II

There were several cultural, social, and political trends that surely contributed to Gifford R. Hart's unease about retirement and manhood. During the 1940s and 1950s, World War II, the Cold War, and expanding incomes and widening chances for upward mobility refocused how men in the United States thought about masculinity. In addition to economic reasons for working, numerous social and cultural pressures assumed great importance. World War II put a heavy emphasis on service and usefulness; American men were expected to serve the nation, subsuming individual ambitions to the war effort. The war also engendered massive economic recovery, pulling the United States out of the Great Depression. Now employed, men of the postwar era pursued seemingly attainable middle-class standards of living: suburban homes, two cars, modern kitchen appliances, and growing paychecks. The rise of the Cold War—the heated political and cultural tensions between the United States and the Soviet Union—redefined American political culture. "Real" men took a hard line against Communist expansion. In contrast, men who refused to stand tough against the Soviet Union were conveniently labeled "soft" on Communism and deemed unfit for political office. During the immediate postwar period, men needed to be, at once, good soldiers, productive workers, selfless team members, capable leaders, and successful providers of affluent middle-class lifestyles. With so much to take care of, pundits bemoaned men's unease: "What happened to the American male?"[4]

While various period writers and some historians have since argued that men became increasingly ambivalent about their jobs during the fifties, working and the workplace actually became more important to men as the core of manhood.[5] Some men believed that corporate employment transformed them into unoriginal and anonymous "organization men"; but work, as Gifford Hart suggested, allowed men to live up to new social and cultural imperatives and to escape from the perceived feminizing domesticity of the home. As discussions of retirement illustrated, men wanted to remain ensconced in the corporate boardroom, offices, and even the factory; they did not want to abandon these familiar touchstones of manhood. However, expanding mandatory retirement programs forced older men out. In an era where women seemed to wield too much influence through their ascribed status as domestic caregivers, and world affairs required men to be active in "public" matters, men wanted to remain on the job. Work gave married men a space where wives' influence did not reach and where corporate hierarchies subordinated women to men. Employment also yielded a sense of usefulness, made vital by World War II and the burgeoning Cold War. Finally, men remembered the "forgotten men" of the Great Depression. In the past, employment was unattainable; and as a result of postwar opportunity and prosperity, most men determined they would work as long as they could.

World War II sharpened the relationship between hard work and manliness. The revival of the US manufacturing economy during the war years threw open once again the doors to the factories and offices that had been largely silent during the depression decade, bringing in legions of workers and staffers. The war helped to reopen the factory and the office to aging workers, as many young men went off to war in the Pacific, North Africa, and Europe. Older Americans found new job opportunities.[6] But in addition to bolstering men's access to jobs and thus to male breadwinner status, the experience of global war emphasized the importance of team work and productive service to the nation. To be "men," males could not be idle individuals; real men had to be useful and beneficial team players. During the war, men faced a Herculean task: to defeat fascist aggression in two vast theaters of war. World War II made usefulness and national service the "template for postwar manhood."[7] When the war ended in August 1945, President Harry S. Truman rewarded men with a new mission: "We are faced with the greatest task we've ever been faced with [rebuilding war-torn Europe and Asia]. It is going to take the help of all of us to do it."[8] Americans' willingness to conform during the 1950s suggests how service and usefulness were made important by the exigencies of the war years. In *The Organization Man* (1956), a critique of postwar men's obsession with conformity, William Whyte, Jr., observed: "Man exists as a unit of society.

Of himself, he is isolated, meaningless; only as he collaborates with others does he become worth while, for by sublimating himself in the group, he helps produce a whole that is greater than the sum of its parts."[9] The underlying logic of postwar conformity, however, was the stuff of culture not rational equations. As psychologist Erich Fromm once wrote, and later quoted by David Riesman in his *The Lonely Crowd* (1950), "In order that any society may function well, its members must acquire the kind of character which makes them *want* to act in the way they *have* to act as members of the society . . . They have to *desire* what objectively is *necessary* for them to do. *Outer force* is replaced by *inner compulsion*, and by the particular kind of human energy which is channeled into character traits."[10]

Personal memories of the Great Depression also affirmed men's eagerness to work and earn in offices and factories. As a man in his sixties, Gifford R. Hart surely remembered the difficulties men faced during the 1930s; postwar men, especially older men, could recall the troubles they and others experienced during the "lean years" of the depression decade. Men viewed World War II as the beginning of a brighter economic future. The work of war ultimately paid off. In 1942, 101st Airborne Private Carwood Lipton looked forward to the personal and economic opportunities afforded by the army and the end of the depression. "The Depression was over," he noted. "I was beginning a new life that would change me profoundly."[11] The war also afforded new opportunities to New Yorker Robert Lekachman. He told the oral historian Studs Terkel that "The army provided me with my first steady job."[12] Men knew joblessness during the depression, and they wanted to leave those turbulent years behind. Some servicemen worried the end of the war would bring about a new depression in the economy, leading to more "ditch digging and bread lines" and "11 million apple salesmen" on American streets.[13] In truth, new opportunities abounded for men in the 1940s and 1950s. The 1944 GI Bill of Rights, for example, made it possible for 7.8 million US veterans to pursue college degrees and job skills training after the war, while 3.8 million veterans took advantage of low-interest GI Bill home loans; in addition, during the twenty year period after World War II, the US economy created over 20 million new blue- and white-collar jobs.[14] When he returned home from Europe after World War II, a wartime friend offered Major Richard Winters the job of personnel manager at his family's nitration works. By 1950, he was general manager of the factory. Carwood Lipton, who left the US Army as a lieutenant, also found employment opportunities after the war. When he returned home, he went to college and later found work in a glass manufacturing business. Eventually, he went on to become a major executive with the company.[15] With so many new opportunities to finally work and earn, post-depression men did not want to leave their jobs. Now more and than ever, a man who wanted a job could find and keep one, it seemed. Male breadwinner status seemed both achievable and sustainable in postwar America.

Despite increasing confidence among many Americans about the present and the future, the unfolding Cold War contributed to new anxieties about gender and sexuality in the years after World War II. During the late 1940s and 1950s, Americans worried about Communists and homosexuals as sources of effeminacy and subversion. Gender ideology of the 1950s mirrored the Cold War ideology of "containment,"[16] and the perceived pervasiveness of homosexuality led to new worries about the erosion of manhood. In response, politicians were quick to redraw the national and gender boundaries of the United States. For example, Republican Party politicians in Washington, DC, affirmed heterosexuality as the national sexual identity when Undersecretary of State John E. Puerifoy complained in 1950 that the State Department was staffed by a large population of homosexuals. Politicians called for investigations into the presence of gay men in government posts, demanding their prompt removal.[17] In 1950, Senator Joseph McCarthy characterized Democrats as sexual nonconformists: "Communists and queers" in the Truman Administration "lost" China; "prancing mimics of the Moscow party line" worked for the State Department; and officials such as Dean Acheson and UN Ambassador-at-Large Phillip Jessup were "dilettante diplomats" who "cringed" before the Soviet colossus.[18]

Americans worried that manhood was ebbing under geopolitical and sexual forces. Were men tough enough to handle the Communist threat, especially since they lived in suburbs and, as Kinsey suggested, dabbled in homosexuality?[19] During the early years of the Cold War, American political culture took a "hard" turn. "Peace," Truman asserted, "has to be built on power."[20] In this era of anxiety about gender and sexuality, as reflected in Cold War rhetoric, work provided men with an established way to prove their manliness.

Expanding postwar mass consumption and increasing paychecks reorganized masculinity around middle-class standards of attainment. To be "men" after World War II, males needed to work in order to provide the many accoutrements of suburban comfort. While ideals about masculinity before World War II emphasized work as a pathway to breadwinning and family stability, postwar masculinity reflected newfound desires for upward mobility—now apparently within reach. Working-class men expected that unions and employers would offer them high wages and job stability in exchange for "peace" on the shop floors of industry. The 1950 "Treaty of Detroit," for instance, the United Automobile Workers' (UAW) contract with General Motors, symbolized a bargain between labor and management: amiable labor relations in exchange for high wages, generous benefits, and middle-class standards of living.[21] As editors of *Fortune* magazine remarked, the unions of the Congress of Industrial Organizations helped blue-collar working men ("to an amazing degree") become "middle-class member[s] of a middle-class society."[22] To be men in the postwar years, males also needed to establish new suburban roots. "My next step," an auto industry welder noted in the 1950s, "is a nice little modern house of my own. That's what I mean by . . . getting ahead."[23] Higher wages meant additional discretionary income, which helped working people enjoy, to a much greater degree, the expanding postwar consumer economy. The "embourgeoisment" of the working class (and American culture writ large) reinforced the importance of work for men.[24] During the 1950s, roughly 60 percent of families earned a "middle-class" income ($3,000–$10,000 annually). During the 1920s, in contrast, only 31 percent earned so much.[25] There were powerful cultural and economic incentives for men to continue working; retirement to a fixed, and reduced, income would not suffice as a foundation of manhood. While a working man could retire on a pension during the 1920s and not view the pension as a marker of diminished manhood, men of the postwar years worried that fixed and reduced incomes could undermine their status in a society that now guaranteed so much to men who could work.

Men could not stop working in their later years—even if they wanted to. In the boardrooms of the white-collar office, male executives complained that the women at home pushed them too hard to work and succeed, demanding more and more of the good life: cars, homes, appliances. "More and more wives," journalist J. Robert Moskin argued, "identify economic achievement with masculinity . . . and men are unsexed by failure."[26] The renewed emphasis on domesticity for women after World War II, coupled with the household management and technological overtones of housework, made the home a space where women wielded and voiced great influence; women expertly cooked, cleaned, shopped, cared for children, and even fixed household gadgets. Men worried that women wielded too much power in this space, controlling a range of issues: including sexual intercourse and consumption patterns.[27] If that was the case, men need to continue working in order to retain their status as income providers.

The widening of the American middle-class after the Second World War and culture producers' insistence that the postwar United States was a middle- and not working-class nation greatly contributed to the new white-collar/ middle-class overtones in discussions of retirement. In *Fortune* magazine during the late 1940s, writers trumpeted, as economist Michael Zweig noted, "the arrival of middle-class America and the end of the working class."[28] Writing in the *Atlantic Monthly*, writer Herbert Gold claimed in 1957: "Now there are no workers left in America; we are almost all middle class as to income and expectations."[29] Retirement observers readily drew upon, as well as reinforced, middle-class cultural overtones in their analyses of manhood in later life. Thus, the making of a middle-class retirement culture around the figure of the male white-collar worker would closely dovetail the broader reworking of American culture around the figures and symbols of middle-class standards of living and white-collar work.[30] Experts characteristically now envisioned the older man as a white-collar and middle-class, no longer blue-collar working-class, man. During the interwar period, discussions of aging, men, and work hinged on older working-class men's struggles with the economic foundations of manhood, systematically denied them by employer discrimination and assembly line speedups. These earlier discourses hinged on a stern social critique of class inequalities and ageism that had plagued working men as they reached later life. In the post-World War II period, however, discussions of men and manhood pointed to a new preoccupation with upper-class executives and white-collar professionals as representative men in a predominantly middle-class culture. Experts retreated from discussions of older working-class men in the factory; they now focused on the retiring professional—who worried more about personal fulfillment, lifestyle choices, and the preservation of an affluent standard of living than the injustices of age discrimination and old-age poverty. Discussions of manhood and retirement began with the assumption that most men were financially stable, and they tended to focus on individuals' emotions and anxieties, building on the growing influence of popular psychology.[31] Postwar intellectuals largely ignored class inequalities in their writings and proclamations about age, retirement, and gender.

Another reason why middle-class overtones pervaded discussions of retirement after World War II was the shifting career interests and the deaths of key authors and activists. Authors of the interwar period who once focused on aging working-class men or downwardly mobile middle-class men had either died or moved on to other subjects in the postwar years. Most significantly, Isaac Max Rubinow and Abraham Epstein, two of the most prominent old age pension advocates and commentators on older working-class men's struggles, passed away in 1936 and 1942 respectively. At the time of his death of pneumonia in 1942, Epstein, who was only fifty years old, was teaching courses on social insurance at both New York University and Brooklyn College. He also served as a consulting economist with the Social Security Board. Former ironworker, Secretary of Labor, and United States Senator James J. Davis died after a long struggle with a kidney ailment in 1947.[32] Ray Giles, who once wrote articles about jobless professionals and Forty Plus Clubs during the Great Depression, had lost interest in older men's organizing efforts by the time he wrote *How to Retire—and Enjoy It* in 1949: a lifestyle advice book for retiring white-collar professionals. He was no longer concerned with

economic justice for aging men; he now focused on leisure opportunities that
had to be considered and planned for before a (successful) man retired from a
business career.[33] A loss of interest in the blue-collar working-class was very
noticeable in the postwar retirement literature.

By the late 1940s and early 1950s, a major change had occurred in the
ways authors wrote about aging men and retirement. A new generation of
intellectuals and self-proclaimed experts (such as Gifford R. Hart and others)
began to move conversations about men's worries about gender in later life
from the factory and the poorhouse to the affluent suburb, the white-collar
office, and the country club golf course. Now more than ever, employment
mattered deeply as the basic way for men like Gifford Hart to secure manhood, even as they aged. Employment allowed men to work toward financial
rewards and social ambitions, allowing them to secure middle-class status
and affluence in the booming post-World War II economy. The workplace
also provided a crucial site that helped men to prove their productive worth in
an era that valued service, team work among men, and usefulness. Lastly, the
pursuit of postwar manhood promised to bring men away from the feminized
space of the home, a space too closely associated with women, leisure, and
the absence of paid employment in this era of expanding suburban affluence.
The sociologists Eugene A. Friedmann and Robert J. Havighurst argued that
men worked because they wanted to very much prove they were active and
productive. Work constituted "a purposeful activity," they remarked, "which
is expected of . . . adult males in our society."[34] As other scholars noted at a
conference on aging during the early 1950s, work

> is the symbol of worth, success, and achievement. It confers status and prestige
> on the worker which he can acquire in no other way. It is the evidence of his
> acceptance by and contribution to society, and the source of most of his mean-
> ingful social contacts.[35]

In the years after World War II, men embraced an intensifying culture of in-
dustriousness and hard work enshrined in a "strong Puritan tradition" and the
Protestant work ethic.[36] Work allowed men to prove their mettle in a new and
changing culture, just as the ruggedness of the newness of the frontier once
challenged earlier generations of men. Thus, retirement from work seemed
to undermine manhood in a productive postwar America. "The lack of self-
maintaining work in old age," scholars noted, "is a symbol of failure."[37]

DEFINING RETIREMENT

Gifford R. Hart was very familiar with retirement writers' warnings about
the difficult transition from work to retirement, citing his knowledge of "the

literature of retirement" in his 1957 memoir and advice book.[38] During the 1940s and 1950s, experts in sociology and gerontology and popular magazine writers gave a lengthy list of potential dangers that lied in wait for men in old age. "Retirement shock," the loss of sexual ability, sudden illness, social isolation, gender inversion within the home, and declining living standards, for example, were all cited as problems that retiring men could expect. When Hart returned home from work for the last time and collapsed on his bed in a nervous heap, he was certainly aware of experts' warnings that retirement seemed to signify of the end of manhood.

Retirement was a new concept during the 1940s and 1950s.[39] Before Social Security, most men remained active in the labor market until they were prevented from doing so by ill-health, injuries, hiring age limits, firings, institutionalization, or death; men usually did not "retire." Beginning in the 1940s, however, Americans expected men to stop working in their later years, presumably to live quietly and humbly on small pensions and savings. As the Townsend Movement's logo once proclaimed during the 1930s, "Youth for work. Age for leisure."[40] On the economic foundations of Social Security and an expanding postwar system of company pensions, more and more men did retire during the 1940s and 1950s. In 1950, 45.8 percent of men over 65 held jobs; by 1955, the number had declined to 39.6 percent; in 1960, it was 33.1 percent.[41] Some men actually wanted to retire, but many more worried about the potential impact of the new social and cultural institution of retirement on their personal and financial well-being. Most men did not decide when they left their jobs; in many cases, company policies forced men out of work or prevented them from finding new full–time employment. As men continued to live longer, retirement became a common and enduring part of the life cycle: by the 1950s, men could very well live into their 70s and 80s. Despite the growing regularity of retirement, experts in gerontology and sociology and advice authors worried that retirement was a danger to men—especially since work was the bedrock of masculinity.

What exactly did "retirement" mean? How could retirement jeopardize manhood if Social Security and company pensions had become more and more available in postwar society? During the 1940s and 1950s, the term "retirement" described the withdrawal of a man from his previous full-time occupation due to age.[42] Three factors led to retirement: (1) company policies that required men to leave work at a certain age; (2) disability or illness that made it no longer possible to work; and/or (3) an individual's willingness to retire and the financial ability to do so. For men, retirement meant "old age," which they equated with sickness, isolation, the loss of prestige and status, vulnerability, sexual failure, and death.

Men understood retirement to mean "disengagement" from society. As company retirement policies more and more stipulated during the 1940s and

1950s, employers expected the older men in their service (and those women who worked) to, in essence, withdraw from their usual full-time employments and thus from the core of their daily lives. Sociologists and gerontologists described this as "disengagement theory" during the 1950s and 1960s. As men aged, the ties between older persons and society's institutions would be severed. Many older men absolutely hated the idea that retirement meant "disengagement." Disengagement theory was a thorny problem for retirees because it seemed to disregard the "public" and "private" components of postwar gender identities and identity. Working away from the home for wages and salaries now defined masculinity more than ever in post-World War II America, and by working, men believed they were meaningfully "engaged" with society. If retirement meant disengagement and a permanent retreat into the home's domesticity, then men wanted no part of it. Observers and retirees highlighted stark and jarring themes—death, illness, and the destruction of "men's" and "women's" spheres—to express their disapproval of retirement as "disengagement."[43]

More and more companies inaugurated pension programs for their workers and executives in the postwar years. Surveys indicated during the 1950s that over 90 percent of firms in the United States featured pension plans for their blue- and white-collar workers.[44] Harkening back to pre-World War II industrial pension plans, postwar managers viewed pensions as useful ways to regulate workforce composition. Mandatory retirement ages and pensions allowed managers to move outmoded (i.e., older) men out, and create room for the advancement of younger staffers and workers. As managers claimed in previous decades, young men supposedly brought vitality and new ideas to business in the form of "new blood."[45]

By the 1950s, most US companies featured mandatory retirement rules, typically at the familiar age of 65. The National Industrial Conference Board estimated that 48 percent of firms in the United States featured mandatory retirement policies.[46] In New Jersey, a survey of 82 industrial companies in the state showed that 73 percent featured mandatory retirement for workers who reached 65.[47] In a survey of reasons why men retired, 50 percent of the men cited "discharged by employer" as the reason why they stopped working. By the 1950s, roughly half of retired men had been summarily dismissed in this fashion.[48]

Many older men, while they often sympathized with young men's need to advance, disliked the compulsory loss of their jobs. An executive at a New Jersey firm reported that retiring men—blue collar and white collar—seldom embraced retirement. "Since we've had compulsory retirement in our shop," the man noted, "I've seen an awful lot of guys, big brass and no brass, go on the skids."[49] In Chicago, Albert T. Sands, who worked in the fields of pensions and insurance, wrote in 1951 about a disgruntled sixty-five year-old man who visited his office to complain about his forced retirement. "He was terribly dejected," Sands wrote, "and he even urged me to intercede on his behalf." Sands said that he was aware of the company's compulsory retirement policy, but could do nothing to help. He asked the man if ever thought about retirement before the day of his ouster arrived. "I did not like to think of retirement," the now-retired man admitted.[50] In retirement advice author Irving Salomon's survey sample of 21 retired men, 7 of the men reported they did not choose to retire.[51]

Since the late-nineteenth century, sixty-five had been typically imposed as the age when aging men would be deemed eligible for pension benefits (if their employers offered them, of course) and subsequently retired. Employers chose the age of 65 because they did not want to pay benefits to men who were, in their estimation, too young and would thus live (and remain a cost burden) for many more years. Presumably, a man at age 60 would live longer and collect pension benefits for a significantly longer period of time than a man who was 65. It was simply cheaper to set the pension age as high as possible. The Roosevelt White House, the architects of Social Security, also adopted the age of 65 when they designed old age insurance provisions during the mid-1930s. In the years after World War II, employers continued to embrace these precedents when they created new mandatory retirement programs. Postwar employers created a process that allowed them to move older men out, while at the same creating room for the promotion and hiring of younger men. These programs facilitated a more subtle form of age discrimination, smoothed over by pension checks and Social Security benefits. Standard Oil, General Electric, and the American Telephone & Telegraph Company, for instance, argued that mandatory retirement for workers created a more equitable workplace, making it possible for young men's careers to go forward within the company. Under mandatory retirement, the worker "knows where he stands"; he knows he will retire at age 65.[52]

"DEATH COMES AT RETIREMENT"

While aging men knew better where they stood with their employers in the postwar workplace, most worried a great deal about the many implications of the looming transition from employment to retirement. Financially, socially, and even medically, retirement seemed to tear at the fabric of men's lives in grim ways.

Gifford R. Hart feared retirement because, as many experts believed, the abrupt end of work could cause older men to die prematurely. Work defined the basis of men's identities, and the arbitrary retirement of a man at age sixty-five could, as many men apparently believed, abruptly and literally kill him—the most horrifying outcome of "retirement shock."[53] Robbed of their cherished routines, self-esteem, friendships, and economic status, retired men allegedly became ill and depressed; soon, they died. "Forced retirement can be a man's death sentence," the editors of *Nation's Business* announced to the reading public in 1949.[54] Gifford Hart heard numerous tales of retirement shock as his own final day of work approached. He collapsed this "folklore" into the story of a fictional man, "John." John was a successful white-collar worker who dearly loved his job, but in a tragic turn of events, John "dropped dead" the day after he retired.[55] Some narratives ended in suicide, perhaps evoking memories of the 1920s. Writing in the *New York Times Magazine*, John L. Springer claimed that a vice president of an important corporation committed suicide after a year of "uselessness" and "loneliness" in retirement.[56] Among white-collar staffers, these narratives of retirement shock proliferated. "I daren't retire," an aging executive remarked in 1956. "I'd be dead in a couple of years."[57]

No valid research underpinned the assertion that retirement led to higher death rates among older men, but some experts claimed that doctors' "clinical observations" proved that older men who worked longer *lived* longer than retired men.[58] The assumption that retirement killed men was ubiquitous. Dr. Edward J. Stieglitz, a hospital chief of staff, argued, "It is an axiom of clinical medicine that forcing the one-track mind executive to retire is tantamount to signing his death certificate within the year." Dr. Roger I. Lee, once a president of the American Medical Association (AMA) tersely concluded: "Death comes at retirement."[59] This argument was often based on unsubstantiated stories and rumors passed on among coworkers. Experts' sustained use of these urban legends highlights a strong current of male anxieties about retirement, manhood, and growing old. Perhaps retirement signified to Gifford Hart, and other men, how they were closer to the end of life than the beginning—or the middle. Retirement was the same as the final phase of life. "Could it be," Hart wondered, "that his [the aging man's] retirement is at least partly compounded of his own fears for the future? Is his retirement unwelcome not so much because it is retirement but because it is an inescapable reminder of something else?"[60] The transition to retirement "reminded" aging men of their mortality, especially since at age 65 they were only expected to live another 3 to 5 years during the 1950s.[61]

As discussions of "retirement shock" suggested, the medical reasoning behind the dangers of retirement reinforced widespread unease among men about growing old and leaving work. Even if death did not result, experts worried that retirement would lead to chronic illness, as boredom, inactivity, and isolation caused physical decline in men. In a 1952 advice pamphlet, writer Kathryn Close wrote about "Andy Smith" and how this man's poorly planned retirement contributed to constant illness and physical deterioration. Smith was a successful man who rose through the ranks of his company, becoming a vitally important and powerful man in the firm. Once a factory hand, he retired as a highly paid and well-regarded executive. But retirement, due to rigid company rules, "sunk" him. With no work, he quickly became bored, lonely, and restless. After so many inactive months spent listening to the radio and sitting home alone, he began experiencing acute pains in his chest. Smith's heart was failing, and he soon became an "invalid."[62] David D. Stonecypher, who wrote for the *New York Times Magazine*, argued in 1957 that the retired man "fears his body is degenerating." Retired men feared arthritis, cataracts, heart disease, stroke, "and other frightening things."[63] They worried that persistent health troubles would consign them to a permanent convalescence in the domestic sphere. After suffering heart trouble, Bill Biggers, a railroad worker, sarcastically asked his physician: "Doctor, do you know where there's furniture having a bargain sale on rocking chairs? Maybe I'll learn to knit and crochet."[64] Now living with a bad heart, he was no longer able to exert himself as he once could and had to retire. Illness and the loss of employment meant for Biggers a loss of manhood as well. While men surely experienced health troubles in later life, retirement was certainly not the principal cause of ill health. Lifestyle choices, such as tobacco use, poor diet, or drinking, surely contributed to older men's health troubles.

Men also worried about retirement because of the loss of overall physical strength they associated with aging. Since healthy bodies and physical ability were major vehicles for the demonstration of manliness, both at work and at play, declining strength and waning physical ability pointed to the loss of manhood. "On the physical side," British author Carlton Wallace wrote of growing old, "there is the obvious reduction of muscular strength and of bodily endurance. It is no longer possible to perform great feats of weight-lifting, and it is no longer possible to maintain a high degree of physical performance over prolonged periods."[65] Older men worried their bodies would deteriorate even faster when they retired. Physical decline in later life frightened aging men. Some older men even thought of their bodies as "inferior," and as a result, they did not take adequate care of themselves.[66]

In addition to death, decline, and illness, retiring men worried about the erosion of separated spheres of activity for men and women.[67] In 1952, a retired white-collar worker told *Business Week* that retirement brought him "from a man's world into a woman's world."[68] Men envisioned themselves as "public" beings who worked in paid occupations away from the home, while women occupied the "private" realm within it. Despite the fact that women also worked in offices and factories, retiring men of the 1950s and those who wrote about them understood gender in terms of a rigid ideology of separated spheres.[69]

In the new postwar literature on retirement, scholars in sociology and gerontology seldom wrote about women as retiring "workers." Rather, women appear as discontented housewives, uncertain about, if not opposed to, husbands' retirements. Why did retirement experts focus on men's struggles with aging? As journalism professor Walter B. Pitkin explained during the mid 1940s, retirement occurred within the "man's world" of business and industry. He said women were "lucky" because they did not work in paid employments long enough to ever retire. For women who (unfortunately, according to Pitkin) did work away from the home, the author urged them to prepare for retirement by reading what experts said about men: "let them read what we have to say about men. It will apply to them too."[70]

Although much less frequently discussed in the literature on aging and retirement during the 1950s, experts occasionally linked men's fears of aging to anxieties about continued sexual performance. The gerontologist Edward J. Stieglitz described how men invested heavily in youth and sexual performance as important components of what it meant to be a physically functioning man. To answer the question, "Why fear senescence?" he noted: "Not infrequently these fears [of aging] are associated with a distorted outlook about the anticipated decline of sexual vigor and enthusiasm." David D. Stonecypher of the *New York Times* agreed, concluding that the loss of "sexual drive" could only "arouse thoughts intensely painful."[71]

In addition to the spatial, economic, and performative dimensions of gender, Gifford Hart worried about the relationship between time and gender—specifically, the productive sense of manhood derived as a result of men's career-long daily routines. Social ideas about gender arranged the way men imagined the structure of their days; for roughly eight or ten hours everyday, most men worked away from the home, while women remained behind as domestic caregivers. For years, working men woke, dressed, ate a breakfast that was prepared for them by a spouse, and ventured out to work. At the end of the working day, tired men returned home to hot dinners, evening papers, and sleep. This arrangement of time defined their daily experiences and sense of self as men. Retirement, it seemed, would destroy the underpinning structures and rhythms of their daily lives; in retirement, their days would, they believed, look exactly like a woman's world: kitchens, noisy vacuum cleaners, laundry, cooking. As retirement writer Paul Boynton argued, the jarring end of a man's routine could shock him into physical decline. The loss of a man's routine was a "just plain understandable fear," according to Irving Salomon. As Gifford Hart wrote, older men did not want to confront the end of their cherished routines: "A certain world, which may have meant even more to them than they are aware, has suddenly evaporated. The discovery is shocking. In a sense, the man has lost his identity; he has become a nobody instead of a somebody, and he doesn't like it."[72]

Retirement robbed men of acquaintances and friendships, as men's social relationships with other men were often rooted in the workplace. Retirement redefined these relationships along unequal lines or led to their conclusion. For white-collar workers who wrote about their retirement experiences suggested that the men still at work treated retired men differently once they had stopped working. As coworkers, men could be equals; but in retirement, older men were now has-beens, relics of bygone eras, dinosaurs. Retiree authors explained to readers how former coworkers rebuffed them when they visited the office. Lonely and eager for companionship, retired men often returned only to discover their former colleagues had no desire to talk with them. When retiree Paul Boynton visited his old office, "Joe" shook his hand asked how he was doing. While he was polite enough, Boynton realized that his one-time friend was not paying attention to him. "Bill" behaved the same way. The (former) co-worker met him "with his old friendly grin but when you sit down for a moment's chat you see that he is working on something that is new to you. The job has moved, the scene has changed. Bill pushes aside his work and devotes himself to your concerns but you know, just the same, that you are in the way; you no longer fit this picture, you have fallen way behind the play."[73]

Gifford Hart was financially well off, but other men feared a significant loss of income when they retired. Pensions from companies and the federal government, even if men received benefits from both sources, paid less than the salaries and wages earned while working. While the number and amount of Social Security payments and private pensions increased during the 1950s, especially in election years, the sums of money remained low.[74] Retirement signaled a social and financial setback, a major reduction of living standards for older men and families. Less money meant less food, shelter, travel, and leisure. Aging men also worried about funds to cover unforeseen health expenses. As pension scholars and retired professionals pointed out throughout the 1950s, "financial fears" and "worry about economic security" constituted major sources of retirement anxiety for men.[75] Experts in social provision lamented Social Security shortcomings, demanding increased benefits; and the Congress of Industrial Organizations' constituent unions, especially the United Automobile Workers, insisted that working-class men should retain middle-class standards of living when they retired.[76]

As mandatory retirement became common during the 1950s, Gifford Hart and other men worried what lied ahead for them in a life without work. Experts in gerontology and sociology, as well as retired professionals, popular magazine writers, and newspaper writers, cited numerous problems and dangers that retiring men would confront. Men worried about sudden death, the loss of sexual ability, boredom, illness, physical decline, the loss of working routines, the loss of middle-class incomes and lifestyles, and the destruction of separated spheres for men and women. The view of aging-as-loss would fuel gerontologists' work in the years to come. In 1970, for example, gerontologists Leon A. Pastalan and Daniel H. Carson concluded that the ages 65–75 would be characterized by "Loss of job, spouse, friends, income, some body image loss," while ages 75–87 would be marred by "Increased loss of sensory activity, health, strength, and independence." At the extreme end of the adult life-cycle (the ages of 85 and beyond) they could expect to confront and contend with the "Serious loss of health and independence."[77] Faced with such daunting prospects in old age, retirement planning became a widely discussed topic during the 1950s. Men would need to ready themselves for retirement because if they did not prepare, they risked the loss of so much—so quickly. To have any chance at surviving a life without work, aging men would need to carefully ready themselves.

ON-THE-JOB RETIREMENT PREPARATION

At the Esso Standard Oil Company, managers surveyed 1,000 employees at its New Jersey refineries during 1951, and they found that new retirees experienced "retirement shock," hostility from spouses, and overall boredom and isolation after leaving their jobs.[78] Because so many employers instituted mandatory retirement ages during the 1940s and 1950s, and anxieties about retirement became so widespread, prominent companies and labor unions began to explore and implement new retirement preparation programs. Companies such as Allis-Chalmers, Pitney-Bowes, Eastman Kodak, Lockheed Aircraft, Wrigley, American Rolling Mills, US Rubber, Western Electric, Shell Oil, and Esso Standard Oil, as well as prominent union leaders such as Walter P. Reuther of the United Automobile Workers, believed that aging working men needed to be prepared for retirement. Companies explored ways to counsel their retirees on the economics of retirement, but they also devoted considerable time and resources to lifestyle considerations. Companies knew that men worried about the loss of productive manhood, and the growth of these programs was substantial. By the early 1950s, 20 percent of American companies offered pre-retirement counseling and training programs to older workers.[79] Gifford Hart agreed with the principle of retirement preparation, pointing out that retirement would be less daunting if aging men had assistance with this momentous transition.

Corporate programs addressed the widespread medical fears of retirement by urging older men to stay busy and "productive" (and thus manly) once they left their jobs. Companies hoped to foster continuity between the working years and the twilight years by educating older men in the weeks and months leading up to their retirements to consider alternative activities that would supplant their jobs as the foundation of their daily lives and routines. If retirement would be made into a healthy and enjoyable experience, corporate retirement trainers of the 1950s, like other experts, insisted that productivity would have to be carefully reconstructed in later life. As the Standard Oil Company of New Jersey noted of its retirement training program in 1950, the goal was to help working men stay well in old age by preparing for what they termed "post-retirement careers."[80]

How did companies design retirement preparation programs? What did they teach aging blue- and white-collar workers? Observers who wrote for *Business Week* and the *New York Times* cited the Esso Standard Oil program at its Bayonne, New Jersey, refinery as a model retirement training program. Established in 1950, Esso organized a series of informational seminars and presentations, where they implemented "scientific" advice from gerontologists and psychologists about aging men's anxieties and needs.[81] Esso's program stemmed from the company's proud history of rewarding long-serving employees and its avowed respect for the "dignity" and "welfare" of older workers and retirees.[82] At the Esso refinery, there were 2,425 workers and staffers on the payroll, and roughly 150 retired from the company every year. The Esso Standard program emphasized 2 goals: (1) to warn aging men about the personal troubles (economic and health issues) they could confront in retirement; and (2) to help them cultivate a set of interests ("plotting post-retirement careers") before they retired.[83] The program functioned as a tutorial on how to ironically reinvent work in retirement.

Refinery superintendents at Esso Standard introduced aging workers to the retirement program through the mail. Exactly one year before the worker's retirement date, the man (signified as the typical gender of the Esso worker) received a letter of notification and an invitation to attend the series of seminars about retirement. There would be five meetings, all of them offered during the man's working hours. Attendance was not required, but as *Business Week* pointed out, "nobody has turned down the chance."[84] The meetings were ongoing, and brought men together who were scheduled to retire during the same month. The typical session size ranged from six to fifteen men. Esso Standard's retirement seminars also integrated salaried and hourly workers into the same classes.[85] Managers devoted the first session to getting acquainted: managers, workers, and speakers. Subsequent meetings were organized thematically: such as defining retirement, physical health and aging, finances, retirement leisure activities, individual success stories, and a summary session.[86]

After the initial meeting, the retiring Esso Standard man began the actual program by attending the "What is Retirement?" session. Along with other men, he heard speakers explain, in broad terms, about how aging affects "basic human needs"; and speakers told their audiences about the importance of defining retirement on their own terms. Would they disengage from society, or would they find new interests to replace the job? During the second session, the Esso men listened to a physician on the subject of "Retirement and Your Health." Doctors warned their audience about the dangers of unhealthy lifestyles, as well as the benefits of proper medical care. Bad habits and neglected health led directly to serious illness and an early grave.[87]

The second half of the Esso Standard program focused on lifestyle choices. The third session, "Planning for Retirement," emphasized that retiring men needed to find other productive activities to stay active in later life and to replace the role of the job in their daily lives. "The program is based on translating job satisfactions experienced by employes [sic] nearing retirement age into post-retirement careers," an article in the *New York Times* reported. "Some of the job satisfactions taken into account are feeling of activity, importance, belonging, usefulness, achievement, being needed, companionship and desires for creative work and physical change."[88] The fourth meeting presented Esso retirement success stories: men who made the most of their retirements through civic affairs, hobbies that became businesses, and frequent church activities that provided the men with personal fulfillment (and a crowded schedule of many activities). The meetings also featured Esso "Ex's" who "got off on the wrong foot" with their retirement, but had righted their course by finding ways to get out of the house and become active and productive again. Esso Standard counseled its retirees to find activities that were consonant with the idea that ongoing productivity was the basis of successful aging. "One thing is stressed," *Business Week* noted in 1951: "A man ought to plan something to keep his hands busy."[89] The final session was the "roundup." Here, the Esso man presented his own plans for retirement (in particular, how he intended to spend his time). Additionally, Esso Standard hoped that the retirement planning sessions would help new retirees build social contacts with other men who shared their interests that would continue once they left the company: for instance, "a man who likes gardening can be introduced to another man who has a similar hobby."[90]

After the Esso man retired, the company continued to check on him. Through correspondence and personal meetings, company officials kept themselves abreast of men's retirement choices. Beginning in the 1950s, companies used a variety of means to involve themselves in workers' retirements. By doing so, companies wanted older men to feel they still had ties to the workplace (and perhaps their manhood). "Most companies," sociologists Elon H. Moore and Gordon F. Streib remarked, "seek to retain for the worker the sense of belonging."[91] Other companies sent company newsletters and Christmas cards to retirees. Some companies offered special benefits to retirees. Phone companies offered discount phone services, while some railroad firms offered travel discounts. Most significantly, some firms made a point of offering life insurance and health benefits to retirees.[92]

Companies who offered retirement preparation programs ("nearly all") emphasized that husbands and wives needed to prepare for men's retirement together, since it would affect them both in significant ways. Retiring men and the observers who wrote about them believed that retirement undermined the daily arrangement of gender, necessitating a difficult process of renegotiation. Now reintegrated into the home on a full-time basis, men and women would need to work together on how men would occupy their time (and not be "under foot"). Companies encouraged women to participate in their husbands' retirement preparation; husbands and wives needed an opportunity to work on the ground rules of life in retirement.[93]

In addition to the ambitious Esso Standard Oil program, numerous other companies offered their own programs; these programs focused on retirees' needs for productive lifestyle choices. For example, the Pitney-Bowes firm in Connecticut created an arts-and-crafts program that allowed its working men to explore various hobbies and handicrafts as their retirements approached. Lockheed Aircraft hired a retirement counselor named Ray H. Geist to oversee a similar crafts program for soon-to-be-retiring men. These programs were large enough to include not only the oldest blue-collar and white-collar workers, but also younger men whose retirement was in the distant future. Both firms agreed with gerontologists, psychologists, and workers about men's unease about retirement, concluding that new activities to occupy aging men's minds, time, and hands would help them successfully adjust to lives without work. Joseph Morrow, P-B's personnel relations director during the early 1950s, insisted that "a man with a hobby finds retirement one of the happiest times of his life." Without some form of purposeful activity, the retiring man would surely become despondent and die after he left the workplace. Morrow evoked pervasive discussions of "retirement shock," concluding "the chances are he will die soon" without some form of activity to occupy himself.[94]

The expansion of retirement preparation programs after World War II signaled the revival of corporate paternalism. Once, historians generally argued that corporate paternalism and welfare capitalism began during the turn of the twentieth century and declined during the Great Depression, as the economic collapse, massive unemployment, and the rise of CIO unionism undermined employer benevolence and ushered in a new era of collective bargaining.[95] But more recent work has shown that employers continued to pursue welfare capitalism after the heyday of the New Deal and the end of the Second World War.[96] After the depression decade, numerous companies rebuilt paternalism within the context of these new retirement programs. While some companies (especially the Chrysler Corporation) resisted the expansion of retirement benefits, other firms (such as the titanic General Motors) tried to assume control over worker retirement politics by publishing advice pamphlets and designing seminars of their own.[97] The expansion of company retirement programs throughout the 1950s illustrates how employer paternalism adapted to the labor liberalism of the New Deal era.

In the postwar years, the Congress of Industrial Organizations challenged companies' new enthusiasm for retiree paternalism. During the 1950s, Walter P. Reuther and the UAW launched numerous initiatives on behalf of older men. While the UAW focused on autoworkers, the union leadership envisioned their programs as models for the entire country. Under Reuther's direction, the UAW advocated and instituted retiree social centers (called "Drop-In Centers") in Detroit. The union also pushed for the expansion of pension programs, increased Social Security payments, expanded health coverage, and pre-retirement training programs. As its retired membership expanded throughout the 1950s, the union devoted more and more funds on their behalf. To fund its new retirement training initiative, the UAW earmarked more than $14,000 per month. The purpose of the program was "to begin to prepare workers for the change that retirement will bring into their lives so that they can make the emotional adjustment and . . . [make] full use of the new leisure which their years of productive work have earned for them." By 1957, the UAW boasted a retired membership of over 78,000 former autoworkers.[98]

In their efforts to preclude the ominous fate that medical experts insisted awaited men in retirement, company retirement counselors reinforced the idea that perpetual activity could help men best navigate the treacherous transition from work to retirement. Retirement seminars and training programs, such as the influential Esso Standard Oil program, functioned as tutorials on the important connections between productivity and manhood. Even if older men could not work, corporate retirement trainers suggested that new routines of crafts and hobbies and other activities could help men produce improved health and ensure longevity, while simultaneously keeping the stress of "retirement shock" at bay.

SAYING GOODBYE: THE LAST DAYS OF WORK

Many of the themes related to postwar men's anxieties about retirement came together in discussions of the last days of work and, for some, retirement ceremonies. Retiring white-collar office workers such as Gifford R. Hart, as well as others like Paul Boynton and Raymond Kaighn, wrote extensively about their anxieties regarding the loss of sacred routines, changing relationships with co-workers, and the coveted sense of purpose and status they derived from work. Retiring men talked about how they, as Kaighn put it, "hate[ed] to give it all up."[99] In the postwar advice literature on retirement, aging men wrote about the last days of work and the retirement day as a disquieting time that seemed to, at once, affirm the intensely productive core of postwar manhood while at the same menacing its foundations. The retirement day itself encapsulated a stark contradiction: on one hand, employers and coworkers tried to honor retirees' service and hard work with kind farewells and gifts; on the other, retirement meant the sudden end of a man's long career. It was simultaneously a time of tragedy and commemoration. Retirees seized upon retirement ceremonies to affirm their worth as useful men, men whose labors defined themselves as well as supported families and the company. The retirement day and the last days of work proved to be uneasy cultural terrain, as retiring men struggled to reconcile their sense of manhood and identity with the reality that their literal life's work would now abruptly and anti-climatically come to an end. White-collar retiree and author Paul Boynton described the day of a man's retirement as the "dividing line between the old life and the new."[100] It seemed nothing would ever be the same again.

    White-collar/middle-class executives and professionals figured most prominently in discussions of retirement ceremonies in the advice literature and the newspaper notices of retirements during the 1940s and 1950s. However, other appearing figures included long-serving mail carriers, policemen, military leaders, school board officials, and elite businessmen—prominent members of communities who would have piqued the interest of newspaper editors and readers. Despite newspapers' overall focus on professionals, steelworkers' retirements sometimes made the pages of the *Chicago Daily Tribune*; the *New York Times* focused on white-collar men's retirements, except for occasional discussions of postal workers' retirements.[101] Overall, published sources suggest that companies and government agencies held frequent retirement ceremonies during the 1940s and 1950s; they ranged from informal gatherings to luncheons and formal evening ceremonials. Retired professionals, who produced most of the retirement advice literature during the 1950s, wrote about their own retirement experiences—ignoring blue-collar men's experiences. Throughout the retirement advice literature, retiring men expressed conflicted feelings of excitement and anxiety about retiring.

One reason why retirees, especially in white-collar occupations, experienced anxiety upon retirement was the chilly, if not rude, reactions of their co-workers to announcements that a man was retiring. When fellow white-collar executives and staffers learned of Gifford R. Hart's upcoming retirement, Hart noted they generally expressed a "mild, inarticulate embarrassment." No one told him they were happy for him, and no one said they were angry with him for leaving. But Hart noticed a palpable change in his co-workers' demeanor. They seemed to lose respect. "Well," a few tersely remarked, "good luck."[102] Hart's co-workers assumed that men belonged in the workplace. There, a man could be a real man; he could be useful and valuable. They typically viewed retirement as a tragedy, but they conceived of voluntary retirement as outright foolishness. Hart, who voluntarily retired because of fragile health, worried that his colleagues thought of him as a quitter. No one envied Hart for leaving.[103]

In their discussions of the last day of work, retirees lamented how relationships with their co-workers and friends changed so quickly. Retirees knew they would miss the shop talk, after-work cocktails, and long lunches shared with (always male) coworkers. Everything would change when they retired. Gifford R. Hart warmly described the farewell luncheon thrown for him by a "big group of my business friends" on his last day of work. "The preliminary cocktails were fine," he recalled, "the group was congenial, the conversation was loud and gay."[104] Men told jokes, fondly recalled old times, patted each other on the back, and vowed to remain close. In retirement, Hart knew he would miss the frequent socializing and the camaraderie. This homosocial world had been a defining part of his, and many other retired men's, manhood.[105] Men depended on their male-exclusive work cultures and social circles to establish boundaries and spaces where women were not present and could not enter. Author Thomas Collins suggested that men were deeply committed to the homosociability found at work; specifically, they were "married" to the daily or weekly lunch meetings with male colleagues and after-hours activities such as company bowling leagues.[106]

Men made comparisons between the last days of work and the ending of a romantic relationship with a woman. Work offered them emotional bonds. Men "loved" their jobs; they were "married" to them. Retirement felt too much like a painful divorce. Thomas Collins wrote in 1956: "You will be leaving your job at sixty-five much as a man might leave his wife after forty years of marriage. Because every man who works for a living is a bigamist of sorts. He is married to his wife, and he is married to his work." He concluded,

"In the closing days . . . you will have some of the emotions of a man who is breaking off a romance."[107]

Rare discussions of working-class men's last days of work before retirement sometimes suggested that retirees would miss the work itself—that is, the specific tasks and skills required of them on the job. In a 1959 study of the "nature" of retirement, a retiring locomotive engineer told two sociologists that it "was not easy putting a good engine on pit for the last time." The aging train man was dismayed by the end of his work rhythms. "I went home that day without even going into the washroom," he commented. He left the grime on his hands, taking with him the dirt and soot he had worn into his pores.[108]

As the retirement day approached, white-collar men wanted to perform their tasks with greater rigor and precision. They wanted to leave a personal imprint on their jobs, proclaiming to coworkers and management that no other man could ever replace them. Gifford Hart noted that he did his best work during his final six months on the job. Since he was retiring, coworkers expected him to slow down, but Hart refused. Despite ailing health, Hart worked harder than ever, noting that his energy level and skill had actually increased. "I want to make my exit with all flags flying," Hart wrote, "and the band playing 'He's a jolly good fellow.'" He felt what he described as an overriding "urge" to leave his mark in the workplace.[109] Perhaps Gifford Hart believed that a final burst of hard work would give him a kind of productive boost that would allow him to take a sense of manhood with him once he retired.

During their last days, aging men asserted their own expertise and a sense of self-importance when they mocked the younger men who would replace them. By ridiculing their naïve and inexperienced replacements, they tried to assert themselves as better professional men. Thomas Collins mused about how his young successor seemed like he could never function as a true replacement. The upstart knew nothing of the job's true complexities, all of which Collins claimed to have mastered. When the self-assured lad boasted of his plans to reform the old man's position, Collins kept his opinions to himself. He knew better; he privately believed no bragadocious youngster could ever attain his level of skill, knowledge, and mastery. As he ventured into the unknowns of retirement, Collins wanted to take with him that sense of importance. He was a man who once mattered in the workplace; yet he actually wanted to be more than that—to be one of a kind.[110]

The last days of work before retirement forced white-collar men to relive their own personal history as they cleaned out their desks—an awkward, forced journey through their many years of work. Paul Boynton described these moments with bittersweet sadness, as they underscored the impending end of his career and his status as a man of the working world. When he cleaned out his desk, Boynton discovered letters he once intended to mail, as well as a forgotten shopping list that caused an "unhappy misunderstanding" with his spouse. Most significantly, he came across an old timetable. The retiring Boynton realized he would never again monitor appointments and meetings with such precision. The timetable symbolized a key component of his working years that he would no longer need when he woke up the next day in retirement. Once he finished cleaning his desk, it was time to leave work for the last time. Boynton wrote, "you go with the same sinking feeling that the only world you know and feel at home in is yours no longer. You are cut adrift. From now on, you are on your own."[111]

Because men worried so extensively about retirement in the years after World War II, many offices and factories held retirement ceremonies for their departing workers as a way to mark the occasion. Workers, experts, and employers viewed the retirement ceremony as an important moment in a man's career. Employers and workers wanted the retirement ceremony to honor men's service in business, to impart meaning and status to a man for many years of hard work. "The recommendation," a retired professional wrote, "is that retirement should be marked by ceremony, by a sequence of deliberate actions which will give definite shape to the changes which are to be made. Certain doors leading to the past should be closed, locked and bolted, even screwed or bricked up; others have to be opened and what is beyond them swept and furbished and otherwise made habitable."[112] As written accounts of retirement ceremonies in newspapers, magazines, and advice books illustrate, ceremonies honored the retiring man's service, loyalty, endurance, and success with a company or agency.

Despite the fanfare, the retirement ceremony also reminded retirees they were no longer members of the working world; retirement "closed" the doors of the workplace. As retired men's writings suggest, ceremonies functioned as a polite but final send off—a way to nicely nudge these old men out the door. Amidst the martinis, lunches, expensive dinners, kind words, and gold watches, retirees lost work as the foundation of manhood. Once the celebrations ended, retirees such as Gifford R. Hart discussed how they experienced terrible feelings of anxiety and loss. "It may be the nearest thing to dying you have ever experienced," Paul Boynton lamented.[113] Employers, workers, and professionals envisioned the retirement ceremony as a way to mark the transition from one momentous part of the life cycle to the next. However, the retirement ceremony encapsulated numerous contradictions and ambiguities.

The structure of retirement ceremonies varied from company to company. Often, retirement ceremonials took place during the lunch hour of a typical workday. However, they sometimes extended over an entire day or even two days. During the retiring white-collar man's last day of work, he often listened to and made speeches at receptions, ate lunches and dinners with coworkers, and had private meetings with his supervisor. When "John Jones" retired from his white-collar job during the 1950s, he enjoyed "the customary farewell party" with colleagues. His employer presented him with a travel bag as a show of gratitude for his many years of service to the company.[114] (Did John Jones have plans to travel in retirement, or was the bag a subtle way for his co-workers to say they were so glad he was leaving that they wanted to help him pack?) As he described his own retirement ceremony, Raymond Kaighn recalled a rapid succession of events: a lunch with friends, laudatory speeches from co-workers and supervisors, letters of praise received from colleagues ("to buck up the ego when it has gone limp"), kisses from a "demonstrative woman or two," and finally the goodbye handshakes and hearty slaps on the back. "God bless you, old scout. Take it easy and enjoy yourself!" coworkers told him. Suddenly, the aging man found himself out on the street, alone.[115]

Retirement ceremonies and the activities of the last day of work did allow retiring men to free themselves from the hierarchies and power relations of the workplace. On any other day, supervisors gave orders; workers and staffers carried them out. Retirement ceremonies gave aging men, who had worked faithfully for their companies for many years, an opportunity to receive honors and praise from superiors. Rather than act in accordance to their boss' every whim, a retiring man would hear the boss give a glowing speech about his successful career, eat a fine meal paid for by the firm, and receive a manly handshake from the boss in thanks for his fine service. The boss also told the retiring worker he would be sorely missed, that the company would not be the same without him. Proceedings always concluded with warm wishes for health, a long life, and a happy retirement. In addition to the ceremony, retiring white-collar staffers particularly remembered farewell meetings with the boss. There, retirees heard more praise about their work. The last day's activities allowed older men to receive acknowledgement, however small, from their supervisors.[116] In addition, it was custom for retirees to enjoy an expensive cigar—lit personally by the boss. Some men even went so far as to take off their shoes during the retirement ceremony, putting their stocking feet on the head table.[117]

During the retirement ceremony, the retiring man generally received a gift from the company. Men received any number of items: gold watches, fishing tackle, golf clubs, scrolls of honor, encyclopedias, and gold medals were common. Most often, retired men went home with fishing poles or golf clubs—a reminder they should now enjoy a work-free life filled with leisure. Companies bestowed a sense of manliness on their retirees by decorating them like soldiers, giving them medals and booty to honor their years of service.[118] Sometimes in front of the entire company, bosses presented retiring workers with service medals and gifts. At a retirement ceremony for a Los Angeles water department worker, colleagues gave the man a "gold-painted" water meter filled with silver dollars.[119]

The gifts made some men uneasy. For example, men pondered why employers would send them away with a wrist watch. After all, some men remarked, when a man retired he no longer needed to keep track of time. Some men disliked encyclopedias (intended to be a light-hearted gift) because the retired man would now "have so much time to read."[120] Retirees did not want to be reminded they would no longer work. At the end of retirement ceremonies, retirees gave "awkward" speeches to offer thanks.[121] In 1950, office worker Tom Jenkins was noticeably uncomfortable during his farewell dinner. "There was Tom," another man, soon to retire himself, sympathetically observed, "up front, fiddling with the gold watch just given him, and trying to find the right words for what he was feeling inside." He was not only overwhelmed to receive the fine watch; he was worried about what he would do next.[122]

Some retiring men avoided ceremonies and formal goodbyes. Paul Boynton observed: "For some men this is a day to get through as painlessly as possible. They prefer to say nothing about it, to avoid any unnecessary fuss." Retirement ceremonies, for some older men, conveyed an uneasy sense of finality and loss—despite the company's intent to honor and celebrate men's careers. Boynton argued that all retiring men, even those who left their jobs quietly, experienced the same anxieties. He wrote, "Whether you prefer to go out as unostentatiously as an invisible man or with fanfare and gifts and speeches, the last day will have the same quality of finality, the same realization as you perform familiar tasks, 'I won't be doing this again.'"[123] When New York City's postmaster general retired in 1952, he refused to attend any ceremony. He would only receive a small group of colleagues in his office for a private (and brief) goodbye.[124] In 1949, James E. Shaw, a city clerk at the Los Angeles Superior Court, hoped his upcoming retirement would pass quickly without comment. He hoped to "retire from his labors . . . without fanfare," to leave his post, as a journalist noted, "without ado." However, his long-time colleagues failed to grant him his last wish. "However there was ado," the *Los Angeles Times* noted. "There were flowers and gifts. There were handclaps and well wishes all the day. There were telephone calls and letters from his friends and associates of bench and bar."[125]

Faced with the loss of their cherished careers, some men tried to reassert a sense of authority and independence by proclaiming their antipathy towards the boss or the company. Retirement could bring out years of pent-up frustration. In 1949, a retiring executive named John Bassett bitterly wrote "SITBE" on the calendar entry for the day of his retirement. ("SITBE" stood for "Spit in the boss' eye."[126]) Bassett's long history with the company left him with much resentment: the early retirement of a friend (and his replacement with a younger and less-effective man), unrecognized efforts, and failed departmental improvements. When the boss, named JC Gower, invited Bassett into his office to talk about his upcoming retirement, Bassett never SITBE. The two men spoke frankly about Bassett's grievances and managed to clear the air. Gower even gave the executive an extension of his employment with the department—which is what Bassett apparently wanted now more than ever.[127]

Other, less angry men announced the activities they planned to explore once they retired. Some men discussed long-postponed vacations (often to warmer climates), hobbies to be explored, or new employment opportunities they would seek. When Morris Warschauer, a member of the New York City school board, retired in the early 1950s, he vowed he would remain "active in educational affairs."[128] In Chicago, a retiring policeman, Joseph Sychowski, bragged to friends he would take a long vacation in the South to get away from the chilly winter in the Windy City.[129] Retired LA city clerk James E. Shaw told the *Los Angeles Times* that he wanted to begin a new life as "an automobile bum": exploring the East Coast, venturing to Quebec to see family, and finally making his way west again. By doing so, he wanted to find new places where he could hunt and fish at his leisure.[130] In the Midwest, company newsletters provided some information about what working-class men planned to do when they retired. Leo "Dutch" Wendt, a German immigrant who retired from his job as a machinist at Detroit Steel Products in 1956, told coworkers he planned to rest during the winters and visit his daughter's house (with its large backyard garden) in the nearby suburb of Mt. Clemens. Another retiring DSP worker, Roman Cichowski, planned to simply "rest and relax."[131]

Women, specifically wives, played key roles during the last days of work and the retirement ceremony. Women constituted an audience for the affirmation of manhood: they dutifully attended their aging husbands' retirement ceremonies, marveling with pride to hear praises of their husbands' fruitful endeavors in the workplace. In white-collar working men's writings, wives marveled at the sights and sounds to be experienced at the retirement ceremony. Surely grateful for his partner's support as his retirement approached, Raymond Kaighn remarked that "your wife is right there at the head table with a special hairdo, a new gown, and an orchid, treasuring in her heart every kind thing said about her hero and not missing the smallest item of the great occasion. In a glow of happiness, you have your great moment in the spotlight."[132] Women remembered everything about the experience: the excellent food, the speeches, the new clothes, and the company's "generous" parting gift. Impressed with the company's admiration for her husband, the woman continued to talk about the experience when she arrived home.[133] Retirement ceremonies allowed retirees to show their partners they were real men—males who had accomplished a great deal during their working years. In addition, retirement ceremonies allowed men to affirm separated spheres for men and women as a signifier of gender. Men worked in offices and factories, and women admired them for their labor.

Even though businessmen carefully choreographed women's roles in their male colleagues' retirement ceremonies, men could never fully claim retirement celebrations as sites that privileged and protected manhood. Professional women, too, retired from white-collar and executive posts, and their co-workers provided luncheons and formal ceremonies to honor their hard work and service. As "Lucille" wrote to the author of the "White Collar Girl" column at the *Chicago Daily Tribune* in 1952, older women ended their own careers with the familiar "dinners and speeches of praise" that men also enjoyed on the day of the retirement. Lucille suggested that retirement was not uniquely male, noting "it's the oldster's farewell to business."[134] When May D. Lahey, a Municipal Court judge in Los Angeles, California, retired in 1947 after 28 years of service, her male and female colleagues gave her a well-attended send-off. Leading members of the Los Angeles and state bar associations attended, and numerous California judges participated in the ceremony. The former assistant US Attorney General, Mabel Walker Willebrandt, and Judge Frank B. Tyrell of the Municipal Court in Los Angeles, feted Lahey with speeches that honored her reputation as "a highly intelligent, strong woman."[135] Given aging men's anxieties about how retirement and growing old could undermine manhood and the social divisions between men and women, retiring men probably did not find any comfort in these celebrations of retiring professional women. Retirement ceremonies not only reminded men of the impending end of their identities as workers; the ceremonies themselves were rituals that were subject to reinterpretation by women themselves. When Judge Lahey retired, those who honored her emphasized her femininity, reframing the retirement ceremony as a celebration of professional womanhood rather than manhood. "She represents woman in the highest embodiment of mind," Willebrandt noted. The judge was "an admirable woman."[136]

In the advice literature of the 1950s, narratives of the retirement day usually concluded with tones of burgeoning isolation, confusion, and depression. Once the parties concluded and it was time to go home, now-retired men described jarring moments of grim realization. After years of work, they were no longer employed workers and professionals. They would no longer wake up every morning and venture out to work. They would no longer earn salaries, and the future looked grim. As Harold R. Hall, a professor of business at Harvard University, wrote in 1953, *"One day later he is—nobody."*[137]

The next morning, retired men confronted more intense feelings of dread. Drawing on his personal experiences, Raymond Kaighn discussed how retired professionals quickly lamented the loss of their daily routines and the feelings of economic usefulness and meaning they derived from work. "Yesterday," he wrote, "you were helping to keep the wheels of economic life whirling. They are whirling alright this morning, but without your help. That is not a comfortable feeling. They don't need you out there anymore. That is still more uncomfortable to think about. You are through."[138] Some men enjoyed the first morning of their retirement. They slept in, smiling as they turned off their alarm clocks. One man, who slept past noon, enjoyed a hearty breakfast. However, grim realities soon clouded over new retirees' initial satisfaction. Men felt "queer" as they watched spouses cleaning and cooking.[139]

Discussions of the retirement day show the extent to which white-collar workers and middle-class professionals now embodied the figure of the "retired" man. White-collar men generated the advice literature on retirement during the 1950s, defining "work" and "retirement" through the prism of their own lives and experiences. Retired men such as Raymond Kaighn, Gifford R. Hart, and Paul Boynton wrote about retirement as they experienced it. They worried most about fulfillment and purpose, since they themselves had retired with the security afforded by hefty pensions and benefits. And retirement ceremonies, while laden with subtly contradictory and ambiguous interpretations of masculinity, conveyed gratitude and respect to these white-collar retirees. Since the retirement advice literature focused so heavily on the middle class, we do not know as much about working-class men's experiences with retirement ceremonies and the last days of work. By the 1950s, discussions of men's troubles with growing old reflected (and reinforced) a broader cultural reorientation in post-World War II America towards a middle class cultural framework, displacing entirely earlier views of aging which emphasized older blue-collar working men's troubles with growing old in the factory. By the 1950s, talk of social justice for older men had receded far into the background.

HANGING ON: RETIREMENT AVOIDANCE

Faced with anxieties about the supposed dangers found in retirement, many men concluded they would not retire voluntarily, choosing to cling to their jobs for as long as possible. Employment defined manhood, and men were not willing to abandon their coveted status as workers and professionals. "I'd rather wear out than rust out," some men stubbornly argued.[140] At Columbia University, scholars at a conference on aging spoke about how many men refused to accept or consider retirement. Even if a man was financially secure, they noted, he still did not want to stop working. The group concluded that men

> will sometimes cling tenaciously to a job in order to avoid or at least postpone assumption of the dreaded role assigned to old age. Driven by cultural forces which make a job the symbol of his continuing worth as an individual, the worker is loathe to surrender it, even when he is financially secure, even when his health makes continuing inadvisable. He is afraid to stop, afraid of being inactive . . . Retirement represents to him emptiness, loneliness, boredom, and a generally devalued existence.[141]

Since work was "the symbol" of a man's "continuing worth as an individual," we should not be surprised to see that statistical evidence suggested that a majority of working men hoped to avoid retirement. For example, in a 1952 *Business Week* survey of retired men's opinions in Cleveland, Ohio, nearly 52 percent opposed corporate retirement policies.[142] Men did not want to give up the social and economics dividends they derived from work. (Nor did they want to die prematurely, or lapse into ill-health and isolation.) They viewed retirement as something that real men could never intelligently or safely accept.

Retirement avoidance occurred among both blue- and white-collar working men. Clark Tibbitts, who worked with the US Department of Health, Education, and Welfare, noted that "salaried workers" and "wage-earners" preferred to avoid retirement if they were healthy enough to work. Other scholars talked about determined men from many different occupations—including postmen, businessmen, carpenters, and janitors—who planned to avoid retirement. They were, as some experts remarked, made of "sterner stuff."[143] These men planned to "die in harness" rather than retire from work.[144]

Some writers suggested that women encouraged men's retirement avoidance. Raymond Kaighn met with the spouse of a retired man who told him about how her husband briefly tried retirement. Hating it immediately, the older men quickly went back on the job. The man believed he was no longer himself without work; he became, according to his wife, "a caged animal tramping about." Once he was working again, the household returned to a state of calm. "No, I hope never again to 'retire,'" the woman told Kaighn. "We'll die with our boots on."[145] For men who wanted to stay on the job, however, company rules and mandatory retirement policies often precluded their plans and spouses' possible preferences.

Hollywood screenwriters and filmmakers took notice of many aging men's hopes to avoid retirement. Twentieth Century-Fox's film *As Young As You Feel* (1951) captured men's unease about the end of their careers and Americans' ambivalence toward postwar corporate retirement policies. Starring Monty Woolley, Thelma Ritter, David Wayne, and a young newcomer named Marilyn Monroe, the film—a story written by Paddy Chayefsky—is a comedy about an aging printer named John R. Hodges (played by Woolley) and his struggle to avoid retirement. "Acme Printing Services," the company where Hodges had worked for many years, abruptly greeted him at the punch clock one afternoon with a retirement notice. "No! Oh no! By the eternal, no!" Hodges exclaimed. He loved "the art" of printing, yet his company had "fired" him. What could he do now? Hoping to somehow hold onto his job, the wily Hodges devised a bold and imaginative scheme: He would impersonate the president of "Consolidated Motors," the massive and important automobile manufacturing firm that owned ACME Printing Services, Mr. Harold P. Cleveland, and order the printing firm to abandon its "absurd" retirement policy—thereby allowing him to remain at work. (The film not-so-subtly alludes to auto manufacturing as a hugely impersonal industry known for a history of blatant discrimination against older men.) Hodges concealed his true identity (and his age) by dying his beard and hair from gray to black—perhaps another nod to older working men and their ongoing struggles in mass production industry. The next day, he posed as Mr. Cleveland, "the prexy of CM," and surprised the top brass at ACME with a "routine inspection tour" visit.

Initially, the plan works. Louis McKinley, the president of ACME, falls over himself to please the impostor. After the ACME top brass (and the new CM "prexy") had toured the factory, the men marched into a company boardroom for a meeting. Hodges expressed his displeasure about ACME's "asinine policy" of retiring men at sixty-five, complaining there was "not one single white-haired man on the job." For the company to thrive, he insisted the firm needed to embrace older men, "the artisans, yes, those artists," who honored the trade and industry as a whole (and the principle of good work itself). He told McKinley to stop running his print shop like an automobile factory and to bring back the retired men immediately. While automobile manufacturing "perhaps required youth rather than experience," Hodges remarked, "the art of printing" demanded cool-headed veterans who possessed skill, stability, and experience. For the company to thrive, they needed these men's expertise in the factory. Eager to please, McKinley abolished the policy on the spot, ordering his secretary (Marilyn Monroe) to call all of the retired men back to work, "provided they wished to return."

Before Hodges could excuse himself and end the ruse, however, McKinley whisked him away to a crowded Chamber of Commerce lunch. There,

Mr. Cleveland (still Hodges) delivered an impromptu speech condemning retirement policy trends, describing men over sixty-five as "a great fund of stability" that would ensure the present and future of American economic growth, curb inflation, and prevent another depression. The speech is well-received by the audience and even discussed in the press. When the real Mr. Cleveland learned of the speech, he sought out the strange pretender. Once they met, Cleveland and Hodges, both men of advancing age, quickly developed a mutual respect. Asked why he put on the hoax that caused such uproar, Hodges simply said, "I wanted my job back." Impressed by the printer's logic and native intelligence, Cleveland offered Hodges a new job as a "consultant" with Consolidated Motors, but the printer politely declined. In the final scene, Cleveland promised Hodges he could return to his old job at ACME Printing Services.[146] Problem solved. Amidst the humorous absurdity, the film *As Young As You Feel* pointedly questioned and criticized company policies during the 1940s and 1950s that forced aging men into retirement—policies that ignored workers' valuable contributions and dedication to the companies they served.

Retirement avoidance pointed to the heightened importance of work as the basis of manhood in postwar America, and many men's determination to resist company pressures to retire. It was difficult for older men to envision life without labor. In various magazine articles and Hollywood films such as *As Young As You Feel*, observers argued that productivity would have to be somehow reconstructed for later life, as many men concluded that masculinity could only be found on the job—not on a park bench.

"The retired man," a writer noted in 1954, "is a marooned sailor watching the ship in which he once served disappearing behind the skyline."[147] Gifford Hart certainly felt that way, as he collapsed in a heap on his bed after his retirement dinner. Retirement became a widespread source of anxiety about manhood during the 1940s and 1950s. Taken together, the remaking of manhood within the context of a popular middle-class culture and its emphasis on the attainment of affluence, memories of the Great Depression, the experience of world war, and the rise of the Cold War affirmed productive work as the core of ideals of manhood. As the new cultural and economic institution of retirement took shape in the postwar years, retiring men were determined to safeguard manhood in this increasingly prevalent and uneasy phase of life.

Company retirement policies, which typically forced men out at age sixty-five, undermined men's ties to the workplace as they aged and jeopardized the central role of work in their notions of self. Discussions of "retirement shock" and sudden death, the loss of income, the erosion of separated spheres for men and women, and physical decline in later life underscored men's uncertainty regarding manhood in old age.

Anxiety about manhood in retirement was so prevalent that major companies explored retirement training preparation programs for their older workers. Frequent discussions of retirement ceremonies and the last days of work highlighted not only how postwar men eagerly wanted to remain at work, but also how they viewed retirement as a dangerous phase of life where their identities became unstable. Since the possibilities for productive manhood in retirement were unclear, many men avoided saying goodbye to the workplace.

The final chapter examines how men, once retired, tried to secure a new sense of productive manhood. But how could older men preserve ongoing productivity in retirement—a time when, at least theoretically, men no longer worked?

NOTES

1. Gifford R. Hart, *Retirement: A New Outlook for the Individual* (New York: Harcourt, Brace and Company, 1957), 163.

2. *About Schmidt*, dir. Alexander Payne, New Line Cinema, 2002. See the conclusion of this book for an analysis of the film.

3. In particular, see James Gilbert, *Men in the Middle: Searching for Masculinity in the 1950s* (Chicago: University of Chicago Press, 2005), esp. 34, 46, 48–49.

4. For overviews of World War II at home and abroad, see David M. Kennedy, *Freedom From Fear: The American People in Depression and War, 1929–1945* (New York: Oxford University Press, 1999); and Eric Foner, *The Story of American Freedom* (New York: WW Norton & Company, 1998), 219–247. For background on the early Cold War, see Walter LaFeber, *America, Russia, and the Cold War, 1945–1992*, 7th edition (New York: McGraw Hill, 1993); HW Brands, *The Devil We Knew: Americans and the Cold War* (New York: Oxford University Press, 1993); William L. O'Neill, *American High: The Years of Confidence, 1945–1960* (New York: Free Press, 1986); William H. Chafe, *The Unfinished Journey: America Since World War II* (New York: Oxford University Press, 1986); and Foner, *Story of American Freedom*, 259–273. On postwar consumption and mass culture, see Lizabeth Cohen, *A Consumer's Republic: The Politics of Mass Consumption in Postwar America* (New York: Vintage Books, 2003). The question comes from Arthur M. Schlesinger, Jr., "The Crisis of American Masculinity" (1958), in *The Politics of Hope* (1949; repr., Boston: Houghton Mifflin Company, 1962), 237.

5. See Arthur Miller, *Death of a Salesman* (1949; repr., New York: Penguin Books, 1998); and William H. Whyte, Jr., *The Organization Man* (New York: Simon and Schuster, 1956); as well as Michael Kimmel, *Manhood in America: A Cultural*

History (New York: Free Press, 1996), esp. 240; and Richard L. Ochberg, "The Male Career Code and the Ideology of Role," in *The Making of Masculinities: The New Men's Studies*, ed. Harry Brod (Boston: Allen & Unwin, 1987), 173–174. Historian James Gilbert downplays popular anxieties about masculinity during the 1950s. See Gilbert, *Men in the Middle*, 220–221.

6. Kenneth Walker, *Living Your Later Years* (New York: Oxford University Press, 1954), 168–169.

7. Susan Faludi, *Stiffed: The Betrayal of the American Man* (New York: HarperCollins Publishers, 1999), 16 (quote); Naoko Shibusawa, *America's Geisha Ally: Reimagining the Japanese Enemy* (Cambridge: Harvard University Press, 2006), 89–91. On male bodies, military service, and masculinity during World War II, see Christina Jarvis, *The Male Body at War: American Masculinity during World War II* (DeKalb, IL: Northern Illinois University Press, 2010).

8. Faludi, *Stiffed*, 19.

9. Whyte, *Organization Man*, 7.

10. David Riesman, *The Lonely Crowd* (New Haven: Yale University Press, 1950), 5. Emphases in original. On Riesman's interest in Erich Fromm's work, see Gilbert, *Men in the Middle*, 41–42.

11. Stephen E. Ambrose, *Band of Brothers* (New York: Simon & Schuster, 2001), 17.

12. Studs Terkel, *"The Good War": An Oral History of World War II* (New York: Pantheon Books, 1984), 66.

13. Christopher P. Loss, "'The Most Wonderful Thing Has Happened to Me in the Army': Psychology, Citizenship, and American Higher Education in World War II," *Journal of American History* 92:3 (2005): 886.

14. Loss, "'Most Wonderful Thing,'" 888, 887; Kennedy, *Freedom from Fear*, 857.

15. Ambrose, *Band of Brothers*, 306–307, 303.

16. Elaine Tyler May, *Homeward Bound: American Families in the Cold War Era* (New York: Basic Books, 1988).

17. KA Cuordileone, "'Politics in an Age of Anxiety': Cold War Political Culture and the Crisis in American Masculinity, 1949–1960," *Journal of American History* 87:2 (2000): 532, 536; Gilbert, *Men in the Middle*, 18.

18. Lawrence S. Wittner, *Cold War America: From Hiroshima to Watergate* (New York: Praeger, 1974), 95.

19. Cuordileone, "Politics in an Age of Anxiety," 529, 532–533, 538; Gilbert, *Men in the Middle*, 85.

20. Cuordileone, "Politics in an Age of Anxiety," 516; Wittner, *Cold War America*, 15.

21. Cohen, *Consumer's Republic*, 155.

22. Quoted in Meg Jacobs, *Pocketbook Politics: Economic Citizenship in Twentieth-Century America* (Princeton: Princeton University Press, 2005), 250.

23. Cohen, *Consumer's Republic*, 161.

24. Ibid., 155.

25. Stephanie Coontz, *The Way We Never Were: American Families and the Nostalgia Trap* (New York: Basic Books, 1992), 24–25.

26. J. Robert Moskin, "Why Do Women Dominate Him?" in *Look Magazine*, ed., *The Decline of the American Male* (New York: Random House, 1958), 16; Schlesinger, "Crisis of American Masculinity," 238, 240–241.

27. Moskin, "Why Do Women," 8–9; Schlesinger, "Crisis of American Masculinity," 238. On 1950s wives as "handywoman," see Gilbert, *Men in the Middle*, 153.

28. See Michael Zweig, *The Working Class Majority: America's Best Kept Secret* (Ithaca: Cornell University Press, 2000), 57.

29. Herbert Gold, "The Age of Happy Problems," *Atlantic Monthly*, March 1957, 60.

30. Historians James Gilbert and Miriam Forman-Brunell also observed the middle-class cultural orientation in their analyses of men, women, and gender in postwar America. See Gilbert, *Men in the Middle*, esp. 2, 8; and Miriam Forman-Brunell, *Babysitter: An American History* (New York: New York University Press, 2009), esp. 73.

31. See Eva S. Moskowitz, *In Therapy We Trust: America's Obsession with Self-Fulfillment* (Baltimore: Johns Hopkins University Press, 2001); as well as Rachel Devlin, *Relative Intimacy: Fathers, Adolescent Daughters, and Postwar American Culture* (Chapel Hill: University of North Carolina Press, 2005), esp. 20–22; and Forman-Brunell, *Babysitter*, 70.

32. "Dr. Isaac Rubinow, Social Expert, Dies," *New York Times*, 3 September 1936, 21; "Abraham Epstein Is Dead Here at 50," *New York Times*, 3 May 1942, 53; "James Davis, 74, Former Senator," *New York Times*, 22 November 1947, 15.

33. See Ray Giles, *How to Retire—and Enjoy It* (New York: McGraw-Hill Book Company, 1949).

34. Eugene A. Friedmann and Robert J. Havighurst, *The Meaning of Work and Retirement* (Chicago: University of Chicago, 1954), 1, 3.

35. Thomas Parran, Harwood S. Belding, Antonio Ciocco, James A Crabtree, Theodore F. Hatch, Adolph G. Kammer, and Violet B. Turner, "Monograph I," in *Criteria for Retirement: A Report of a National Conference on Retirement of Older Workers*, ed. Geneva Mathiasen (New York: GP Putnam's Sons, 1953), 66. This book is a report from a 1952 meeting on aging at Columbia University. For additional material, see Otto Pollack, *The Social Aspects of Retirement* (Philadelphia: Pension Research Council of the Wharton School of Finance and Commerce, University of Pennsylvania, 1956), 5, 20; and Robert J. Havighurst, "The Impact of Retirement of the Individual," in *Unions and the Problems of Retirement: Proceedings of a Conference* (University of Chicago, 3–4 April 1959), booklet (Chicago: Union Research and Education Projects, 1959), 13, in vertical files ("Retirement"), Institute of Labor and Industrial Relations (hereafter ILIR), University of Illinois at Urbana-Champaign (hereafter UIUC).

36. On the longer history of the Protestant work ethic, see, of course, Max Weber, *The Protestant Ethic and the Spirit of Capitalism* (1905; repr., New York: Scribner, 1958); as well as Daniel T. Rodgers, *The Work Ethic in Industrial America, 1850–1920* (Chicago: University of Chicago Press, 1978). Another useful discussion is found in GV Davis, "Work Ethic," in *Encyclopedia of US Labor and Working-Class History*, Volume 1 (A-F), ed. Eric Arnesen (New York: Routledge, 2007), 1518–1521.

37. See Parran, et al, "Monograph," 66. On the fear of failure in American cultural history, see Scott A. Sandage, *Born Losers: A History of Failure in America* (Cambridge: Harvard University Press, 2005).

38. Hart, *Retirement*, 27.

39. Ibid., 12.

40. Russell Porter, "Looking for Utopia Along the Townsend Trail," *New York Times Magazine*, 5 September 1939, 5.

41. Patrick J. Purcell, "Older Workers: Employment and Retirement Trends," *Monthly Labor Review*, October 2000, 21; see also "The Older Worker," *Time*, 19 October 1953, 100; and Dora L. Costa, *The Evolution of Retirement: An American Economic History, 1880–1990* (Chicago: University of Chicago Press, 1998), 174.

42. Clark Tibbitts, "Retirement Problems in American Society," *American Journal of Sociology* 59:4 (1954): 302; Donald H. Kausler and Barry C. Kausler, *The Graying of America: An Encyclopedia of Aging, Health, Mind, and Behavior*, 2nd edition (Urbana: University of Illinois Press, 2001), 343.

43. See Stanley Parker, *Work and Retirement* (London: George Allen & Unwin, 1982), 13; and Nancy C. Morse and Robert S. Weiss, "The Function and Meaning of Work and the Job," *American Sociological Review* 20:2 (1955): 191.

44. James R. Morris, *Employment Opportunities in Later Years* (Burlingame, CA: Foundation for Voluntary Welfare, 1960), 75.

45. See, for example, "Preparation for Retirement," *Personnel Journal*, November 1951, 211; and Close, "Getting Ready to Retire," 3.

46. Jack F. Culley and Fred Slavick, *Employment Problems of Older Workers*, booklet (Iowa City: State University of Iowa, 1959), 22, in vertical files ("Retirement"), ILIR, UIUC.

47. Charles R. Naef, *Pre-Retirement Programs in New Jersey* (New Brunswick, NJ: Institute of Management and Labor Relations, Rutgers University, 1960), 6.

48. Wilcock, "Who's Too Old To Work?" 8; see also "Most Persons Over 65 Have Little Income," *Chicago Daily Tribune*, 9 January 1956, C5.

49. Mutual Benefit Life Insurance Company of Newark, New Jersey, *Helping Employees Get Ready to Retire*, booklet (Newark: Mutual Benefit Life Insurance Company of Newark, New Jersey, 1952), 1, in vertical files ("Retirement"), ILIR, UIUC.

50. Albert T. Sands, "Preparation for Retirement," *Chicago Daily Tribune*, 13 October 1951, 8.

51. Irving Salomon, *Retire and Be Happy* (New York: Greenberg, 1951), 174–205.

52. "Should You Be Forced to Retire at 65?" *US News & World Report*, 13 September 1957, 95.

53. Harold R. Hall, *Some Observations on Executive Retirement* (Boston: Graduate School of Business Administration, Harvard University, 1953), 91–95; Mutual Benefit Life Insurance Company, *Helping Employees*, 1; A. Barr Comstock and Sydney Morrell, "Need 65 Be Time To Retire?" *Nation's Business*, June 1949, 47–48; "Training Is Urged on How To Retire," *New York Times*, 30 November 1949, 25.

54. Comstock and Morrell, "Need 65 Be Time To Retire," 48; "When and How Retirement? Problem for Leaders," *Newsweek*, 12 July 1954, 48.

55. Hart, *Retirement*, 27; Salomon, *Retire and Be Happy*, 3; Mutual Benefit Life Insurance Company, *Helping Employees*, 1; Philip L. Seman, "Hobbies as Recreation for Older People," *Recreation*, August 1944, 254; Havighurst, "Impact of Retirement of the Individual," 12; Elon H. Moore, "Preparation for Retirement," *Journal of Gerontology* 1:2 (1946): 206.

56. John L. Springer, "What Is the Right Time To Retire?" *New York Times Magazine*, 15 February 1959, 13; Nancy E. Gross, *Living With Stress* (New York: McGraw-Hill Book Company, 1958), 148.

57. Carlton Wallace, *How to Retire Successfully* (London: Evans Brothers Limited, 1956), 90.

58. "Work Long and Live Longer," *Science Digest*, June 1946, back cover.

59. Comstock and Morrell, "Need 65 Be Time," 47.

60. Hart, *Retirement*, 74–75; Hall, *Some Observations on Executive Retirement*, 177.

61. Martin Gumpert, "We Can Live Longer—But for What?" *New York Times Magazine*, 22 March 1953, 14; Harry J. Johnson, "How To Retire and Be Happy," *US News & World Report*, 1 February 1957, 38.

62. Kathryn Close, "Getting Ready To Retire," Public Affairs Pamphlet No. 182, New York: Public Affairs Committee, Inc., 1952, 1; "Retirement May Uncover Hidden Emotional Defects," *Science Digest*, September 1958, 25; Frank Howard Richardson, "Retirement: Tonic or Slow Poison?" *Today's Health*, June 1953, 19, 70; Hans Selye, *The Stress of Life* (New York: McGraw-Hill, 1956), 265; Milton L. Barron, Gordon F. Streib, and Edward A. Suchman, "Research on the Social Disorganization of Retirement," *American Sociological Review* 17:4 (1952): 479–482.

63. David D. Stonecypher, "You Can Grow Old Gracefully," *Science Digest*, December 1957, 64; see also "How To Retire and Be Happy," *US News & World Report*, 1 February 1957, 38; and Jesse F. Ballenger, *Self, Senility, and Alzheimer's Disease in America: A History* (Baltimore: John Hopkins University Press, 2006), 57–60.

64. Bill Biggers, "You're Never Through Till You Quit," *Today's Health*, November 1957, 32.

65. Carlton Wallace, *How to Retire Successfully* (London: Evans Brothers Limited, 1956), 19; Selye, *Stress of Life*, 265.

66. Gross, *Living With Stress*, 147; Stonecypher, "Old Age," 68.

67. I use the term "separated spheres" to acknowledge critiques of "separate spheres" models in gender and women's history. During the 1950s, for example, experts used ideologies about separated spheres to make sense of gender in retirement, as men's return to the home, they believed, undermined gender arrangements between husbands and wives. For insightful critiques of separate spheres ideology, see Linda K. Kerber, "Separate Spheres, Female Worlds, Woman's Place: The Rhetoric of Women's History," *Journal of American History* 75:1 (1988): 9–39; and Nancy Isenberg, *Sex and Citizenship in Antebellum America* (Chapel Hill: University of North Carolina Press, 1997), esp. 8–10. For important discussions of women's public activities and gender politics during the 1950s, see the various essays in Joanne Meyerowitz, ed., *Not June Cleaver: Women and Gender in Postwar America, 1945–1960* (Philadelphia: Temple University Press, 1994).

68. "Retirement Not Always Happy," *Business Week*, 5 April 1952, 50; Jacob Tuckman and Irving Lorge, *Retirement and the Industrial Worker: Prospect and Reality* (New York: Teachers College Columbia University, 1953), 68, 69; Salomon, *Retire and Be Happy*, 152; William Attwood, "Why Does He Work So Hard?" in *The Decline of the American Male*, ed. *Look Magazine* (New York: Random House, 1958), 58.

69. Elaine Tyler May, "Pushing the Limits: 1940–1961," in *No Small Courage: A History of Women in the United States*, ed. Nancy Cott (New York: Oxford University Press, 2000), 492–493.

70. Walter B. Pitkin, *The Best Years: How to Enjoy Retirement* (New York: Current Books, 1946), 44.

71. Edward J. Stieglitz, *The Second Forty Years* (Philadelphia: JB Lippincott Company, 1946), 2; Stonecypher, "Old Age," 67.

72. Salomon, *Retire and Be Happy*, 3; Paul W. Boynton, *Six Ways to Retire* (New York: Harper & Brothers, 1952), 23; Hart, *Retirement*, 70.

73. Boynton, *Six Ways to Retire*, 49; see also Barron, Streib, and Suchman, "Research on the Social Disorganization of Retirement," 479–482; Giles, *How to Retire*, 227; and George Lawton, "Will Your Old-Timers Be Ready To Retire?" *Factory Management and Maintenance*, January 1950, 117.

74. See Costa, *Evolution of Retirement*, 174–176.

75. Robert K. Burns, *Meeting the Challenge of Retirement*, booklet (Chicago: Industrial Relations Center, University of Chicago, n.d., 1959?), 42; Salomon, *Retire and Be Happy*, 3; Thomas Parran, Harwood S. Belding, Antonio Ciocco, James A Crabtree, Theodore F. Hatch, Adolph G. Kammer, and Violet B. Turner, "Monograph I," in *Criteria for Retirement: A Report of a National Conference on Retirement of Older Workers*, ed. Geneva Mathiasen (New York: GP Putnam's Sons, 1953), 68.

76. See Dillard Stokes, *Social Security—Fact and Fancy* (Chicago: Henry Regnery Company, 1956). On the UAW and postwar Social Security demands, see, for instance, Seth Wigderson, "How the CIO Saved Social Security," *Labor History* 44:4 (2003): 483–507; and Timothy G. Borden, "'Toledo Is a Good Town for Working People': Richard T. Gosser and the UAW's Fight for Pensions," *Michigan Historical Review* 26:1 (2000): esp. 51, 64; as well as "Report to the Membership," *United Automobile Worker*, April 1957, 4; and "The Steady Push for Pensions," *Fortune*, June 1959, reprinted in *Social Security: Programs, Problems, and Policies*, ed. William Haber and Wilbur J. Cohen (Homewood, IL: Richard D. Irwin, Inc., 1960), 184.

77. Quoted in Victor Regnier, "Neighborhood Planning for the Urban Elderly," in *Aging: Scientific Perspectives and Social Issues*, ed. Diana S. Woodruff and James E. Birren (New York: D. Van Nostrand Company, 1975), 298 (Table 14.1).

78. "What to Do For Retirement," *Business Week*, 14 April 1951, 34, 36.

79. "Retirement Not Always Happy," *Business Week*, 5 April 1952, 52.

80. Alfred R. Zipser, Jr., "Elderly Workers 'Taught' To Retire," *New York Times*, 17 September 1950, 131.

81. "What to Do For Retirement," 36; Zipser, "Elderly Workers," 131.

82. "Preparation for Retirement," 211.

83. Zipser, "Elderly Workers," 131.

84. "What to Do for Retirement," 36; "Should You Be Forced To Retire at 65?" *US News & World Report*, 13 September 1957, 96.

85. "What to Do for Retirement," 36; Mutual Benefit Life Insurance Company, *Helping Employees*, 10.

86. "What to Do for Retirement," 36.

87. "What to Do for Retirement," 36; Mutual Benefit Life Insurance Company, *Helping Employees*, 10; Elon H. Moore and Gordon F. Streib, *The Nature of Retirement* (New York: Macmillan Company, 1959), 197–198.

88. Zipser, "Elderly Workers," 131.

89. "What to Do for Retirement," 36; Mutual Benefit Life Insurance Company, *Helping Employees*, 10; Moore and Streib, *Nature of Retirement*, 198.

90. "What to Do for Retirement," 36; Mutual Benefit Life Insurance Company, *Helping Employees*, 10.

91. Moore and Streib, *Nature of Retirement*, 199.

92. Ibid.

93. Moore and Streib, *Nature of Retirement*, 198; "What to Do for Retirement," 36.

94. "To Retire Happily, Get a Hobby First," *Business Week*, 22 December 1951, 36, 38.

95. On corporate paternalism and welfare capitalism before the era of the CIO, see William Littmann, "Designing Obedience: The Architecture and Landscape of Industrial Capitalism, 1880–1930," *International Labor and Working-Class History* 53 (1998): 88–114; Lizabeth Cohen, *Making a New Deal: Industrial Workers in Chicago, 1919–1939* (New York: Cambridge University Press, 1990); James D. Rose, *Duquesne and the Rise of Steel Unionism* (Urbana: University of Illinois Press, 2001); Nikki Mandell, *The Corporation as Family: The Gendering of Corporate Welfare, 1890–1930* (Chapel Hill: University of North Carolina Press, 2002); Wayne A. Lewchuk, "Men and Monotony: Fraternalism as a Managerial Strategy at the Ford Motor Company," *Journal of Economic History* 53:4 (1993): 824–856; and Lisa M. Fine, "'Our Big Factory Family': Masculinity and Paternalism at the Reo Motor Car Company of Lansing, Michigan," *Labor History* 34 (1993): 274–291.

96. On the continuation of welfare capitalism beyond the 1930s, see, for instance, Sanford M. Jacoby, *Modern Manors: Welfare Capitalism Since the New Deal* (Princeton: Princeton University Press, 1997); as well as Jennifer Klein, *For All These Rights: Business, Labor, and the Shaping of America's Public-Private Welfare State* (Princeton: Princeton University Press, 2003).

97. "What to Do For Retirement," 34; Zipser, "Big Business Tries to Aid Retirement," F9.

98. "UAW Plans Center," *New York Times*, 19 April 1957, 24; Elvira Delaney, "After the Job—What?" *Recreation*, May 1958, 154–155; "UAW's Drop-Ins Woo Pensioners," *Business Week*, 17 April 1954, 158–160, 162, 164; "Auto Union to Bargain for Retired Workers," *Business Week*, 1 June 1957, 130; photo essay on UAW Drop-In Centers, *United Automobile Worker*, June 1954, 6–7.

99. Kaighn, *How to Retire and Like It*, 16.

100. Boynton, *Six Ways to Retire*, 46.

101. See "Plants Honor 4 South Side Steelmakers," *Chicago Daily Tribune*, 4 June 1950, 2; and "Ten Employes of Wisconsin Steel Retire," *Chicago Daily Tribune*, 24 July 1952, 1. See also "Charles E. Hill Honored," *New York Times*, 27 June 1946, 31; "Two Surety Veterans Retiring," *New York Times*, 31 December 1947, 26; "Dr. Bayne Is Honored By 1,000 Educators," *New York Times*, 8 May 1949, 69; "5th Ave. Group Hails Leadership of Terry," *New York Times*, 26 October 1949, 29; "Worthington Sales Chief Retiring After 59 Years," *New York Times*, 19 September 1951, 51; "Judge Conger, 70, Honored," *New York Times*, 8 January 1952, 29; "Dr. Gartlan, Retiring, Honored at Luncheon," *New York Times*, 8 June 1952, 63; "Justice Davis at 70 Retires This Week," *New York Times*, 28 December 1952, 24; "Fete For Hungerford," *New York Times*, 29 January 1953, 30; "To Fete Retiring School Aide," *New York Times*, 15 May 1953, 25; "700 Educators Bid Dr. Ernst Good-By," *New York Times*, 17 May 1953, 68; "Tobin Retiring from Erie," *New York Times*, 20 October 1954, 43; and "Gillroy is Honored By Building Groups," *New York Times*, 11 November 1958, 48, as well as other citations discussed below.

102. Hart, *Retirement*, 149.

103. Ibid., 143.

104. Ibid., 158.

105. On the tensions between heterosocial and homosocial leisure among men and women, see, for instance, Howard P. Chudacoff, *The Age of the Bachelor: Creating an American Subculture* (Princeton: Princeton University Press, 2000); and Randy D. McBee, "'He Likes Women More Than He Likes Drink and That Is Quite Unusual': Working-Class Social Clubs, Male Culture, and Heterosocial Relations in the United States, 1920s–1930s," *Gender & History* 11:1 (1999): 84–112.

106. Thomas Collins, *The Golden Years: An Invitation to Retirement* (New York: John Day Company, 1956), 249.

107. Ibid.

108. Moore and Streib, *Nature of Retirement*, 17.

109. Hart, *Retirement*, 145.

110. Collins, *Golden Years*, 249; see also James A. Michener, "Out to Pasture," *Nation's Business*, April 1949, 33.

111. Boynton, *Six Ways to Retire*, 46–47.

112. Wallace, *How to Retire Successfully*, 119.

113. Boynton, *Six Ways to Retire*, 46.

114. Theodor Greene, *How to Enjoy Retirement for the Rest of Your Life* (New York: Exposition Press, 1957), 54.

115. Kaighn, *How to Retire and Like It*, 16.

116. Collins, *Golden Years*, 249; Boynton, *Six Ways to Retire*, 46; Hart, *Retirement*, 159; Kaighn, *How to Retire and Like It*, 16; Close, "Getting Ready To Retire," 1.

117. See "A Postman 29 Years Takes His Ease on Retirement," *New York Times*, 2 May 1956, 33.

118. Ethel Sabin Smith, *The Dynamics of Aging* (New York: WW Norton & Company, 1956), 125; "Gold Watch Given Refinery Employe On Job for Half Century," *Chicago Daily Tribune*, 13 June 1948, S5; "Seven Oil Co. Vets Retire," *Chicago*

Daily Tribune, 15 July 1956, S5; Michener, "Out to Pasture," 70; Kaighn, *How to Retire and Like It*, 16; Herbert Corey, "Will Retirement Be a Bore to You?" *Nation's Business*, July 1947, 39.

119. "Water Division Retirant Trades Meter for Pole," *Los Angeles Times*, 14 December 1958, 5.

120. Corey, "Will Retirement Be a Bore," 39.

121. Wallace, *How to Retire Successfully*, 119; "Should You Be Forced to Retire at 65?" *US News & World Report*, 13 September 1957, 95; Boynton, *Six Ways to Retire*, 46; Close, "Getting Ready To Retire," 1; "Honored At Retirement," *New York Times*, 26 February 1944, 5.

122. "Will Your Old-Timers Be Ready to Retire?" *Factory Management and Maintenance*, January 1950, 115.

123. Boynton, *Six Ways to Retire*, 46.

124. "Goldman Retires As Head Mailman," *New York Times*, 29 April 1952, 20.

125. "Retirement Day for Court Clerk is Busy Affair," *Los Angeles Times*, 22 September 1949, 29.

126. Michener, "Out to Pasture," 33.

127. Ibid., 70–74.

128. "Career Man Ends Long City Service," *New York Times*, 16 January 1958, 25.

129. "Retiring Today," *Chicago Daily Tribune*, 29 January 1952, 15.

130. "Retirement Day for Court Clerk," 29.

131. "Dutch Retires," *DSP Folks*, March 1956, 5; "Roman Retires," *DSP Folks*, March 1956, 5. Newsletter copies in possession of the author.

132. Kaighn, *How To Retire and Like It*, 16.

133. Ibid.

134. "Lucille" letter to Ruth MacKay ("White Collar Girl"), quoted in "Retirement Can Be A Pleasure," *Chicago Daily Tribune*, 26 March 1952, B2.

135. "Judge May Honored By Two Clubs At Luncheon," *Los Angeles Times*, 28 February 1947, 5.

136. Ibid.

137. Hall, *Some Observations*, 94. Emphasis in original.

138. Kaighn, *How to Retire and Like It*, 17.

139. Boynton, *Six Ways to Retire*, 47–48.

140. Richardson, "Retirement," 19; Alfred R. Zipser, "Big Business Tries to Aid Retirement," *New York Times*, 12 March 1950, F9.

141. Thomas Parran, Harwood S. Belding, Antonio Ciocco, James A Crabtree, Theodore F. Hatch, Adolph G. Kammer, and Violet B. Turner, "Monograph I," in *Criteria for Retirement: A Report of a National Conference on Retirement of Older Workers*, ed. Geneva Mathiasen (New York: GP Putnam's Sons, 1953), 66–67.

142. "Retirement Not Always Happy," *Business Week*, 5 April 1952, 52.

143. Moore and Streib, *Nature of Retirement*, 2 (quote); "New York's Desmond Program Moves Forward," *Aging* (US Department of Health, Education, and Welfare), November 1953, 7; Havighurst, "The Impact of Retirement of the Individual," 12; Herbert Corey, "Will Retirement Be A Bore To You?" *Nation's Business*, July 1947, 39; "Judge Inch at 82 Is Going Strong," *New York Times*, 3 August 1955,

55; "The Oldsters Go Back To Work," *Newsweek*, 13 January 1958, 70–71; "When and How Retirement? Problem for Leaders," *Newsweek*, 12 July 1954, 48–51; "Old Hands Snub Pensions," *Business Week*, 18 November 1950, 124–126.

144. This phrase appears in Buckley, *Retirement Handbook*, 33; see also Thomas Parran, "Must You Retire at 65," *Collier's*, 24 May 1952, 75; and "When and How Retirement?" *Newsweek*, 12 July 1954, 50.

145. Kaighn, *How to Retire and Like It*, 88.

146. *As Young As You Feel*, dir. by Harmon Jones, Twentieth Century-Fox, 1951.

147. Walker, *Living Your Later Years*, 99.

Chapter Five

Work, Play, and Gender:
The Making of Retirement Culture

We are a disappointed generation . . . The age of happy problems has brought us confusion and anxiety amid the greatest material comfort the world has ever seen. Culture has become a consolation for the sense of individual powerlessness in politics, work, and love. With gigantic corporations determining our movements . . . we ask leisure, culture, and recreation to return to us a sense of ease and authority. But work, love, and culture need to be connected.

—Herbert Gold, author, 1957[1]

The art of good retirement is to find in leisure, the meanings you get out of work.

—Robert J. Havighurst, sociologist, 1959[2]

Many retired men probably would have agreed with the sentiments of Herbert Gold in his 1957 *Atlantic Monthly* article. Retirees of the 1950s *were* a disappointed generation; they were pushed out of their jobs at a time when material wealth and profitable work seemed within most American men's grasp. Despite increasing material standards, some adult men felt powerless, as pundits often pointed out. Companies, large bureaucracies, and women, men complained, demanded too much of them and undermined their individuality. As Gold suggested, many Americans looked to leisure and recreation to find fulfillment and achievement in a mass society. But Gold warned that leisure, on its own, could not provide men (or women) with the sense of self-esteem and individuality they yearned for. Without work and productivity as the foundations of daily existence, how could a man, for instance, savor his leisure? How could men find meaning and purpose if all they did was play? Men needed work *and* leisure if they were to attain the "sense of ease and authority," or the fulfilling and balanced life that Herbert Gold described. Somehow, the concepts would have to be integrated in men's lives.

Observers of retirement, however, typically believed that leisure could *replace* the role of work in a man's life. During the post-World War II years, the expansion of middle-class affluence transformed Americans' thinking about aging and gender. Earlier discussions of economic justice for aging working-class men in the 1920s and 1930s, gave way to a new preoccupation with leisure activities in an upwardly mobile middle-class society in the late 1940s and 1950s. Those who wrote about retirement during the 1940s and 1950s thought of retiring men as aging white-collar workers and professionals with stable incomes and suburban homes who would now build new lives on a foundation of leisure.

Experts, including University of Chicago sociologist Robert J. Havighurst, urged retired men to think about their avocations as surrogate vocations. If men made "productive" use of their leisure and play, and applied the same seriousness they did when they were working, then male retirees could remain physically and mentally productive—and thus retain their manhood. Furthermore, observers insisted that leisure (like the job) offered men the opportunity to put distance between themselves and women, further ensuring their masculinity in old age. Retirement experts argued that masculinity could only be preserved if old men remained busy and vigorous. But could leisure *work*? Could leisure become a way for men to hold on to their ideals of productive manhood?

"THE HUSBAND MAY BE AROUND THE HOUSE"

The home was a key site where retired men struggled to make sense of manhood in postwar American culture. Retirement made previous gender arrangements less stable because it removed men from their jobs and brought them back home full-time, challenging men's and women's public-versus-private assumptions regarding gender. According to the writings of academics, magazine writers, and advice authors, men were supposed to work in paid occupations away from home, while women remained in the home as domestic caregivers. However, as the spatial and occupational dimensions of gender eroded upon retirement, men and women began working to reconstruct identifiable differences between husbands' and wives' activities—with a focus on labor, leisure, and space in the home.[3]

Gender-specific dichotomies of "work" and "home" informed experts' views of retirement. Male retirement advice authors described scenarios where husbands and wives occupied very different realms of daily experience. Men, as interpreted by these experts, knew nothing about the home since they spent all their time at a paid job located somewhere other than their own houses. They did not cook or clean. Men did not buy groceries, nor were they aware of how money was budgeted for daily expenses. Socially, man and wife did not spend time together. During daylight hours he resided in the workplace (an estimated fifty hours or more every week), returning home at night only to eat and sleep; she stayed in the home, cleaning and cooking in support of her husband (and presumably slept, though observers failed to mention it).[4] Everyday, men and women lived their lives according to the same gendered routines. As retirement advice writer Irving Salomon summarized, "His special domain was his place of work; her province was their home."[5]

Postwar suburban houses—with multiple rooms, garages, and basements on the fringes of urban areas—provided key locations where experts and retirees envisioned spatial and occupational problems (as well as solutions) to retired men's anxieties about manhood. These larger residences were crucial components of the postwar conversation about gender negotiations in retirement; they provided the ample spaces that created literal room for men and women to more easily renegotiate the gendered arrangement of turf in the household. Retirement experts' focus on suburban spaces made sense, given the rapid expansion of suburban communities after World War II. Government subsidies for mortgages and construction, as well as economic growth outside of urban centers, propelled the rapid growth of suburbia during the 1940s and 1950s.[6] Between 1947 and 1953, the US suburban population increased by 43 percent, compared to an overall population increase of only 11 percent. By 1953, 19 percent of Americans (30 million) lived in suburbs. More and more Americans owned single-family dwellings: homeownership jumped from 44 percent (1940) to 62 percent (1960).[7] In New Jersey, for instance, over 70 percent of the state was classified as suburban during the postwar years.[8] In suburban Orange County, outside of Los Angeles, California, the population increased by 385 percent between 1940 and 1960.[9] As historians Elaine Tyler May and Miriam Forman-Brunell write, homeownership was a "middle-class ideal," the "bedrock of the 'American Dream,'" that symbolized "the good life" for "the upwardly mobile postwar generation."[10] For many Americans of the postwar years, the decidedly middle-class orientation of American culture surely made sense; the United States now appeared to be a well-off middle-class nation. Between 1945 and 1960, the Gross National Product (GNP) increased by 250 percent; and nationally, incomes jumped by 60 percent. Postwar Americans enjoyed a much greater supply of discretionary dollars (5 times as many in 1950, as opposed to 1940).[11] Experts who wrote about retirement assumed that men who retired had already acquired affluence and suburban residences.

However, retirement writers failed to notice that few retiring men and women could afford suburban bliss. Despite the rapid expansion of suburbs, houses were a weighty expense—beyond the reach of older men and women who lived on fixed and limited incomes. As historian Lizabeth Cohen suggested, younger people dominated the suburban housing market, buying 70 percent of all houses sold in the 1940s and 1950s.[12] Nationally, when retirees received their Social Security checks in the mail during the 1950s, they opened envelopes that contained sums totaling, on average, between 756 and 840 dollars per year. In poorer Southern states, such as Mississippi, a retired person might receive a paltry 360 dollars per year, or 30 dollars each month. Even in more affluent states, such as New York and Massachusetts, retired men received only 1,200 dollars over the course of a given year.[13] Throughout the US, aging men and women's incomes were very low. As Michael Herrington noted in his study *The Other America*, 68 percent of men and women over 65 had incomes of less than $1,000 per year.[14] (By contrast, only 11 percent of Americans over the age of 65 had a yearly income between $2,000 and $3,000, while 15 percent had an annual income for $2,000 or more.[15]) Home costs were out of the reach of those who depended on Social Security. To buy a home at "Levittown" on Long Island, New York, a buyer needed to able to pay for housing costs ranging from $7,990 to $9,500.[16] Outside of Newark, New Jersey, in Parsippany-Troy Hills, a typical family needed an estimated 2,000 dollars in annual income to support the costs of homeownership.[17]

Postwar notions of separated spheres did not conform to many men's and women's realities, retired or not. First, women could certainly be found in jobs away from the home, laboring in both offices and factories. As World War II drew to a close in 1945, an estimated 80 percent of working women were determined to remain employed in peacetime.[18] By the end of the 1950s, twice as many women were working than in 1940; and 40 percent of women over the age of 16 worked in a paid occupation.[19] Working women's endeavors did not go unnoticed. Men frequently complained about women's expanding presence in the workplace during the 1950s. Some white-collar men grumbled that women no longer confined themselves to the steno pool; they could even be found in managerial posts.[20] Second, many men remained at home in postwar America, complicating the idea of the home space as a woman's unique "sphere." Once they retired, for example, men reentered the home as a more constant presence.

In the home space, women managed daily affairs. Husbands often complained that their spouses disliked their new presence at home. Women viewed the home as their arena of authority and retired men were regarded as interlopers. Experts remarked that women (the "queens") vowed not to "relinquish" authority to their retired husbands, the "dethroned kings."[21]

While men were supposed to wield authority over the home as a result of their breadwinner status, women actually oversaw household management. Men may have ruled in the office, but women ruled on the homefront. Retirement transformed men's and women's relationships, forcing them to share domestic space: "In our society the great majority of marital arrangements before retirement are based on the husband's absence from the home during working hours. His absence necessitates self-reliance and a certain autonomy of decision-making on the part of the wife . . . The wife who in the minutiae of living has built up a position approaching matriarchy may suddenly be confronted with the . . . husband."[22] While surely not every married couple struggled with retiring men's return to the home, there were many husbands and wives who did. Men's retirement compelled men and women to revisit their assumptions about gender relations and gender identity within the contexts of home, marriage, and family. Making sense of gender would be a difficult undertaking, as men and women remained committed to the idea that men belonged to the workplace and the public world beyond the home and hearth. This proved to be a common refrain in retirement advice authors' writings; it was thought to be natural for men to spend their time not at home but at the factory or office.

Conflicts over the arrangement of household tasks in the home (especially cooking and cleaning) showed how men's concerns with productive manhood in retirement collided with women's status as household managers. The expectations placed upon women's labors remained the same once husbands retired. Women often continued to cook and clean just as they had when their husbands worked. A Florida woman complained that her retired husband was "now a gent of leisure," but her schedule "operated just the same as ever."[23] Men were often oblivious to women's routines of household work and management. They spent their days at the office, not observing domestic labor. When they retired, some men tried to assert command over household labor, presuming they were bringing the workplace virtues of efficiency and organization to domestic labor. Men, however, did not understand that women had already established their own routines, work processes, and managerial styles. While men claimed to know how to work faster and save time (after all, "time is money"), women disliked husbands' interference with long-established work processes.[24] Women remarked that husbands made poor co-workers; when men helped in the domestic workplace, their inexperience prolonged tasks. "The routine of running the household," sociologist Otto Pollack remarked, "may be upset by a well-meaning but not necessarily efficient helper."[25] Discussions of retirement highlighted women's complaints about men as intruders in domestic work. Older men came home to stay in retirement, and they became visible and meddlesome fixtures around the house.

The women who lived with retiring men faced their own "retirement shock": how to deal with the continual presence of husbands, the added burdens placed on household work, and the resulting clash of personalities. Observers feared that men's retirement would contribute to a tense atmosphere in the supposedly calm postwar American home.[26] In response to the potential for domestic unrest, experts cautioned men to tread lightly until spouses had adjusted to their continual presence. As Joseph C. Buckley wrote in *The Retirement Handbook* (1953): "During the years when the husband works, the wife sees him for only a few hours during the day, except on weekends and during vacations. After retirement the husband may be around the house a good deal of the time. This may be a new experience for both of them."[27]

Still, other experts who wrote about retirement urged men to assert themselves in the domestic workplace. They suggested to men they could find manliness in what heretofore had been known, in feminized terms, as "housework." Household work was physical work; it was not easy to scrub, cook, and sweep for hours each day. Were retired men "manly" enough to roll up their sleeves and help? Could they handle the work? Faced with retirement and re-entry into the home, Gifford R. Hart, for instance, tried to redefine the gender connotations of housework. Men who refused to use a broom, he suggested, could not really call themselves "men." This was a progressive concept during the 1950s, but observers of retirement were not primarily concerned with easing women's burdens after so many years of domestic labor. Rather, experts envisioned the redefinition of housework as a way for aging men to remain active, busy, and productive. As Hart wrote in 1957: "Unless you are deaf and blind, you will discover, soon after you retire, that you will have to revise some of your ideas about the housewife's day. You [the retiree] have taken the wear and tear of business principally on your nerves . . . she takes the wear and tear of housework principally on . . . a surprisingly wide variety of muscles." Were women tougher than men? Hart suggested that retired men needed to re-demonstrate their strength and utility. Housework was rigorous, consonant with "men's" work: "If you get right in there with her and pitch for a couple of days, you will . . . find, no doubt to your surprise, that there is real satisfaction and pride in doing those jobs around the house."[28]

The necessity of renegotiating household work was not only grounded in shifting ideals about gender in later life, but also rooted in practicality. As women aged, they could not be expected to work as strenuously on cleaning, cooking, and washing—especially if they lived in a large residence that encompassed multiple floors, rooms, tall flights of stairs, and heavy machinery to move around (such as the vacuum cleaner). Retired men's entry into the domestic workplace forced them to revisit the gendered connotations of "women's work." Retired men would need to help. And if their spouses became ill or even passed away, they would have to assume sole responsibility for domestic labor. A retired man who lived with his two daughters spent two to three hours each day on "housework" because his daughters were working away from the home every day.[29] There were many ways for retired men to make a contribution; they made beds, swept floors, hung laundry, and cleaned the kitchen. In addition, writers urged retired men to take their spouses out to restaurants more often, easing women's cooking labors. Some retired men favored wives' familiar cooking, however.[30]

Just as some retirement advice authors urged men to help women with household labor, others ignored changes in housework after retirement, assuming that women would remain the sole domestic caregiver. Men often implicitly presumed that women would never retire, nor did they need to retire. It was widely believed that men struggled in retirement because the end of men's paid employment undermined the daily routines that had previously defined men's and women's lives. Since men assumed that paid employment in public settings defined "work," male retirement observers argued that women did not face the jarring transition of retirement: "His [the retired man's] wife . . . is less affected by the change and will likely keep up her accustomed household duties and interests to the end."[31] These retirement writers presumed that wives' household work was not really "work" at all, and these women would never need to rest or end their domestic chores: they were "accustomed" to their routines, purportedly seeing their household activities as favored "interests" and sacred "duties." Male writers who studied retirement also overlooked the many older married women who worked in paid occupations during the 1950s, and would, theoretically, "retire" from their jobs if they continued working into their 60s and 70s.[32] Did they work not only in a factory or office, but also around the house? Presumably so. What retirement challenges would they face? Retirement advice authors in effect condemned aging women to an unending life of domestic service.

Despite writers' encouragement, most retired men did not want to busy themselves with what they continued to label "women's work." One retired man, immersed it would seem in an unfamiliar routine of domestic labor, described his home as a "chamber of horrors." He told author Ray Giles that retiring men must

Watch out . . . that you don't become a lady's maid. Too many of the men I know who have retired get to dusting the furniture, doing the marketing, sweeping the sidewalks, and even hanging out the wash. Housework was becoming too great a part of my program, and 'It jest ain't natcheral!'[sic][33]

Another man complained how his spouse transformed him into a domestic helper. He warned other retirees to learn from his misfortune.

> Let me give these newly retired brothers a tip. Don't start in doing a lot of household chores. I never made a bed in my life up to my retirement, and now I do two of them every morning. I also volunteered to make the gravy for dinner and the salads for supper, and I have been doing that now for the past ten years. Of course you want to help the little wife, but she has her work inside the house, and you be quick to find something outside before she has you nailed down to some new habits you don't dare break.[34]

Advice writers thus feared that even minimal household work could lead to feminization and submission. Now constantly surrounded by spaces that were sustained by feminized labors and overseen by resident female supervisors, the surroundings of the home were dangerously unmanly spaces for retired men.

"ODD CHORES AROUND THE HOUSE"

Beginning in the home and extending beyond, retired men pursued numerous strategies to reconstruct firmer boundaries between themselves and women. During the 1940s and 1950s, many retiring men turned to work *in the house* (as opposed to "housework") in order to carve out activities that would serve as productive foundations for a new masculinity in retirement. While most men disregarded housework, undertakings historically associated with cleaning, cooking meals, and the women they lived with, they nonetheless used work in and around the home to differentiate themselves from women and the feminine connotations of domestic labor and space, thereby protecting a surer sense of manhood.[35] Furthermore, retired men constructed specific sites *at* and *away* from home where they could further distance and isolate themselves from women. Some retired men built dens and garage workshops where they could be left alone, while some (white-collar) men actually rented office spaces and commuted back to the laboring city. These men did not work; they only wanted to escape.[36]

Retired men often remarked how they worked on repairs, chores, or projects, but they avoided associations with what might be interpreted as "housework." Men's approach to household tasks brought them to the frontiers of their homes. Retirees often envisioned themselves making contributions in the "garden" or "yard"—not necessarily in the home itself. Irving Salomon, who interviewed retirees for a book called *Retire and Be Happy* during the early 1950s, met retired men who were always working "around a home": they were "repairing furniture," "regrad[ing] the lawn," "put[ting] up storage shelves," "working in the garden," "work[ing] in the yard," "tinkering," and/ or simply "do[ing] odd chores around the house."[37] Sociologist Clark Tibbitts described in a 1954 edition of the *American Journal of Sociology* how older men "turn to repair and maintenance of the home" once they retire, and in *Business Week*'s 1952 survey of retired men's choice activities, 64 percent listed working on the house or garden as the principal way they spent their time every day.[38] Moreover, men would cook meals, but only if they could use fiery outdoor barbecue grills. In the suburbs, according to the *Esquire Handbook for Hosts*, "When a barbecue goes into operation, it automatically becomes a masculine project." The handbook noted, "After all, outdoor cooking is a man's job."[39] Men envisioned the yards that surrounded their homes as their domain.

Even though notions of labor continued to define ideals of masculinity, retired men often ironically relied on laziness to further distinguish themselves from women.[40] As women cooked dinner or vacuumed the floor, men admitted to reading the newspaper, listening to the radio, or even napping on the couch. In the house, retired men used productivity *and inactivity* to differentiate themselves from women and fully disassociate themselves from housework. In Cleveland, nearly 20 percent of retired men listed "loafing" as their daily activity of choice, while a study of retiring men's attitudes towards retirement activities conducted by the University of Chicago indicated 58 percent of factory workers and 39 percent of supervisory personnel planned to spend their retirement "taking it easy."[41]

Women were not shy about voicing their opposition to retired men's proclivity toward rest and relaxation. Content to relax, men were angered when women criticized their decisions. Retired men complained that spouses ordered them on errands whenever they turned on the radio or sat down to rest. A newly retired man wanted to spend his time reading the newspaper, but his spouse disliked seeing him doing nothing around the house each and every day. Soon, quarrels erupted between them. "I thought when I retired I would enjoy my life sitting around the house," another retired man noted, but "[w]ithin a few months, my wife started nagging me nearly all the time."[42] Retirement advice writer Raymond Kaighn met a retired office manager who told him about the woman he lived with, "She is always telling me what to do." The nagging wife upset the former executive because he was an important man in his office and was not used to receiving criticism and orders from others—especially women.[43] In the 1951 film *As Young As You Feel*, a retired man complains to a friend in the local park how his spouse violently ordered him to leave the house. "Get out of the house!" she reportedly shouted, and to underscore her seriousness and get him moving, the woman threw his hat at him.[44]

The nagging wife was a familiar theme in American culture during the 1950s. For instance, in Alfred Hitchcock's *Rear Window* (1954), the main character, LB Jeffries (James Stewart), justifies not marrying his long-time girlfriend Lisa Fremont (Grace Kelly) because he worries about coming home everyday to a "nagging wife." A sympathetic male friend corrected Jeffries by saying, "Wives don't nag, Jeff. They 'discuss.'" For Jeffries, nagging wives embodied the trappings of domesticity. If he married Lisa, would she become a nuisance to him, especially since she was so refined and he was not? Confined to a wheelchair with a broken leg for several weeks during the summer, Jeffries could only look out his apartment window and watch his neighbors' lives unfold. He witnesses one couple who argues constantly. Jeffries soon discovers that the husband has murdered his wife and smuggled her out of their apartment. The film cites her nagging as the likely cause of the murder.[45]

The portrait of agitated women in retiree households complicates popular views of women in the 1950s. While Betty Freidan argued that domesticity stifled women, retiring men and advice authors confronted domestic women in retirees' households who were neither stifled nor silent in their frustration.[46] Women "nagged," ordered men out of the house, and sternly retained authority over household labor. Given the ebb and flow of men and women in and out of the realms of home and work, a movement hastened by lengthening life spans and the expansion of a new and uncertain retirement culture, it is no surprise that older men and women of the 1950s were struggling to make sense of gender identities and boundaries between the sexes. Retirement and retirement advice thus became key arenas where writers and retirees struggled to map out postwar gender relations. Advice authors confronted an uneasy tension in their discussions of retirement: If the home was intrinsically dominated by women, then how could retired men, who no longer left their homes for the manliness of the workplace and remained home on a full-time basis, retain masculinity amidst the prevalence of domesticity?

To create a male space within the house and escape from women's supposed nagging, retired men sometimes built "dens" in their homes. Different from communal recreation rooms, these dens were veritable fortresses of solitude for men. Many men wanted a room (or even rooms) of the house that was their own, a space where the aging patriarch could retreat from the din of the vacuum, the clanging pots and pans, and the ladies' gossip emanating from the kitchen. Since the home constituted a solidly women's space, men used dens to isolate themselves from the feminine meanings attached to the rest of the house. They could literally enter a room, close the door, and separate themselves from the other sex.[47]

In addition to spending time in dens, older men used garages and basements as places where they could withdraw. As historian Kristen Haring writes, these places provided "a masculine refuge in an increasingly feminized household."[48] Many retired men sought out the activity and solitude of tinkering in small workshops; in retirement, the garage and the basement became new "workplaces" for the aging man: men used these spaces to work with tools, often building furniture or making small repairs on household items. As early as the 1930s, architects regarded garages as "essential" components of houses, but they did not become standard in new home construction until the 1950s and 1960s.[49] In contrast with other "proper" rooms of the home, dusty, dirty, and even dingy garages, basements, and attics held a "rugged" and "manly" appeal.[50]

Women even encouraged husbands to build these spaces of isolation and labor, literally giving ground to their spouses. The wife of one retired man said: "I think that a retired man should have a room that is all his own—a den, if you want to call it that—where he can go in and shut the door, and be out of his wife's sight for part of the day . . . What he is doing in there need be none of her concern; nor should her occupation during that time be any of his. They will be seeing plenty of each other as it is."[51]

Garage and basement workshops not only provided retired men with their own spaces; they also allowed older men to regain a lost sense of usefulness and self-importance that evaporated when they retired. "I don't know what my husband would do shut up for hours in a den," the spouse of a retired man noted. "He is not a bookish man . . . But he does like to tinker, and he does well with tools. You should see his workshop in the basement of our house. That is where you will find him every day right after breakfast."[52]

Despite the emphasis on separating men's and women's activities within the house, experts recognized the need for sociability and the solidarity among the members of these opposing sexes. To coexist in the same house on a consistent basis, men and women needed some activities they could do together. While experts delineated "work" along gender lines, certain leisure practices could be more safely shared. Especially when the activities involved the house itself, husbands and wives were advised to do more things together; the house was still a shared space. Leisure that included both men and women required careful planning, however. Experts cautioned that men and women would struggle to find activities they both could take pleasure in—if a man thought he and his spouse could enjoy a woodworking class, he was sorely mistaken. "She goes along like a martyr," fretted Paul Boynton, "watches you show off with a hammer and a saw, tries valiantly to get into the spirit of the thing, and hits her thumb with the hammer."[53]

Retirement writers wanted to imagine women in supporting roles as live-in retirement counselors—dutiful assistants who would help nervy husbands find their footing in a time of stressful upheaval. As retired men struggled to adjust, women were to provide them with ample emotional support. Women were expected not to worsen husbands' anxieties. Wives of retired men had only one task, according to one observer: "It is her responsibility for easing him out of his active habits into his new tapering ways of life, with the least possible upset." Irving Salomon told retiring men to expect women's support. "Her understanding and cooperation," he wrote, "particularly when you first retire, may determine the success of your retirement. The continuation of her cooperation and encouragement will be another prop when and if, at some later time, you should waver."[54] While many women certainly helped their spouses adjust to retirement, observers returned again and again to the figure of the nagging wife, the testy and vocal woman of the home who resented retirees' constant, unusual presence. Only rarely did male retirement observers actually discuss retired men's spouses in positive terms.

Retirement scholars seldom imagined any life beyond the home and hearth for aging women, and when they did, they were careful to connect women's public activities to their private lives at home. In a 1952 survey of men and women's activities in later life, sociologists Evelyn Colby and John G. Forrest discussed how aging women could bring supplemental income into the retired man's household by securing part-time jobs for themselves. The authors did not want to facilitate women's liberation from the drudgery of housework or ease tension between retired husbands and wives; instead, they envisioned women's workforce participation as a way to bolster male-headed households. The older woman's income would help continue the standards of living acquired during the retired man's tenure as the breadwinner. Furthermore, the authors' discussions of occupations for aging women affirmed gendered ideas about work. Older women, the authors wrote, could find positions as babysitters, maids, cooks, housekeepers, laundresses, party planners, among other safely or traditionally "feminine" occupations.[55]

Colby and Forrest's writing on women and retirement, however, pointed to sources of gender subversion in the home—even as the scholars hoped to see women's labors contribute to the financial stability of the male-headed household. In situations where the wife was younger than the husband, Colby and Forrest saw no reason why women should not venture out to work. While this would have supported the overall goal of keeping the male-headed household financially solvent, the sociologists' work evoked not-so-subtle tones of women's liberation. "In many families the wife is younger than the husband," the scholars conceded. "Very often, too, she has educational background that she has never attempted to use, her time being taken up with running a household and rearranging a family."[56] Now that husbands were retired and the kids were grown up, women were free to seek some kind of job. It might be difficult to find employment (due to hiring age limits), but older women—especially those with education—could find job opportunities. Women with schooling might work as substitute teachers, medical laboratory technicians, librarians, dental hygienists, and nutritionists.[57] Theoretically, Colby and Forrest suggested work to women not only as a means to bring additional money into the household, but also as a way to become the dominant breadwinner, assume a new public role (that had formerly belonged to their husbands), and build new social relationships.

Experts often discussed ways for retired men to escape from the home. However, as observers of retirement suggested, it was much easier for white-collar/middle-class men to escape from the home than blue-collar working-class retirees. They possessed the money to travel, as well as the ability to buy or rent distant places of retreat. Some white-collar retirees in the suburban New York City area set up small private offices in the city, even though they were not employed and did not complete any work. Everyday, these men commuted from their homes to these offices, traveling once again from the feminized world of the home to the more male-gendered world of the public sphere. These sentimental journeys allowed men to reconstruct a key part of the earlier working routine: the daily commute. A retired New York professional commuted from his suburban home to a rented office in Manhattan. He did not work there, but the commute allowed him to, as he put it, escape from the "woman's world." Riding the train also allowed the older man to visit with his old commuter cronies. Another man did the same; he traveled from outside the city to a small office to "get out from under the carpet sweeper."[58] These men constructed a fantasy world of commuting, sociability, and simulated work environments. This artificial workaday world allowed them to escape from the home's domesticity, and to retain key elements of earlier (and manlier) endeavors as workers.

Because experts and retiring men thought of the home as a space where women ruled, retirees would look beyond their yards, dens, garages, and basements for new activities and sites that would help them secure new paths to manhood. An older man in Texas, for example, embittered by his retirement, vowed to spend the majority of his time away from home. The Texan quickly plunged into "civic affairs" and local fraternal orders, and frequently bothered his old friends to go fishing, play poker, and attend horse races. "That made him feel like a man again," Ray Giles reported to readers.[59] Like the man in Texas, many other retired men struggled to find new activities that would take them away from the home and give them something that would test and challenge their bodies and minds.

WORKING HARD AT PLAY

How could men get away from the home and the women they lived with? What were the best ways for retired men to spend their time now that they no longer worked? To successfully "adjust" to retirement, experts closely advised men about the possibilities for productivity found, ironically, through leisure. Since the workplace was closed to many older men, experts viewed leisure practices as the most readily accessible way to escape from the home and stay busy everyday. To preserve their masculinity while at play, retired men needed to keep themselves occupied with a rigorous regimen of physical and mental activity: sports, games, crafts, travel, socializing, and collecting— anything and everything to keep their minds and bodies vigorous, strong, and in perpetual motion. Despite their varying health conditions and limited monetary means, retired men needed to work hard at having fun in order to retire "successfully." Games such as shuffleboard and golf were not idle ways to waste time; they were regarded by some as crucially important ways to forge a new productive manhood. The aging journalism professor Walter Pitkin traveled to Florida during the 1940s, where he quickly developed a "loathing" for the game of shuffleboard. Why? Retired men played too seriously. "No doubt it is a noble game and fascinating to those it fascinates. But the grim mouth haunts me," he wrote. "The stern assault of the court every morning after breakfast is like Custer's Last Stand. The player must go on, though he sees no hope. He mutters . . . that perhaps after all the battles worth fighting are those we must lose."[60] Shuffleboard was more than leisure; it was war.

In their discussions of retiree leisure, writers ironically refashioned manhood in old age on the foundations of youthful exuberance and ability, labor and productivity, and monetary means and affluence. The most successful older men were those who not only enjoyed many activities, but were vibrant, energetic, and committed "experts" in their new fields of endeavor. The ideal retired men in postwar culture were former white-collar professionals who enjoyed many physical activities such as golf, shuffleboard, hunting, baseball, and fishing. They also succeeded intellectually as hobbyists and collectors. Access to such opportunities in retirement, however, depended to a great extent on health and income. Free time was not really free, but rather required dollars and the ease they bought, as well as physical ability. Retirement observers assumed that money was not a concern; yet to participate in this culture of retirement and solidify their manhood in old age, older men needed the economic empowerment that accompanied middle-class affluence. For instance, a retired factory foreman was "in for all sorts of recreation," including fishing, hunting, baseball, football, billiards, driving, bowling, trapping, and shooting, among other activities; as a retired professional on a generous pension, he had the time, and the money, needed to work hard at having fun all day. In addition, he was physically rich: able to enjoy such a busy schedule of physical activity.[61]

Retirement experts envisioned leisure as an essential way for aging men to retain physical ability and mental acuity—key foundations of functioning male bodies. Retirement advice author Joseph Buckley pointed to the words of Joseph Lee, the "father" of the modern playground movement, who argued that "We do not cease playing because we are old; we grow old because we cease playing." To avoid "retirement shock" and to keep disability and death at arm's length, retired men needed activity to energize and strengthen their bodies and minds. "All of us need a certain amount of physical exercise to keep our bodies in good shape," Buckley pointed out. Men were told to exercise in order to keep their bodies and emotions strong and fit. "During retirement," he continued, "we should see to it that we get the kind of physical exercise which is beneficial to body structures and to our muscular and nervous systems."[62] A retiree suggested that other men would have to work diligently to learn about how to have fun: "Every man should learn to play and do some of it before he finishes life."[63]

Staying "young" and preserving manhood were synonymous. Some experts and retirees envisioned rigorous physical activity as a fountain of youth, capable of helping a man keep his vigor and vim as he journeyed through his twilight years. The important ties between masculinity and exercise had been centerpieces of middle-class culture in the United States since the turn of the twentieth century, and it was believed that strenuous activity could guard older men against the dangers of growing old. California retiree William Leslie occupied his days with intense physical activities such as roller skating. Leslie pursued this life on wheels because he believed that skating helped him stay young. Others agreed, noting they "subscribe[d] with a rebel yell" to Leslie's contention that exercise sustained youth. Men needed to be careful, however: "one man's activity is another's funeral."[64] If retirees subscribed to William Leslie's view of retirement, they would pursue this form of manhood on the edge of a potentially fine line: they would need to work out their bodies energetically but somehow avoid injury (or worse). For some, perhaps aging bodies could not be made young again without significant risk.

Many "oldsters" seized upon opportunities to play sports such as baseball. Retirement writers discussed aging male ball players with a mix of surprise, worry, and admiration. In Florida, where warm weather permitted year-round play, baseball became a centerpiece of retirement culture. St. Petersburg was one Sunbelt city among many that featured popular retiree baseball leagues. These leagues catered to serious, though less accomplished, athletes: "As is to be expected, these oldsters do not run very fast or throw very well; but they bat and catch nearly as well as anyone and usually use good judgment in their play."[65] Retirement observers marveled at teams that featured men in their seventies and eighties, as they watched these aggressive old men "sass" umpires who made bad calls. In the crowd, a "vociferous" gang of older men watched the action. The games could be intense, and an "ever-alert local undertaker" lurked quietly nearby.[66]

Golf offered a lower-impact workout, becoming a popular retiree activity during the 1950s. Like baseball, the sport brought men out of doors, providing exercise, sociability, and a basis for manly competition. Even though golf was a significantly less physical game than baseball or roller-skating, the difficulty and complexity of golf, the opportunities for competition it afforded, and the length of time needed to finish a series of nine or eighteen holes made golf an attractive substitute for the job in an aging man's retirement lifestyle. "Much of golf's appeal," observed sports writer Arthur Daley in 1953, "lies in the persistent, relentless challenge it offers in the endless search for perfection."[67] Golf demanded the ongoing cultivation of mental acuity, physical ability, and competitiveness and, to succeed, a man would need to play on a routine basis. Observers noted the workaday ethos that old men brought to the otherwise quiet golf courses of their communities. "Some try to duplicate the frenzy of their working days" by playing a lot of golf, *Newsweek* magazine noted in 1954.[68] Moreover, a day on the links might provide a way for retired men to escape from the "nagging" women they lived with and the stifling homes they lived in. Writer and golf lover John P. Marquand claimed that men, after all, once invented golf to "get away from women."[69]

The growing accessibility of golf courses and golf equipment during the 1950s made it a key foundation of male retirement culture, just as the expansion of retirement during the postwar years fueled the growth of golf. Both North and South, the number of public, semi-private, and private courses expanded considerably. In 1953, the state of Florida boasted of 120 golf courses, "one of the experiences most enjoyed by visitors to the Sunshine state."[70] Many courses in Florida were public courses that were accessible to everyone, and private courses were "just as willing and ready to accord you golfing privileges" for a fee.[71] By 1960, there were 3,162 private, 1,997 semi-private, and 852 public golf courses throughout the US.[72] New golf cars (not yet called "carts") made it possible for aging men with limited physical mobility to still enjoy the game. And increasingly affordable golf apparel enhanced men's chosen identities as golfers. A retired man on a fixed income could still afford a $3 golf shirt (in pastel colors), $5 golf pants (35 percent rayon), and $10.95 leather golf shoes (made with the popular "moccasin" leather). "Elmer Dubb," the average golfer of the 1950s, was very happy when scored a 95 on the course, and "can dress economically for all the weathers that strike our golf courses, and dress stylishly, too."[73] In 1957 alone, golfers spent more than $60 million on golf equipment—surpassing the totals spent on equipment for all other sports. The purchase of boxing gloves was at an all-time low.[74]

While many men told of plans to play golf in retirement, they would enter a leisure space that was increasingly popular among women as well. There were so many men and women playing golf that the "total age" of many couples on golf courses "would add up to over three hundred years."[75] Golf courses were not intrinsically male spaces. By 1956, there were 5 million golfers in the United States, and an estimated 25 percent of them were women.[76] Arthur Daley noted many men's complaints about women's "invasion" of golf courses, but reminded them there was nothing they could do to stem the tide. Men "fume and mutter" about women, yet as Daley wrote, "the dolls can't be ruled off the course."[77] Writing in the *Chicago Daily Tribune*, Annette Victorin described how women "have crashed the barriers of most sports once dominated by men": golf, bowling, boating, and even wrestling. Only fishing remained a "closed sanctum" to women in postwar culture, according to Victorin.[78]

Men often said they "want to catch up" on fishing and hunting when they retired.[79] Hunting and fishing were thought to be particularly manly endeavors. Hunting and fishing in woods, lakes, and streams perhaps not only required mental and physical work, but the wooded and watery surroundings perhaps evoked the bygone days of the mythical western frontier, where hardy men once struggled to prove their mettle. Though often confined to decidedly urban and suburban settings, retired men ventured off to local frontiers on the edge of town—the wooded areas, streams, creaks, and lakes that existed on the fringes of their communities. Within these new frontiers of postwar America, many retirees labored to cultivate a new, though familiar, identity as a "sportsman." Aging husbands told spouses that fishing, for example, was "too rugged and rough" for women. "It's the one time he insists I stay home," a woman noted in 1955. "Frankly I don't mind because fishing is . . . ugh!"[80]

Observers of retirement focused on professional men's supposed sporting prowess. For instance a retired professor loved to hunt and fish, hunting birds in particular. Marvin S. Pittman, who wrote for the journal *Recreation*, admired the emeritus professor's skill and single-mindedness; the professor was, in his words, "a real sportsman." Driving along country roads, the professor would stop upon seeing a bird. He would pull over, produce his gun, and fire. "Before the bird knows it," Pittman wrote, "he is only another notch on the professor's game log, which acquires hundreds of new notches every year." This endless hunt along country roads made sense to Pittman. After all,

"This sport with the gun . . . relaxes the nerves and strengthens the body of the professor."[81] As if to solidify his reputation as a sportsman, the professor was also known among other men as a "master fisherman."[82] White-collar retirees were once mental workers and professionals, but in retirement they could become hardy woodsmen of the frontier, testing themselves by hunting and fishing in the wilds. "At last a man would have time to hunt and fish," Pittman remarked of retirement, "not the little bits and moments of these ancient, traditional past times which weekend and vacations now afford, but those long stretches for which every true fisherman and hunter always yearn."[83]

Ideal retirement activities had to be "productive." Gifford R. Hart wrote that retired men needed "interests of a serious, constructive character" if they were to enjoy a "successful" retirement. Leisure activities needed to "[p]erform some useful function," "produce a financial result of some sort," and "make some use of the retired man's principal skill or experience." Sociologist Robert J. Havighurst told an audience at the University of Chicago in 1959 that the "activity theory" of retirement was far more beneficial than the rest and ease of the "rocking chair." Older men, he noted, "must look for in retirement the same satisfactions he received from his work life," while *Changing Times* told readers in 1953 to "Make sure you'll get the rewards, tangible or intangible, you anticipate." Observers of retirement completely agreed that ideal retirement activities needed to produce personal dividends that recreated the functions of work.[84] Scholars told older men to prepare for their retirement by studying leisure activities as future jobs. Retired men, after all, would rely heavily on these activities to define their new "careers." As Elon H. Moore asked gerontologists in 1946, "To what then shall an individual retire? Whatever his choice, the prospective retiree should make a careful job analysis of his intended activity and then determine his interest in such activity."[85]

Once they retired, many older men organized their new activities into new daily and weekly routines. Just as routines defined their working lives, aging men brought this ethos with them into retirement. In lieu of work, retired men pursued routines of leisure; the best aging men resembled harried professionals who occupied nearly every hour of the day with an intense routine of varied activities. Robert Havighurst wrote, "He [the retired man] may make a routine out of his leisure to fill the void left by the loss of routines centered about his job."[86] For example, "RES" retired from his job as a factory superintendent to a demanding, self-imposed routine. During his working years, RES did not enjoy leisure. Worried he would hate retirement, the former superintendent organized a program "much as he did at his job."[87] He described the progression of a typical week during a conversation with Irving Salomon:

MONDAY:
Morning: Reading Sunday's *New York Times*. (He never had time to really read it on a Sunday.)
Afternoon: To the farm. (He and another man own a ninety-acre farm, forty-two miles out of town.)
Evening: (And it is noted that although he planned evenings, they are all the same.) Television, picture show, friends, cards, etc.

TUESDAY:
Morning: Reading. Primarily, technical publications.
Afternoon: Exercise/and or grandchildren.

WEDNESDAY:
Morning: Reading of books
Afternoon: Helping at the YMCA

THURSDAY:
Morning: At desk taking care of personal matters and miscellaneous reading.
Lunch: With friends
Afternoon: Ball game or movie

FRIDAY:
All day: Work at the farm.

SATURDAY:
Morning: Take care of grandchildren.
Afternoon: Visit friends, go to a show, take a ride with wife.
For emergency when insufficient to do, start a workshop, or more time for YMCA.[88]

Once he was only a factory superintendent, but now he was a Renaissance man. RES's new routine hinged on a dizzying assortment of activities, ranging from pursuits that stimulated his mind (reading and socializing) to those that allowed him to exercise his body and acquire additional income (farming). He also busied himself with charitable volunteer work or visits with his grandchildren. Another retired man followed a similar routine of activities that included helping people in his neighborhood. He reported that he even drove women in his neighborhood to the local "mental institution" when needed.[89]

When Morton H. Anderson, of Bethlehem Steel, retired from his post as an executive, he and his spouse moved to Los Angeles to enjoy a well-deserved rest "after a long and strenuous business career." But in retirement, Anderson was actually busier than ever; the *Los Angeles Times* dubbed him the "Busiest Retired Man." While he initially anticipated a retirement that would be characterized by rest and relaxation, he could not let go of his notions of a rigorous daily routine. He became a member of the board of education, joined the California Shoreline Planning Association, worked with local and state highway committees, joined the Santa Monica Chamber of Commerce, and worked on behalf of the War Bond drive, the Salvation Army, and the Community Chest, among seventeen other posts he held. But before beginning his daily whirlwind of activities, he always managed to play a quick round of golf by "starting at dawn."[90]

Even retired men who pursued only leisure activities in retirement conceptualized their play as part of productive daily and weekly routines. While RES needed to devote time to his farm, and Morton H. Anderson was active in numerous community activities and local government, a retired telephone company supervisor (referred to as "XXXXXXXXX" by Irving Salomon) embraced a rigorous routine composed almost entirely of sociability, pleasure, and play. His daily and weekly checklist included:

Daily:
1. Shop for daily needs of the house.
2. Prepare breakfast for wife and self.
3. Listen to radio programs.

Weekly:
1. Have lunch with friend in New York City.
2. Attend meeting of the Old Guard.
3. Attend bowling match of Church League.

Other Activities:
1. Attend Men's Club meeting at church.
2. Attend lectures and parties sponsored by Telephone Company.
3. Attend theater and movies and some travel lectures.
4. Take trips for picture material (photography).
5. Visit my sons and grandchildren.
6. Entertain at home.
7. Plan and take automobile trips.[91]

Despite experts' frequent discussions of the personal productivity that could be derived from leisure, some older men dismissed hobbies and games as "childish" or "womanish," appropriate only for "sissies." Aging men worried about stigmas attached to not working, despising the perception they were "playing" and wasting their time. Against the backdrop of World War

II and the Cold War, which put a premium on usefulness and service, aging men worried about losing connections to their notions of productivity. Men also worried about not living up to new cultural standards that celebrated the maintenance of middle-class affluence. Some retired men preferred the terms "outside-of-work interests" to describe their leisure pursuits. The term "hobbies" connoted for some a lack of seriousness.[92]

However, many retired men did not view recreation as "womanish"; these men viewed retirement as an opportunity to free themselves from the troubles and burdens of the working world. No longer tied to machines, offices, and assembly lines, men savored the chance to live on their own terms. One retired man noted that all men should look forward to retirement because it afforded them time "relax, reflect, and have time to enjoy living. Get away from the grind."[93] Now, as superannuated men, they could finally explore other interests. The sociologist Warner Bloomberg, Jr., talked with aging working-class men in a mass production factory who told him they were especially eager to retire. "There was so much to do in life besides work in a factory!" some exclaimed. "At last a man could furnish his home and landscape his yard, and even be able to 'piddle' at it instead of having to drive himself to get done all that he could on a one- or two-day weekend." A sixty-five year-old former corporate director of research, who fully enjoyed his newfound freedom, noted, "If a man has something in mind he wishes to do, retire and do it."[94] Some men relished the chance to never work again.

A move to the Sunbelt states of Florida or California symbolized the most significant expression of personal freedom. No longer bound to the North and its industrial jobs, retired men began moving south during the 1950s in greater numbers. *Business Week* polled retirees in 1951 and discovered that "many" wanted to pack up and move to Florida. Between 1940 and 1950, the US census showed that substantial numbers of older men and women were relocating to the Sunbelt. California gained 130,000 new older residents, while Florida and Arizona drew 66,000 and 8,900 respectively.[95] Even if they did not permanently relocate, many aging men and women took extended vacations in the Sunbelt. Observers often talked with retired men who spent part of their time every year in California or Florida. Florida and California were "thronged" with older men and women. If they had the means, retirees wanted to take advantage of their freedom. An aging man told the sociologist Alonzo F. Myers that he did "not want to die in Pittsburgh"; he wanted to live out his years under the warm Florida sun.[96]

Moving to Florida was not a privilege enjoyed only by wealthy men. Due to the expansion of retiree trailer parks in the Sunbelt, aging working men were also able to enjoy the chance to dip their toes in the sand and surf of Florida. In a 1954 survey of a Florida trailer park, for example, sociologists discovered a cross-class mixture of older couples. Men who once worked in occupations such as factory work (30.9 percent), farming (24.7 percent), retail (22.2 percent), and managerial work (8.2 percent) lived in the park's 100 units. Many of these men and women came from the wintry regions of the East and Midwest.[97]

Due to physical decline in later life, which could prevent some men from enjoying the sports of golf, shuffleboard, or baseball, retirement experts recognized the need for activities that relied less on the body and utilized the mind to a greater degree. Some experts suggested that retired men could reinvent themselves as hobby enthusiasts. Collecting and other crafts, retirement writers suggested, were far more worthy pursuits than other less-serious undertakings such as lawn bowling or sitting in the park. Plagued by chronic back pain, a seventy-four year-old retired dentist, for instance, reported that he focused his energies on collecting favorite poems because he could no longer enjoy sports.[98]

Hobbies such as collecting and crafts did more than simply pass the time; rather, these activities helped retired men nurture a new expertise, new skills for their hands, and meet other men who shared their interests. Serious hobbies allowed older men to have "both minds and hands full."[99] In the realm of collecting, there was much to explore: stamps, coins, ship models, furniture, and firearms, to name a few. Firearms provided the collector's item of choice for older men during the 1950s. In addition to the importance of guns in hunting, firearms connected their collectors to a familiar touchstone of masculinity, as these weapons overlapped with American histories of frontier expansion, war, and technology.[100] Gun collecting and knowledge of weapons, according to George H. Preston, were an "ideal retirement activity" and a "fascinating" choice for retired men to explore.[101] Yet collecting did not require extensive physical movement or strength. Many of these activities could even "be done from a wheelchair." Most importantly, hobbies kept men mentally and socially engaged, and led to new social contacts: "No matter what you collect other people are collecting the same things. See to it that part of your collecting includes collecting other collectors."[102] Hobbies could provide retiring men with absorbing new activities—much as their jobs had once done.

Men regarded leisure as a necessary way to stay busy (and manly) in retirement. They believed that serious physical and mental activity in the realm of play would help men remain youthful and personally productive as they aged. To claim identities that were consonant with ideals of productivity, retiring men would need to stay physically active and busy everyday. Older men organized their leisure activities into new routines, recreating key aspects of their earlier working lives for their twilight years. By doing so, ideals of productive manhood became the centerpiece of postwar retirement culture.

SOCIAL CLUBS FOR RETIRED MEN—AND WOMEN

In their examinations of American culture at the turn of the twentieth century, historians of masculinity point out that social organizations for boys and adult men typically affirmed rough cultures of aggression and excluded women; these organizations—The Boy Scouts, college fraternities, Young Men's Christian Association (YMCA) sports, Odd Fellows, Freemasons, and even street gangs—were key social sites where men constructed "brutish" and separatist forms of masculinity. They wanted to refashion male dominance and apartness amidst the rapid economic changes, multiculturalism, and the breaking down of traditional gender boundaries between men and women that accompanied the rise of mass society. This aggressive turn-of-the-twentieth-century masculinity gained considerable influence in American culture and would continue to lurk in the American cultural landscape for the remainder of the twentieth century.[103] However, the formation of social clubs for retired men—and women—during the 1940s and 1950s offered a noteworthy challenge to the deep connections between homosocial organizations and the formation of twentieth-century masculinity.

During the post-World War II years, retired men looked, in part, to collective sites for leisure, sociability, and the preservation of manhood. But retired men's organized avenues for sociability demonstrated a significant degree of flexibility that challenged the cultures of male exclusivity that defined so much of twentieth-century masculinity. While male retirees did create male-exclusive social organizations in the 1940s and 1950s, they also supported and embraced social clubs that endorsed heterosocial activities. Social organizations such as Golden Age Clubs provided sociability among older men as well as women. Through these organizations, aging men and women could talk with each other, participate in numerous social activities, and feel like they were members of a community. Hardly exclusive, these clubs provided a basis for organized male sociability that made room for women.

However, retired men and women, as well as municipal governments, churches, and schools, carefully organized numerous retiree social activities along gender lines. Men and women shared the Golden Age Club, but many retired men (who were often anxious to distance themselves from women) utilized the male-exclusive Old Guard as a social organization that could be firmly delineated as male. Men enjoyed the cards and small talk found at the

Golden Age Clubs, but many also embraced the competition and homosocial surroundings stressed by the Old Guard.

Oskar Shulze started the first Golden Age Club in Cleveland, Ohio, in 1940. Numerous Golden Age Clubs soon appeared around Cleveland, and new clubs spread throughout the United States within only a few years. By the early 1950s, observers of retirement trends frequently discussed their significance in the lives of men and women. The federal government, the *New York Times*, gerontologists, and sociologists all celebrated the success and potential of the Golden Age Clubs.[104] They provided men and women with many social outlets, games, and activities to occupy their time. Who organized the clubs? Local churches, municipal governments, or recreation agencies provided meeting places, as well as staff members who helped with activities and planning. At the Ossining, New York, Golden Age Club, undergraduates from a nearby college coordinated social activities each week, and meetings took place at the Ossining Recreation Commission hall. The club began in 1946, when Andrew A. Sargis, superintendent of the commission, met a group of older men languishing on the steps of a local church. Sargis and "the boys" started the group together. Membership varied; some groups (such as the Ossining group) featured as many as ninety members.[105]

Golden Age Clubs constituted a flexible site where retired men and women could socialize and enjoy themselves. Meetings often began in the early afternoon. Proceedings began with small talk over checkers, cards, or dominoes; the majority preferred these entertainments, but others headed for the television. Later, meetings proceeded into group activities: singing, parties, crafts, movies, dancing, lectures, amateur theatre, or planning outings. Also during the meetings, older men and women enjoyed refreshments. Members loved the food and drink because it gave them a chance to have a meal with friends—rather than alone at home. Meetings usually ended before 5:00 p.m., allowing members to walk home before dark. The "club season" lasted between September and May, but in the summer members continued to spend time together on weekly picnics, boat trips, and sight-seeing tours.[106]

Observers who studied the Golden Age Clubs often remarked how the members were invigorated by the social opportunities and activities; the clubs were "therapeutic."[107] Journalist Merrill Folsom, who visited the Ossining, New York, Golden Age Club in 1951, met a retired actor who thrived on the activities and social environment. The eighty-eight year-old thespian was so energized that he often spontaneously launched into Shakespearean monologues. He was "[a]lways ready to recite Hamlet." When asked about his ongoing dedication to the theatre, the aging actor wryly noted, "Some people think I'm acting my last scene. It's not so. I'm just getting ready for the final scene in front of St. Peter."[108]

Golden Age Clubs provided educational opportunities, which retirees enjoyed. The clubs offered men and women, many of whom were working class, "educational value," since members could talk with so many other retirees, hear lectures, participate in plays, and explore crafts. "Mr. N.," member of Cleveland, told a visitor: "Isn't it wonderful that we have our club! You see, my parents were very poor; therefore, I could go to school only three years. Then I had to go to work and ever since my life has been hard work. I never had time to study. Now I am lucky that I have my club where I can learn so many things."[109]

While material related to gender difference in leisure practice within the Golden Age Clubs is admittedly scant, evidence from community recreation centers, which fostered a similar social environment, suggests that programmers and retirees made room for gender difference in the retirees' shared leisure space. In Philadelphia, a writer for *Recreation* visited a community center that catered to older visitors where she carefully noted how men and women chose different activities, affirming their choices as natural. "We find that men are adept at playing games and finding things to fill their leisure (smoking, checkers, horseshoes, watching excavations, sitting around the store or square, politics)," she wrote. However, "Women have spent their young years being housewives and mothers, with their major handwork sewing." When communities designed facilities for the aged, the observer suggested, the program of events should include a workshop and tools for men and kitchen activities for women.[110] Another observer noted that recreation centers should provide bocce ball for aging men, while offering places where older women could explore jewelry making and dressmaking.[111]

Despite the gendered structure of many leisure activities at social clubs and recreation centers, the organizations provided aging and sometimes widowed men and women with vital social contacts. For example, sociability helped to preclude more intense feelings of isolation and depression after the loss of a spouse. Social clubs brought widowed men and women out of their homes at least part of the week. In 1952, a retired man talked with a visitor about the death of his wife and the loss of his home since he could no longer take care of himself. Widowhood brought the man into his son's household. The Golden Age Club provided him with a new place to go and new friends. It gave him something to do, something to look forward to every week. "Last year I lost my wife," the man remarked. "I am now living with my son and his family. They try to be kind, but their friends are young and I am only in the way. In my Golden Age Club, I take part in activities with folks my own age and am happy."[112]

Golden Age Clubs allowed older men to leave their homes and socialize with other retired men—and women. But during the late 1940s and 1950s, a time when retired men were very eager to draw firmer boundaries between men and women because of the loss of their jobs in retirement and their relegation to domestic space, heterosociablity actually brought men and women together rather than pushed them apart. The presence of women in the Golden Age Clubs, despite the ways the organization (and other sites such as recreation centers) were careful to organize various activities along gender lines, probably did not allow all men to view retiree groups as organizations that drew firmer boundaries around manhood.

MEN ONLY: THE OLD GUARD

To create social spaces that were more exclusively male, some retired men turned towards a new organization called the Old Guard Club. Unlike the Golden Age Clubs, only aging men could join the Old Guard. The organization, founded by Samuel Johnson, a medical doctor, espoused the idea that homosociability among men guaranteed a gentler transition from work to retirement, as well as the idea that social interactions kept men mentally sharp. Retirement writer Joseph Buckley, for example, said the Old Guard "cultivate[d] good fellowship" and "preserve[d] mental alertness." As a result, retirees could feel younger—and live longer. As Samuel Johnson once wrote, "If a man does not make new acquaintances as he advances through life, he will soon find himself alone. A man, sir, must keep his friendships."[113]

The organization first appeared in Summit, New Jersey, in 1930, but the group steadily expanded during the 1940s–1950s. By 1951, the Old Guard boasted of 23 chapters in 8 states; and some of the clubs featured as many as 250 members. In addition to more than 16 clubs in New Jersey, Old Guard organizations could be found in Ohio, Pennsylvania, New York, Texas, and Florida; nationally, there were 5,100 men in the group during 1959. To join, men needed to be at least 50 years old and retired. While the organization was small when compared to the Golden Age Clubs, writers and scholars often cited the Old Guard as an ideal setting for men's retirements. Observers such as Joseph Buckley celebrated Old Guard members as men who "refused to take their retirement lying down."[114]

Men viewed the Old Guard Clubs as an important way to overcome isolation. Irving Salomon described how retirement was, for some, a release from daily routines, but how for others it meant isolation. "Retirement often points toward solitude by change of direction from active duties and the daily contact one has had with others," Salomon wrote. "[It] imposes a situation which is rather bewildering and frustrating. And, to some, a feeling of oppressive loneliness and solitude, as age advances and friends pass away." Men needed to take Dr. Johnson's advice: "Association with those of one's own age has its distinct virtues, as a tonic for loneliness, a quickener of stagnated thinking, a brightener of the gloom which often afflicts old age, a spur to lagging endeavors in any chosen line of old age activity. Nothing can be more conducive to give zest to living than such intercourse and regular contact with one's own class."[115] (While Johnson used the word "class," he meant gender.) Through social contacts with other men, retirees could be energized and able to better ensure their health.

Socially, the Old Guard allowed men to retreat to an exclusively male space. The typical meeting combined homosociability with structured procedural matters, business, and entertainments. During the first part of a meeting, men met "informally." Next, the actual meeting began with ten minutes of singing favorite old songs, moving then into business matters. Guests were introduced and welcomed by an executive committee, and birthdays were announced. Members also provided reports on the progress (or decline) of members who were ill. Members read correspondence from other clubs, as well as summarized new and old "business." For activities, the Old Guard featured guest speakers, often members who spoke on topics from "his own background and experience." A retired history professor, for instance, gave a lecture on the American Revolution at one club meeting. In addition, Old Guard men enjoyed fishing trips, movies, and shuffleboard—a favorite game among members.[116]

Old Guard Clubs boasted of a cross-class membership, comprising blue-collar and white-collar men, as well as men of the economic elite. A range of men from the comfortable classes—bankers, chemists, engineers, editors, attorneys, manufacturers, merchants, clergymen, doctors, and salesmen—all joined the Old Guard. But the group also brought in men from working-class occupations. When Irving Salomon visited an Old Guard meeting in New Jersey, he remarked, "Here you see men who are executives of large organizations, men in "Who's Who," a bank president or an ex-governor, sitting next to and fraternizing with the man who was a former policeman, a barber, or a bricklayer."[117]

Male bonding and manly competition infused the organization's culture. First, chapters competed against one another for members. During the late 1950s, *New York Times* reporter Joseph G. Haff wrote about a competition for members between the Point Pleasant, New Jersey, chapter and the Minneapolis chapter—the largest in the United States. The men of the Old Guard of Greater Point Pleasant saw their club as a rugged upstart, challenging the largest of the Old Guard for national prominence. (Haff did not report whether or not the Minneapolis group acknowledged the competition with the New Jersey men.) The men of Point Pleasant, however, were still 6 short of surpassing the Minnesota group when Haff visited. But the group had certainly grown, from 4 to 516 men.[118]

Second, Old Guard chapters competed in sports. The Point Pleasant chapter bragged that the older men on its bowling team could handle any challenger of any age. They regularly, according to Joseph Haff, competed against teams where the average age was "thirty years under their own." This surprised the *New York Times* reporter, especially since two men on the Old Guard Team were seventy-one years old. Besides bowling, Old Guard Clubs often challenged each other on the shuffleboard courts. Point Pleasant's Old Guard shuffleboard team bragged they had never been defeated by another team; and within the chapters, members competed against each other "to determine the club's champion." In the Old Guard, men could—every week—flex their aging muscles on the shuffleboard court.[119]

When Old Guard men named their chapters, the name choices suggested how they wanted to view themselves in later life. Old Guard chapters deployed a variety of nicknames: In Evanston, Illinois, men organized the "Retired Live Wires"; in Oak Park, Illinois, men called themselves the "Borrowed Time Club"; older men in Montclair, New Jersey, started the "Dunworkin Club"; and the "Old Timers' Club" appealed to men in East Orange, New Jersey.[120] The names, such as the "Dunworkin Club" or the "Retired Live Wires," celebrated, rather than lamented, how many retired men no longer worked. Others parodied their advancing years, as suggested by the men in Oak Park who called themselves the "Borrowed Time Club."

Social clubs for retired men and women were popular during the 1940s and 1950s. As retirement became more and more common, retirees busied themselves with numerous social commitments. Golden Age Clubs were the most prominent. These groups offered weekly opportunities for heterosocial leisure, which many older men and women enjoyed. Club activities and programs provided a much-needed social outlet that transported older Americans away from the lonelier confines of their homes. The prevalence of heterosocial leisure, however, created a counter-current among some retired men. Preoccupied with creating male-exclusive social spaces, some retirees looked to the Old Guard Club, which promised a social setting that guaranteed a steady diet of homosocial leisure and manly competition.

RETIRING FROM RETIREMENT

Despite the possibilities for manliness that experts attached to leisure activities, many retired men decided they could only regain their productive masculinity around working and the workplace. Employment provided retired men with the most familiar way to reconstruct differences between themselves and women as well as reconstruct their notions of productivity and daily routines. During the 1940s and 1950s, some older men "retired" from retirement by making their way back to work. Though retired, some older men, especially former white-collar professionals, looked for new job opportunities as a way to ensure productive manhood—preferring in some cases to look for jobs (and continuity in their sense of masculinity) in their earlier fields of employment. Leisure did not easily replace work in men's lives. Professional men often dismissed the idea of retirement after confronting life without work. As they pointed out, not all older men liked shuffleboard, fishing, and tinkering.[121] Some men who went back to work claimed that labor bolstered their health and prolonged life. Walter Pitkin knew a retired man who became a distraught hypochondriac. Without work to occupy his mind and his time, the ex-businessman was a "total wreck, breaking to pieces on the sands of time." The older man's former colleagues, however, quickly "came to the rescue." They invented a problem at work, and invited the aging man to help them resolve it. Returning to work brought the man out of his depression. Pitkin happily noted, "He is now pretty well, thank you."[122]

Available statistical data indicates that substantial numbers of retired men returned to work during the 1950s. In a 1952 *Business Week* survey of retired men in Cleveland, over 10 percent of their sample had already returned to work full-time; 16 percent of the sample worked part-time. Even among the retired men who were not currently employed (perhaps due to health reasons or troubles with hiring age limits), 37 percent noted they would prefer to work.[123] In Jacob Tuckman and Irving Lorge's 1953 survey of retired blue-collar men in the New York needle trades, they found that 36 percent did not plan to retire unless they became too sick to work.[124] In a 1954 survey conducted by Penn State University, significant numbers of older men reported they planned to work instead of retiring. Nearly 59 percent planned to continue working full-time for their current firm; 22 percent planned to work full-time, but in another occupation.[125] While numbers varied from study to study, the data suggests that many older men did not want to stop working.

For many professional men, "hobbies" could not suffice as a foundation for manhood. These men envisioned work and leisure as absolutely dissimilar concepts. In the 1940s and 1950s, when usefulness, productivity, and service became cardinal virtues in American culture, many aging men could not envision themselves without work. "For me hobbies are like desserts," an aging white-collar man remarked in 1954. "I have to have some meat and potatoes of work for my main fare."[126] Other professional men—used to the busy routines of the corporate office—condemned retirement as "loafing" and "a stupid way to live."[127] While writers sanctioned productive leisure as a way to

demonstrate manhood during the 1940s and 1950s, other men rejected retirement and went back to work.

Eager to remain working, some men offered up their services during their
retirement ceremonies. After twenty-four years of teaching at City College's
(New York City) Bureau of Business Research, administrators retired Professor Ernest S. Bradford. He had reached the mandatory retirement age of
seventy years. During the well-attended luncheon to honor Bradford for his
years of service to the college, the feisty professor offered his experience to
"any college which needs a young man on its staff." Apparently, someone
at the luncheon forwarded his bold declaration to the administrators at Manhattan College. Very quickly, Bradford was teaching again, as Manhattan
College made him Professor of Business. Bradford did not see himself as an
"old man," ready for retirement. Rather, he thought of himself as a young
man—ready and able to continue working at his post. When Milton Bernet
retired as vice president for Mountain States Telephone and Telegraph Company, he bragged how his phone began ringing with job offers. "I have had
a number of jobs offered to me," Bernet bragged. "I intend to accept one of
them. I wouldn't think of retiring from productive work."[128]

It was more common for retiring men to place ads in local newspapers,
soliciting employers for job offers. As several examples suggest, retiring men
preferred to remain in their previous occupations; continuity between old
and new kinds of work shaped retired men's views of masculinity. "I regret
this retirement," a former public relations man complained. "I am in perfect,
vigorous health, and I am tired of golf and play, and north and south resorts,
and I find that my efforts at "do-gooding" do not keep me keen." Nothing
but employment in his old line of work would suffice. "I wish again to work,
and work hard, at business," he wrote. He took out a large advertisement in a
newspaper, offering up his experience. The ad announced to readers: "THIS
ADVERTISEMENT IS DIRECTED TO THE PRESIDENT OF A COR-
PORATION WHOSE PROSPEROUS BUSINESS LIFE DEPENDS UPON
THE ESTEEM AND GOODWILL OF THE GENERAL PUBLIC." The man
urged any employer in need of a PR man to contact him; he even offered to
work without pay.[129]

"Retirement is a bore," a retired man wrote in another classified newspaper
ad. "I want to work again. Reputation unquestionable. If you have an opening I'd like to talk it over."[130] The classified columns of major newspapers
became an ongoing record of many retired men's desires to escape from
retirement, as well as the obstacles to their reemployment. But column after
column in the help wanted ads of the *New York Times* listed plentiful job possibilities for *young* male applicants in industry, offices, and sales. In 1955,
for example, the classified columns of November 21 featured 37 job ads

that asked for a "Young Man"—and none that called for retired or "mature" men.[131] Also contained in these pages of classifieds were retired men's calls for work opportunities. A typical ad read:

> RETIRED business man . . . seeks interesting position, full time: salary secondary. 1449 Times Fordham 56.[132]

We do not know if the "RETIRED" man found his "interesting" job or not, but his succinctly worded ad tells us something of his desire to escape from retirement. He was willing to ignore the salary issue in exchange for the chance to work again. However, he may have done himself a disservice by starting his ad with the phrase "RETIRED" in full capital letters. Perhaps he wanted employers to feel sorry for him, or perhaps he underestimated the continued importance of young men in employer choices for new hires.

While "RETIRED business man" disclosed his status to newspaper readers and potential employers, other aging men downplayed their backgrounds as retirees by using other labels to discuss their age and experience. In 1958, for example, "Man, matured" placed an ad in the *New York Times* that asked for employers to consider him for positions in management or sales. He chose to describe himself as "matured," avoiding risky associations with a word like "retired," which may have suggested to employers that he was in his sixties, collecting Social Security, and stuck in a rocking chair. "Man, matured" tried to further sell himself by asking for a "moderate" salary and explaining that he owned a car.[133] "Man, matured" wanted potential employers to see him as an experienced (but not "old") man who was willing to work for minimal salary and was able to travel ample distances for work. Perhaps the aging man thought this would be a swifter path out of retirement and back into the workplace.

Employers seeking labor in the want ads were often stunned by the volume of retirees' requests for work. In 1951, a business executive placed an ad for a messenger boy in his "large company" and received a surprising 245 applications, mostly from aging and retired men who wanted or needed to return to work. The executive was overwhelmed by what he read on the battered penny postcards, old greeting cards, and hand-written loose-leaf sheets he received in his mailbox. "Can you give a fellow (55) a chance to earn a living? Formerly an auditor," one man wrote, while another said, "I am well educated and am retired with a small income which is not enough to make ends meet due to the increase of living costs." The man in charge of the job search noted that many of the applicants hated retirement and wanted out. One note he received said, "I am 63 years of age, in very good health and I am not pleased with my retirement." But in the end, only one man would be hired. "Only one guy's gonna win the sweepstakes," the executive noted, "and somebody's gonna get hurt."[134]

Hiring age limits continued to prevent many of these retired men from working again. In Houston, 52 percent of job notices in early 1952 contained age requirements, while in Columbus, Ohio, 4/5 of employer requests for workers asked for men under the age of 45; and 2/5 of these requests were for men under 35.[135] Age limits struck hard at former industrial workers. For instance, "Jim" was a typical retired factory worker who could not find work. Though business was good in the postwar economy, no factory would hire him, even on a part-time basis. Jim had a good record with his previous company; he was a "trained" and "experienced" worker, with over twenty years spent at his post. But no hiring officer bothered to ask him about his record; Jim was just too old. "Employers in his town and in those around preferred to hire young men," the US Bureau of Employment Security concluded.[136]

New non-profit organizations worked to reintroduce retirees into the labor market. In 1953, retired Chicago businessmen and leaders of the YMCA formed an organization they called "Senior Achievement," an organization devoted to helping older retirees (both men and women) find new forms of employment. Inspired by the Junior Achievement program that helped teens avoid juvenile delinquency with organized activities, the organizers of Senior Achievement furthered the idea that new job opportunities could preclude retirement shock and thwart idleness, isolation, and illness. As Joseph K. Wexman, the chairman of Senior Achievement "industries," said, "Most people after retirement go to pieces because they lose their self-respect. Many workers associate life with work, and without work they tend to feel worthless. We plan to provide these people with useful work which will fit their skills and physical energies, and give them a renewed confidence in their place in society."[137]

More than half of participants in Senior Achievement programs were men of previous white-collar backgrounds. An estimated 425 aging Chicago workers responded to a Senior Achievement interest survey in July 1955, and 73 percent of them were men; more than 250 of the respondents worked in a white-collar occupation before retirement, including commercial sales, industrial and business management, accounting, advertising, and engineering. The remainder (175 respondents) had once labored in fields such as textiles, metal work, carpentry, clerking, and sales.[138] In practice, Senior Achievement industries emphasized door-to-door sales and petty commodity production in a new Chicago workshop space. Newspaper articles described eighty-year old men venturing door-to-door selling manufactured tie racks and wire bacon drainers, and older men and women manufacturing children's' toys for sale. In addition, among the 100 employees of Senior Achievement industries, the "white-collar personnel" were "loaned to outside businesses," as determined by their marketable skills and demand.[139] Senior Achievement leaders reported their jobs program helped older retirees (especially men) evade the boredom of retirement and remain "busy and useful." For example, retired department store owner Eugene A. Ricker "is now an office man . . . for a busy . . . brokerage firm" in Chicago, while Senior Achievement hired William Wilhelm, a retired manager of a metal factory, to run the organization's workshop. As David E. Sonquist, the Senior Achievement executive director, noted in 1956, "I think we can show that a man can be . . . young at 80."[140]

In addition to helping older men and women reenter the labor market, Senior Achievement aimed to recreate working daily routines for retirees. Typically, a member of Senior Achievement worked on a steady part-time basis, which usually meant a thirty-hour week. For their varied labors, Senior Achievement retiree workers earned $100 per month or less—a sum that allowed retirees to avoid conflicts with Social Security regulations which mandated that pensioners could earn no more than that sum.[141]

Retirement advice writers frequently wrote about retirees who launched themselves into successful entrepreneurial ventures. In 1944, retiree Roy Adams began building tables in his garage, while his wife sold the pieces to local stores. "Business was so good"; the man found investors, and the business grew. The couple even moved the operation to a larger building on a different site.[142] In Florida, Paul Bryant also found success in the furniture business, turning his affinity for antiques into a manufacturing concern. He built a small factory to make copies of early American furnishings.[143] Farming was another favorite enterprise among retirees.[144] Some retired men wanted to get back to the land, as if to escape from the urban/industrial/corporate surroundings of their earlier years—and they wanted to bolster their incomes. Some operations were substantial. Dan Belding, an aging white-collar worker at an advertising firm, bought a citrus ranch near San Diego. Operating the ranch constituted his plan for a "productive" retirement.[145] A retired postal worker bought a twelve-acre farm. Between April and November, the ranch kept him busy, but the seasonal work provided some time to rest.[146]

Aging white-collar staffers frequently launched consulting firms after they retired. In the 1940s, Alfred L. Hart retired from his salaried position with General Electric, but he quickly concluded that he disliked the quiet and boredom of life in retirement. Initially he tried farming, but he did not enjoy the work. Hart, however, refused to retreat to the rocking chair. "Still full of business drive," the aging man formed, with the aid of several retired colleagues, a successful management consulting firm. By the 1950s, Hart's firm boasted of a staff of fifty "top management men" with a combined 2,000 years of experience. They advised business and government on "practically everything."[147]

As aging men confronted retirement and the end of work, they frequently interpreted productive manhood in literal terms: they insisted that manhood could only be found in the familiar arenas of paid employment and the workplace. Retirement created new questions about gender relations and gender identity in men's minds, as they faced the prospect of consignment to domestic space and doubt about finding manhood through play. For many, the surest path to manhood remained in the workplace. Even small charitable organizations for the aged, such as Senior Achievement, built their program around the idea that retirees needed to be "busy" and productive in later life. Many old men rejected the idea of retirement altogether, trying to battle their way out of permanent layoff. In the process, they deepened the ties between productivity and masculinity in twentieth-century American culture.

During the 1940s and 1950s, older men viewed retirement as a crucial arena where manliness and productivity needed to be carefully reconnected. However, retirement never became safe for aging men, as observers of retirement trends envisioned manhood in a contradictory way. As men aged and retired from work, manhood still very much depended on staying mentally and physically youthful, maintaining productivity, and sustaining upper-class affluence and suburban standards of living. However, aging bodies and fixed incomes proved to be unstable foundations for manliness. How could aging males remain "men" if they would be obligatorily retired to a fixed income, and their bodies would continue to age? And could leisure and play, even if rigorously pursued on a daily, routine basis, ever truly supplant work as the basis of manhood? Play never fully became a sure path to productive manhood in postwar culture; golf, baseball, shuffleboard, fishing, hunting, and collecting never became adequate surrogates for work as the foundation of manhood. Instead, many men sought ways to return to the workplace.

By going back to work, these retired men underlined how productivity defined twentieth-century masculinity. In discussions of both employment and leisure in old age, we see notions of productivity situated at the very center.

NOTES

1. Herbert Gold, "The Age of Happy Problems," *Atlantic Monthly*, March 1957, 61; also quoted in KA Cuordileone, *Manhood and American Political Culture in the Cold War* (New York: Taylor & Francis, 2004), 103.

2. Robert J. Havighurst, "The Impact of Retirement on the Individual," in *Unions and the Problems of Retirement: Proceedings of a Conference*, booklet (Chicago: Union Research and Education Projects, 1959), 14, in vertical files ("Retirement"), Institute of Industrial and Labor Relations (hereafter ILIR), University of Illinois at

Urbana-Champaign (hereafter UIUC). The conference was a meeting on aging at the University of Chicago in April 1959.

3. For additional discussions of the spatial arrangement of gender in the home after World War II, see in particular Kristen Haring's excellent work in "The 'Freer Men' of Ham Radio: How a Technical Hobby Provided Social and Spatial Distance," *Technology and Culture* 44:4 (2003): 734–761; as well as Kristen Haring, *Ham Radio's Technical Culture* (Cambridge: MIT Press, 2007).

4. For the statistic on the duration of men's work week, see Rachel Devlin, *Relative Intimacy: Fathers, Adolescent Daughters, and Postwar American Culture* (Chapel Hill: University of North Carolina Press, 2005), 10; see also Miriam Forman-Brunell, *Babysitter: An American History* (New York: New York University Press, 2009), 107.

5. Irving Salomon, *Retire and Be Happy* (New York: Greenberg, 1951), 148.

6. Christopher P. Loss, "'The Most Wonderful Thing Has Happened to Me in the Army': Psychology, Citizenship, and American Higher Education in World War II," *Journal of American History* 92:3 (2005): 887–888; Elaine Tyler May, *Homeward Bound: American Families in the Cold War Era* (New York: Basic Books, 1988), 169; Kenneth T. Jackson, *Crabgrass Frontier: The Suburbanization of the United States* (New York: Oxford University Press, 1985), 233; Lisa McGirr, *Suburban Warriors: The Origins of the New American Right* (Princeton: Princeton University Press, 2001), 26–29; Thomas J. Sugrue, *The Origins of the Urban Crisis: Race and Inequality in Postwar Detroit* (Princeton: Princeton University Press, 1995), 140–141.

7. Lizabeth Cohen, *A Consumers' Republic: The Politics of Mass Consumption in Postwar America* (New York: Vintage Books, 2003), 195.

8. Ibid., 197.

9. McGirr, *Suburban Warriors*, 28.

10. May, *Homeward Bound*, 166; Forman-Brunell, *Babysitter*, 74.

11. Statistics come from Osgerby, "Pedigree of the Consuming Male," 762; May, *Homeward Bound*, 165.

12. Cohen, *Consumers' Republic*, 194–195.

13. "Social Security," in *The World Book Encyclopedia*, vol. 16 (Chicago: Field Enterprises Educational Corporation, 1960), 457; Michael Herrington, *The Other America: Poverty in the United States* (1962; repr., New York: Penguin Books, 1981), 110.

14. Herrington, *Other America*, 110.

15. "Most Persons Over 65 Have Little Income," *Chicago Daily Tribune*, 9 January 1956, C5.

16. Jackson, *Crabgrass Frontier*, 236.

17. Cohen, *Consumers' Republic*, 202–203.

18. William H. Chafe, "America Since 1945," in *The New American History*, ed. Eric Foner (Philadelphia: Temple University Press, 1997), 161.

19. William H. Chafe, *The Unfinished Journey: America Since World War II* (New York: Oxford University Press, 1986), 126.

20. Sloan Wilson, "The Woman in the Gray Flannel Suit," *New York Times Magazine*, 15 January 1956, 8.

21. Margaret S. Gordon, "Work and Patterns of Retirement," in *Aging and Leisure: A Research Perspective Into the Meaningful Use of Time*, ed. Robert W. Kleemeier (New York: Oxford University Press, 1961), 44; Elon H. Moore, Elon H. and Gordon F. Streib, *The Nature of Retirement* (New York: Macmillan Company, 1959), 119.

22. Otto Pollack, *The Social Aspects of Retirement* (Philadelphia: Pension Research Council of the Wharton School of Finance and Commerce, University of Pennsylvania, 1956), 7; idem, *Positive Experiences in Retirement* (Philadelphia: Pension Research Council of the Wharton School of Finance and Commerce, University of Pennsylvania, 1957), 37.

23. Salomon, *Retire and Be Happy*, 181.

24. Raymond P. Kaighn, *How to Retire and Like It* (New York: Association Press, 1951), 91; Pollack, *Positive Experiences in Retirement*, 37.

25. Pollack, *Social Aspects of Retirement*, 7.

26. Moore and Streib, *Nature of Retirement*, 119.

27. Joseph C. Buckley, *The Retirement Handbook: A Complete Planning Guide to Your Future* (New York: Harper & Brothers, 1953), 5; Harold R. Hall, *Some Observations on Executive Retirement* (Boston: Graduate School of Business Administration, Harvard University, 1953), 228.

28. Hart, *Retirement*, 97–98; Pollack, *Social Aspects of Retirement*, 7.

29. Salomon, *Retire and Be Happy*, 195.

30. Kaighn, *How to Retire and Like It*, 36, 93.

31. Theodor Greene, *How to Enjoy Retirement for the Rest of Your Life* (New York: Exposition Press, 1957), 53–54; Hall, *Some Observations on Executive Retirement*, 230–231; Buckley, *Retirement Handbook*, 5; David D. Stonecypher, Jr., "Old Age Need Not Be 'Old,'" *New York Times Magazine*, 18 August 1957, 66–67.

32. By 1960, there were 10 million married women in the workforce in the United States. See Elaine Tyler May, "Pushing the Limits: 1940–1961," in *No Small Courage: A History of Women in the United States*, ed. Nancy Cott (New York: Oxford University Press, 2000), 495. *Readers' Guide to Periodical Literature* citations on "retirement" focused consistently on men. Only sporadically did advice writers, themselves typically men, write about women as retirees. Of 160 articles on "retirement" between 1947 and 1961, only 18 focused on women as retiring workers or professionals.

33. Ray Giles, *How to Retire—and Enjoy It* (New York: McGraw-Hill Book Company, 1949), 226.

34. Kaighn, *How to Retire and Like It*, 124. On postwar men's ambivalence toward housework, see James Gilbert, *Men in the Middle: Searing for Masculinity in the 1950s* (Chicago: University of Chicago Press, 2005), 65.

35. For a brief summary of the association between women and housework in US history, see Michael Goldberg, "Breaking New Ground, 1800–1848," in *No Small Courage: A History of Women in the United States*, ed. Nancy Cott (New York: Oxford University Press, 2000), 187.

36. Hall, *Some Observations on Executive Retirement*, 260. On escape as a theme in the history of manhood, see Michael Kimmel, *Manhood in America: A Cultural History* (New York: Free Press, 1996), 59–70, 87–89, 251–257, 309–325; and Haring, "'Freer Men' of Ham Radio," 734, 752.

37. Salomon, *Retire and Be Happy*, 75, 197, 186, 200.

38. Clark Tibbitts, "Retirement Problems in American Society," *American Journal of Sociology* 59:4 (1954): 306; see also Haring, "'Freer Men' of Ham Radio," 744. *Business Week* statistic found in "Retirement Not Always Happy," 52; see also "Planning for Retirement," *Today's Health*, January 1958, 15.

39. Quoted in Kimmel, *Manhood in America*, 246.

40. See also Haring, "'Freer Men' of Ham Radio," 734–761. Analyses of gender divisions and leisure practices typically focus on sites away from the home. See, for example, Kathy Peiss, *Cheap Amusements: Working Women and Leisure in Turn-of-the-Century New York* (Philadelphia: Temple University Press, 1986); and Howard P. Chudacoff, *The Age of the Bachelor: Creating an American Subculture* (Princeton: Princeton University Press, 2000).

41. See "Retirement Not Always Happy," 52. The second statistic appears in Ernest W. Burgess, Lawrence G. Corey, Peter C. Pineo, and Richard T. Thornbury, "Occupational Differences Toward Aging and Retirement," *Journal of Gerontology* 31:2 (1958). The authors conducted their study at Standard Oil facilities in Indiana.

42. Salomon, *Retire and Be Happy*, 152.

43. Kaighn, *How to Retire and Like It*, 89.

44. *As Young As You Feel*, dir. by Harmon Jones, Twentieth Century-Fox, 1951.

45. *Rear Window*, dir. by Alfred Hitchcock, Universal Pictures, 1954.

46. Betty Friedan, *The Feminine Mystique* (1963; repr., New York: WW Norton & Company, 1974), esp. 15. For another critical reading of Friedan, see Joanne Meyerowitz, "Beyond the Feminine Mystique: A Reassessment of Postwar Mass Culture, 1946–1958," in *Not June Cleaver: Women and Gender in Postwar America, 1945–1960*, ed. Joanne Meyerowitz (Philadelphia: Temple University Press, 1994), 229, 231–237

47. Similar themes appear in Haring, "'Freer Men' of Ham Radio," 752.

48. Haring, "'Freer Men' of Ham Radio," 753; Kimmel, *Manhood in America*, 158.

49. Jackson, *Crabgrass Frontier*, 252; Haring, "'Freer Men' of Ham Radio," 753.

50. Haring, "'Freer Men' of Ham Radio," 753.

51. Kaighn, *How to Retire and Like It*, 92; Hall, *Some Observations on Executive Retirement*, 131.

52. Kaighn, *How to Retire and Like It*, 93. See also *Salomon, Retire and Be Happy*, 175, 177; and Pollack, *Positive Experiences in Retirement*, 25.

53. Paul W. Boynton, *Six Ways to Retire* (New York: Harper & Brothers, 1952), 111.

54. Walter B. Pitkin, *The Best Years: How to Enjoy Retirement* (New York: Current Books, 1946), 44; Salomon, *Retire and Be Happy*, 147. The term "helpmates" dates back to the colonial period. On wives as "helpmates," see Jeanne Boydston, *Home and Work: Housework, Wages, and the Ideology of Labor in the Early Republic* (New York: Oxford University Press, 1990).

55. Evelyn Colby and John G. Forrest, *Ways and Means to Successful Retirement* (New York: BC Forbes and Sons Publishing, 1952), 134–142.

56. Ibid., 182.

57. Ibid., 182–189. See also Iphigene Bettman, "A Second Career for the Older Woman," *New York Times Magazine*, 10 October 1948, 22, 28; and "Early Planning To Retire Urged," *New York Times*, 29 June 1954, 23.

58. "How Old Executives Fade Away," *Fortune*, June 1952, 174; Hall, *Some Observations on Executive Retirement*, 131. On travel as a form of male retreat, see Gilbert, *Men in the Middle*, 66.

59. Giles, *How to Retire*, 226–227; Kaighn, *How to Retire and Like It*, 122; Salomon, *Retire and Be Happy*, 148.

60. Pitkin, *Best Years*, 55–56.

61. Salomon, *Retire and Be Happy*, 186.

62. Buckley, *Retirement Handbook*, 101.

63. Salomon, *Retire and Be Happy*, 184.

64. Pitkin, *Best Years*, 54. On masculinity and exercise at the turn of the twentieth century, see Clifford Putney, *Muscular Christianity: Manhood and Sports in Protestant America, 1880–1920* (Cambridge: Harvard University Press, 2001).

65. Henry S. Curtis, "The Other Half of the Playground Movement," *Recreation*, August 1947, 247.

66. Kaighn, *How to Retire and Like It*, 49.

67. Arthur Dailey, "3,265,000 Reasons for Playing Golf," *New York Times*, 31 May 1953, reprinted in *New York Times Encyclopedia of Sports*, vol. 5 (Golf), ed. Herbert J. Cohen and Richard W. Lawall (New York: New York Times Company, 1979), 88. For an overview of the history of golf in the United States, see George B. Kirsch, *Golf in America* (Urbana: University of Illinois Press, 2009).

68. "When and How Retirement?" *Newsweek*, 12 July 1954, 49.

69. Quoted in Edmund Fuller, "Fun For Golfing Fan-Atics," *Chicago Daily Tribune*, 16 June 1957, C5.

70. "Golfing in Florida," *Chicago Daily Tribune*, 30 September 1953, 18. On the postwar expansion of golf, see Kirsch, *Golf in America*, esp. 128–130, 141.

71. "Summer Fun is Wide in S. Florida," *Chicago Daily Tribune*, 12 June 1955, J10.

72. Nevin H. Gibson, *The Encyclopedia of Golf* (New York: AS Barnes and Company, 1964), 51.

73. Kirsch, *Golf in America*, 133–134; "Golf Garb Plentiful, Inexpensive," *Chicago Daily Tribune*, 14 May 1956, D2.

74. "Golf Equipment First in '57 Sales," *New York Times*, 23 April 1958, reprinted in *New York Times Encyclopedia of Sports*, vol. 5 (Golf), ed. Herbert J. Cohen and Richard W. Lawall (New York: New York Times Company, 1979), 105.

75. Hall, *Some Observations on Executive Retirement*, 212; Kaighn, *How to Retire and Like It*, 49.

76. Herbert Warren Wind, *The Story of American Golf: Its Champions and Its Championships* (New York: Simon and Schuster, 1956), 6.

77. Daley, "3,265,000 Reasons for Playing Golf," 89.

78. Annette Victorin, "Wife's Advice to Wives: Take Your Husband Fishing!" *Chicago Daily Tribune*, 12 June 1955, L44.

79. "What To Do For Retirement," *Business Week*, 14 April 1951, 36; Salomon, *Retire and Be Happy*, 65. On the links between masculinity and hunting, see Lisa

Fine, "Rights of Men, Rites of Passage: Hunting and Masculinity at Reo Motors of Lansing, Michigan, 1945–1975," in *Boys and Their Toys? Masculinity, Class, and Technology in America*, ed. Roger Horowitz (New York: Routledge, 2001), 251–271.

80. Victorin, "Wife's Advice to Wives," L44.

81. Marvin S. Pittman, "After Retirement—What?" *Recreation*, July 1943, 223.

82. Ibid.

83. Warner Bloomberg, Jr., "Automation Predicts Change: For the Older Worker," in *The New Frontiers of Aging*, ed. Wilma Donahue and Clark Tibbitts (Ann Arbor: University of Michigan Press, 1957), 23; see also Buckley, *Retirement Handbook*, 100–101; Alonzo F. Myers, "Essential Elements of a Good Retirement Plan," *Journal of Educational Sociology*, 31:8 (1958): 323; Hall, *Some Observations on Executive Retirement*, 131, 260; LC Michelon, "The New Leisure Class," *American Journal of Sociology* 59:4 (1954): 375; Ethel Sabin Smith, *The Dynamics of Aging* (New York: WW Norton & Company, 1956), 132; Pollack, *Positive Experiences in Retirement*, 25; "What To Do For Retirement," 36; Salomon, *Retire and Be Happy*, 65, 67; and "Retirement Without A Wrench," *Business Week*, 29 May 1954, 70.

84. "How To Retire," *Changing Times*, February 1953, 42; Hart, *Retirement*, 82; Havighurst, "Impact of Retirement," 14; David Riesman, "Some Clinical and Cultural Aspects of Aging," *American Journal of Sociology* 59:4 (1954): 381.

85. Elon H. Moore, "Preparation for Retirement," *Journal of Gerontology* 1:2 (1946): 209; "What Will You Do When You Retire?" *Changing Times*, March 1956, 18

86. Robert J. Havighurst, "Flexibility and the Social Roles of the Retired," *American Journal of Sociology* 59:4 (1954): 310.

87. Salomon, *Retire and Be Happy*, 72.

88. Ibid., 72–73.

89. Ibid., 72–73, 188.

90. "'Busiest Retired Man' Title Won By Ex-Steelman," *Los Angeles Times*, 22 February 1944, 8.

91. Salomon, *Retire and Be Happy*, 188.

92. George H. Preston, *Should I Retire?* (New York: Reinhart & Company, 1952), 76; Buckley, *Retirement Handbook*, 75.

93. Salomon, *Retire and Be Happy*, 195.

94. Bloomberg, "Automation Predicts Change," 22–23; Salomon, *Retire and Be Happy*, 183.

95. Homer L. Hitt, "The Role of Migration in Population Change Among the Aged," *American Sociological Review* 19:2 (1954): 196.

96. "What To Do For Retirement," *Business Week*, 14 April 1951, 36; Robert H. Guest, "Work Careers and Aspirations of Automobile Workers," *American Sociological Review* 19:2 (1954): 162; Kaighn, *How to Retire and Like It*, 49; Sally Doyle, "Retiring Postman to Miss Friends—and Dogs—on Route," *Chicago Daily Tribune*, 26 April 1953, 12; Preston, *Should I Retire?* 52; Alonzo F. Myers, "Essential Elements of a Good Retirement Plan," *Journal of Educational Sociology* 31:8 (1958): 322.

97. GC Hoyt, "The Life of the Retired in a Trailer Park," *American Journal of Sociology* 59:4 (1954): 363.

98. Salomon, *Retire and Be Happy*, 181–182.

99. Preston, *Should I Retire?* 77.

100. For further insight into the connections between manhood and the history of gun ownership, see Jacqueline M. Moore, *Cow Boys and Cattle Men: Class and Masculinities on the Texas Frontier, 1865–1900* (New York: New York University Press, 2010), 63.

101. Preston, *Should I Retire?* 73.

102. Ibid., 74–75.

103. See Kimmel, *Manhood in America*, esp. 157–188.

104. Oskar Shulze, "Recreation for the Aged," *Journal of Gerontology* 4:4 (1949): 310; Merrill Folsom, "Ossining Oldsters' Club So Good Other Cities Rush to Emulate It," *New York Times*, 24 February 1951, 15; "When the Older Citizens, Themselves, Carry the Ball," *Aging* (published by the US Department of Health, Education, and Welfare), January 1954, 3.

105. Folsom, "Ossining Oldsters' Club," 15.

106. Shulze, "Recreation for the Aged," 311; Folsom, "Ossining Oldsters' Club," 15; "When the Older Citizens," 3. Elon H. Moore and Gordon F. Streib, *The Nature of Retirement* (New York: Macmillan Company, 1959), 178; Buckley, *Retirement Handbook*, 93. Golden Age Clubs did not have a monopoly on heterosocial leisure activities for retired men and women. For example, Older Adult Klubs were a different (and smaller) organization, but featured similar activities. See Howard G. Danford, *Recreation in the American Community* (New York: Harper & Brothers, 1953), 12.

107. Riesman, "Some Clinical and Cultural Aspects of Aging," 381.

108. Folsom, "Ossining Oldsters' Club," 15.

109. Shulze, "Recreation for the Aged," 311–312.

110. Jeanne H. Barnes, "Not Too Old To Enjoy Life," *Recreation*, September 1944, 312–313.

111. "Recreation for Older People," *Recreation*, October 1940, 432.

112. "Fun Doesn't Stop At Sixty," *Recreation*, December 1952, 416.

113. Buckley, *Retirement Handbook*, 94–95; Boynton, *Six Ways to Retire*, 124; Hall, *Some Observations on Executive Retirement*, 268.

114. Buckley, *Retirement Handbook*, 95; Salomon, *Retire and Be Happy*, 97, 99; Joseph G. Haff, "Retirement Club Eyes US Record," *New York Times*, 13 September 1959, 123.

115. Salomon, *Retire and Be Happy*, 97–98; quote taken from Haff, "Retirement Club Eyes US Record," 123.

116. Salomon, *Retire and Be Happy*, 99; Haff, "Retirement Club Eyes Us Record," 123.

117. Buckley, *Retirement Handbook*, 94–95; Salomon, *Retire and Be Happy*, 99.

118. Haff, "Retirement Club Eyes US Record," 123.

119. Ibid.

120. Hall, *Some Observations on Executive Retirement*, 268; Salomon, *Retire and Be Happy*, 104.

121. Walker, *Living Your Later Years*, 99.

122. Walter B. Pitkin, *The Best Years: How to Enjoy Retirement* (New York: Current Books, 1946), 113.

123. "Retirement Not Always Happy," *Business Week*, 5 April 1952, 48.

124. Jacob Tuckman and Irving Lorge, *Retirement and the Industrial Worker: Prospect and Reality* (New York: Teachers College Columbia University, 1953), 21.

125. Joseph H. Britton and Jean O. Britton, "Work and Retirement for Older University Alumni," *Journal of Gerontology* 9:4 (1954): 471.

126. Harold R. Hall, "Activity Programming for Retirement By Executives," *Journal of Gerontology* 9:2 (1954): 217.

127. Kaighn, *How to Retire and Like It*, 126; "What Will You Do When You Retire?" *Changing Times*, March 1956, 18.

128. "Takes Teaching Job at 70," *New York Times*, 22 July 1947, 25; "Should You Be Forced To Retire at 65?" *US News & World Report*, 13 September 1957, 97.

129. Moore and Streib, *Nature of Retirement*, 35. Emphasis in original.

130. LC Michelon, "The New Leisure Class," *American Journal of Sociology* 59:4 (1954): 372.

131. "Help Wanted—Male," *New York Times*, 12 November 1955, 53.

132. "Situations Wanted—Male," *New York Times*, 16 April 1959, 64.

133. "Situations Wanted—Male," *New York Times*, 23 July 1958, 53.

134. "245 'Over 45' Rush to get $34 Job," *New York Times*, 18 January 1951, 29.

135. "Man Living Longer But Working Less," *New York Times*, 1 July 1952, 19.

136. US Bureau of Employment Security (Dir. Robert C. Goodwin), *Workers Are Young Longer: A Report of the Findings and Implications of the Public Employment Service Studies of Older Workers in Five Cities*, booklet (Washington, DC: US Bureau of Employment Security, 1952), 3, in vertical files ("Age and Employment"), ILIR, UIUC.

137. "Workers Over 60 Offered Job in Retirement," *Chicago Daily Tribune*, 1 June 1955, 24.

138. "Hope of Work Proves Allure for Oldsters," *Chicago Daily Tribune*, 11 July 1955, B14.

139. "Seniors Form Achievement Group of Own," *Chicago Daily Tribune*, 26 February 1956, 28; "Two Achievers Display Skills," *Chicago Daily Tribune*, 13 May 1956, A9; "Senior Group Expanding Its Working Space," *Chicago Daily Tribune*, 9 September 1956, 30.

140. "Seniors Form Achievement Group," 28; John R. Thomson, "For the Young at Heart," *Chicago Daily Tribune*, 7 October 1956, G48.

141. "Seniors Form Achievement Group," 28.

142. Buckley, *Retirement Handbook*, 81.

143. "Down in Florida, Retired Men Find New Careers Making Furniture," in *Aging* (published by the US Department of Health, Education, and Welfare), November 1953, 2.

144. Pollack, *Positive Experiences in Retirement*, 40; "What Will You Do When You Retire?" 18; Salomon, *Retire and Be Happy*, 72–73.

145. "One Man's Retirement Program," *Newsweek*, 12 July 1954, 48; see also Bloomberg, "Automation Predicts Change," 23.

146. Moore and Streib, *Nature of Retirement*, 3.

147. "How Old Executives Fade Away," *Fortune*, June 1952, 174.

Conclusion: Beyond the
Masculinity of Youth?

There seems to be a release from the old imperatives of dominance and power, of competitive appearance and performance, of self-abnegation and manipulation, of conformity and mask, of illusion and self-deceit. There is a new ease of responsiveness and an unarmored vulnerability that relaxes old, no longer necessary defenses.

—Betty Friedan, 1993[1]

The aging feminist and author Betty Friedan found reasons for optimism as she interviewed older men and women for her 1993 book, *The Fountain of Age*. As oldsters aged in the late-twentieth century, they pursued new lives in retirement that defied familiar definitions of age and gender. While "old age" was assumed to be a period of decline, the reality of lengthening life in the twentieth century, she argued, compelled many older people to define the categories of "old," "man," and "woman" on their own terms; and the freedom and wisdom of age offered new possibilities for enrichment. Friedan's book offered a poignant comment on aging in twentieth-century America that remains relevant in the twenty-first: many older men and women often avoid retreating to the rocking chair when they "retire," and by staying active, they try to forge new ways of defining what it means to grow old. Why fear retirement if it offers personal freedom and the chance to create new ways of living? Friedan bluntly defied the negative connotations that accompanied many assumptions about age:

we will create a new image of age—free and joyous . . . saying what we really think and feel at last—knowing who we are, realizing that we know more than we ever knew that we knew, not afraid of what anyone thinks of us anymore, moving with wonder into that unknown future we have helped to shape for the generations coming after us. There will not have to be such dread and denial for them in living their age if we use our own age in new adventures, breaking the old rules and inhibitions, changing the patterns and possibilities of love and work, learning and play, worship and creation, discovery and political responsibility, and resolving the seeming irreconcilable conflicts between them.[2]

Friedan herself concluded, "I have never felt so free."[3]

Even as *The Fountain of Age* tore down the usual thinking about age as a period of decline, Friedan's writing pointed to the continuing importance of individual productivity as the foundation of cultural ideals of manhood, for instance, and successful aging. The book's content owed much to the mid-twentieth-century history of productive manhood and its middle-class/professional cultural and economic foundations—even as the book challenged it. Even as retiring men could retreat from their careers, formulas for successful retirement, in Friedan's view, depended on working hard at staying active and productive: this meant new jobs, new challenges, new activities. Friedan continued to note the importance of these activities for men in particular, urging older men to look "beyond the masculinity of youth" in retirement.[4] For aging men, retirement afforded opportunities to create identities by embracing new attitudes and new endeavors. Based on interviews with mainly professional men, Friedan noted that men's careers had been all-encompassing; and that in retirement many men found ways to rethink their life-long relationships to work and activity. "It is not easy for men to shift from the power race," Friedan argued, as her predecessors did during the 1950s. "Yet some men do."[5] She discussed aging males who, in her view, had transformed manhood and old age by retreating from the intensity of the daily working grind when they retired, seeking new ways to be active. Mogey Lazarus, a retired finance officer at a major department store chain, noted he had "changed a lot" since his retirement. After leaving his long career in business, he joined the board at a local hospital—and later "retired" from that post at the age of seventy-two. As Betty Friedan suggested, staying busy (and thus staying productive) in old age provided Lazarus with a new way to grow old as a man. "I had to find something I could zero in on, some concentrated productive activity, if I was going to keep mentally engaged, or I would fritter away my age with distractions," Lazarus told Friedan. "You have to divorce yourself from your former business."[6] But he continued to look for new activities that would replace the role of career in his life. While Friedan discussed old age as a time of "release," a time to move "beyond the masculinity of youth," there was real continuity between the productive masculinity of the working years and the retirement years; productive manhood still mattered. As observers of retirement originally argued in the 1940s and 1950s, working hard at new vocations (and avocations) would sustain manhood in later life. To remain "men," retiring males needed to stay energetic, engaged, busy, and active. They needed to find some new vocation that would stimulate and challenge them. As Mogey Lazarus noted, "I think the more comfortable you become in old age, the faster you age. You've got to stay a little uncomfortable, keep the antenna out."[7]

You've got to stay a little uncomfortable . . . Productivity continued to matter greatly in "successful" men's retirements throughout the remainder of the twentieth century. Still, I wouldn't discount Friedan's assertion that manhood in later life diverged from the "masculinity of youth." As Friedan's research indicated, retiring men did try to define staying busy doing something on their own terms and according to their own circumstances. In the process, they expressed some ambivalence regarding the life-long connection between working and male identity and the expectations placed on them as a result of their professional pasts.

In her interviews, Friedan met several older men who claimed that retirement was "for the birds," but she encountered others who embraced the idea of finding new ways of living.[8] A "government administrator" described how he felt a "tremendous burning ambition" as a younger man, but now observed that his career had "peaked out." He told Friedan that he had "reconciled" himself to the fact that career, success, and ambition no longer mattered so much to him. The man had mellowed with age. The administrator noted he was "reasonably content" to conclude his career in his current post, and he no longer felt the need to compete with younger colleagues. He was, in fact, "content" to "bring younger people along."[9] Another man, a veteran Air Force officer, discussed his hope to find "new goals" in his twilight years, while another complained about his career as a senior trade commissioner: "What happens if I do this the rest of my life?"[10] An aging college professor in California retired from his post as chair in a large university department and accepted a less labor-intensive post in the lab. However, the emeritus professor quickly retired completely when his spouse broke her hip. At home, he "took over the shopping" and cooking until her death a few years later. After his wife passed away, the professor resumed some of his old routines at the lab, returning to "[his] office at the lab every morning, Monday to Friday, [to] read the new scientific papers."[11]

Betty Friedan rightly argued "it is never pointed out that all our assumptions and definitions of masculinity are based on *young men*," and *The Fountain of Age* was an iconoclastic text that moved older men to the center of conversations about gender.[12] However, the history of productive manhood and retirement in the twentieth century showed that ideals of masculinity *were* based on younger men, as aging men continued to pursue their notions of productivity over the entire span of adulthood, however revised—even as they hoped to challenge them. As men aged, productive manhood would be made and remade.

While older men's pursuit of productive manhood fundamentally shaped experts' and observers' framing of aging and retirement culture in postwar America, the actual gender foundations of work and retirement have changed considerably since the 1950s. In the years since 1960, women and men have increasingly shared "retirement" as a phase of the life cycle; significant numbers of women have retired not as housewives but as employed blue-collar workers and white-collar professionals, collecting Social Security benefits, drawing workplace pensions, and seeking ways to remain busy and active in new lives without employment. Mirroring these gender changes in work and retirement, the *New York Times*, for instance, published a series of articles on "Women and Retirement" in 1986. While retiring men remain committed to the pursuit of productive manhood in later life, they would now do so in more and more social and cultural spaces they shared with retiring women. Men no longer have a monopoly on retirement, real or imagined. Between 1955 and 1967, the number of working women who were eligible for Social Security retirement benefits increased from 1.2 to 4.8 million.[13] By 1970, 25 percent of aging widows, single women, and divorcees received pension benefits, a number that would increase to 43 percent by 1986. In 1986, retired women collected $49 billion dollars per year in benefits from Social Security.[14] By 1983, 1 of 5 older women (20 percent) received a pension from their employer, compared to 42.6 percent of men.[15]

After the 1950s, productivity, too, became a concept that retired men had to share, if not concede, to older women. While aging men's labor participation dropped markedly in the second half of the twentieth century, declining from 50 percent of men 65 and up in 1950 to 16.3 percent in 1984, aging women's labor force participation remained steady for those over the age of 65 while increasing for women between the ages of 55 and 64. In 1950, 10 percent of women over the age of 65 worked away from home, and the number declined to only 7.5 percent in 1984. For women in their 50s and early 60s, workforce participation expanded dramatically in these years: 27 percent worked in 1950, and the number leapt to 41.7 percent by 1984. By 1990, this number would increase to 45 percent.[16]

There were several factors that contributed to aging women's expanding presence in the labor market since the 1950s: the employment of women in lower-paying jobs that lack benefit packages that would facilitate women's retirement; many women's decision to go back to work after raising their children; and women's need to sustain greater incomes once their (frequently older) husbands retired.[17] In the end, the danger of poverty in old age proved to the deciding factor that spurred aging women to remain at work. Through 1986, women comprised 71 percent of the aged poor in the United States.[18]

As aging women continue to take their place alongside older men in work and retirement, tensions over gender roles and relationships in retiree marriages have once again become a topic of discussion. While men retire, many women continue working into their later years and marital tensions emerge, despite Friedan's insistence that men and women could transcend the "old restrictions of masculine and feminine competition" in later life.

For example, Robert Waskover and his spouse, Barbara, faced a dilemma that began when Robert retired from his direct-mail business in 1990, and Barbara decided to explore new opportunities in research and public speaking. He retired to the golf course, while Barbara assumed new identities as a professional and intellectual. "He felt threatened because my life was so exciting and his wasn't," she observed. "It was constant bickering. When we did go out, he wouldn't dance with me. I guess he was trying to assert himself." Robert admitted he felt unsure about their relationship since their previous relationships to work had shifted. He said,

When you work your whole life, and all of a sudden you stop, it's like you lose something. She's doing all these things. I became insecure. I did nothing but criticize, which I never did before. All of a sudden, I didn't like the way she was rolling my socks.[19]

Tensions quickly reached a tipping point.

Barbara threatened her husband with divorce unless he secured a new job and thus restored the old feeling of balance to their relationship (and Robert's bruised notions of manly purpose). Robert first took a job as a telemarketer and then a second position in the insurance business. By going back to work (a lot), the frustrated husband found a firmer sense of identity and purpose in their heretofore strained relationship. Working restored Robert's sense of manhood amidst the upheavals of retirement and restored calm to the marriage. Finding work of his own helped him to "[support] his wife's work" and "to get over it."[20]

While labor, productivity, and staying busy have consistently defined the American culture of successful aging and retirement, adult Americans continue to worry deeply about the impact of growing old on their understandings of self—despite several decades of cultural production that stresses how, for men, working through later life (in its various guises) provides the surest paths to masculinity, health, and longevity. We suffer from a kind of cultural amnesia, though surrounded by a culture that stresses productivity as the lighthouse beacon that will prevent aging men from crashing into the rocky shoals of isolation, ill-health, and distress found in old age. Exploring the twentieth-century history of retiring men in America should help us in the twenty-first to feel less fearful of retirement and what lies beyond labor.

The 2002 Hollywood film *About Schmidt* highlights something of our lack of a sense of knowledge about aging, gender, and self. The narrative introduces us to everyman Warren R. Schmidt (Jack Nicholson), a retiring insurance actuary of Omaha, Nebraska, whose transition into retirement would be quickly overrun by anxiety, tragedy, and dissatisfaction. The film's earliest scenes are very reminiscent of 1950s conversations about the last days of work, retirement ceremonies, and the unsettling aftermath, raising age-old questions about the masculinity of life-long labor and the stifling isolation of retirement. The film begins in Schmidt's office, as he quietly watches the clock on the wall signal 5 p.m. and thus the end of his final day. As he follows the minute hand on the clock, he sits behind a now-empty desk, flanked on his right by several cardboard boxes of files (the sum total of his life's work?). The barrenness of the walls, the dreary cold rain outside, and the darkened office as Schmidt walks out of the room for the last time set a lonely, empty, and even despairing mood. With his wife Helen, he drives in silence to an impressively well-attended retirement dinner at a local steakhouse restaurant. As Gifford R. Hart and others experienced during the 1950s, Warren and Helen Schmidt sit at the center of the head table and enjoy a lavish dinner, gifts, and words of praise. After a brief toast given by "the new guy" who will take over Schmidt's duties, long-time friend Ray Nichols stands up to speak. As he talks to the assembled diners, Nichols insists upon the manliness of a life devoted to purposeful work as the ultimate kind of wealth for a man. A little drunk and very candid as a result, he says:

Hey Warren, how do you fell about these young punks taking over our jobs? Seems like some kind of conspiracy to me. Now, I have known Warren here probably long than most of you people have been alive. Warren and I go way back. Way back to the horse-and-buggy days at Woodmen's [Woodmen of the World, an Omaha-based insurance company and Schmidt's long-time employer] . . . Anyway, I know something about retirement and what I want to say to you out loud, so all these young hot shots can hear, is that all those gifts over there don't mean a goddamn thing. And this dinner don't mean a goddamn thing. None of these superficialities mean a goddamn thing. What means something . . . is the knowledge that you devoted your life to something meaningful, to being productive, and working for a fine company . . . At the end of his career, if a man can look back and say "I did it. I did my job," then he can retire in glory and enjoy riches far beyond the monetary kind. So, all of you young people here, take a good look at a very rich man.[21]

But his silence on what follows for the retiring man fails to answer the questions that so troubled Gifford R. Hart, Raymond Kaighn, and others: How could a retired man maintain this "wealth" without work? Can he ever be a full man again? For Schmidt, this new retired life was uncomfortable and wholly unfamiliar. (Couldn't anyone read or recall Gifford Hart's advice book on retirement?) Memories and celebrations of a job well-done and a family supported seemed to ring hollow, as he woke up the next day without his old routine, without the job that had defined his life and his identity for so long.

Soon listless and bored, Schmidt gravitates back to his old office. The film presents viewers with old assumptions about retired men at home: that they want to get away from this unfamiliar place, to somehow get back to work. Unannounced, he visits his successor, who has settled nicely into Schmidt's old duties. Schmidt hopes he can offer some kind of advice or assistance, but his help is not needed; the young man can get along without him. Schmidt leaves the building only to see his old boxes of files in the dumpster.

Schmidt's burgeoning retirement ennui is thrown into utter chaos by the sudden death of his spouse, the result of a blood clot in her brain. His entire world collapses during the same week—the purpose he once found at work ruined by retirement, and the domestic security he enjoyed at home undermined by Helen's death. He had been away from the house when she died, first visiting the post office and then stopping off at the local Dairy Queen for a Blizzard ice cream treat. His life shattered, Schmidt desperately tries to reconstruct some semblance of purpose in his life by driving across the vast Middle West from Omaha to Denver, Colorado, initially in order to "help out" with his beloved daughter Jeannie's wedding preparations but ultimately to convince his daughter not to marry her fiancé, a dimwitted salesman named Randall. After a series of misadventures and bizarre encounters during his journey, Schmidt fails in his quest to convince Jeannie to cancel the wedding. He even grows to quietly accept his daughter's choice of a future with the lackluster Randall. Schmidt returns home. In the final scene, he is brought to tears by a letter he received from a religious missionary in Tanzania, where he had been sponsoring a young "foster" child, 6-year-old Ndugu. In a series of earlier letters he wrote to the boy, the result of his desire to appropriately include "personal information" with his donations, Schmidt filled pages of legal pad paper with details and anecdotes about his life, his frustrations and problems. In the letter he receives from Tanzania, the nun tells Schmidt that his sponsorship had made a major difference in Ndugu's life, and that Ndugu thought of him fondly and often. Schmidt is brought to tears, realizing that his lonely life did matter after all. His co-workers moved on, and his family was gone, but he had been able to give help to this little boy.

Perhaps in our forgetfulness lies possibility: the chance to further imagine alternatives to ongoing productivity as the basis of male purpose. Warren R. Schmidt had to ultimately look beyond work, family, and home (and his own problems) to renew his life. The film begins a narrative that strongly echoes the retirement narratives of the 1950s, but abruptly departs into surprising directions: the accidental and painful discovery of his wife's long-ago infidelity with friend Ray Nichols; a near-escape from an RV campground where he foolishly tried to kiss another man's wife, a terribly injured and cramped neck incurred during a difficult night spent on a sloshing waterbed (and, to make matters worse, a later bad drug reaction to some very-old prescription pain killers), and a night-time hot tub encounter with the (naked) groom's mother, to list a few of Schmidt's experiences. In the end, he finds peace and meaning in his "72 cents a day" assistance to Ndugu in faraway Tanzania.[22]

As the fictional Warren R. Schmidt discovered, his retirement forced him to rethink the standards of defining a successful man. Would he be measured by the paper files in the dumpster, or the grateful young boy he helped overseas? Some men such as Austen A. Ettinger, the retiring advertising executive and dental patient we met at the beginning of this book, tried to seize upon retirement as an opportunity to begin redefining themselves on their own terms. "I'm determined to avoid the expectations trap," a frustrated and even defiant Ettinger noted, "accepting someone else's ideas about what I am, and what I should do, instead of shaping my own standards and setting my own pace."[23] Everyone around the aging white-collar man told him, in no uncertain terms, that manhood would be defined by ongoing work, staying busy, and remaining active—even, ironically, in retirement. Ettinger, however, voiced ambivalence to the idea that his identity would have to be defined by continued labor of some sort. Other men repeatedly asked him whether or not he was "keeping busy." Ettinger was torn between his determination to define himself and retirement on his own terms, with the constant, unrelenting reminders that to be a man, even in old age, he must continue to "produce." In the end, he committed himself to "[set] his own pace."[24] He would at least compromise.

The making of productive manhood for older men over the twentieth century, ironically, stemmed from the aging of the American population, the lengthening of the adult life cycle, and the establishing of retirement as a commonly accepted phase of life. As men aged, work, and more broadly the concept of productivity, became more and more important as the core of male identity. Workers, professionals, reformers, journalists, and advice authors struggled to map gender identities and relations across the expanding life cycle; and as a result, they did broaden the depth and extent of gender difference in culture, politics, public policy, the family, and the workplace. But by doing so, they did provide alternatives to the visceral masculinities that defined youth. As sociologist David Riesman once wrote in his book *The Lonely Crowd* (1950): "I like to interpret the conception that 'Man is born free; and everywhere he is in chains,' to mean that man is born a slave—a slave to his biological and cultural inheritance—but that he can become, through experience and experiment, increasingly free."[25]

Today's young men who live in what the noted sociologist and historian Michael Kimmel calls "Guyland" will someday grow up, grow old, and perhaps even liberate themselves from this "inheritance" as a result. In fact, for both the young and old, aging provides opportunities and reasons to look for new beginnings.

NOTES

1. Betty Friedan, *The Fountain of Age* (New York: Touchstone, 1993), 169.
2. Ibid., 637.
3. Ibid., 638.
4. Ibid., 165.
5. Ibid., 171.
6. Ibid., 231.
7. Ibid., 232.
8. Ibid., 170.
9. Ibid.
10. Ibid., 171.
11. Ibid.
12. Ibid., 165. Emphasis in original.
13. Alice Kessler-Harris, *In Pursuit of Equity: Women, Men, and the Quest for Economic Citizenship in 20th-Century America* (New York: Oxford University Press, 2001), 162, 336.
14. Glenn Collins, "More Women Are Retiring, and Doing Better," *New York Times*, 20 March 1986, C1. An estimated 73 percent of eligible older women received Social Security benefits during the 1980s. See Jill Quadagno, *The Transformation of Old Age Security: Class and Politics in the American Welfare State* (Chicago: University of Chicago Press, 1988), 2.
15. "Most Depend on Social Security," *New York Times*, 20 March 1986, C8.
16. Glenn Collins, "As More Men Retire Early, More Women Work Longer," *New York Times*, 3 April 1986, C1; Elizabeth T. Hill, "The Labor Force Participation of Older Women," *Monthly Labor Review*, September 2002, 39.
17. Collins, "As More Men Retire Early," C1.
18. Glenn Collins, "Bright Futures For Some, Bleak Prospects For Many," *New York Times*, 26 March 1986, C1; Louise Saul, "When Men Retire but Wives Do Not," *New York Times*, 30 September 1984, NJ1.

19. John Leland, "He's Retired, She's Working, They're Not Happy," *New York Times*, 23 March 2004, A1.

20. Ibid.

21. *About Schmidt*, dir. Alexander Payne, New Line Cinema, 2002.

22. Ibid.

23. Austen A. Ettinger, "The Retiring Kind," *New York Times*, 28 May 1989, 18.

24. Ibid.

25. David Riesman, *The Lonely Crowd* (New Haven: Yale University Press, 1950), 300.

Bibliography

ARCHIVAL SOURCES

Institute of Labor and Industrial Relations Library, University of Illinois at Urbana-
Champaign, Urbana, Illinois
    Vertical files
        Age and Employment
        Retirement
Walter P. Reuther Library, Wayne State University, Detroit, Michigan
    Joe Brown Papers
    Robert W. Dunn Papers
    UAW Oral History Transcripts

NEWSPAPERS AND PERIODICALS

AC Sparkler
Aging
Amalgamated Journal
American Federationist
American Journal of Sociology
American Labor Legislation Review
American Magazine
American Sociological Review
Atlantic Monthly
Auto Workers News
Baltimore Sun
Boston Daily Globe
Boston News Gazette

Buick Worker
Business Week
Changing Times
Chicago Daily News
Chicago Daily Tribune
Chicago Evening Post
Chicago Record-Herald
Collier's
Commonweal
Detroit Labor News
Detroit News
Dodge Main News
DSP Folks (Detroit Steel Products company newsletter)
Factory Management and Maintenance
Forum
Fortune
Harpers Magazine
Hygeia
Journal of Educational Sociology
Journal of Gerontology
Journal of Political Economy
Labor Age
Life
Los Angeles Times
Modern Crusader
Monthly Labor Review
Nation
Nation's Business
National Labor Tribune
New York Times
New York Times Magazine
Newsweek
Outlook
People's Press
Personnel
Personnel and Guidance Journal
Pittsburgh Post-Gazette
Public Opinion Quarterly
Reader's Digest
Recreation
Review of Reviews
Science Digest
Searchlight
Social Forces
Survey

Survey Graphic
Survey Midmonthly
Today's Health
UE News
United Automobile Worker
USA Today
US News & World Report
Vital Speeches of the Day
Voice of Local 212
Wall Street Journal
Washington Post

OTHER PUBLISHED PRIMARY SOURCES

Anderson, John W. "How I Became Part of the Labor Movement," in *Rank and File: Personal Histories by Working-Class Organizers*, Alice Lynd and Staughton Lynd, ed., 2nd edition. Princeton: Princeton University Press, 1981.

Anderson, Nels. *The Hobo: The Sociology of the Homeless Man*. Chicago: University of Chicago Press, 1923.

Attwood, William. "Why Does He Work So Hard?" in *The Decline of the American Male*, ed. *Look Magazine*. New York: Random House, 1958.

Bakke, E. Wight. *The Unemployed Worker: A Study of the Task of Making a Living without a Job*. New Haven: Yale University Press, 1940.

Bell, Thomas. *Out of this Furnace* (1941). Pittsburgh: University of Pittsburgh Press, 1976.

Bloomberg, Warner Jr. "Automation Predicts Change." in *The New Frontiers of Aging*, ed. Wilma Donahue and Clark Tibbitts. Ann Arbor: University of Michigan Press, 1957.

Bonosky, Philip. *Brother Bill McKie: Building the Union at Ford*. New York: International Publishers, 1953.

Boynton, Paul W. *Six Ways to Retire*. New York: Harper & Brothers, 1952.

Brock, Harold L. *The Fords In My Past*. Warrendale, PA: Society of Automotive Engineers, 2000.

Buckley, Joseph C. *The Retirement Handbook: A Complete Planning Guide To Your Future*. New York: Harper & Brothers, 1953.

Burns, Robert K. *Meeting the Challenge of Retirement* (booklet). Chicago: Industrial Relations Center, University of Chicago, n.d.

Catlin, Warren B. *The Labor Problem in the United States and Great Britain*. New York, Harper & Brothers Publishers, 1926.

Chamberlain, Neil W. ed. *Sourcebook on Labor*. New York: McGraw-Hill Book Company, 1958.

Chinoy, Ely. *Automobile Workers and the American Dream* (1955). Boston: Beacon Press, 1965.

Close, Kathryn. "Getting Ready To Retire." Public Affairs Pamphlet No. 182. New York: Public Affairs Committee, Inc., 1952.

Cohen, Herbert J., and Richard W. Lawall, eds. *New York Times Encyclopedia of Sports*. Vol. 5 (Golf). New York: New York Times Company, 1979.

Colby, Evelyn, and John G. Forrest. *Ways and Means to Successful Retirement*. New York: BC Forbes and Sons Publishing, 1952.

Commons, John R., and John B. Andrews. *Principles of Labor Legislation*. New York: Harper & Brothers Publishers, 1916.

Conroy, Jack. *The Disinherited: A Novel of the 1930s* (1933). Columbia: University of Missouri Press, 1991.

Cully, Jack F. and Fred Slavick. *Employment Problems of Older Workers*. Iowa City: Bureau of Labor Management, State University of Iowa, 1959.

Danford, Howard G. *Recreation in the American Community*. New York: Harper & Brothers, 1953.

Davis, Horace B. *Labor and Steel*. New York: International Publishers, 1933.

de Caux, Len. *Labor Radical: From the Wobblies to CIO*. Boston: Beacon Press, 1970.

Dunn, Robert W. *Labor and Automobiles*. New York: International Publishers, 1929.

Dunn, Robert W. and Jack Hardy. *Labor and Textiles*. New York: International Publishers, 1931.

Epstein, Abraham. *Insecurity: A Challenge to America*. Introduction by Frances Perkins. New York: Harrison Smith and Robert Haas, 1933.

———. *The Challenge of the Aged*. Introduction by Jane Addams. New York: Vanguard Press, 1928.

———. *Facing Old Age: A Study of Old Age Dependency in the United States and Old Age Pensions*. New York: Alfred A. Knopf, 1922.

Epstein, Pierre. *Abraham Epstein: The Forgotten Father of Social Security*. Columbia, MO: University of Missouri Press, 2007.

Federal Security Agency. *Fourth Annual Report of the Social Security Board*. Washington, DC: Government Printing Office, 1940.

Fitch, John. *The Steel Workers* (1910). Pittsburgh: University of Pittsburgh Press, 1989.

Ford Motor Company. *A Tour of the Remarkable Ford Industries during the Days When the End Product Was the Matchless Model A, with 150 Photographs* (1929). Lockport, NY: Lincoln Publishing Company, 1961.

Foster, William Z. *The Great Steel Strike and Its Lessons* (1920). New York: DaCapo Press, 1971.

Fountain, Clayton W. *Union Guy*. New York: Viking Press, 1949.

Friedan, Betty. *The Fountain of Age*. New York: Touchstone, 1993.

———. *The Feminine Mystique* (1963). New York: Dell, 1975.

Friedmann, Eugene A. and Robert J. Havighurst. *The Meaning of Work and Retirement*. Chicago: University of Chicago, 1954.

Freud, Sigmund. *Civilization and its Discontents*. Translated by James Strachey (1930). New York: WW Norton & Company, 1961.

Gibson, Nevin H. *The Encyclopedia of Golf*. New York: AS Barnes and Company, 1964.

Giles, Ray. *How to Retire—and Enjoy It*. New York: McGraw-Hill Book Company, 1949.

Golden, Clinton S. and Harold J. Ruttenberg. *The Dynamics of Industrial Democracy*. New York: Harper & Brothers Publishers, 1942.

Gompers, Samuel. *Labor and the Employer*. New York: EP Dutton & Company, 1920.

Gordon, Margaret S. "Work and Patterns of Retirement." In *Aging and Leisure: A Research Perspective Into the Meaningful Use of Time*, ed. Robert W. Kleemeier. New York: Oxford University Press, 1961.

Greene, Theodor. *How to Enjoy Retirement for the Rest of Your Life*. New York: Exposition Press, 1957.

Gross, Nancy E. *Living With Stress*. New York: McGraw-Hill Book Company, 1958.

Gulick, Charles A. *Labor Policy of the United States Steel Corporation*. New York: Longmans, Green & Co., 1924.

Gumpert, Martin. *You Are Younger Than You Think*. New York: Duell, Sloan and Pearce, 1944.

Haber, William and Wilbur J. Cohen, eds. *Social Security: Programs, Problems, and Policies*. Homewood, IL: Richard D. Irwin, Inc., 1960.

Hall, Harold R. *Some Observations on Executive Retirement*. Cambridge: Graduate School of Business Administration, Harvard University, 1953.

Hardy, Jack. *The Clothing Workers: A Study of the Conditions and Struggles in the Needle Trades*. New York: International Publishers, 1935.

Hart, Gifford R. *Retirement: A New Outlook for the Individual*. New York: Harcourt, Brace and Company, 1957.

Havighurst, Robert J. "The Impact of Retirement of the Individual." in *Unions and the Problems of Retirement: Proceedings of a Conference*. University of Chicago, 3–4 April 1959, booklet. Chicago: Union Research and Education Projects, 1959.

Herrington, Michael. *The Other America: Poverty in the United States* (1962). New York: Penguin Books, 1981.

Howe, Irving, and BJ Widick. *The UAW and Walter Reuther*. New York: Random House, 1949.

Interchurch World Movement. *Report on the Steel Strike of 1919*. New York: Harcourt, Brace & Howe, 1920.

Kaighn, Raymond P. *How to Retire and Like It*. New York: Association Press, 1951.

Kausler, Donald H. and Barry C. Kausler. *The Graying of America: An Encyclopedia of Aging, Health, Mind, and Behavior*, 2nd edition. Urbana: University of Illinois Press, 2001.

Komarovsky, Mirra. *The Unemployed Man and His Family—The Effect of Unemployment Upon the Status of the Man in Fifty-Nine Families* (1940). New York: Octagon Books, 1973.

Korth, Philip A. and Margaret R. Beegle. *I Remember Like Today: The Auto-Lite Strike of 1934*. East Lansing: Michigan State University Press, 1988.

Kraus, Henry. *The Many and the Few: A Chronicle of the Dynamic Auto Workers.* Los Angeles: Plantin Press, 1947.

Latimer, Murray Webb. *Industrial Pensions in the United States and Canada.* New York: Industrial Relations Counselors, 1932.

Lynd, Robert S. and Helen Merrell Lynd. *Middletown: A Study in American Culture.* New York: Harcourt, Brace, and Company, 1929.

———. *Middletown in Transition: A Study in Cultural Conflicts.* New York: Harcourt, Brace and Company, 1937.

Marquart, Frank. *An Auto Worker's Journal: The UAW from Crusade to One-Party Union.* University Park, PA: Pennsylvania State University Press, 1975.

Massachusetts Commission on Pensions. *Report on Old Age Pensions.* Boston: Commission on Pensions, 1925.

Mathewson, Stanley B. *Restriction of Output Among Unorganized Workers.* New York: Viking Press, 1931.

McElvaine, Robert S., ed. *Down and Out in the Great Depression: Letters from the Forgotten Man.* Chapel Hill: University of North Carolina, 1983.

Miller, Arthur. *Death of a Salesman* (1949). New York: Penguin Books, 1998.

Millis, Harry A. and Royal E. Montgomery. *Labor's Risks and Social Insurance.* New York: McGraw-Hill Book Company, 1938.

Moore, Elon H. and Gordon F. Streib. *The Nature of Retirement.* New York: Macmillan Company, 1959.

Morris, James R. *Employment Opportunities in Later Years.* Burlingame, CA: Foundation for Voluntary Welfare, 1960.

Moskin, J. Robert. "Why Do Women Dominate Him?" in *The Decline of the American Male*, ed. *Look* Magazine. New York: Random House, 1958.

Naef, Charles R. *Pre-Retirement Programs in New Jersey.* New Brunswick, NJ: Institute of Management and Labor Relations, Rutgers University, 1960.

Nassau, Mabel Louise. *Old Age Poverty in Greenwich Village.* New York: Fleming H. Revell Company, 1915.

National Center for Health Statistics. *Health, United States, 2004, with Chart Book on Trends in the Health of Americans.* Hyattsville, MD: US Department of Health and Human Services, 2004. http://www.cdc.gov/nchs /data/hus/hus 04trend.pdf#027.

National Labor Relations Board. *Decisions and Orders of the National Labor Relations Board: Volume IV.* Washington, DC: Government Printing Office, 1938.

Nelson, Steve, James R. Barrett, and Rob Ruck. *Steve Nelson: American Radical.* Pittsburgh: University of Pittsburgh Press, 1981.

Niebuhr, Reinhold. *Leaves from the Notebook of a Tamed Cynic.* Chicago: Willet, Clark & Colby, 1929.

Parran, Thomas, Harwood S. Belding, Antonio Ciocco, James A Crabtree, Theodore F. Hatch, Adolph G. Kammer, and Violet B. Turner. "Monograph I." In *Criteria for Retirement: A Report of a National Conference on Retirement of Older Workers*, ed. Geneva Mathiasen. New York: GP Putnam's Sons, 1953.

Pitkin, Walter B. *The Best Years: How to Enjoy Retirement.* New York: Current Books, 1946.

Pollack, Otto. *The Social Aspects of Retirement*, booklet. Philadelphia: Pension Research Council of the Wharton School of Finance and Commerce, University of Pennsylvania, 1956.

Preston, George H. *Should I Retire?*. New York: Reinhart & Company, 1952.

The Public Papers and Addresses of Franklin D. Roosevelt, with a Special Introduction and Explanatory Notes by President Roosevelt: Volume IV: The Court Disapproves, 1935 (1938). New York: Random House, 1969.

Riesman, David. *The Lonely Crowd*. New Haven: Yale University Press, 1950.

Rubinow, Isaac Max. *Social Insurance, with Special Reference to American Conditions*. New York: Henry Holt, 1913.

Salomon, Irving. *Retire and Be Happy*. New York: Greenberg, 1951.

Schlesinger, Arthur M., Jr. "The Crisis of American Masculinity" (1958). In *The Politics of Hope*. Boston: Houghton Mifflin Company, 1962.

Selekman, Ben M. *Employes' Representation in Steel Works: A Study of the Industrial Representation Plan of the Minnequa Steel Works of the Colorado Fuel and Iron Company*. New York: Russell Sage Foundation, 1924.

Selekman, Ben M. and Mary Van Kleeck. *Employes' Representation in Coal Mines: A Study of the Industrial Representation Plan of the Colorado Fuel and Iron Company*. New York: Russell Sage Foundation, 1924.

Sinclair, Upton. *The Jungle (1906)*. New York: Bantam Books, 1981.

Smith, Ethel Sabin. *The Dynamics of Aging*. New York: WW Norton & Company, 1956.

"Social Security." In *The World Book Encyclopedia*. Vol. 16. Chicago: Field Enterprises Educational Corporation, 1960.

Social Security Board. *First Annual Report of the Social Security Board*. Washington, DC: Government Printing Office, 1937.

Squier, Lee Welling. *Old Age Dependency in the United States: A Complete Survey of the Pension Movement*. New York: The Macmillan Company, 1912.

Steele, James [Robert Cruden]. *Conveyor: A Novel*. New York: International Publishers, 1935.

Stieglitz, Edward J. *The Second Forty Years*. Philadelphia: JB Lippincott Company, 1946.

Stokes, Dillard. *Social Security—Fact and Fancy*. Chicago: Henry Regnery Company, 1956.

Stolberg, Benjamin. *The Story of the CIO*. New York: Viking Press, 1938.

Sweeney, Ed. *Poorhouse Sweeney: Life in a County Poorhouse*. New York: Boni & Liveright, 1927.

Terkel, Studs. *"The Good War": An Oral History of World War II*. New York: Pantheon Books, 1984.

Tuckman, Jacob and Irving Lorge. *Retirement and the Industrial Worker: Prospect and Reality*. New York: Teachers College Columbia University, 1953.

Twentieth Century Fund, Inc. *More Security for Old Age: A Report and A Program*. New York: Twentieth Century Fund Inc., 1937.

US Department of Commerce. *Historical Statistics of the United States: Colonial Times to 1970*. Washington, DC: Government Printing Office, 1975.

US Bureau of the Census. *Fifteenth Census of the United States, Population, Vol. IV: Occupations, By States.* Washington, DC: Government Printing Office, 1933.

Vorse, Mary Heaton. *Men and Steel.* New York: Boni & Liveright, 1920.

Wallace, Carlton. *How to Retire Successfully.* London: Evans Brothers Limited, 1956.

Walker, Charles R. and Robert H. Guest. *The Man on the Assembly Line.* Cambridge, MA: Harvard University Press, 1952.

Walsh, J. Raymond. *CIO: Industrial Unionism in Action.* New York: WW Norton & Company, 1937.

Weber, Max. *The Protestant Ethic and the Spirit of Capitalism* (1905). New York: Scribner, 1958.

West, Kenneth B. "'On the Line': Rank and File Reminiscences of Working Conditions and the General Motors Sit-Down Strike of 1936–37." *Michigan Historical Review,* 12 (Spring 1986).

Whyte, William H., Jr. *The Organization Man.* New York: Simon and Schuster, 1956.

Wind, Herbert Warren. *The Story of American Golf: Its Champions and Its Championships.* New York: Simon and Schuster, 1956.

Wolman, Leo, and Gustav Peck. "Labor Groups in the Social Structure." In *Recent Social Trends in the United States: Report of the President's Research Committee on Social Trends.* With a foreword by Herbert Hoover. New York: McGraw-Hill, 1933.

FILMS

About Schmidt, dir. Alexander Payne. *New Line Cinema.* 2002.

As Young As You Feel. dir. Harmon Jones. Twentieth Century-Fox. 1951.

Rear Window. dir. Alfred Hitchcock. Universal Pictures. 1954.

SECONDARY SOURCES: BOOKS AND ARTICLES

Achenbaum, W. Andrew. *Old Age in the New Land: The American Experience Since 1790.* Baltimore: Johns Hopkins University Press, 1978.

Ambrose, Stephen E. *Band of Brothers.* New York: Simon & Schuster, 2001.

Amenta, Edwin. *When Movements Matter: The Townsend Plan and the Rise of Social Security.* Princeton: Princeton University Press, 2006.

Andrews, Thomas G. *Killing For Coal: America's Deadliest Labor War.* Cambridge: Harvard University Press, 2008.

Arnesen, Eric. "'Like Banquo's Ghost, It Will Not Down': The Race Question and the American Railroad Brotherhoods, 1880–1920." *American Historical Review,* 99:5 (1994).

Asher, Robert, and Ronald Edsforth, eds., with the assistance of Stephen Merlino. *Autowork.* Albany: State University of New York Press, 1995.

Ballenger, Jesse F. *Self, Senility, and Alzheimer's Disease in America: A History.* Baltimore: John Hopkins University Press, 2006.

Baron, Ava. ed. *Work Engendered: Towards a New History of American Labor.* Ithaca: Cornell University Press, 1990.

———. "Questions of Gender: Deskilling and Demasculinization in the US Printing Industry, 1830–1915." *Gender & History,* 1:2 (1989).

Baron, Ava, and Eileen Boris. "'The Body' As a Useful Category for Working-Class History." *Labor: Studies in Working-Class History of the Americas,* 4:2 (2007).

Barrett, James R. *William Z. Foster and the Tragedy of American Radicalism.* Urbana: University of Illinois Press, 1999.

———. "Americanization from the Bottom Up: Immigration and the Remaking of the Working Class in the United States, 1880–1930." *Journal of American History,* 79:3 (1992).

———. *Work and Community in the Jungle: Chicago's Packinghouse Workers, 1894–1922.* Urbana: University of Illinois Press, 1987.

Bederman, Gail. *Manliness and Civilization: A Cultural History of Gender and Race in the United States, 1880–1917.* Chicago: University of Chicago Press, 1995.

———. "'The Women Have Had Charge of the Church Work Long Enough': The Men and Religion Forward Movement of 1911–1912 and the Masculinization of Middle-Class Protestantism." *American Quarterly,* 41 (1989).

Benson, Susan Porter. *Household Accounts: Working-Class Family Economics in the Interwar United States,* afterword by David Montgomery. Ithaca: Cornell University Press, 2007.

———. *Counter Cultures: Saleswomen, Managers, and Customers in American Department Stores, 1890–1940.* Urbana: University of Illinois Press, 1986.

Benton-Cohen, Katherine. *Borderline Americans: Race and Labor War in the Arizona Borderlands.* Cambridge: Harvard University Press, 2009.

Bernstein, Irving. *The Lean Years: A History of the American Worker, 1920–1933* (1960). Boston: Houghton Mifflin Company, 1972.

———. *Turbulent Years: A History of the American Worker, 1933–1941.* Boston: Houghton Mifflin Company, 1970.

Blair, Cynthia M. *I've Got To Make My Livin': Black Women's Sex Work in Turn-of-the-Century Chicago.* Chicago: University of Chicago Press, 2010.

Blewett, Mary H. *Men, Women, and Work: Class, Gender, and Protest in the New England Shoe Industry, 1780–1910.* Urbana: University of Illinois Press, 1988.

Blumberg, Barbara. *The New Deal and the Unemployed.* Cranbury, NJ: Associated University Presses, 1979.

Boydston, Jeanne. *Home and Work: Housework, Wages, and the Ideology of Labor in the Early Republic.* New York: Oxford University Press, 1990.

Brands, HW. *The Devil We Knew: Americans and the Cold War.* New York: Oxford University Press, 1993.

Braverman, Harry. *Labor and Monopoly Capital: The Degradation of Work in the Twentieth Century.* New York: Monthly Review Press, 1974.

Brody, David. *Steelworkers in America: The Nonunion Era* (1960). Urbana: University of Illinois Press, 1998.

Brody, David. *Labor in Crisis: The Steel Strike of 1919.* New York: JB Lippincott Company, 1965.

Brown, Kathleen M. *Good Wives, Nasty Wenches, and Anxious Patriarchs: Gender, Race, and Power in Colonial Virginia.* Chapel Hill: University of North Carolina Press, 1996.

Calasanti, Toni. "Bodacious Berry, Potency Wood and the Aging Monster: Gender and Age Relations in Anti-Aging Ads." *Social Forces,* 86:1 (2007).

Calasanti, Toni M. and Kathleen F. Slevin. *Gender, Social Inequalities, and Aging.* Lanham, MD: Rowman & Littlefield, 2001.

Carnes, Mark C. and Clyde Griffen, eds. *Meanings for Manhood: Constructions of Masculinity in Victorian America.* Chicago: University of Chicago Press, 1990.

Carter, Susan B. and Richard Sutch. "Myth of the Industrial Scrap Heap: A Revisionist View of Turn-of-the-Century American Retirement." *Journal of Economic History,* 56:1 (1996).

Casebeer, Kenneth. "Aliquippa: The Company Town and Contested Power in the Construction of Law," *Buffalo Law Review,* 43:3 (1995).

Chafe, William H. "America Since 1945." In *The New American History,* ed. Eric Foner. Philadelphia: Temple University Press, 1997.

———. *The Unfinished Journey: America Since World War II.* New York: Oxford University Press, 1986.

———. *The American Woman: Her Changing Social, Economic, and Political Roles, 1920–1970.* New York: Oxford University Press, 1972.

Chandler, Alfred D. *The Visible Hand: The Managerial Revolution in American Business.* Cambridge, MA: Harvard University Press, 1977.

Chauncey, George. *Gay New York: Gender, Urban Culture, and the Making of the Gay Male World, 1890–1940.* New York: Free Press, 1994.

Chudacoff, Howard P. *The Age of the Bachelor: Creating an American Subculture.* Princeton: Princeton University Press, 2000.

Cohen, Lizabeth. *A Consumer's Republic: The Politics of Mass Consumption in Postwar America.* New York: Vintage Books, 2003.

———. *Making a New Deal: Industrial Workers in Chicago, 1919–1939.* New York: Cambridge University Press, 1990.

Connell, R W. *The Men and the Boys.* Berkeley: University of California Press, 2001.

———. *Masculinities.* Berkeley: University of California Press, 1995.

Coontz, Stephanie. *The Way We Never Were: American Families and the Nostalgia Trap.* New York: Basic Books, 1992.

Cooper, Patricia. *Once a Cigar Maker: Men, Women, and Work Culture in American Cigar Factories, 1900–1919.* Urbana: University of Illinois Press, 1987.

Costa, Dora L. *The Evolution of Retirement: An American Economic History, 1880–1990.* Chicago: University of Chicago Press, 1998.

Cott, Nancy, ed. *No Small Courage: A History of Women in the United States.* New York: Oxford University Press, 2000.

Cuordileone, KA. *Manhood and American Political Culture in the Cold War.* New York: Routledge, 2005.

———. "'Politics in an Age of Anxiety': Cold War Political Culture and the Crisis in American Masculinity, 1949–1960." *Journal of American History,* 87:2 (2000).

Dabakis, Melissa. "Douglas Tilden's Mechanics Fountain: Labor and the 'Crisis of Masculinity' in the 1890s." *American Quarterly*, 47:2 (1995).

Davis, Clark. *Company Men: White-Collar Life and Corporate Cultures in Los Angeles, 1892–1941*. Baltimore: Johns Hopkins University Press, 2000.

Davis, GV. "Work Ethic." In *Encyclopedia of US Labor and Working-Class History*, ed. Eric Arnesen. New York: Routledge, 2007.

De Hart, Jane Sherron, and Linda K. Kerber. "Introduction: Gender and the New Women's History." In *Women's America: Refocusing the Past*, 5th edition. New York: Oxford University Press, 2000.

Denning, Michael. *The Cultural Front: The Laboring of American Culture during the Twentieth Century*. New York: Verso, 1996.

Devlin, Rachel. *Relative Intimacy: Fathers, Adolescent Daughters, and Postwar American Culture*. Chapel Hill: University of North Carolina Press, 2005.

Dublin, Thomas. *Women at Work: The Transformation of Work and Community in Lowell, Massachusetts, 1826–1860*. New York: Columbia University Press, 1979.

Dumenil, Lynn. *The Modern Temper: American Culture and Society in the 1920s*. New York: Hill and Wang, 1995.

Edsforth, Ronald and Robert Asher, with Raymond Boryczka. "The Speedup: The Focal Point of Workers' Grievances, 1919–1941." In *Autowork*. eds. Robert Asher and Ronald Edsforth, with the assistance of Stephen Merlino. Albany: State University of New York Press, 1995.

Estes, Steve. "'I AM a Man!' Race, Masculinity, and the 1968 Memphis Sanitation Strike." *Labor History*, 41:2 (2000).

Faler, Paul. *Mechanics and Manufacturers in the Early Industrial Revolution: Lynn, Massachusetts, 1780–1860*. Albany: State University of New York Press, 1981.

Faludi, Susan. *Stiffed: The Betrayal of the American Man*. New York: HarperCollins Publishers, 1999.

Faue, Elizabeth. *Community of Suffering and Struggle: Women, Men, and the Labor Movement in Minneapolis, 1914–1945*. Chapel Hill: University of North Carolina Press, 1991.

Feimster, Crystal N. *Southern Horrors: Women and the Politics of Rape and Lynching*. Cambridge: Harvard University Press, 2009.

Filene, Peter G. *Him/Her/Self: Sex Roles in Modern America* (1978). Baltimore: Johns Hopkins University Press, 1986.

Fischer, David Hackett. *Growing Old in America*. New York: Oxford University Press, 1978.

Fine, Lisa. "Rights of Men, Rites of Passage: Hunting and Masculinity at Reo Motors of Lansing, Michigan, 1945–1975." In *Boys and Their Toys? Masculinity, Class, and Technology in America*, ed. Roger Horowitz. New York: Routledge, 2001.

———. "'Our Big Factory Family': Masculinity and Paternalism at the Reo Motor Car Company of Lansing, Michigan." *Labor History*, 34:2–3 (1993).

Fine, Sidney. *Sit-Down: The General Motors Strike of 1936–1937*. Ann Arbor: University of Michigan Press, 1969.

——. The *Automobile Under the Blue Eagle: Labor, Management, and the Automobile Manufacturing Code*. Ann Arbor: University of Michigan Press, 1963.

Foley, Neil. *The White Scourge: Mexicans, Blacks, and Poor Whites in Texas Cotton Culture*. Berkeley: University of California Press, 1997.

Foner, Eric. *The Story of American Freedom*. New York: WW Norton & Company, 1998.

Fones-Wolf, Elizabeth. *Selling Free Enterprise: The Business Assault on Labor and Liberalism, 1945–1960*. Urbana: University of Illinois Press, 1994.

Forman-Brunell, Miriam. *Babysitter: An American History*. New York: New York University Press, 2009.

Friedlander, Peter. *The Emergence of a UAW Local, 1936–1939: A Study in Class and Culture*. Pittsburgh: University of Pittsburgh, 1975.

Gabin, Nancy. *Feminism and the Labor Movement: Women and the United Auto Workers, 1935–1975*. Ithaca: Cornell University Press, 1990.

Gilbert, James. *Men in the Middle: Searching for Masculinity in the 1950s*. Chicago: University of Chicago Press, 2005.

Gilmore, David. *Manhood in the Making: Cultural Concepts in Masculinity*. New Haven: Yale University Press, 1990.

Gilmore, Glenda Elizabeth. *Gender and Jim Crow: Women and the Politics of White Supremacy in North Carolina, 1896–1920*. Chapel Hill: University of North Carolina Press, 1996.

Glenn, Evelyn Nakano. "Protest, Resistance, and Survival in the Jim Crow South." *Labor History*, 39:2 (1998).

Glickman, Lawrence B. "The Strike in the Temple of Consumption: Consumer Activism and Twentieth-Century American Political Culture." *Journal of American History*, 88 (2001).

——. *A Living Wage: American Workers and the Making of Consumer Society*. Ithaca: Cornell University Press, 1997.

Goodwin, Joanne L. *Gender and the Politics of Welfare Reform: Mothers' Pensions in Chicago, 1911–1929*. Chicago: University of Chicago Press, 1997.

——. "'Employable Mothers' and 'Suitable Work': A Re-Evaluation of Welfare and Wage-Earning for Women in the Twentieth-Century United States," *Journal of Social History*, 29:2 (1995).

Gordon, Linda. "US Women's History." In *The New American History*, ed. Eric Foner. Philadelphia: Temple University Press, 1997.

——. *Pitied But Not Entitled: Single Mothers and the History of Welfare, 1890–1935*. New York: Free Press, 1994.

——. "Social Insurance and Public Assistance: The Influence of Gender in Welfare Thought in the United States, 1880–1945." *American Historical Review*, 97:1 (1992).

Gorn, Elliot. *The Manly Art: Bare-Knuckle Prize Fighting in America*. Ithaca: Cornell University Press, 1986.

Graebner, William. *A History of Retirement: The Meaning and Function of an American Institution, 1885–1978*. New Haven: Yale University Press, 1980.

Gratton, Brian. "The Poverty of Impoverishment Theory: The Economic Well-Being of the Elderly, 1890–1950." *Journal of Economic History*, 56:1 (1996).

———. "The New History of the Aged: A Critique." In *Old Age in a Bureaucratic Society: The Elderly, the Experts, and the State in American History*, ed. David Van Tassel and Peter N. Stearns. New York: Greenwood Press, 1986.

Greenberg, Joshua R. *Advocating the Man: Masculinity, Organized Labor, and the Household in New York, 1800–1840*. New York: Columbia University Press, 2008.

Greene, Julie. *The Canal Builders: Making America's Empire at the Panama Canal*. New York: Penguin Books, 2009.

Greenwald, Maurine. *Women, War, and Work: The Impact of World War I on Women Workers in the United States*. Westport, CT: Greenwood, 1980.

Grossman, James R. *Land of Hope: Chicago, Black Southerners, and the Great Migration*. Chicago: University of Chicago Press, 1989.

Gutman, Herbert G. "Work, Culture, and Society in Industrializing America, 1815–1919." *American Historical Review*, 78:3 (1973).

Haber, Carol, and Brian Gratton. *Old Age and the Search for Security: An American Social History*. Bloomington, IN: Indiana University Press, 1994.

Hannon, Joan Underhill. "The Generosity of Antebellum Poor Relief." *Journal of Economic History*, 44:3 (1984).

Hapke, Laura. *Labor's Text: The Worker in American Fiction*. New Brunswick: Rutgers University Press, 2001.

Haring, Kristen. *Ham Radio's Technical Culture*. Cambridge: MIT Press, 2007.

———. "The 'Freer Men' of Ham Radio: How a Technical Hobby Provided Social and Spatial Distance." *Technology and Culture*, 44:4 (2003).

Higbie, Frank Tobias. *Indispensable Outcasts: Hobo Workers and Community in the American Midwest, 1880–1930*. Urbana: University of Illinois Press, 2003.

Hirshbein, Laura Davidow. "William Osler and *The Fixed Period*: Conflicting Medical and Popular Ideas About Old Age." *Archives of Internal Medicine*, 161 (24 September 2001).

Hoganson, Kristin. *Fighting for American Manhood: How Gender Politics Provoked the Spanish-American and Philippine-American Wars*. New Haven: Yale University Press, 1998.

Hunter, Tera. *To 'Joy My Freedom: Southern Black Women's Lives and Labors After the Civil War*. Cambridge, MA: Harvard University Press, 1998.

Isenberg, Nancy. *Sex and Citizenship in Antebellum America*. Chapel Hill: University of North Carolina Press, 1997.

Jacobs, Meg. *Pocketbook Politics: Economic Citizenship in Twentieth-Century America*. Princeton: Princeton University Press, 2005.

Jacoby, Sanford M. *Modern Manors: Welfare Capitalism Since the New Deal*. Princeton: Princeton University Press, 1997.

Jackson, Kenneth T. *Crabgrass Frontier: The Suburbanization of the United States*. New York: Oxford University Press, 1985.

Jaher, Frederic Cople. "White America Views Jack Johnson, Joe Louis, and Muhammad Ali." In *Sport in America: New Historical Perspectives*, ed. Donald Spivey. Westport, CT: Greenwood Press, 1985.

Jarvis, Christina. *The Male Body at War: American Masculinity during World War II*. DeKalb, IL: Northern Illinois University Press, 2010.

Johansson, Ella. "Beautiful Men, Fine Women and Good Work People: Gender and Skill in Northern Sweden, 1850–1950." *Gender & History*, 1:2 (1989).

Johanningsmeier, Edward P. *Forging American Communism: The Life of William Z. Foster*. Princeton: Princeton University Press, 1994.

Johnson, Christopher H. *Maurice Sugar: Law, Labor, and the Left in Detroit, 1912–1950*. Detroit: Wayne State University Press, 1988.

Jones, Kathleen W. "When a Young Woman Dies: Gender, Youth, and Suicide in the Jazz Age." In *Death and Dying: Inter-Disciplinary Perspectives*, Asa Kasher, ed. London: Rodopi Press, 2007.

Jones, William P. *The Tribe of Black Ulysses: African American Lumber Workers in the Jim Crow South*. Urbana: University of Illinois Press, 2005.

Kaplan, Michael. "New York City Tavern Violence and the Creation of a Working-Class Male Identity." *Journal of the Early Republic*, 15 (1995).

Kasson, John F. *Houdini, Tarzan, and the Perfect Man: The White Male Body and the Challenge of Modernity in America*. New York: Hill and Wang, 2001.

Kaster, Gregory L. "Labour's True Man: Organised Workingmen and the Language of Manliness in the USA, 1827–1877." *Gender & History*, 13:1 (2001).

Katz, Michael B. *In the Shadow of the Poorhouse: A Social History of Welfare in America* (1986). New York: BasicBooks, 1996.

Keeran, Roger. *The Communist Party and the Auto Workers' Unions* (1980). New York: International Publishers, 1986.

Kelley, Robin DG. *Hammer and Hoe: Alabama Communists during the Great Depression*. Chapel Hill: University of North Carolina Press 1990.

Kennedy, David M. *Freedom From Fear: The American People in Depression and War, 1929–1945*. New York: Oxford University Press, 1999.

Kerber, Linda K. "Separate Spheres, Female Worlds, Woman's Place: The Rhetoric of Women's History." *Journal of American History*, 75:1 (1988).

Kessler-Harris, Alice. *In Pursuit of Equity: Women, Men, and the Quest for Economic Citizenship in 20th-Century America*. New York: Oxford University Press, 2001.

———. "Providers: Gender Ideology in the 1930s." In *Women's America: Refocusing the Past*, ed. Linda K. Kerber and Jane Sherron De Hart, 5th edition. New York: Oxford University Press, 2000.

———. "Treating the Male As 'Other': Redefining the Parameters of Labor History." Labor History, 34:2–3 (1993).

———. "Gender Ideology in Historical Reconstruction: A Case Study from the 1930s." *Gender & History*, 1:1 (1989).

———. *Out to Work: A History of Wage-Earning Women in the United States*. New York: Oxford University Press, 1982.

Keyssar, Alexander. *Out of Work: The First Century of Unemployment in Massachusetts*. New York: Cambridge University Press, 1986.

Kimmel, Michael. *Guyland: The Perilous World Where Boys Become Men*. New York: HarperCollins, 2008.

———. *Manhood in America: A Cultural History*. New York: Free Press, 1996.

———. "The Contemporary 'Crisis' of Masculinity in Historical Perspective." In *The Making of Masculinities: The New Men's Studies*, ed. Harry Brod. Boston: Allen & Unwin, 1987.

Kirsch, George B. *Golf in America.* Urbana: University of Illinois Press, 2009.

Klein, Jennifer. *For All These Rights: Business, Labor, and the Shaping of America's Public-Private Welfare State.* Princeton: Princeton University Press, 2003.

Kleinberg, SJ. *The Shadow of the Mills: Working-Class Families in Pittsburgh, 1870–1907.* Pittsburgh: University of Pittsburgh Press, 1989.

LaFeber, Walter. *America, Russia, and the Cold War, 1945–1992.* 7th edition. New York: McGraw Hill, 1993.

Laurie, Bruce. *Artisans Into Workers: Labor in Nineteenth Century America.* New York: Hill and Wang, 1989.

Leotta, Louis. "Abraham Epstein and the Movement for Old Age Security." *Labor History*, 16:3 (1975).

Letwin, Daniel. *The Challenge of Interracial Unionism: Alabama Coal Miners, 1878–1921.* Chapel Hill: University of North Carolina Press, 1998.

Lewchuk, Wayne A. "Men and Monotony: Fraternalism as a Managerial Strategy at the Ford Motor Company." *Journal of Economic History*, 53:4 (1993).

Lewis, Earl. "Invoking Concepts, Problematizing Identities: The Life of Charles N. Hunter and the Implications for the Study of Gender and Labor." *Labor History*, 34:2–3 (1993).

Lichtenstein, Nelson. *The State of the Union: A Century of American Labor.* Princeton: Princeton University Press, 2002.

———. *The Most Dangerous Man in Detroit: Walter Reuther and the Fate of American Labor.* New York: Basic Books, 1995.

———. "Conflict Over Workers' Control: The Automobile Industry in World War II." In *Working-Class America: Essays on Labor, Community, and American Society*, ed. Michael H. Frisch and Daniel J. Walkowitz. Urbana: University of Illinois Press, 1983.

———. *Labor's War at Home: The CIO in World War II.* New York: Cambridge University Press, 1982.

Lindaman, Matthew. "Wrestling's Hold on the Western World before the Great War." *Historian*, 62:4 (2000).

Lipsitz, George. *Rainbow at Midnight: Labor and Culture in the 1940s.* Urbana: University of Illinois Press, 1994.

Littmann, William. "Designing Obedience: The Architecture and Landscape of Industrial Capitalism, 1880–1930." *International Labor and Working-Class History*, 53 (1998).

Lorence, James J. *Organizing the Unemployed: Community and Union Activists in the Industrial Heartland.* Albany: State University of New York Press, 1996.

Lorenz, Stacy L., and Geraint B. Osborne. "'Talk About Strenuous Hockey': Violence, Manhood, and the 1907 Ottawa Silver Seven-Montreal Wanderer Rivalry." *Journal of Canadian Studies* 40:1 (2006).

Loss, Christopher P. "'The Most Wonderful Thing Has Happened to Me in the Army': Psychology, Citizenship, and American Higher Education in World War II." *Journal of American History*, 92:3 (2005).

Lubove, Roy. *The Struggle for Social Security, 1900–1935.* Cambridge, MA: Harvard University Press, 1968.

Luskey, Brian P. *On the Make: Clerks and the Quest for Capital in Nineteenth-Century America.* New York: New York University Press, 2010.

Mandell, Nikki. *The Corporation as Family: The Gendering of Corporate Welfare, 1890–1930*. Chapel Hill: University of North Carolina Press, 2002.

May, Elaine Tyler. *Homeward Bound: American Families in the Cold War Era*. New York: Basic Books, 1988.

May, Martha. "The Historical Problem of the Family Wage: The Ford Motor Company and the Five Dollar Day." *Feminist Studies*, 8:2 (1982).

McBee, Randy D. "'He Likes Women More Than He Likes Drink and That Is Quite Unusual': Working-Class Social Clubs, Male Culture, and Heterosocial Relations in the United States, 1920s–1930s." *Gender & History*, 11:1 (1999).

McClelland, Keith. "Masculinity and the 'Representative Artisan' in Britain, 1850–1880." In *Manful Assertions: Masculinities in Britain since 1800*, ed. Michael Roper and John Tosh. London: Routledge, 1991.

———. "Some Thoughts on Masculinity and the 'Representative Artisan' in Britain, 1850–1880." *Gender & History*, 1:2 (1989).

McDevitt, Patrick F. *May the Best Man Win: Sport, Masculinity, and Nationalism in Great Britain and the Empire, 1880–1935*. New York: Palgrave Macmillan, 2004.

McGirr, Lisa. *Suburban Warriors: The Origins of the New American Right*. Princeton: Princeton University Press, 2001.

Messner, Michael. "The Life of a Man's Seasons: Male Identity in the Life Course of the Jock." In *Changing Men: New Directions in Research on Men and Masculinity*, ed. Michael Kimmel. Newbury Park, CA: Sage Publications, 1987.

Mettler, Suzanne. *Dividing Citizens: Gender and Federalism in New Deal Public Policy*. Ithaca: Cornell University Press, 1998.

Meyer, Steve. *The Degradation of Work Revisited: Workers and Technology in the American Auto Industry, 1900–2000*, 2004. http://www.autolife.umd.umich.edu/Labor/L_Overview/L_Overview1.htm.

———. "Workplace Predators: Sexuality and Harassment on the US Automotive Shop Floor, 1930–1960." *Labor: Studies in Working-Class History of the Americas*, 1:1 (2004).

———. "Rough Manhood: The Aggressive and Confrontational Shop Culture of US Auto Workers during World War II." *Journal of Social History*, 36 (2002).

———. *The Five Dollar Day: Labor Management and Social Control in the Ford Motor Company, 1908–1921*. Albany: State University of New York Press, 1981.

Meyerowitz, Joanne, ed. *Not June Cleaver: Women and Gender in Postwar America, 1945–1960*. Philadelphia: Temple University Press, 1994.

Milkman, Ruth. *Gender at Work: The Dynamics of Job Segregation by Sex during World War II*. Urbana: University of Illinois Press, 1987.

Mink, Gwendolyn. *The Wages of Motherhood: Inequality in the Welfare State, 1917–1942*. Ithaca: Cornell University Press, 1995.

Montgomery, David. *The Fall of the House of Labor: The Workplace, the State, and American Labor Activism, 1865–1925*. Cambridge, UK: Cambridge University Press, 1987.

———. *Workers' Control in America: Studies in the History of Work, Technology, and Labor Struggles*. New York: Cambridge University Press, 1979.

Moore, Jacqueline M. *Cow Boys and Cattle Men: Class and Masculinities on the Texas Frontier, 1865–1900*. New York: New York University Press, 2010.

Morgan, Edmund S. *American Slavery, American Freedom: The Ordeal of Colonial Virginia*. New York: WW Norton & Company, 1975.

Moskowitz, Eva S. *In Therapy We Trust: America's Obsession with Self-Fulfillment*. Baltimore: Johns Hopkins University Press, 2001.

Myles, John. *Old Age in the Welfare State: The Political Economy of Public Pensions* (1984). Lawrence: University of Kansas Press, 1989.

Nash, Gary. "Poverty and Politics in Early American History." In *Down and Out in Early America*, ed. Billy Smith. University Park: Pennsylvania State University Press, 2004.

———. "Poverty and Poor Relief in Pre-Revolutionary Philadelphia." *William and Mary Quarterly*, 33:1 (1976).

Nelson, Daniel. *Managers and Workers: Origins of the New Factory System in the United States, 1880–1920*. Madison: University of Wisconsin Press, 1975.

Nevins, Allan and Frank Ernest Hill. *Ford: Expansion and Challenge, 1915–1933*. New York: Charles Scribner's Sons, 1957.

Norrell, Robert J. "Caste in Steel: Jim Crow Careers in Birmingham, Alabama." *Journal of American History*, 73:3 (1986).

Norwood, Stephen H. *Strikebreaking and Intimidation: Mercenaries and Masculinity in Twentieth-Century America*. Chapel Hill: University of North Carolina Press, 2002.

Ochberg, Richard L. "The Male Career Code and the Ideology of Role." In *The Making of Masculinities: The New Men's Studies*, ed. Harry Brod. Boston: Allen & Unwin, 1987.

O'Neill, William L. *American High: The Years of Confidence, 1945–1960*. New York: Free Press, 1986.

Oestreicher, Richard. *Solidarity and Fragmentation: Working People and Class Consciousness in Detroit, 1875–1900*. Urbana: University of Illinois Press, 1989.

Orloff, Ann Shola. *The Politics of Pensions: A Comparative Analysis of Britain, Canada, and the United States, 1880–1940*. Madison: University of Wisconsin Press, 1994.

Osgerby, Bill. "A Pedigree of the Consuming Male: Masculinity, Consumption, and the American 'Leisure Class.'" In *Masculinity and Men's Lifestyle Magazines*, ed. Bethan Benwell. Oxford, UK: Blackwell Publishing, 2003.

Parker, Stanley. *Work and Retirement*. London: George Allen & Unwin, 1982.

Peiss, Kathy. *Cheap Amusements: Working Women and Leisure in Turn-of-the-Century New York*. Philadelphia: Temple University Press, 1986.

Peterson, Joyce Shaw. *American Automobile Workers, 1900–1933*. Albany: State University of New York Press, 1988.

Pettegrew, John. *Brutes in Suits: Male Sensibility in America, 1890–1920*. Baltimore: Johns Hopkins University Press, 2007.

Pomfret, David M. "'A Muse for the Masses': Gender, Age, and Nation in France, Fin de Siecle," *American Historical Review*, 109:5 (2004).

Putney, Clifford. *Muscular Christianity: Manhood and Sports in Protestant America, 1880–1920.* Cambridge, MA: Harvard University Press, 2001.

Quadagno, Jill. *The Transformation of Old Age Security: Class and Politics in the American Welfare State.* Chicago: University of Chicago Press, 1988.

Ransom, Roger L. and Richard Sutch. "The Labor of Older Americans: Retirement of Men On and Off the Job, 1870–1937." *Journal of Economic History,* 56:1 (1986).

Rees, Jonathan. "What If a Company Union Wasn't a 'Sham?' The Rockefeller Plan in Action." *Labor History,* 48:4 (2007):

Regnier, Victor. "Neighborhood Planning for the Urban Elderly." In *Aging: Scientific Perspectives and Social Issues,* ed. Diana S. Woodruff and James E. Birren. New York: D. Van Nostrand Company, 1975.

Reutter, Mark. *Making Steel: Sparrows Point and the Rise and Ruin of American Industrial Might* (1988). Urbana: University of Illinois Press, 2004.

Rodgers, Daniel T. *The Work Ethic in Industrial America, 1850–1920.* Chicago: University of Chicago Press, 1978.

Roediger, David R. *The Wages of Whiteness: Race and the Making of the American Working Class.* New York: Verso, 1991.

Rose, James D. *Duquesne and the Rise of Steel Unionism.* Urbana: University of Illinois Press, 2001.

———. "'The Problem Every Supervisor Dreads': Women Workers at the US Steel Duquesne Works during World War II." *Labor History,* 36:1 (1995).

Rose, Sonya O. *Limited Livelihoods: Gender and Class in Nineteenth-Century England.* Berkeley: University of California Press, 1990.

Rotundo, E. Anthony. *American Manhood: Transformations in Masculinity from the Revolution to the Modern Era.* New York: Free Press, 1993.

Ruiz, Vicki L., and Ellen Carol DuBois, eds. *Unequal Sisters: A Multi-Cultural Reader in US Women's History,* 2nd edition. New York: Routledge, 1994.

Salvatore, Nick. *Eugene V. Debs: Citizen and Socialist.* Urbana: University of Illinois Press, 1982.

Sandage, Scott A. *Born Losers: A History of Failure in America.* Cambridge: Harvard University Press, 2005.

Sass, Steven A. *The Promise of Private Pensions: The First Hundred Years.* Cambridge: Harvard University Press, 1997.

Scharf, Lois. *To Work and To Wed: Female Employment, Feminism, and the Great Depression.* Westport, CT: Greenwood Press, 1980.

Scott, Joan Wallach. *Gender and the Politics of History.* New York: Columbia University Press, 1988.

Sengupta, Gunja. "Elites, Subalterns, and American Identities: A Case Study of African-American Benevolence." *American Historical Review,* 109:4 (2004).

Serrin, William. *Homestead: The Glory and Tragedy of an American Steel Town.* New York: Times Books, 1992.

Shibusawa, Naoko. *America's Geisha Ally: Reimagining the Japanese Enemy.* Cambridge: Harvard University Press, 2006.

Skocpol, Theda. *Protecting Soldiers and Mothers: The Political Origins of Social Policy in the United States.* Cambridge, MA: Belknap Press, 1992.

Slavishak, Edward. *Bodies of Work: Civic Display and Labor in Industrial Pittsburgh.* Durham: Duke University Press, 2008.

Stanley, Amy Dru. *From Bondage to Contract: Wage Labor, Marriage, and the Market in the Age of Slave Emancipation.* New York: Cambridge University Press, 1998.

Stansell, Christine. *City of Women: Sex and Class in New York, 1789–1860.* Urbana: University of Illinois Press, 1987.

Stearns, Peter N. *Be a Man! Males in Modern Society.* New York: Holmes & Meier Publishers, 1979.

Stott, Richard Briggs. *Jolly Fellows: Male Milieus in Nineteenth-Century America.* Baltimore: Johns Hopkins University Press, 2009.

Strom, Sharon Hartman. *Beyond the Typewriter: Gender, Class, and the Origins of Modern Office Work.* Urbana: University of Illinois Press, 1995.

Sugrue, Thomas J. *The Origins of the Urban Crisis: Race and Inequality in Postwar Detroit.* Princeton: Princeton University Press, 1995.

Syrett, Nicholas L. *The Company He Keeps: A History of White College Fraternities.* Chapel Hill: University of North Carolina Press, 2009.

Tentler, Leslie Woodcock. *Wage-Earning Women: Industrial Work and Family Life in the United States, 1900–1930.* New York: Oxford University Press, 1979.

Tomlins, Christopher. "Why Wait for Industrialism? Work, Legal Culture, and the Example of Early America — An Historiographical Argument." *Labor History,* 40:1 (1999).

Tosh, John. "What Should Historians Do With Masculinity? Reflections on Nineteenth-Century Britain." *History Workshop,* 38 (1994).

Vargas, Zaragosa. *Proletarians of the North: A History of Mexican Industrial Workers in Detroit and the Midwest, 1917–1933.* Berkeley: University of California Press, 1993.

Wagner, David. The *Poorhouse: America's Forgotten Institution.* Lanham, MD: Rowman & Littlefield Publishers, Inc., 2005.

Whitehead, Stephen M. *Men and Masculinities: Key Themes and New Directions.* Cambridge, UK: Polity, 2002.

Wilentz, Sean. *Chants Democratic: New York City and the Rise of the American Working Class, 1788–1850.* New York: Oxford University Press, 1984.

Willrich, Michael. "Home Slackers: Men, the State, and Welfare in Modern America." *Journal of American History,* 87:2 (2000).

Wixson, Douglas. *Worker-Writer in America: Jack Conroy and the Tradition of Midwestern Literary Radicalism, 1898–1990.* Urbana: University of Illinois Press, 1994.

Wood, Gregory. "'The Paralysis of the Labor Movement': Men, Masculinity, and Unions in 1920s Detroit." *Michigan Historical Review,* 30:1 (2004).

Zieger, Robert H. *The CIO, 1935–1955.* Chapel Hill: University of North Carolina Press, 1995.

Zweig, Michael. *The Working Class Majority: America's Best Kept Secret.* Ithaca: Cornell University Press, 2000.

UNPUBLISHED SECONDARY SOURCES

Addington, Wendell Phillips. "Reds at the Rouge: Communist Party Activism at the Ford Rouge Plant, 1922–1952." MA Thesis, Wayne State University, 1997.

Burg, Steven B. "The Gray Crusade: The Townsend Movement, Old Age Politics, and the Development of Social Security." PhD diss., University of Wisconsin at Madison, 1999.

Greenwald, Maurine, and Richard Oestreicher. "Engendering US History: Rethinking Masternarratives." Unpublished paper in the author's possession, 2001.

Hirshbein, Laura Davidow. "The Transformation of Old Age: Expertise, Gender, and National Identity, 1900–1950." PhD diss., Johns Hopkins University, 2000.

Kilbourne, E. Michelle. "Self-Made Men: The Margins of Manliness Among Northern Industrial Workers, 1850–1920." PhD diss., Emory University, 2000.

Rees, Jonathan. "Managing the Mills: Labor Policy in the American Steel Industry, 1892–1937." PhD diss., University of Wisconsin at Madison, 1997.

Rose, Sarah. "No Right To Be Idle: The Invention of Disability, 1850–1930." PhD diss., University of Illinois at Chicago, 2008.

Runstedtler, Theresa E. "Journeymen: Race, Boxing, and the Transnational World of Jack Johnson." PhD, diss., Yale University, 2007.

Smith, Thurber M. "The Unemployment Problem: A Catholic Solution." PhD diss., St. Louis University, 1932.

Vargas, Zaragosa. "Mexican Auto Workers at Ford Motor Company, 1918–1933." PhD diss., University of Michigan, 1984.

Wood, Gregory. "'It Made Us Feel Like Men': Gender, Power, and the CIO in Pittsburgh's Steel Valley, 1910–1937." Paper presented at The Working-Class History Seminar, University of Pittsburgh-Carnegie Mellon University, 19 April 2001.

Index

1919 Steel Strike, 41–43
1920s, 59–91; Abraham Epstein and
 pension politics, 83–87; industrial
 pensions, 65–69; institutionalization,
 69–78; overview, 59–61; private old
 age homes, 78–83; savings, 61–65;
 state pensions, 87–91
1930s, 9. *See also* Great Depression

AA (Amalgamated Association), 28, 90,
 104–5
About Schmidt, 230–32
"activity theory" of retirement, 200
Adams, Roy, 215
Addams, Jane, 86
adolescents, socialization of, 7
ads, soliciting work through, 212
advice: on finding escape within home,
 192–94; for older men in consumer
 marketplace, 127–29; on-the-job
 retirement preparation, 156–60;
 regarding leisure, 196–97; on staying
 healthy, 20–21, 124–26
affluence, and manhood after World
 War II, 142–48
AFL (American Federation of Labor),
 30–31, 43, 104
age discrimination in hiring and
 firing, 22–24; after retirement, 214;

attempts to hide age, 46–49; in
 automobile industry, 43–46; formal
 hiring age limits, 35–41; informal
 patterns of discrimination, 41–43;
 statistics regarding, 31–35; towards
 women, 49–51
age entry requirements, for private old
 age homes, 80–81
age limits, hiring, 35–41, 214
age of retirement, 151
ageism. *See* age discrimination in hiring
 and firing
agility, emphasis on at work, 24–31,
 117
aging: attempts to hide signs of, 46–49;
 changing concepts of in twentieth
 century, 225–33; difficulty of mass
 production labor processes, 25–31;
 emphasis on agility at work, 24–31;
 and gender identity, 1–11; manhood
 and work in early twentieth century,
 19–24; overview, 18–19; struggle to
 avoid, 20–21; as threat to ability to
 work, 20. *See also* age discrimination
 in hiring and firing; old age poverty
Aikman, Duncan, 103
almshouses, 69–78
Amalgamated Association (AA), 28, 90,
 104–5

Davis, Horace B., 34, 41, 90
Davis, James J., 29–30, 34, 147
de Caux, Len, 31
death, as result of retirement, 151–52
deception regarding age, 49
Deluse, Otto P., 63
democracy, industrial, 118–20
dens, as space for men, 192
dependence during old age. *See* old age poverty
Depression. *See* Great Depression
Detroit Federation of Labor (DFL), 43
Detroit Labor News, 21–22
Detroit United Railway company, 43
Devine, Edward, 25, 85
Dewees, H., 28
diet, advice on, 126
disease: and ability to acquire savings, 63–64; and mass production labor, 27–29; as result of retirement, 152–53
disengagement theory, 149–51
The Disinherited, 23, 27, 76–77
dismissals. *See* firing, age discrimination in
Dix, Lucien, 112–13
Dodge Motor Company, 46–47
domestic labor: at home after retirement, 184–90; at private old age homes, 81–82
Downey, James F., 37, 38
draft law, 40–41
dress code, Forty Plus Clubs, 114
Dunn, Robert W., 44–45, 47
dyes, hair, as way to hide age, 47–48

early twentieth century, 18–51; emphasis on agility at work, 24–31; manhood and work in, 19–24; overview, 18–19. *See also* age discrimination in hiring and firing
earnings: and ability to acquire savings, 63; after retirement, 155, 186; and age discrimination, 46; Social

Security, 106–7; when working after retirement, 215
economic support for retired persons, 59–91; Abraham Epstein and pension politics, 83–87; industrial pensions, 65–69; institutionalization, 69–78; overview, 59–61; private old age homes, 78–83; savings, 61–65; state pensions, 87–91
educational opportunities, at Golden Age Clubs, 207
electric razors, 126–27
elite contempt for poor, 71
emotions, upon retirement, 161–63, 168–69
employment. *See* work
England: ageist hiring policies in, 36; workhouses in, 70–71
enlistment, age limits for, 37, 40–41
entrepreneurial ventures by retirees, 215
Epstein, Abraham: chronic illness and ability to acquire savings, 64; death of, 147; mass production labor processes, 25; pension politics, 83–87; poorhouses, 72, 78; precariousness of future of aged men, 23–24; state pensions, 90, 91
ER Squibb & Sons Company, 125
Esquire Handbook for Hosts, 191
Esso Standard Oil Company, 156, 157–58
Ettinger, Austen A., 1, 10, 232
escape from home after retirement, 195
exclusivity, of private old age homes, 78–79
executives. *See* retirement culture; white-collar workers
exercise, 196–200
expert advice. *See* advice

Facing Old Age, 84, 86
factories, 22–24, 214. *See also* mass production labor processes
Fairbanks, Douglas, 21

loneliness, 207–9
The Lonely Crowd, 144, 233
Lorge, Irving, 211
Los Angeles Times, 48, 113–14, 166, 201–2
Lubove, Roy, 84
Lynch, James M., 70
Lynd, Helen Merrell, 11, 29
Lynd, Robert S., 11, 29

male bodies, idealization of, 21–22
Maloney, James, 30
management, age of workers in, 34–35
mandatory retirement rules, 150–51
manhood, 98–131; after World War II, 142–48; consumer marketplace, 124–31; Forty Plus Clubs, 110–16; industrial unionism, 116–24; overview, 98–100; and resistance to institutionalization, 76–77; Second New Deal, 100–110; and unemployment, 98–100; views of in nineteenth century, 2–3; and work in early twentieth century, 19–24. *See also* postwar manhood; productive manhood
manufacturing, age of men in managerial positions in, 34–35. *See also* industrial workplaces
Marquand, John P., 198
married couples: gender divisions at home, 190–95; household work, 184–90; in poorhouses, 74–75; in private old age homes, 80; retirement preparation, 159; with working wife and retired husband, 229
Martin, George A., 62
masculinity studies, 5–6. *See also* manhood; productive manhood
mass production labor processes, 18–19; emphasis on agility at work, 24–31; industrial pension programs, 66–67; industrial unionism, 116–24; overview, 22–24. *See also* age discrimination in hiring and firing

Massachusetts Commission on Pensions, 64
matrons, in private old age homes, 82
Maurer, John H., 74–75
May, Elaine Tyler, 185
McCarthy, Joseph, 145
McKie, William, 49
McMahon, Thomas F., 30–31
meatpacking industry, industrial pension programs in, 68–69
medical advice, focus on in consumer marketplace, 124–28
Men and Steel, 43
mental activity, 204
middle-class lifestyles, 6, 142–48. *See also* retirement culture
Middletown: A Study in American Culture, 11, 29
"Milady's Beauty Table" column, *Los Angeles Times*, 48
military, age limits in, 37, 40–41
military veterans, state pensions for, 88
Millarde, Harry, 75–76
Modern Crusader, 103, 104
Moeser, Kate J., 48
Montana state pension plan, 89
Monthly Labor Review, 80, 122
Moore, Elon H., 159, 200
Morris & Co. meatpacking firm, 68–69
Morrison, Samuel, 126
Morrow, Joseph, 159
mortality, retirement as reminder of, 152
Moskin, J. Robert, 146
mothers' pensions, 88–89
moustaches, and age discrimination, 47
movies, depiction of retirement in, 21, 171–72, 230–32
Moving Forward, 33

nagging wives, 191–92, 194
National Civic Federation, 64
National Industrial Conference Board, 150
National Labor Relations Board (NLRB), 119

Index